INSIDE THE STRIKE ZONE

By
Randal A. Hendricks

EAKIN PRESS ★ Austin, Texas

FIRST EDITION

Copyright © 1994
By Randal A. Hendricks

Published in the United States of America
By Eakin Press
A Division of Sunbelt Media, Inc.

ISBN 0-89015-982-3

1 2 3 4 5 6 7 8 9 10

Library of Congress Cataloging-in-Publication Data:

Hendricks, Randal A.
  Inside the strike zone / by Randal A. Hendricks.
      p.   cm.
  Includes bibliographical references and index.
  ISBN 0-89015-982-3 : $24.95
  1. Trade-unions — Baseball players — United States. 2. Collective bargaining — Baseball — United States.   I. Title.
GV880.2.H45   1994
331.89'0417963570973 — dc20   94-16985
                                                                CIP

Contents

Foreword

Over the years, sports agents have been feared and on occasion loathed. Some have earned respect — from their adversaries as well as their clients. At the top of this list is Randal A. Hendricks, lawyer, scholar, aging but still dedicated softball player, sports analyst, and author.

Hendricks achieved his star status as an agent not by being diplomatic, nor by his eagerness to compromise. He earned it by being truthful, consistent and, most of all, by being right an uncanny percentage of the time.

To his players, Randy's word is better than government savings bonds. And he looks at baseball the way an old world jeweler studies the facets of a precious stone.

As the saying goes, diamonds are forever.

Hendricks does not set out to embarrass an owner or a front office honcho, although the temptation must be difficult at times to resist. He sees the give-and-take between management and labor as a trial, bordering on combat. He isn't a bully. He isn't a screamer. He doesn't threaten. His intensity is his trademark. A student of military history, he knows that while Patton enjoyed matching wits with Rommel, he never laughed off the loss of a tank.

He has been called a double agent, a sly reference to his partner and older brother, Alan. He has been called a not-so-secret agent, a reference to his talent for making news, and waves. But mostly, the Hendricks brothers have been called with frequency by players who rate among the game's rich and famous: Roger Clemens, Doug Drabek, Greg Swindell, Norm Charlton, Mitch Williams, Chuck Knoblauch, Jay Buhner, and Chuck Finley. They represent a significant number of major leaguers and many of the highest paid pitchers.

It is against this backdrop that *Inside the Strike Zone* takes the reader into a world beyond fantasy, a feast for every Rotisserie Leaguer and numbers cruncher. This is the arena where the real combustion of baseball takes place, the money pit, and class warfare in the age of high tech. Here are the take-no-prisoners collisions of arbitration. Here are the economic issues that shape the new reality: one strike and everybody is out.

Randy Hendricks puts you in the batter's box.

Professional ethics would not permit Randy, or Alan, to respond to an owner's offer by saying, "No, that's too much." But the Hendricks brothers believe in free enterprise. They are not against big business. They are against bad management. General managers no longer deal with agents by keeping a can of Flit on their desks, but a sense of humor is still essential.

An interesting fact about Randy is that you can ask him a baseball question, and en route to the answer he may pause to drop off a football anecdote. He was interrupted one day during his spring training travels, his mobile phone at his fingertips. He excused himself from a dinner meeting with a client, a pitcher for the Texas Rangers.

When asked if the call was inconvenient, he asked if we knew how the San Francisco 49ers discovered one of their former stars. No, we did not.

"They sent a scout to check out a quarterback at Clemson," he said, "and the scout came away raving about the guy catching all the passes. So they drafted the receiver instead, and that's how the 49ers got Dwight Clark."

Randy knows the feeling. He once went to observe a potential first round draft choice, a high school pitcher he had been hearing about, at a ballpark near his office. The game was a regional playoff game, and proved to be a pitchers' duel. Randy was impressed with the slider of the first rounder, but repeated to brother Alan the next day the Dwight Clark story. Randy's Dwight Clark was a skinny, righthanded sophomore. And that was how, a few years later, the Hendricks brothers happened to sign Roger Pavlik, the Texas Rangers pitcher Randy was meeting with when the phone rang.

As happens in real life, their players get hurt, lose their stuff, grow old, retire or get released. But the human stories and the backstage skirmishing goes on.

Both brothers graduated from the University of Houston, Alan with a degree in finance and Randy with degrees in finance and law. It was in late 1970 that one of the football coaches suggested they talk to a player who was about to be drafted by the NFL. Elmo Wright, a wide receiver who played six years for the Kansas City Chiefs before an injury ended his career, became their first client. Elmo had another claim to fame: he is said to be the first player to celebrate a touchdown by performing a dance in the end zone, inspiring the craze that continues to this day.

In 1976 they moved into baseball, predicting correctly that baseball players were in for big bucks. They also like the idea of representing clients who were less likely to wind up crippled. By the end of the 1970s, they decided to concentrate their future efforts almost entirely on baseball.

At this point, allow me, please, a personal reference. As a writer for the *Houston Post*, I have known the Hendricks brothers since they first began to be described by the media as "power brokers." By coincidence, during the period of their emergence I assisted the late Bob Woolf, the first nationally recognized sports agent, with a book he wrote called *Behind Closed Doors*.

You could hardly find two personalities less alike than Bob or Randy (or, for that matter, Randy or Alan). Woolf was almost Talmudic in how he deliberated. It thrilled him just to have the unlisted numbers of his clients, never mind representing them. Randy is the militant, a keeper of causes, who typically can go days with almost no sleep while preparing a case. All had this in common: they have been important figures for their time, and honorable men.

Now Randy Hendricks has put on paper how the game has changed and with it the financial strike zone. He has been a key player in those changes. The advocate who rises from these pages is neither wide-eyed fan nor hero worshipper. He is an astute observer, who believes that victory comes not from acquiring the most money, but in winning for the players a voice in their own futures.

— MICKEY HERSKOWITZ
Houston, Texas

Introduction

I started representing professional athletes in late 1970. It did not take long for me to realize that the salary mechanisms operating in Major League Baseball and the National Football League severely restricted my clients' bargaining power.

Unlike doctors, lawyers, economists, accountants, engineers, school teachers, construction workers, you name it, athletes were drafted into their professions by whatever team happened to select them. Once signed, a player became the property of his club for as long as the club desired. Player movement from one team to another was accomplished by direct trade or by outright release and reentry, also solely at the discretion of the teams.

And so from the very beginning of his career, the professional baseball or football player had no say in where he would ply his trade. What's more, the baseball owners' control over player movement was perfectly legal, protected by antitrust exemptions sanctioned by the Supreme Court of the United States and ratified by congressional inactivity.

When confronted with the opportunity to affirm that baseball players have the same rights that are accorded to other American workers, the Supreme Court in 1972 instead upheld the reserve system in baseball. The court did not want to disturb the precedential value of the 1922 Federal Baseball Club of Baltimore case, in which Oliver Wendell Holmes stated that baseball games, "although made for money, would not be called trade or commerce in the commonly accepted use of those words."

In the National Football League, it was the Rozelle Rule that worked as a barrier against player movement. In Major League Baseball there simply was no freedom of movement, at all. In both systems the players were assignable property, indentured servants, whose professional lives were totally governed by the members of a cartel — namely, the owners of the teams.

It is not surprising, then, that few players earned more than an average white-collar income or that the majority were distinctly underpaid relative to the revenues of their sport.

As a consequence of the restrictions that existed in both sports, the players' right to freedom of choice with respect to salary and locale — free agency — became the overarching issue in my professional career. For I recognized that without this basic right, otherwise fundamental to American workers, players would never choose where and for whom they would work, and they would never realize their true market value, whatever that value might be.

I also learned early in my career that without the bargaining power that comes from the freedom to choose one's employer, teams seldom show respect to either players or their agents. A club operating without the possibility of ever losing a player will operate on its own schedule, within its own predetermined salary scale, and invariably in a patronizing manner. And so the right to meaningful free agency creates not only bargaining leverage and fair salaries for the players, but it also engenders respect between the parties.

I have marveled throughout my years in sports why many well-educated analytical people, including economists, lawyers, and judges, will abandon their belief in traditional free-market capitalism when evaluating the salary systems of baseball or football. It is as if they disengage their rational faculties and let their emotional perspectives take over. Consequently, they embrace the view held by many team owners and most sportswriters and commentators that professional athletes are a collection of prima donnas, who lead carefree lives while indulging themselves in the games of childhood.

Overlooking the thousands of low-paid minor leaguers and marginal major leaguers who never get to cash in on their still significant talents, many observers believe that because the top few hundred players are now paid extremely well relative to the rest of the populace they should not have the same rights that are guaranteed to other citizens of the United States. From this lopsided promanagement perspective, when a player leaves a team as a free agent, he is considered disloyal. But when a team trades or releases a player, it is considered to be for the good of the team.

By implication, then, it would be perfectly acceptable to return to the days before free agency, when players were the rented livestock of the owners, to be admired or chastised and inevitably put out to pasture in the name of "the team."

When I first analyzed the systems of baseball and football, I was struck with their similarity to the former Soviet system of government. In the name of lofty ideals, the Soviet government controlled its subjects in a manner akin to the way ball players were manipulated. In both cases, the "citizens" could not freely exit and reenter or move within the system. There were controls on where one worked and lived.

The producers were governed by a pseudo-ruling class, the official state bureaucracy, which lived off the productive labor of the workers while publicly extolling the virtue of those workers. Worse still, the ruling class was subsidized by public money that was deemed necessary to make the system work "for the benefit of all the people," in much the same way that the folks in several major league cities have been forced by baseball owners to subsidize ball clubs with stadium bond issues to keep those clubs in their hometowns.

The Soviet system was founded on unrealistic and unattainable economic and social ideals, implemented on the backs of the workers who fueled the system and supported for years by a "captive" press. As an attorney, I found it to be a legal outrage that the United States of America would follow that Soviet model in the sports industry.

Thanks to the leadership, skill, and dedication of baseball's union leaders, Marvin Miller and Richard Moss, and to the nearly unwavering support of the players, baseball players were emancipated on December 23, 1975. Their freedom sprang from arbitrator Peter Seitz's decision in the Messersmith-McNally case.

The case hinged on the arbitrator's interpretation of the renewal clause contained in the standard player contract. At the heart of the matter was the idea that clubs could "reserve" a player perpetually by unilaterally renewing his contract year after year. This was a fancy way of making a player an indentured servant in the baseball world.

Seitz ruled in the Messersmith-McNally case that ALL players were free to offer their services to other clubs after playing for one year under a renewed contract. However, after this landmark decision, the owners and the union agreed in 1976 to a new collective bargaining agreement, or "Basic Agreement." The new Basic Agreement provided that, subject to the right of every player to play under a renewed contract in 1977 and then become a free agent, a player could elect to become a free agent only after he completed six years of major league service.

Even the very best professional ball players, those select few who move up to the big leagues, typically go through two to four years of minor league training and development before they get to the majors. Thus, the 1976 Basic Agreement meant that most major leaguers would have to play professionally for eight to ten years before they could obtain the freedom to sell their services to an interested club of their own choosing.

Though the Basic Agreement has been amended in numerous ways, the six-year free agency system remains intact as the driving force in the salary system. Ironically, after seventeen years under the new system, it is still the case that only about 30 percent of major league players ever complete the six seasons needed to elect free agency.

*　　*　　*

Growing up in the Shawnee Mission suburb of Kansas City, I was not exposed to labor-management confrontations, though they did occur in other parts of greater Kansas City. There was nothing predominant in my upbringing to make me focus on labor issues, let alone choose which of the two camps I would naturally align myself.

The baseball players' union was organized in order to utilize the advantages afforded to unions by federal labor law. I suspect that most baseball fans have a difficult time considering major league baseball players to be union men. When asked to picture a union man, it is more likely that one will picture a factory worker with a lunch pail in hand, rather than a baseball player dressed in pin stripes, bat or glove in hand. The principles and goals which guide the organization of a union of factory workers are the same ones that guide the union of baseball players — the creation of a bargaining unit to offset the power of ownership.

I was unsure of what to expect when I first dealt with Marvin Miller at the baseball players association. I had dealt with the football union for the prior five years, and it had demonstrated the flavor of an organization run by campus radicals, rather than by mature professionals. Dealing with Marvin Miller turned out to be quite a contrast. He was exceedingly measured and analytical. The word "professional" described him perfectly. He was the George Washington, or Abraham Lincoln, if one prefers, of the baseball players' freedom movement.

Contrasts between the two unions could be made in many ways. The football union had a large staff; the baseball union had a small staff. The football union operated like a political organization; the baseball union operated like a professional organization. The professionals in the football union were dreamers and radicals; the professionals in the baseball union were pragmatists. The professionals in the football union appealed to emotion; the professionals in the baseball union appealed to logic. The professionals in the football union gave inflammatory speeches and hoped that those speeches would produce results; the professionals in the baseball union hit the law books and planned how they would utilize the law to gain victory over their opponents. The professionals in the football union were dysfunctional in organizing and unifying their membership; the professionals in the baseball union were skillful in organizing and unifying their membership. Unsurprisingly, baseball players achieved meaningful free agency seventeen years before football players achieved a beneficial form of free agency.

*   *   *

What follows are unique stories which illustrate and explain why repetitive labor struggles continue in baseball nearly two decades after the players were liberated by arbitrator Seitz's decision.

CHAPTER 1

The Reasons for Labor Conflict in Baseball

Why have all seven negotiations since 1972 between major league owners and players produced a combined four strikes and three lockouts? At the heart of the problem are the divergent attitudes of the owners and the players in three fundamental areas of their common existence. Unfortunately, these attitudes produce, metaphorically speaking, a cacophony of sound, rather than the familiar refrain, "Take Me Out to the Ballgame."

The culture of baseball is the first and foremost area in which divergent attitudes produce conflict. Ownership has traditionally viewed its role as one in which it rules, governs, and controls. That mindset produces an attitude which regards the players, their agents, and the leaders of the players' union as inferiors in the culture, as people who, however talented, lack the "status" to be treated as equals to the twenty-eight lords of baseball.

The players, as one might suspect, are a heterogenous group, whose focus historically has been on freedom and economic gains. That focus created a commitment to achieve those goals. The players have been interested in receiving a greater share of the economic pie, as well as in securing the freedom to lead their lives as they individually choose. These preeminent goals mean that players do not seek to control the game or the owners, but seek, rather, the freedom to play baseball in cities of their choosing at salaries reflective of their abilities and the gross income generated by the business of baseball.

The division of the revenues produced by the sport between the owners and the players is the second area of conflict. At its most fundamental level, this is a simple power struggle over the portion each group should receive out of the income generated by the sport. While each side recognizes that it needs the other to play the games on the field, the parties nevertheless forever fight over how to "cut the pie." This type of economic fight is as old as mankind itself and reflects a viewpoint which narrowly defines economic self-interest.

Given that economic negotiations are a game which, like the sport of baseball itself, pit fellow travelers against each other in a series of one-on-one contests, one should be tolerant of these inevitable clashes. Whether in collective bargaining between the owners and the players' union, or in individual negotiations between a club and a player, the relative abilities of each party, as well as the merits of their positions, are matched against each other. It should not be particularly surprising that people who compete for a living will exert all of their competitive abilities toward producing the best economic result for themselves or for their group.

The legal structure of the off-the-field game is the third area of contention. Unsurprisingly, the structure has a major impact upon the rights and economic benefits which accrue to each group. While their widely divergent views of the proper legal structure may appear to be a natural consequence of their different perspectives, the ownership view has at its root a preoccupation with control.

The owners have carefully constructed their oligarchy in order to control the number and location of franchises. The owners are most interested in maximizing franchise values, while jealously guarding against any expansion or franchise relocation unless the existing owners receive a substantial economic benefit. The shameless way in which the Tampa–St. Petersburg area has been repeatedly teased is the most glaring example of how the owners manipulate the supply and location of franchises.

The players are interested in job growth and in major league baseball being played in geographic areas which can support a major league team. More importantly, though, the players oppose the judicially sanctioned oligarchy and its insulation from the application of the antitrust laws.

The parties also disagree over the office of the commissioner. Until the unceremonious dumping of Commissioner Fay Vincent, one could still find a large number of people who believed that the office broadly represented the owners, the players, and the public. In reality, the commissioner has always represented just the owners.

The players would like a legitimate voice in choosing a commissioner who would truly represent the owners, the players, and the public. If the prior role of the commissioner is to continue, the players prefer that the commissioner be publicly recognized as an arm of ownership and not be cloaked with a false public image.

The system under which players are disciplined is also a subject of disagreement. Historically, due process of law has been a concept about which the owners, their lawyers, the league presidents, and the commissioner lacked conviction when applied to player rights. Either that, or they failed to grasp the subject in their professional or legal training.

In many areas of dispute, Marvin Miller negotiated the right of a player to file a grievance. The permanent arbitrator, who is selected by joint agreement of ownership and the union, serves as the neutral judge in those areas of dispute. He is familiar with the concept of due process of law and applies it in his decisions.

Discipline for on-the-field conduct is another subject. The league presidents and the commissioner enforce discipline in the forms of fines and suspensions. If a player is displeased with a fine or suspension, his sole recourse is to appeal to the very party who rendered the decision in the first place. Thus, in such cases the league presidents serve as prosecutor, judge, jury, and then appellate judge. Even if it does not comport with due process of law, it makes for some interesting cases, such as the discipline imposed upon Roger Clemens for what happened in the fourth game of the 1990 American League playoffs.

The different attitudes exhibited by the owners and the players in the three areas of their common existence come into play in the current debates over revenue sharing and a salary cap.

Current financial pressures on clubs have resulted in a focus on the system under which clubs divide revenue. Clubs operate in differently sized markets and as a consequence have different revenue streams, especially from local television and radio contracts. The franchise value of each club is closely tied to its revenue stream and market size. Unsurprisingly, the large market clubs have been reluctant to change the current system to reallocate greater revenue to clubs in smaller markets.

The players do not have an official position on the subject of revenue sharing, since they believe the subject is one for ownership to address. However, Richard Ravitch, the owners' labor negotiator, has stated that a change in the system under which revenues are shared between the clubs must be accompanied by the union's agreement to a salary cap.

The reasons cited for a salary cap include the need of the clubs to control costs, the need to prevent the industry from becoming unprofitable, and the need to prevent the bankruptcy of small market clubs. Prior experience naturally makes the players both suspicious of such claims of need and unsupportive of the notion that the players should be responsible for solving those needs. Under labor law, the clubs can plead inability to pay and open up their books if they believe that they are collectively in a hardship situation. Of course, while the owners have historically made such claims in the media, they have not done so in collective bargaining.

Home clubs pay very little to visiting clubs, 20 percent or less of each ticket sold. Given inflation and the significant increases in revenues from television, radio and merchandising over the recent past, the exercise of a little common sense and compassion would increase this amount if the wealthier owners have a genuine concern for the welfare of their poorer relations.

Many other options of revenue reallocation are available to the clubs. However, all options require that the more prosperous clubs transfer some income, if not some wealth, to the less prosperous clubs. The tying of a salary cap to revenue sharing is meant to placate the large market clubs by giving them a cost control mechanism in exchange for redistributing some of their revenue. This means that the owners expect the players to pay the price for the needed reallocation of income between the clubs.

The position of Ravitch on the link in bargaining between revenue sharing and a salary cap can be summarized thusly: the owners will do that which the owners need to do and have the independent power to do, only if the players will do that which the players do not need to do.

The current player compensation system has been in place since 1976. The players are essentially pleased with the current system. The owners, of course, are not. The owners have adopted an alternative way of expressing the concept of a salary cap by stating that players can be paid a share of designated revenues. Given that the National Basketball Association has been sued by the National Basketball Players Association for manipulating defined revenues so as to underpay the players, there should be little wonder as to why baseball players lack enthusiasm for this disguised salary cap proposal.

More fundamentally, baseball players do not see the need for a change in the current system. Every baseball club now cites budgetary restraints in dealing with player acquisitions and salaries. Instituting a salary cap would undoubtedly restrict player movement, and it would be unnecessary if clubs would act in a prudent financial manner.

Ravitch's pronouncements regarding the needs of ownership are accompanied by statements that the owners and players should become partners. Such a catchy proposal invites one to examine how true partnerships operate. If the owners' idea of a partnership means sharing power over such matters as selecting the commissioner and negotiating national television contracts, as well as serving together on a board of governors which is responsible for the game as a whole, then the players have an interest in such a partnership. On the other hand, if the owners' idea of a partnership is revenue participation implemented through a salary cap under the guise of a partnership, then the players have no interest in such a pseudo-partnership. In the latter case, the owners would continue their time honored tradition of bargaining in a patronizing manner, with their true goals being a reduction of the rights presently enjoyed by players and an increase in the owners' control over all aspects of the game.

A true partnership is intriguing, as well it should be. In areas such as licensing, both parties have gone their respective ways, while earning considerable income for their constituents. Licensing efforts could be easily consolidated in a true partnership.

A harmonious future in baseball between the owners and the players can only be achieved by a true partnership. The challenge for both sides is to achieve a substantive partnership, rather than toy in bargaining over a partnership which would be true only in name.

Chapter 2

The Commissioner
and the Lockout

Shortly after the 1985 Basic Agreement was agreed to by the owners and the players on August 7, 1985, the owners organized a scheme to thwart the movement of free agent players starting with the post-1985 season free agent market. The scheme lasted four years and came to be known as "collusion." The purpose was to control player movement and to control player salaries.

The commencement of collusion by the clubs, operated under the guise of fiscal responsibility, constituted a group boycott of free agent players. The operating principle of collusion was that each club agreed not to sign a free agent player from another club if that player's former club wanted to re-sign him. The market for that player was therefore limited to only one club — his former club — and he was therefore forced to return to his former club at a "fiscally responsible," noncompetitive, nonmarket value salary.

If not for immunity from the antitrust laws granted by the United States Supreme Court in 1922 and reaffirmed in 1952 and 1972, the collusive behavior of the clubs would have constituted criminal and civil misconduct under federal law. The collusive behavior, however, constituted a breach of contract under Article XVIII(H) of the existing Basic Agreement, which provided that neither clubs nor players can act in concert in the free agent market.

The post-1985 season "free agent market" constituted a dramatic change from the free agent markets of the past. Rather than experiencing the fulfillment of a dream, a good player, who would otherwise have had bargaining leverage in an honest free agent market, was put in limbo. The expectations of players and player agents were dashed. Calls to club officials were made, and the response was almost always the same: "We might have some interest, but we aren't sure how much and at what level. We'll let you know."

The owners proffered fancy labels and simple reasons to explain the sudden change in the free agent market. It would "not do" to offer collusion as the reason why so much money was being saved on player salaries. It was preferable to describe a "change in the culture" as the reason. Commissioner Peter Ueberroth was quoted as saying that there had been a cultural change in the way the owners conducted business. Barry Rona, head of the Player Relations Committee (PRC), the owners' labor bargaining arm, explained the reason as a product of the owners finally exercising "fiscal responsibility."

Following the post-1985 season free agent market, the Major League Baseball Players Association filed a grievance charging that the owners were committing collusion in violation of the Basic Agreement. This case became known as Collusion I. Following the post-1986 season free agent market, the union filed another grievance charging that owners had again committed collusion. This grievance became known as Collusion II.

The question of whether the owners were colluding was debated in the media. Ownership's party line continued to be that at long last the clubs were exercising fiscal responsibility. The union and agent position was that it was hardly plausible that all clubs "got religion" at the exact same time and to the exact same degree.

There was no doubt in my mind that collusion was taking place. There was ample evidence for a veteran agent. All clubs suddenly changed the way they had been doing business. Telephone calls were no longer routinely returned. Contrary to my experience in prior free agent markets, clubs no longer showed interest in signing free agent players for whom they had an obvious need. Clubs dramatically cut back on negotiating contract extensions for players on the verge of becoming eligible for free agency. Clubs exhibited a general indifference toward the prospect that a player would become a free agent. Some clubs even advised players to "test the market" to determine their market value.

Club officials no longer showed apprehension when negotiating with players on the verge of becoming eligible for free agency or with their former players who were free agents. Either owners and club officials had learned to "love the bomb"—or the practice of collusion had become rampant.

Club officials showed less respect for players and agents. Some management personnel developed cavalier or condescending attitudes. Overall, the conduct of club officials reminded me of the management attitudes I had encountered when I first started representing professional athletes prior to the era of free agency.

Arbitrator Tom Roberts rendered his decision on Collusion I in favor of the players on September 21, 1987. While the decision in favor of the players on Collusion II would not be issued by arbitrator George Nicolau until August 31, 1988, the clubs anticipated another loss in that case. Accordingly, following the Roberts decision in Collusion I, the clubs modified their approach. Rather than continue a group boycott of free agents, the clubs replaced the boycott with a price fixing scheme, implemented through the use of an information bank run through the Player Relations Committee.

The clubs were obviously testing "how close to the line" they could get without being found guilty of a violation of the Basic Agreement. Under the new scheme, a player could move from one club to another, but only if he were willing to accept a lower salary than the one that was offered to him by his former club.

Offers made by a club to a player and offers made to a club by an agent were reported to the PRC. A club could call the PRC information bank and learn everything it needed to know about what its "competitors" were offering to a particular free agent player. Thus, the clubs knew every move and countermove being made in the marketplace. The player's former club would hardly offer a market value salary, knowing that its "competitors" would inevitably make a lower offer.

Slowly, but surely, word leaked out about the existence of the information bank. As the free agent season progressed, club officials became quite cavalier about the new approach and their use of the information bank. Several club officials admitted to me that they knew the exact offers made by other clubs. When pressed by me, these same club officials ultimately confirmed the existence of the information bank. The use of the information bank by the owners in the post-1987 season free agent market resulted in the union filing a grievance known as Collusion III.

The experiences of the top free agent players clearly demonstrated that the latest version of the collusion conspiracy continued to depress salaries. While a player could move from one club to another, he could do so only at the cost of a reduced salary.

Absent a significantly higher salary offer from a new club, it makes no sense for a top player to leave his club unless he is very unhappy. This is unlikely, since a lot of playing time and production is required to become a top free agent. Thus, the top free agents, and most other free agents, were financially trapped by the practices of the clubs during the "price fixed" free agent market. The clubs thus continued to "love the bomb," operating without much fear of losing a free agent player.

The owners believed that because players could change clubs, their newly contrived scheme would pass the scrutiny of the permanent arbitrator. As usual, they were wrong, although the decision in Collusion III was not rendered by arbitrator Nicolau until July 18, 1990.

Many players were severely damaged by collusion. The union, agents, and players expended considerable time and money in prosecuting the three grievances in order to secure the clubs' compliance with the Basic Agreement. Collusion caused much frustration and hostility toward ownership, for it taxed our time, our resources, and our sense of justice.

The 1989 postseason period marked the end of the collusion era, as free agents proceeded to again move freely. While the decision in favor of the players in Collusion III would be rendered in July 1990, and all three collusion cases would be settled for $280 million on December 21, 1990, negotiations for a new collective bargaining agreement were scheduled to begin in late November 1989.

Against this late 1989 backdrop, collective bargaining talks would commence. Collusion may have just ended, but the damages from its practice had not been precisely determined, nor had any money been paid to a single player. The Basic Agreement had been flaunted. "Sacred rights" had been violated. A new agreement was to be negotiated with the very people who had just egregiously violated the prior one.

Negotiations for the new collective bargaining agreement commenced on November 28, 1989. Chuck O'Connor replaced Barry Rona as the head of the Player Relations Committee. While Rona was replaced for unstated reasons, many observers viewed the move by Baseball Commissioner Fay Vincent and the owners as symbolic that collusion was over and a new day in labor relations had commenced.

Murray Chass of the *New York Times* followed the labor negotiations for the *Times* and *The Sporting News*. Chass reported from the first bargaining session:

> "They expressed a desire to find a way to end the hostility," said Donald Fehr, executive director of the Major League Baseball Players Association. "We expressed the countervailing feeling that we hope to become persuaded that that's what they mean. But that takes substance, not words. They know that."

According to Chass, Chuck O'Connor reported after the meeting that PRC chairman and Milwaukee Brewers owner Bud Selig had indicated to Fehr that the owners wanted a "civil, credible and an honest labor-management relationship."

By December 8, the bargaining positions of both sides had come clearly into focus. Among other things, the union wanted assurance against a repeat of collusion. The union also wanted eligibility for salary arbitration rolled back from three years of major league service to two years. Prior to the 1985 collective bargaining agreement, eligibility had been two years of major league service. Based upon the representations of ownership in 1985 that ownership was suffering financial distress, the union agreed to a change in eligibility requirements from two years to three years of service.

The owners had a new plan to exercise control over the players and the game. The new scheme was to be achieved through collective bargaining and it had a name—Pay For Performance (PFP).

The owners wanted to implement PFP and by early December had tendered to the union their proposal. Don Fehr called the concept of a pool of money to be divided by the players "by definition a salary cap." Fehr knew that a salary cap limits salaries to below that which would otherwise be paid to the players in a free market.

The early reports of the PFP proposal indicated that it was to apply to all major league players with less than six years of major league service. While players with six or more years of major league service would remain eligible for free agency, revenues allocated under the owners' proposal for total player salaries would be divided between the PFP and free agent groups. If a club exceeded a stipulated payroll limit, that club would be ineligible to sign any free agents other than its own players who had become free agents.

Dave Nightengale of *The Sporting News* reported from the winter meetings in Nashville, Tennessee, held in early December 1989.

In the December 18 issue of *The Sporting News,* he wrote an article which included Chuck O'Connor's response to the question of whether the owners would initiate a lockout:

> "Will the owners lock out the players in spring training if there's no new Basic Agreement at that time? Well, we have discussed with the owners the use of economic pressure in collective bargaining. That is the catalyst that drives our system. Lockouts and strikes are what make people serious.
>
> Let me just say in regard to any discussion about a February 15 lockout date: We (the owners) want an agreement in place in time to protect spring training."

Don Fehr called a meeting of the players in December in Scottsdale, Arizona, to discuss the PFP proposal and the overall status of negotiations. This meeting was especially important, given the seemingly contradictory statements emanating from O'Connor that ownership wanted a "civil, credible and an honest labor-management relationship" while stating "the use of economic pressure in collective bargaining . . . is the catalyst that drives our system. Lockouts and strikes are what make people serious."

Murray Chass was at the Scottsdale meeting and wrote in the January 1, 1990, issue of *TheSporting News*:

> During the Scottsdale meeting, the players wondered how deeply they could trust the owners, in spite of O'Connor's stated intentions. One morning, the players opened their newspapers and saw puzzling comments attributed to Commissioner Fay Vincent.
>
> Vincent, who spoke with reporters at the owners' sessions during baseball's winter meeting in Nashville, Tennessee, was quoted as using the term "economic warfare" and talking about a negotiating deadline "sometime after the middle of February."
>
> "I find it odd and troubling," said Donald Fehr, executive director of the Major League Players Association, "that as negotiations begin and on the heels of announcements of 'we've got to have trust, we have to form a new partnership, we're going to persuade players things are going to be different,' that words like 'economic warfare' are coming out of their mouths and suggestions of setting deadlines, which means lockouts, are coming out. It doesn't seem to be a very auspicious way to begin discussions."

In individual player contract negotiations for the three years leading up to the 1990 collective bargaining talks, club negotiators insisted on lockout clauses in guaranteed contracts. While three versions of a lockout clause existed, all three versions were drafted by PRC lawyers and effectively provided that a player would not be paid his guaranteed salary during the period of a club initiated lockout which complied with the requirements of labor law.

The owners' desire to "get it on" could not have been more clear to those of us close to the scene, their rhetoric about ending hostilities notwithstanding.

On January 9 the PRC presented the union more details of the PFP proposal. The clubs offered 48 percent of the income from tickets and broadcasts. Income from concessions, parking, and postseason play was excluded. Players with less than six years of major league service would be paid based upon statistical criteria. There would be no salary arbitration, no guaranteed contracts for younger players, no multiyear contracts for younger players, and no maximum salary cut provision. At the same time, the PRC announced that it had advised all clubs not to open spring training camps on February 15 until further notice from the PRC.

The union responded by advising the PRC that the players were not interested in the PFP system. Further, the union said that if the owners expected the players to become partners in the proposed revenue sharing plan, then the players expected to be made full partners in all areas of economic decision making—including when, where, and at what price expansion of the leagues should take place.

On February 1 Chuck O'Connor stated that the "camps will not open" unless an agreement was reached before February 16. O'Connor continued to say that the clubs would discuss the players association's proposals only in the context of the players agreeing to revenue sharing. This position, if accepted by the players, would have rendered moot the issue of the service time necessary to qualify for salary arbitration. More details of the PFP proposal were reported. Players would be divided into four categories:

1) Starting Pitchers
2) Relief Pitchers
3) Outfielders, First Basemen, Third Basemen, Designated Hitters
4) Catchers, Second Basemen, Shortstops

Joe Goddard reported in *The Sporting News* that PFP was modeled on the Chicago White Sox salary plan for its young players. That "plan" contained a complex grid system of performance criteria, which determined the compensation for players through their fourth year of major league service. A player who elected the White Sox system forfeited one year of salary arbitration eligibility in exchange for the "opportunity" to enter the plan.

If a player elected not to enter the plan, the salaries for his first three years of service were preset by the White Sox at very low levels. The White Sox salaries for such "obstinate" players were far lower than the salaries paid by other clubs to comparable young players.

Other reports credited the authorship of PFP to PRC lawyer Rob Manfred, Mets executive Frank Cashen, and Brewers executive Harry Dalton.

*   *   *

The entire Pay For Performance concept was simplistic and — to borrow a favorite phrase of the owners — "not in the best interests of baseball." When I heard the letters PFP, I recalled the old advertisements for PF Flyer shoes for kids. After studying PFP, I pictured it as the creation of some kids wearing PF Flyers while playing rotisserie baseball, rather than as the creation of the best minds working for ownership.

Under the PFP system, ownership would annually contribute a fixed sum of money to be divided by players with less than six years of service based upon a set of statistical criteria. The statistics to be used were basic and simplistic. No credit would be given for moving a runner from second to third with nobody out. No consideration would be given for a catcher's prowess at calling a game or for other important components of defensive ability.

Except for free agents, individual contract negotiations would become obsolete. Instead of negotiating individual player contracts through agents, based upon the myriad of factors, including intangibles, which are presently utilized, simplistic statistics would be used to determine a player's salary. During collective bargaining sessions, PRC negotiators told the players in attendance that one of the benefits of PFP would be the elimination of agent fees for nonfree agent players.

Most owners and a few general managers hailed PFP as a revolutionary idea and described it as both innovative and efficient. They did not bother to add that they would be relieved of the difficulties associated with sophisticated contract negotiations. Some club executives conceded that they did not care how players were paid as long as there was a system upon which everyone could agree. More sagacious general managers recognized the foolishness of PFP and publicly distanced themselves from the entire proposal.

The PFP system represented a zero-sum game for the players. Since the pool of money would be fixed, the better one player did, the less money available from the pool for other players. PFP would have pitted player against player — probably a happy thought for most owners, but bad for the game of baseball.

Under PFP every player would know in advance the exact statistics upon which his salary would be determined. In such a circumstance, it would be unrealistic not to expect a player to alter his approach to the game in order to maximize the statistics by which he would be paid.

Move a runner over by making an out? "No way." Call for a breaking ball with a runner on first base? "Gimmee a fast ball." Come out of the game and jeopardize a win by turning the ball over to a weak bull pen? "The manager and I will have to talk." Pitch for the Cubs? "No thanks, I'm going to the Astros." Hit in the Astrodome? "Sure, right after they move the fences in; otherwise I'll play in Fenway Park."

The Sunday papers would have posted not only the usual player statistics, but how each player was faring under PFP. The team concept of baseball would have been dealt a severe blow. PFP embodied all the components necessary to create the ultimate, selfish baseball player. It would have likely created a league full of such players. One could envision a player celebrating an over-the-wall catch by an opposing outfielder in a 5–1 game. While the catch might have robbed a teammate of a solo home run, it would keep the pool of money from being reduced "needlessly." A player would have understood that the best financial scenario for him would have been to have a good day while everyone else had a bad day. PFP welcomes the PGA tour to baseball.

In my judgment PFP threatened the integrity of the game and the way baseball is meant to be played as a team sport. Player and fan reaction to such a system would have been appropriately negative.

The players, the Major League Baseball Players Association (MLBPA), and the agents all opposed PFP. I did not talk to one single player, union official, or agent who approved of this hare-brained scheme the owners planned to cram down our throats.

*   *   *

Murray Chass reported in *The Sporting News* that Commissioner Fay Vincent had chaired a series of three meetings between negotiators for both sides in late January and early February. Nothing was achieved.

The owners met on February 9 and stated that spring training camps would not open on February 16 without a new agreement in place. As the showdown loomed one week away, Associate General Counsel Gene Orza of the players association said:

> The only reason we're in this situation is because of their deadline. They knew they wouldn't have an agreement by this date when they made their proposal. When you make a proposal you know we can't accept, somebody has to ask himself if it was made with the idea of having it rejected. It was designed to effect a confrontation, and they'll get one.

Sure enough, the lockout started on February 15. It was the third lockout initiated by ownership over the past six collective bargaining agreements. The other two occurred in 1973 and 1976.

In the February 26 *Sporting News*, Murray Chass reported that Commissioner Vincent had entered directly into negotiations on February 16, just as the lockout began. Vincent offered his own plan for solving the labor impasse. His plan included:

1. A four-year agreement with an option of the clubs to reopen the agreement after two years.
2. A Revenue Sharing Commission to be appointed and issue a report by April 1, 1991.
3. The owners would drop the PFP proposal.
4. Free agency would remain as is.
5. A minimum salary for players for their first three years of major league service. Those salaries would be:

first year	—	$ 75,000
second year	—	125,000
third year	—	200,000

6. Salary arbitration for players after three years of service but with a limit on awards of no more than a 75 percent raise.
7. Pension contributions by clubs would remain at $39 million.

Don Fehr's reaction was immediate. He noted that during the 1985 negotiations the owners proposed a 100 percent limit on raises in salary arbitration and minimum salaries for young players not yet eligible for salary arbitration. The players rejected those proposals in 1985 and would do so again in 1990, Fehr said.

Fehr noted that Vincent's proposal would reduce salaries for players with service of less than three years. The plan would also take away the incentive for clubs to sign players to multiyear contracts. Fehr said the proposal "is far more regressive than what they started with."

When asked if he had a problem accepting input from the commissioner, who was an employee of the owners, Fehr told Murray Chass:

> I'll take input from anybody I can find. I don't think this commissioner has made any pretense of who he works for. As he has explained to us, it's pretty hard to hide the fact that he's in their meetings and he isn't in ours. That, coming from a commissioner of baseball, is a refreshing thing.

Commissioner Vincent responded to the union's rejection of his proposal: "I don't think we are going to get it done. It's clear to me it's going to be very difficult to get an agreement in the short term."

Bob Hertzel reported Don Fehr's summary of the then current state of affairs in *The Sporting News*: "The issue is whether we are going to have a mechanism of fixed costs for salaries or if we are going to let the market determine salaries."

Hertzel summarized the dichotomy that existed in negotiations:

> The owners have talked about salary caps and limiting arbitration awards, while they have talked revenue sharing and pay for performance, while they have talked about the eventual decline of competitive balance because of unbalanced payrolls, Fehr has steadfastly held to his association's belief that only minor adjustments are needed in the system.

Those minor adjustments included a 50 percent increase in the minimum salary to $100,000, roster sizes of twenty-five men per major league club, increased pension contributions because of the increase in revenues to the owners from the new national television contract, and salary arbitration eligibility after two years of major league service.

During the lockout, players remained unified and avoided "hanging around" the spring training camps. St. Louis outfielder John

Morris spoke for many baseball players when he compared their unity to that of their football counterparts during the ill-fated 1987 football strike:

> You're not going to see 20 guys in matching uniforms out there working out like they did in the NFL. The football guys killed themselves. To show ownership how anxious they were to make a mistake.

Hertzel expressed the disconsolate mood of many observers when he wrote:

> It seems there's nothing anyone can do to put an end to the lockout. This is just how it was in 1976, when the owners locked out the players in the wake of conflicts over free agency.
>
> As the issues were resolved in '76 (after Commissioner Kuhn ordered the camps reopened), both sides vowed that there would be peace in the baseball world.

As Don Fehr observed, "It turned out to be peace in our time the same way it did for Neville Chamberlain."

On February 21 the owners made a new proposal. PFP was nowhere to be found in that proposal. The owners agreed to continue salary arbitration but demanded the following changes:

1. Players could not use for comparative purposes
   a. contracts of free agents
   b. multiyear contracts of players near free agency
2. Players could use only salaries of players at their specific position and within their service group
3. The 20 percent maximum cut rule would no longer be in effect for players eligible for salary arbitration
4. All salary arbitration hearings would be at one location
5. Three arbitrators would hear each case
6. All cases would be heard before any decisions were announced

The owners proposed the following minimum salaries for the first three years of a player's major league career:

First Year	—	$ 75,000
Second Year	—	100,000
Third Year	—	250,000

The owners also proposed an $8 million bonus pool for players in their second or third year of major league service. Bonuses would be paid based upon the following broad performance categories:

Pitchers — Games Pitched, Victories, Saves

Hitters — Games Played, Times on Base, Total Bases

Don Fehr's response to the proposed changes in salary arbitration criteria was quick and to the point. The owners, he said, "have been trying to break the connection between free agency and salary arbitration ever since I've been in baseball." Needless to say, the union summarily rejected the owners' proposal.

The day after the owners' proposal was rejected, a dramatic change in negotiations occured. Commissioner Vincent was back in the role of chief negotiator for the owners. The proposal of the previous day was withdrawn. Under the owners' proposal of February 22, salary arbitration was to be left unchanged. The minimum salary would increase to $85,000. The first year contribution to the pension plan would be $42.6 million and total contributions would equal $179.3 million over four years.

Don Fehr's response was upbeat: "From where the clubs were the suggestions put forward today indicate they have come a substantial way. They are not there yet. It is obviously a step in the right direction, but there's still a long way to go."

Murray Chass reported in *The Sporting News*:

> The back-to-back changes in proposals marked the second and third times in 10 days that the owners had changed their offer significantly. The first time was the previous week, when they removed their revenue sharing plan from the table and replaced it with an intention to negotiate a more conventional Basic Agreement. The first change marked the entry of the commissioner as the man seemingly in charge of the owners' team. Seeing that the owners' revenue sharing effort was failing to elicit even a hint of interest, Vincent stepped in with his proposals.

Chass opined that, "the indication from the owners' side was that the chief aim was to get an agreement now, create labor peace, restore the players' trust in the owners and return to the revenue sharing plan in the future."

The optimism did not last long. On February 25 Commissioner Vincent said, "This is really tragic, and the season is in very heavy jeopardy." Negotiations soon adjourned due to a lack of progress. Murray Chass reported that Commissioner Vincent was on Cape Cod, Deputy Commissioner Steve Greenberg was in Los Angeles, Chuck O'Connor was in New York City, and Don Fehr was in Tampa, Florida.

Salary arbitration eligibility was clearly the key issue keeping the two sides apart. The players association wanted eligibility returned to two years of major league service. The owners were adamant that eligibility remain at three years of major league service.

Bob Verdi, writing in *The Sporting News*, summarized the situation thusly:

> How deep into the twilight zone is our national pastime? Well, the argument about 1990 is so bizarre that we keep hearing tales of horror from 1985, when the players relented and voted the other way, from two years to three on arbitration. The players contend that they did so only because management sold them a platform of imminent economic strife.
>
> Nothing of that kind materialized. The game prospered, and now the players want back what they surrendered under false pretenses. Meanwhile, in Reaganesque fashion, the owners can't recall any dire forecasts. They say they won the concession fair and square. So then, here are management and labor fighting over what happened five years ago, as if they don't have enough to fight over now. Beautiful.

Chuck O'Connor reported that the owners' position had hardened. Fehr responded by saying, "What are they going to do — have a double lockout?" Besides the issue of salary arbitration, other important, unresolved issues existed — the pension contribution, the minimum salary, and roster size.

Negotiations resumed on March 5. Don Fehr said that O'Connor had "clearly ceased being the chief management spokesman. The commissioner is the chief management spokesman."

The commissioner was not upbeat, however, at the end of the March 5 session. Murray Chass reported the commissioner's assessment of the status of negotiations:

> "We are in a very *bad* situation," Vincent said. "The season is in very heavy jeopardy. There's a major risk of serious confrontation here. It looks to me like it is approaching the unavoidable."
>
> "I have spent my life negotiating deals. I know how to do it. When the other side doesn't want to negotiate, I know you're wasting your time. There's no point in meeting without a willingness to negotiate."

According to Chass, Vincent was extremely critical of the players association for being unyielding in its determination to secure the return of salary arbitration eligibility after two years of major league service. Said Vincent:

> Without compromise, obviously from very firmly held positions, there's no point in having a meeting. You can't just sit and talk about the same things. There should be a basis for progress.

Gene Orza did not take kindly to Vincent's comments, and responded with the union's position:

> We have been waiting to negotiate for 18 months. They spent 17 of them on rotisserie baseball for lawyers. Finally, they make a meaningful proposal in the last 10 days. We stand ready to negotiate. They are the ones who closed the camps, not us. What he (Vincent) is saying is just public relations posturing. He really means that what the players association is unwilling to do is memorialize three years for salary arbitration eligibility. If that's what he means by not being willing to negotiate, he's damn right.

*   *   *

I had been consumed through February 20 with the resolution of contracts for salary arbitration eligible clients. I successfully tried the cases of Pirates players Doug Drabek and John Smiley during the latter part of the salary arbitration season. Despite my victories in those cases, I was, as usual, mentally drained by February 21. By February 26 I was regenerated, so I turned my attentions to the collective bargaining negotiations. It was obvious that the lockout was very serious and that the confrontation between the owners and the union would not be a short one.

I followed the "progress" of the negotiations for a week. After the March 5 meeting, I telephoned Don Fehr. I did not call him to seek a status report on the negotiations. Rather, my purpose was to offer "to make myself useful" in the negotiations.

I was well aware that over the years many people had volunteered to become involved in labor negotiations. Neither labor nor management lacked for offers from such well-intentioned volunteers. Nor did they lack for offers from grandstand artists, who always had the perfect solution for everyone.

Over the history of baseball's labor negotiations, certain individuals have occasionally served as intermediaries outside of the traditional bargaining arena. Lee McPhail had done so in the past. My brother, Alan, communicated a very important message during the

1981 strike. I understood that respected people could prove useful. I understood, though, that without proper "authorization," intermediaries, whether potentially effective or potentially meddlesome, were a nuisance to everyone directly involved in the negotiations.

I believe that during the pressure-filled times in labor negotiations, it is the natural inclination of each side to seek out the "peaceniks" on the other side to help broker a deal. While this practice might produce some useful dialogue, I believe that enlightened warriors, not peaceniks, make peace.

Though I offered to be useful to Don Fehr to help solve the impasse, I also had a specific proposal for him. I proposed to call Jerry Reinsdorf, the owner of the White Sox and the Chicago Bulls of the NBA, but only with the union leader's express authorization. I told Fehr that I had been in his position so many times that I knew the "locked into battle" feeling well. He laughed and agreed we both knew the "feeling" well. Precisely for that reason, I said, I believed I could help broker a settlement.

Fehr knew that I had been a militant over free agency and that every Hendricks client had "held the line" during the protracted 1981 strike. He also knew that I had been adamantly opposed to PFP. While we both regarded PFP as a hare-brained scheme, Fehr and others in the union regarded it as a defeated Trojan Horse designed to prevent the union from achieving any meaningful gains in collective bargaining. I could not disagree with that judgment.

The union was not in the mood to accept a status quo agreement. Collusion had cost the players hundreds of millions of dollars, while profits had soared for clubs and franchise values had appreciated rapidly. Collusion and the PFP proposal served to unify the players, who were by now frustrated that nothing positive had been achieved.

While the union was angry and frustrated, the owners were very embarrassed and frustrated by the easy defeat of the PFP proposal. The failure of the PFP proposal was a major setback for those owners who had spent a considerable amount of time building internal support, only to see it unceremoniously scrapped by the commissioner on February 16. Those owners were in no mood to have humiliation heaped upon embarrassment. They were prepared to continue the battle over salary arbitration eligibility in order to maintain, if nothing else, their pride. The idea of a "giveback" was to them non-negotiable.

In my judgment, strong feelings and minor economic issues were now driving the negotiations. Securing or protecting free agency, maintaining the salary arbitration system, and defeating collusion — holy wars for sure — were not at issue. Rather, the question of the precise timing for salary arbitration eligibility was threatening the regular season. The resolution of that question, I believed, could be produced through a thorough economic analysis.

I was quite sympathetic to the union's position. After all, the increase in service from two years to three years to qualify for salary arbitration had been secured under false pretenses. Collusion had followed for half a decade, and the bogus PFP proposal had just been repelled. The players, the union, and the agents were all tired of being on the defensive.

Fehr asked if I thought that Reinsdorf would really listen to me or agree to use me as a go-between. "If you authorize it, I believe he will. What do we have to lose?" I said. Fehr agreed that there was nothing to lose, so he authorized my mission.

Like the Hendricks brothers, Don Fehr grew up in the Shawnee Mission area of Kansas City. Many people believe that he replaced Marvin Miller as executive director. He actually replaced Kenneth Moffett, who followed Marvin Miller. Fehr is a first rate lawyer and strategist. He is forever vigilant in his defense of the union and is blessed with uncommon common sense and good judgment. He is often viewed uncharitably because of the scowl or furrowed brow he usually exhibits in front of television cameras. People forget that those are not leisured times, and Fehr's expression reflects the measured style in which he delivers his position.

Many owners and general managers fear Fehr. They believe that either he does not want to make a deal, or he does not know how to make a deal. Fehr is more than willing to make the *right* deal. Unfortunately, the owners always adopt a negotiating position to obtain a deal which only a weak or foolish leader would accept.

I called Jerry Reinsdorf and told him that I was calling with the knowledge and authorization of Fehr. "Things have gone too far," I said. "It's time to put emotionalism aside and find a pragmatic solution to a pragmatic problem." Reinsdorf was receptive to my call but hesitant to believe that a solution could be brokered in the easy manner I had proposed. The more we talked, though, the more it became clear to me that he wanted to make a deal, but not one that would humiliate the owners. Reinsdorf said that they had been embarrassed by the failure of PFP, and they believed that the union wanted to "rub in" the defeat. He wanted to be sure that I was for real. I assured him that I was.

Reinsdorf said he would talk to Bud Selig, the head of the PRC and owner of the Milwaukee Brewers, and call me back. Within hours, Jerry called back. Selig and he were prepared to proceed with my offer to serve as an intermediary. I now had their permission to work behind the scene to help achieve an agreement.

It was clear to me that some part of the two year class of players would have to become eligible for salary arbitration in order to reach an agreement. I decided to calculate the economic consequences of this issue to both parties. I looked at the differential between what players with two years of major league service would earn with and without salary arbitration eligibility. While my conclusions were based upon estimates, those conclusions reinforced my belief that the issue was a relatively minor economic one.

Over the prior five seasons, an average of 87 players each season had played with two years of service. I evaluated the players who were in those five "two year classes," and concluded that the cost to clubs of a reasonable compromise on the issue of two year salary arbitration eligibility would be about 5 percent of current payroll. In any given year, there would be almost one player per club who would be a major player and thus earn a superior salary.

If a compromise were reached making the high end, by service days, of players with two years of service (2+ players) eligible for salary arbitration, the following players would have been eligible. In the 2+ class of 1990, quality players with a high number of service days included Ellis Burks and Joe Magrane. In 1988, the 2+ class with a high number of service days included Ivan Calderon and Kirk McCaskill. The 2+ class of 1987 contained a banner crop of "seniored" 2+ players — Roger Clemens, Scott Garrelts, Tony Fernandez, Kirby Puckett, Joe Carter, John Franco, and Jose DeLeon.

I reported to Fehr my belief that the only logical solution to the dispute would be an agreement of salary arbitration eligibility at a service point greater than two years and less than three years. While this was the obvious solution, Don advised me that there was strong sentiment among the negotiating committee to secure the return of salary arbitration eligibility for the entire group of players with two years of service.

After reviewing my numbers with the union leader, I suggested that the union run its own numbers to see what conclusions it reached. Don agreed that the union would do this.

I phoned Reinsdorf and told him of my analysis and conclusions. He told me that there remained extreme sentiment among the owners not to give back their major gain from the 1985 negotiations. Because the owners had lost so many battles with the union, I did not believe that Jerry was overemphasizing the recalcitrance of his group. I nevertheless urged the White Sox owner to have the PRC run its own numbers to see if they agreed with my conclusions. He agreed they would run the numbers.

The owners and the players met shortly after my discussions with Don Fehr and Jerry Reinsdorf. The gap suddenly narrowed on the four major issues. The respective positions of the two sides were as follows:

Salary Arbitration:	Players	Top 50 percent, by seniority, of the two year class would become eligible for salary arbitration
	Owners	No change in eligibility from three years of service
Minimum Salary:	Players	$105,000
	Owners	90,000
Pension Contributions:	Players	$ 57 million
	Owners	50 million
Roster Size:	Players and Owners	25 men in 1991 and thereafter; 1990 season undecided.

On March 9, 1990, the owners rejected the compromise on salary arbitration eligibility proposed by the union. Murray Chass reported in *The Sporting News* that the owners "were dismayed that the players even made" the compromise proposal on salary arbitration eligibility. He reported that "the owners refused to budge on the eligibility level."

PRC member Fred Wilpon of the New York Mets recalled at a March 9 press conference that Commissioner Vincent had suggested a token number of players be eligible out of the two year class. "That number, at most, was 10," Wilpon said. According to Chass, "Wilpon totally ignored the arbitration issue" and instead suggested that negotiations continue either over the amount of money in the pool the owners had previously proposed or on some other new concept.

On March 8, Commissioner Vincent proposed that the owners

lift the lockout on the express condition that the players pledge not to strike. The union quickly responded by labeling the offer a blatant public relations ploy. The commissioner responded that he would not order the spring training camps opened, unlike what former Commissioner Bowie Kuhn did in 1976.

Fehr and Vincent met on March 10 at Vincent's home in Greenwich, Connecticut, but no progress was made. Said Vincent:

> Obviously, they are far apart in principle. The clubs just aren't going to give that year back on arbitration and the union wants half of that year. It's no longer a matter of ideas. It's a matter of force. Someone has to change his position.

Not only was Opening Day of the 1990 season now in jeopardy, but the first several weeks of the regular season as well. Mathematically, the owners and the players were approximately 43 players apart on salary arbitration eligibility. That worked out to 1.65 players per club, or slightly less than 7 percent of the major league roster. In any given year, it was unlikely that many of those 43 players would be major players. Despite the difficulties that lay ahead, I remained unyielding in my belief that I could bridge the relatively small difference between the parties.

Because the owners had not budged, I telephoned Reinsdorf first. I asked what his research had revealed. He said that the PRC's research tracked mine. "So give me a proposal on salary arbitration eligibility of less than three years of service," I said. He reminded me of the intractable position held by some members of the PRC. I gently but firmly reminded Reinsdorf, who I knew to be a big fan of baseball, that he, Selig, Fehr, and I all had a responsibility to preserve the integrity of the season when such a relatively modest amount of money was at stake. "This is not principle, this is money," I said, while railing against the hard-liners of the PRC.

Reinsdorf agreed to poll his troops but suggested that I talk directly to Bud Selig. Bud thanked me for my efforts and listened to my ideas about a compromise solution. He said he would review the numbers with Jerry and the other members of the PRC.

Fehr was frustrated over the owners' outright rejection of the union's compromise proposal. I told him that I remained optimistic and to keep studying the numbers to see where a deal could be made. I gave him the same "pep talk" I gave Reinsdorf and Selig about our responsibilities. I not only gave that pep talk, I believed that pep talk.

By March 12 the lockout had become the longest in baseball history. On that date the PRC removed its muzzle from owners, allowing them to speak out about the labor dispute. Predictably, the owners offered a stream of comments. Neil Hohlfeld of the *Houston Chronicle* reported the comments of Astros owner John McMullen, a hard-liner on the salary arbitration eligibility issue:

> The reason I'm pessimistic is that I've been in the meetings, trying to get it done and it just doesn't happen. I'm convinced we're faced with a situation where it is old-time unionism that's dominating instead of intelligence, brains and understanding.
>
> They (the players' union) seem incapable of making a deal. The owners surrendered unconditionally, and now they refuse to accept the surrender. This is nothing more than just power. It's just taking and taking and taking.
>
> The issue over two years or three years (arbitration eligibility) is a hoax. What they want to do is take back what they negotiated away five years ago. Only because that proves that they're stronger than we are.

Hohlfeld reported that McMullen did not believe players should be involved in the negotiating sessions. McMullen went on to say:

> You've got players in there, who when they have an argument with their wives, they've got to call their agent to settle it. And they're up negotiating a major league contract. They should not be in there. They have to hire a guy to do their own contract, and they're negotiating a labor agreement. It's crazy.
>
> We're not trying to screw these guys; we're not trying to defeat the union. We're trying to put some enlightened concepts into this thing. I was dragged kicking and screaming into the revenue-participation plan, because I don't happen to be a disciple of Karl Marx and sharing with workers. I believe in the capitalistic system. But there's no question revenue sharing is the future of this sport. Otherwise, we're going to end up with a continual fighting, bickering relationship. That's not in the interest of fans or baseball.

On March 14 Royals owner Ewing Kaufman said, "We have given, given, given. I'm tired of giving. I think we've gone our share down the road." Kaufman threatened to shut down the season if the players did not accept the owners' proposal on salary arbitration. He cited concessions by the owners on free agent mobility, changes in the waiver rules, minimum salary concessions, player benefits, and roster sizes. Kaufman said that the union's stubbornness "over 80 players" was inappropriate.

Carl Pohlad, owner of the Twins, said of Don Fehr, "I don't think he really understands the economics of baseball. And I don't think he wants to."

George W. Bush, Rangers managing general partner, said he wanted the union to have a secret ballot on the PRC $4 million bonus pool, saying, "If, in fact, there is disgruntlement among the rank and file, as the rumors say, union leadership will hear about it. And one way is a private ballot."

Jeff Smulyan, the Mariners owner, said, "I'm fervently in favor of the way the PRC is handling it (the lockout). I see more unity in the owners at this point because of all that's happened the last two months."

I concluded that while all of these comments represented convictions sincerely held, they constituted saber rattling for public consumption. I was unmoved by this public relations rhetoric.

About that time, I had convinced Fehr, Selig, and Reinsdorf to cease making hostile public comments about the other side's position in the negotiations or about the other side's negotiators. Rude comments to the press were no longer to be a part of the daily ritual. Everyone viewed the contemporaneous public comments made by the owners as the handiwork of the hard-liners in the PRC.

By March 12, I was convinced that Fehr, Selig, and Reinsdorf truly wanted to make a deal. I pointed out to them that if two to three days of the regular season were lost, the resulting economic losses to everyone would exceed the economic gains that either side was now trying to achieve. "Let's do it now, while everyone can win," I said, rather than two weeks later "when everyone will have lost."

The discussions between Reinsdorf, Selig, Fehr, and I now revolved around the percentage of the two-year class that would become eligible for salary arbitration.

Reinsdorf proposed 12 percent, which represented an average of ten players per year. The PRC was now prepared to follow Vincent's suggested compromise of ten eligible players, only Vincent's role and influence had by now diminished according to Reinsdorf and Selig. I had not heard Vincent's name mentioned by any of my contacts during my entire mission. The commissioner had long ago alienated the PRC hard liners, while not being able to persuade the union to reach a compromise.

Fehr was again negotiating with Chuck O'Connor, who was

irritated by my presence in the negotiations. Fehr elected to stay with my line of communication and authorized me to present to Selig and Reinsdorf a new proposal. That proposal was as follows:

1990 — no change in salary arbitration eligibility, since the salary arbitration season had already been completed

1991 — the top 20 percent, by seniority, of the two-year class would become eligible for salary arbitration

1992 — the top 25 percent, by seniority, of the two-year class would become eligible for salary arbitration

1993 — the top 35 percent, by seniority, of the two-year class would become eligible for salary arbitration

The proposal would likely produce 16 to 17 eligible players in 1991, 21 to 22 eligible players in 1992, and 27 to 28 eligible players in 1993.

Reinsdorf responded with the position that his 12 percent offer represented a compromise in principle, and that the PRC would not agree to a higher percentage of the two-year class. I pointed out the obvious, which was the number of players over which the labor dispute now continued.

1991 —   6
1992 — 11
1993 — 17

I separately suggested to each side that it consider reaching an agreement at 20 percent for all three years, but both sides dismissed that number out of hand.

It was now Friday, March 16. I was optimistic, but I knew that if a full season were to be played in 1990, the upcoming weekend would be crucial. Marvin Miller was to meet with the players' negotiating committee and the player representatives at the union offices in New York City. The PRC would be meeting several blocks away.

During the prior week, several news reports had suggested that a settlement was imminent. Other reports had indicated that the players were about to abandon their position on salary arbitration eligibility. I was furious, especially after learning that certain players, perhaps well-intentioned, had said inaccurate things to the media.

I spent a good part of the week of March 12 trying to convince Reinsdorf that those news reports were bogus. Still, he knew that the player representatives or the negotiating committee was going to vote on March 16 or 17. I later learned that he and Selig routinely talked with certain key, naïve players on the White Sox and the Brewers. These players did not recognize that while they were talking to their "friends," they were also "sleeping with the enemy."

On March 16 Marvin Miller met with the negotiating committee. On Saturday, March 17, Marvin met with the player representatives. Fehr believed that the players needed to hear directly from Miller, lest the owners get the idea that a deal could be had on their terms.

Don believed that my efforts had been productive and that an agreement might be close, but he could not be sure. He also wanted more than 12 percent of the two-year class to become eligible for salary arbitration.

The negotiating committee turned down the owners' proposal late at night on March 16. On Saturday, March 17, Reinsdorf was aware of this fact when he told me that the owners were stuck at 12 percent. Fehr advised me the same day that the negotiating committee was stuck at 25 percent "across the board." "They won't go to your suggested 20 percent," he told me.

I replied that I had reworked the numbers on both sides and had the "17 percent solution," a takeoff on the movie, "The 7% Solution." "Why 17 percent?" Don asked. "Because it's about halfway between your two positions, slightly below my compromise, and has a nice ring to it. At this point, any reasonable number will do," I said. He laughed and said he would keep me posted. I told him I would remain chained to my desk for as long as it took. I did not tell him that since childhood I had considered seventeen my lucky number.

I talked to both sides again in midafternoon on March 17. I hit Reinsdorf with my "17 percent solution," but he seemed indifferent to it, although I detected the feeling that he wanted to make a deal. Still, both sides told me to tell the other side that it had "their best offer."

At that point, I did not know whether to laugh or cry. I was locked in to a pragmatic solution, but the remaining disagreement over less than 2 percent of the players looked as if it would prevent the other 98 percent from playing a full season.

Since 1976, I had not been in Houston during March for more than a couple of days each year. The weather in March 1990 was exceptionally beautiful, but I could not enjoy it. I might as well have been literally chained to my desk, either at the office or in my study at home.

During the weekend of March 17, my two youngest children stopped in my study to ask why I continually sat at my desk, waiting for the phone to ring. My daughter Daehne kidded me that I had a phone "sewn in my ear," a reference to a family phrase I had coined years earlier when I discovered that then teenage daughter Kristin could talk incessantly on the telephone. Daehne, by the way, had followed in her steps quite nicely.

My son, Bret, was actively involved in his high school debate program and was pointing toward an eventual state championship. He stopped in my study on the way to a tournament and asked in a concerned voice, "Dad, don't you ever leave your study?" I told him I could not leave my post until the lockout was over.

After talking to both parties Saturday night and making no progress, I went to bed with the knowledge that secret meetings were scheduled for Sunday morning. I also knew that I had delivered final ultimatums to each side prior to those meetings.

Fehr phoned me early Sunday afternoon to tell me that he was pessimistic. The players had dropped to 20 percent and the owners had come to 15 percent. The minimum was agreed at $100,000, and the pension was agreed at $55 million. Still, the 5 percent differential seemed like an unbridgeable gap. The eligibility of four players was now holding up the season for everyone. I wished Don luck and said I would be in my study all day. I talked to Reinsdorf, who confirmed the status of negotiations. Since both Fehr and Reinsdorf were together in the league offices on Park Avenue, I concluded that there was nothing more I could do on that crucial day.

Don called an hour later and said the PRC members were caucusing. He passed the phone to Gene Orza. Gene was relaxed and thanked me for my efforts. I told him that I hoped they would "put the deal to bed." He said the next few hours would be telling.

At approximately 5:23 P.M., central standard time, Don called. He said he was in the commissioner's vacant office, and that I deserved to be the first to know that the 17 percent solution had been agreed to by both sides. "You have a deal?" I asked. "Yes," he said, "and you named it." We laughed as he filled me in on the final events of the day. While he was meeting with the players' negotiating committee, and the PRC members were caucusing, Orza and Mark Belanger of the union struck the compromise with Chuck O'Connor and Steve Greenberg. Orza accepted the 17 percent solution with the words, "Let's play ball."

I facetiously complained about how both sides had been intractable over the past twenty-four hours. "Both sides used me as a tool to test the other side, not just as a mediator," I said. "Of course," said Fehr. "You knew that was part of the role." Indeed, I had. I just wished that I could have been more confident that a deal would have been reached that last day.

A news conference was convened at 1:15 A.M., eastern standard time, on Monday, March 19, to announce the settlement. Spring training would start on March 20, with most players reporting on March 21 and 22. The season would open on April 9, a delay of one week. However, it appeared that a full complement of 162 games could be played by working in over the course of the season the games missed during the first week.

Roster sizes would be 24 in 1990, and expand to 25 in 1991. Salary arbitration would remain as it existed, except that the most senior 17 percent of two-year players, who also had at least 86 days of major league service during the previous season, would become eligible. This meant that approximately 15 additional players would become eligible for salary arbitration beginning in 1991. The minimum salary would be $100,000, with cost of living escalators in later years. The pension contribution would be $55 million.

The agreement could be reopened after three years. To further evaluate the state of the industry, an economic study committee would be appointed to report to both sides. Finally, the owners would be liable for treble damages if they were again found liable for colluding.

On the afternoon of March 19, I received a telephone call at my office from Jerry Reinsdorf. He said he was at the airport in New York and was ready to board a plane bound for Chicago. He said he wanted to call and thank me for my assistance. "I didn't think you had it in you, Randy," he said. I told him I appreciated his thanks and his comment, and replied, "You see too much of me in the role of an advocate. How do you think I have represented such a diverse group of players for so many years, or have led an organization, if I didn't have 'it' in me?"

We exchanged pleasantries for a few more minutes, and Jerry conveyed Bud Selig's thanks as well. Reinsdorf told me that there had been a healthy and extended debate over the compromise and that the PRC vote had not been unanimous. It was not an easy task, he said. I told him I appreciated the fact that his and Bud's interest in the game of baseball had transcended the possibility of a needless and costly battle to everyone, including baseball fans throughout the world.

Both Don Fehr and Gene Orza telephoned the next day. While we reviewed the events of the prior weeks, their main purpose in calling was to express their appreciation for my intervention. Orza said, "You have served the interests of the players well, and you are to be commended." For my part, I expressed my appreciation for the outstanding leadership they had continually demonstrated at the players association. Without the type of vigilance they had consistently demonstrated, player rights would have eroded, I said.

By the end of the day on March 19, my brother Alan already had our spring training travel schedule. We would leave within a few days and head first to Kissimmee, Florida, the spring training headquarters for the Astros.

As I sat in the chair by my desk, I reflected on the hectic and tension filled days of the prior weeks. Those days had been different for me, for by assuming the role of a diplomat or mediator, I had played a role distinctly different from the one I usually played in the baseball world. I felt very satisfied, content in the knowledge that I had done something that, perhaps, no one else on the scene could have accomplished.

Very few people knew of my mission. The first day at spring training Terry Puhl of the Astros came over to where I sat in the bleachers, watching batting practice. He told me that every player owed me a thank you, and he wanted to convey his thanks personally. While acknowledging his appreciation, I wondered how many other players knew the full story. I need not have been concerned, for no other player approached me on the subject during that abbreviated spring training trip.

*   *   *

While the record is reasonably clear, one reads in books and newspapers and hears on television that one of the reasons former Commissioner Fay Vincent was fired was because he intervened during the 1990 lockout to effectuate the final compromise. It has become a part of baseball lore to credit Vincent with resolving the 1990 labor dispute. Typical of this view is the headline found in the June 12, 1992, *USA Today* International Edition: "Vincent comes to the rescue, saving the game again." Under the headline, baseball columnist Hal Bodley wrote:

In August 1985, players went on strike for 24 hours before a compromise was reached and the game resumed.

Certain owners were angered. They felt their brethren had caved in. They were willing to let the players stay out, insisting that was the only way to restore financial sanity to the sport.

Jump ahead to 1990. If not for Vincent's involvement in negotiations, the owners' spring training lockout would have lasted much longer. Instead, the season was delayed only a week, and it was business as usual. It was during this settlement that either side was given the option to reopen in December of 1993, a year earlier than the agreement expired, if necessary.

This same group of owners, led by Chicago White Sox chairman Jerry Reinsdorf, sincerely believes that had Vincent not orchestrated their deal, they were close to breaking the union.

Foolish thought. The Major League Players Association is so well-organized and has so much expertise at its fingertips that most owners are no match.

Perhaps because major league club owners have worked hard to earn the opprobrium of most sportswriters, many of those writers rallied around the embattled commissioner during his dispute with the dissident owners. Due to either intentional revisionist writing, faded memories, or lack of knowledge, many of those writers have romantically revised the history of what transpired during the lockout. Those revisions include ignoring the commissioner's active role on behalf of the owners during negotiations, as well as crediting the commissioner with the settlement in which he did not participate.

Vincent was accommodating to the press and interviewed sympathetically. Because of press support, he was elevated to martyr status during the dispute and after his resignation.

A fundamental question, though, deserves an answer: How did Vincent succeed in alienating his employers to the point that he was forced to resign? The answer is that Vincent persuaded his employers that they could neither trust his judgment nor his decisions.

Vincent was essentially correct on several of his decisions, such as realignment and fighting to retain the power of the commissioner to intervene in matters where the best interests of baseball are at stake. However, it was not simply the power that Vincent possessed that concerned many owners. Rather, it was the way Vincent exercised that power which caused those owners to seek to dismiss their employee.

Despite appearances, Vincent was anything but judicious in most of his major decisions. His decision on the division of the proceeds from expansion succeeded in alienating nearly every club in both leagues. While ostensibly "taking care of" the American League clubs by giving each club $3 million out of the money from National League expansion, he also required each American League club to surrender three players in the expansion draft. Because American League clubs valued their three lost players at a higher value than $3 million, the American League clubs did not consider the decision beneficial to them.

The National League clubs were offended, because they believed that all of the proceeds from National League expansion should be divided exclusively within their league. Historically, expansion proceeds were divided by the clubs within the league which was expanding. In seeking to reach a compromise acceptable to clubs in both leagues, Vincent instead managed to alienate nearly every club because of his decision.

Vincent correctly recognized that realignment was necessary for the game. Yet, the manner in which he handled realignment created a firestorm within his own constituency. The results included insubordinate public comments by National League President Bill White. The Associated Press reported on July 7, 1992:

> Commissioner Fay Vincent's decision to order National League realignment drew immediate criticism from NL President Bill White along with the Chicago Cubs, Los Angeles Dodgers and Cincinnati Reds.
>
> "We believe the commissioner's decision is wrong, bad for baseball and especially bad for baseball fans here in the Chicago area," the Cubs said in a statement. "We are presently considering alternatives available to us."
>
> Vincent ordered the Cubs and St. Louis Cardinals to the West next season, and Atlanta and Cincinnati to the East. The divisions had not been altered since the league split in two in 1969, and the Cubs had blocked realignment when a vote was taken in March.
>
> "I am very disappointed with the commissioner's extraordinary decision to override the National League constitution," White said in a statement. "By this act, the commissioner has jeopardized a long-standing, working document which has governed the National League for decades. Although we worked to attain realignment, we did so within the guidelines of the constitution."
>
> Los Angeles owner Peter O'Malley issued the most critical statement, saying "the Dodgers believe that the commissioner has

exceeded his authority under the Major League Agreement by attempting to revoke what is, in effect, a business decision made by the National League clubs in accordance with the National League constitution."

"Even though the Dodgers voted in favor of realignment and have traditionally been supportive of the office of the commissioner, the Dodgers do not concur with the commissioner's decision in this instance because it undermines the National League constitution. This decision could establish a dangerous precedent for the future of both the National and American Leagues."

Cincinnati voted in favor of the plan, but owner Marge Schott criticized Vincent's decision.

"Can somebody who doesn't own a team, is not an owner and is really an employee—do we want to be set where that person has the right to do anything he wants to?" Schott said. "I don't think that's fair to ownership because, after all, it's the owners who should make the decisions."

The Cubs, owned by the *Chicago Tribune*, elected to sue Vincent to stop his edict on realignment. Vincent had expressed a desire to limit the power of "superstations," such as the *Tribune* owned WGN, but it was not known whether that played a role in his decision on realignment. Vincent had said that "superstations suck up advertising," a reference to CBS and ESPN having difficulties generating higher advertising revenue because of the superstations.

Rudy Martzke of *USA Today* evaluated the motives behind the Cubs' lawsuit and Vincent's decision on realignment. Martzke wrote in his July 9, 1992, column:

> Commissioner Fay Vincent might not know a way out of baseball's TV contract rights-fees mess, but he knows the correct side of the plate when it comes to logical alignment of the National League.
>
> The Chicago Tribune Co.-owned Cubs, who have revenues at WGN driving their lawsuit, are in the minuscule minority in challenging Vincent's "best interests of baseball" decision to move the Cubs and St. Louis Cardinals to the NL West in 1993.
>
> Certainly, the Cubs are upset. In the schedule the NL most likely will reveal Aug. 1, the league favors 16 games against clubs within the division and nine outside the division.
>
> That would mean a 78% increase in games the Cubs play in the Mountain and Pacific time zones, from the current 18 to 32. Advertising executives downplay the amount of ad revenue that

the popular Cubs would lose by the increase in West games. Where WGN figures to take a revenue hit is when its lucrative 9 p.m. CT news is delayed past 10 p.m.

The larger point: A move that is greeted warmly by most observers and fans (the NL agreed with Vincent, earlier, by a 10-2 vote) should not be blocked by one market.

The NFL has a similar situation. Its "three-fourths approval" rule meant a small minority of NFL owners was able to reject a two-year extension of the TV contract that the league hierarchy wanted.

The difference is that Vincent has a "best interests" power the other commissioners don't have, and that baseball has an antitrust exemption the other leagues don't enjoy.

Baseball is the statistical sport. Here's one stat for the Cubs: No legal challenge to the commissioner's "best interest" power has been upheld.

The Cubs prevailed in federal district court in Chicago, and the commissioner was enjoined from imposing his plan of realignment. During the commissioner's appeal from that decision, Vincent was forced out of office by the owners.

Ironically, months earlier Vincent had won "Round 1" in his fight to preserve his authority to invoke the powers of the commissioner. Hal Bodley reported in the *USA Today* International Edition of June 13, 1992:

> Baseball's owners tiptoed out of the Waldorf-Astoria hotel Thursday afternoon looking like children who just had their wrists slapped.
>
> Normally, their biggest priority on the final day of quarterly meetings is to make their flights home. Thursday was different. These owners were numb.
>
> They'd just been lectured by Commissioner Fay Vincent, caretaker of the national pastime, about unity and how only one agenda in baseball can succeed, and that loose cannons firing in different directions seldom hit the target.
>
> Vincent wrestled with the idea of such a speech Wednesday night. Could he walk away from the huge split among owners, one in which he was sitting in the middle, or face his employers head-on?
>
> There was really no choice.
>
> Seldom do club owners pay as much attention to sermons as they did Thursday. Most of them came to New York Monday

unaware that a small faction within their fraternity had tried to greatly reduce the commissioner's role in labor negotiations.

They were shocked and embarrassed, but Vincent rebuffed the attempted power play. Round 1 to the commish.

Wednesday, a verbal battle erupted during a hastily called joint meeting when Player Relations Committee chairman Bud Selig, who orchestrated last week's move, tried to explain his reasoning.

Selig, president and CEO of the Milwaukee Brewers, hired Richard Ravitch last fall as management's chief negotiator. Ravitch suggested the change to strengthen the owners' side in the next labor negotiations, which will occur after the '92 or '93 season.

Some owners, led by the Mets' Nelson Doubleday, blasted Selig for his tactics.

"I obviously made clear that I have no intention of changing my authority under the Major League Agreement," Vincent said. "But I also made it clear I understand baseball has a PRC and Mr. Ravitch was hired to handle the negotiations. I've said many times I know my role, but I also know under the Major League Agreement I have authority and I am not going to surrender it during my commissionership."

At Wednesday night's dinner, one owner after another approached Vincent, shook his hand, and congratulated him for his leadership of the past 10 days. Owners who had been on the fence were now solidly in his corner. It was precisely at that moment the commissioner realized he must issue an additional wake-up call.

"There is no way baseball succeeds on any front with dissension and disunity," Vincent said. "There are a lot of places to go, but we have to go together. It's a lesson baseball has never learned."

What the owners need to do is take a good, hard look in the mirror. Stop throwing darts at the commissioner, stop blaming their problems on Don Fehr and the players union.

If the owners are left with an empty feeling from the events of the past 10 days, they've no one to blame but themselves.

Come on, gentlemen, look at those who have handled negotiations in the past. Stop finding fault and start finding solutions, one of which might be to shake up the membership on key committees.

Trying to break the union, locking out players and looking for scapegoats only serve to damage this wonderful game.

After all, it was the failed strategy — put into place by the same men who tried to rebuff Vincent — that cost all owners $280 million in collusion damages. Some clubs are still paying the bill.

It's time baseball owners moved into the 1990s. Innovative thinking and a common agenda is the only solution. Club owners demand their players answer to the manager. Maybe they should follow the same philosophy.

"It seems to me my responsibility continually is to say, 'Let's try, or maybe now,'" said Vincent. "Maybe, given the enormous problems facing these people, they will finally recognize this kind of discord and bickering and relatively undistinguished behavior is not productive."

Vincent ultimately learned that an employee, however powerful, cannot effectively perform his job without the confidence and support of his employer. Vincent alienated the majority of his constituency over a number of his decisions and his public pronouncements of power. Perhaps because he publicly flaunted that "power," the owners felt compelled to remind him that he served at their discretion. In the final analysis, it may well be that his removal had less to do with the power of the commissioner than with his lack of "feel" for how the inside game of baseball is played. As one owner told me, Vincent made enemies needlessly by how he made decisions and by the public manner in which he defended those decisions.

A good example was Vincent's handling of the Yankee officials — Gene Michael, Jack Lawn, and manager Buck Showalter — who testified on behalf of Steve Howe. The following wire service report appeared in the July 2, 1992, *Houston Chronicle*:

> One day after serving as character witnesses at the grievance hearing for suspended pitcher Steve Howe, New York Yankees manager Buck Showalter, general manager Gene Michael and vice president of baseball operations Jack Lawn were called on the carpet and threatened with suspensions Wednesday by an angry Fay Vincent.
>
> The commissioner apparently charged that by testifying on Howe's behalf, the three Yankees employees were testifying against baseball's drug policy and thereby ran the risk of suspension.
>
> "This is a kick in the (deleted) to the commissioner's office," Vincent told the trio, according to a source familiar with the hearing.
>
> In separate meetings with the three, Vincent made it clear, the source said, that suspension was a definite possibility and they would have to "sweat it out" until Monday.
>
> The commissioner used three phrases, according to the source, to emphasize his anger: "You've effectively resigned from baseball . . . You've quit the game . . . You're out of baseball."

Vincent's reaction to the testimony by the Yankee officials, including his keeping Buck Showalter at the commissioner's office even though the Yankees were beginning a game at Yankee Stadium, persuaded many owners that Vincent was abusing his power. Needless to say, Vincent's reaction did not endear him to either the union or player representatives.

I was not endeared to Vincent by his decision on Roger Clemens' appeal of his fine and suspension, which arose from his ejection during the last game of the 1990 American League playoffs. Clemens was the starting pitcher in game four of the 1990 playoffs. Umpire Terry Cooney ejected Clemens during the bottom of the second inning based upon Cooney's belief that Clemens was trying to "show up" Cooney before the world. Roger was incredulous that he had been ejected and "lost it" after realizing that he had been thrown out of a championship game for no apparent cause.

The question of exactly what Clemens said and did prior to his ejection became a major issue during the appeals of the $10,000 fine and five game suspension imposed by American League President Robert Brown. Chapter 4 details the appeal to the American League president. After Dr. Brown upheld his original fine and suspension, Roger appealed that decision to Commissioner Vincent.

Gene Orza and I represented Clemens during his appeal before Commissioner Vincent. Orza secured a super slow-motion tape of the incident from Phoenix Communications. He hired Deborah Copeland, a professional teacher and lip reader affiliated with the New York Society for the Deaf, to serve as an expert witness. Ms. Copeland was herself deaf and was prepared to testify as to exactly what Roger said to Cooney. Because the tape secured from Phoenix Communications came from a camera focused directly on Clemens for the entire duration of the incident, it was impossible to miss anything that he said or did prior to his ejection.

Ms. Copeland's expert testimony was quite convincing. Orza and I thereafter argued that because Cooney's basis for ejection was improper, no discipline should be imposed on Clemens. With respect to Ms. Copeland's testimony and our argument, Vincent wrote in his decision:

> Clemens has claimed that there is an inadequate basis for the discipline imposed because there was no justification for his ejection and the events subsequent to the ejection should be viewed in and to some extent excused by that context. I have given careful

consideration to this argument. After a review of the videotapes of the incident and the expert testimony of the professional lip-reader, whose testimony was not available to Dr. Brown, it is my opinion that the report submitted by umpire Cooney contains some inaccuracies. It is my view that some of the statements Cooney asserted he heard Clemens make prior to the ejection were not, as I view the record before me, uttered at that time. The videotapes and the testimony of the lip-reader convince me that Clemens did not say . . . before he was ejected.

Intent on finding out why he had been ejected and determined to voice his displeasure at being ejected, Clemens "overstayed his welcome" on the field. In the heat of his passion at being unfairly ejected from a playoff game, he made inappropriate threats to umpires Cooney and Jim Evans.

Near the end of the hearing, it had become clear that Gene and I had proved to Vincent that Roger had been improperly ejected. Vincent asked us for our opinion of how he should rule. I suggested that he rule that Clemens had been improperly ejected, but direct him to make a charitable contribution as penance for his inappropriate conduct after the ejection.

Vincent left Gene and me with the impression that we would be pleased with his ruling. We were not. The commissioner completely upheld Brown's fine and suspension. Vincent probably believed that, as lawyers, Orza and I would be pleased to read in his written opinion that we had "won" our argument and "proved up" our case that Roger had been improperly ejected. The commissioner rationalized his decision to uphold the fine and suspension:

> Notwithstanding my findings regarding the events prior to the ejection, I am not persuaded that the discipline imposed should be eliminated or reduced. Regardless of the basis for an ejection — or any other decision, right or wrong, made by an umpire on the field — a player must comport himself during games within certain accepted norms.

As far as I was concerned, Roger Clemens had been "falsely arrested," but was being convicted for resisting arrest. The punishment being assessed for resisting arrest was the same punishment for the crime for which he had been falsely arrested.

Gene Orza, Don Fehr, and I all went ballistic. According to Fehr, Vincent was surprised that we were upset. He believed that the acknowledgement in his decision that Clemens did not deserve to be ejected would satisfy us. Of course, the press reports of the decision indicated that Dr. Brown's discipline had been upheld and that our appeal had been rejected. However, we were supposed to be pleased.

As an attorney, Vincent should have had more respect for traditional American notions of justice. Don Fehr felt compelled to memorialize his displeasure with the decision. Fehr wrote to the commissioner:

> In deciding the matter, the arbitrator must decide if the penalty can be upheld, on the basis of the original charges and evidence adduced in support of such charges. No arbitrator (or judge or jury, for that matter) has the discretion to change the basis for the discipline imposed in the process of upholding it. To do so is fundamentally unfair in the most elemental sense.
>
> • • •
>
> A way was found to uphold the penalty imposed, even though you clearly determined that the umpire was simply wrong in ejecting Clemens when he did: Clemens simply did not engage in the conduct upon which Cooney based his ejection. How, then, is the penalty sustained? The decision holds that even if the original basis for the imposition of discipline is erroneous, it is entirely appropriate for the arbitrator to review the evidence, seeking to find some other act(s) for which discipline can be imposed, and then to say, in effect, the player is guilty of something other than what he was charged with, and so the penalty will be upheld. In other words, the judge becomes the prosecutor.

Orza and I had argued that umpires are supposed to be like good parents—above the emotional fray, meting out discipline objectively, dispassionately, and even-handedly. One expects players to be emotional, we said, which was all the more reason for umpires to demonstrate poise on the field.

Fehr addressed this point in his letter to Commissioner Vincent:

> Here we have a case in which it has been demonstrated that the best pitcher on a team contending for the American League Championship was ejected by an umpire who, it now seems clear, was emotionally involved in the game, and erroneously rushed to the judgment that Clemens was verbally insulting him. Players are suppose to be emotionally involved in games, umpires are not. This was the most crucial game of the year. Under these circumstances

could anyone have reasonably expected that Clemens would simply say "OK", hang his head and meekly walk to the bench? Of course not. On the other hand, it cannot be argued seriously that it is appropriate for the umpire to eject a player because he, the umpire, becomes emotionally involved. Yet, such is precisely what happened here.

*   *   *

Under certain circumstances, Commissioner Vincent rode to the rescue of an owner in distress. Such an owner was John McMullen, the highly visible and mercurial principal owner of the Houston Astros. Despite bringing Nolan Ryan home in 1980 by signing him to the first $1 million contract in baseball, McMullen is more remembered in Houston for the bitter contract dispute he had with Ryan following the 1988 season. That dispute led to Ryan leaving the Astros to sign with the Texas Rangers.

Astros fans will never forgive McMullen for not agreeing to Ryan's terms. While Ryan preferred to remain with the Astros, he was unwilling to do so on McMullen's terms. The final score of the Ryan contract dispute was a big "W" for the Rangers, a big "L" for the Astros, and a big "$" for Nolan. To make matters worse for McMullen, the Astros club went downhill after Ryan left, and Nolan pitched two more no-hitters — in a Rangers' uniform. Every time Ryan did something good for the Rangers, the fans and press in Houston let the Astros owner know of their continued displeasure.

McMullen started out like many new owners — giddy to be in the limelight and desirous of accommodating his players. He left like many owners — embittered and disillusioned that his dreams had not been fulfilled. Baseball is, after all (would that Oliver Wendell Holmes knew) a business "in the commonly accepted use of" the word.

McMullen readily communicated his contempt for Houston during his tenure as the owner of the Astros. While the city certainly benefited from his purchase of the Astros from two corporate creditors who had been running the club, his public air was patronizing and reminiscent of the movie style of a nineteenth century British general visiting one of the colonies. Whether or not Houstonians were "colonials," they certainly knew they were being treated as such.

The Ryan incident changed McMullen from patronizing to bitter, and he complained repeatedly of his "mistreatment" by the press. To McMullen, Ryan was the villain for leaving town. The Astros had paid Nolan quite handsomely, the owner argued, so the "Express" should not have left the club over a monetary disagreement. No one in Houston sided with the Astros owner, primarily because the Rangers paid Ryan more than he had asked from the Astros.

After a decade of ownership, McMullen decided to sell the Astros in 1990. He was unwilling to accept a sale at less than fair market value. The Astros baseball club was part of a larger enterprise, which included the lease on the Astrodomain complex and the ownership of neighboring hotels. This made valuing the club more difficult than usual. To further complicate matters, a number of interested parties did not want to purchase the hotels.

Frustrated by his inability to consummate a sale to a group of local investors interested in purchasing the Astros, McMullen became increasingly impatient to sell. Drayton McLane, Jr., of Temple, Texas, had been a member of the "local" group which had declined to meet McMullen's terms. McLane was primarily a football fan and had little interest in baseball as a fan. But having sold his company to Wal-Mart, he had time and money.

McLane was involved in negotiations to purchase the Astros for his own account when Commissioner Fay Vincent came to Houston on June 1, 1992, to speak to the Houston Forum Club. I was in the audience and heard Vincent's speech, which dealt with recent events in baseball, including Pete Rose's banishment from baseball.

After the speech, I approached Vincent to thank him for coming to Houston. Vincent headed toward the side doors of the large Westin Galleria ballroom as I left via the main entrance and exit doors. I had no inkling that Vincent was headed to a press conference in one of the anterooms adjacent to the ballroom. At the press conference, Vincent would give a different speech and reveal his true reason for coming to Houston.

The *Houston Chronicle* ran a front page story of Vincent's press conference in its June 2 edition. Under the headline: "Vincent takes swings at Astros fans, McMullen critics," reporter David Barron wrote:

> Baseball Commissioner Fay Vincent warned Houston fans Monday that criticism of Astros owner John McMullen is hampering efforts to sell the team and nudging baseball's hierarchy "toward unattractive conclusions" about the sport's future in Houston.
>
> Vincent emphasized that McMullen has not asked to move the Astros from Houston and said he believes it is in the best

interests of baseball to keep the team here. However, he criticized fans and media representatives who he said are "trying to punish baseball or John McMullen because they don't like his style of ownership."

"By demeaning John (McMullen) and by failing to support the team, I wonder whether the people of Houston have not made the sale more difficult," Vincent said at a Westin Galleria news conference. "I wonder why the people of Houston believe they can punish John and not harm the prospects of a sale to other owners."

"We simply can't sit and watch baseball being devalued, if you will, over a period of time," he said. "And so I say the people of Houston, the media, the baseball fans, ought to support this team while the sale takes place. Only if a new owner can obtain support from fans and the corporate community will a proper sale be possible."

"To continue as we are going is, in my judgment, to push baseball toward a wall, and I don't think that is in the interests of the fans here or of baseball generally." Vincent added.

Vincent, accompanied by McMullen, was in Houston to speak to the Houston Forum Club but did not touch on the controversial Astros owner and his efforts to sell the team until a subsequent news conference.

The commissioner praised McMullen's 13-year record as owner of the team and said he "deserves better treatment than he has obtained in this community." Vincent said the last-place Astros "have a fine group of young players, and they, if not John, deserve better treatment."

And while emphasizing that "baseball ought not to threaten," Vincent called the history of Houston's National League franchise into question by saying, "Houston has never reached the level of attendance that one might have expected."

Unmentioned in the commissioner's remarks was the fact that attendance was up 57,528 over last season entering Monday's game despite the Astros' 21-27 record. However, a season-low 7,544, including McMullen and Vincent, attended Monday night's 7-1 Astros loss to Montreal.

McMullen, who lives in Montclair, N.J., purchased the Astros out of receivership in the late 1970s but fell into disfavor with many fans because of the dismissal of popular team executive Tal Smith in 1980 and his refusal to re-sign local hero Nolan Ryan after the 1987 season.

McMullen announced in November 1990 that the Astros and their parent Houston Sports Association, which controls the lease on the county-owned Astrodome, were up for sale. Retired Texas Commerce Bancshares Chairman Ben Love and his son, Jeff, headed a group that offered $86.5 million for the team only, but that offer was rejected.

Temple businessman Drayton McLane, a member of the Love group and one of the largest shareholders in Wal-Mart Inc., has been mentioned as a potential buyer. Both Vincent and McMullen, however, said Monday that a sale is not imminent.

Attendance has dropped from 2.3 million in 1980, when the team won the National League West title, to 1.2 million last season, when the team lost 97 games and finished last in the NL West.

Vincent, however, defended McMullen's stewardship of the team and questioned why fans and critical media representatives are "forcing John and all of us toward unattractive conclusions."

"I am concerned that the attitude toward John is so negative that it begins to affect baseball, and I don't think that is fair to baseball, to say nothing of being fair to John," he said. "Those who are trying to punish baseball or John McMullen because they don't like his style of ownership are missing the point."

"It's not a case of can we punish John or show him that we don't like him or that we're mad about Nolan Ryan. The point is that we have to have a decent sale to people in this community who can see that there's going to be support."

The Astros came on the market as two National League expansion franchises were awarded to Denver and Miami, leaving rejected bidders such as St. Petersburg, Fla., eager to attract an established team.

McMullen's critics have suggested the Astros could be ripe for a move, but Vincent said the owner "has never asked me to move the team." He declined to assess the chances of the Astros being moved, saying, "I don't think baseball ought to threaten."

"What this community can do is what all other communities who care about baseball do, and that is support the team, support the franchise and support, if you will, the mechanism by which the ownership transfers," he said.

During a late-afternoon visit to the Astrodome, Vincent said he does not believe McMullen plans to sell the team to a buyer who would move it to another city.

"I don't think it's his intention. I know it's not mine," he said.

It did not take veteran Houston sports columnists or Astros fans long to react to Vincent's speech. Ed Fowler of the *Houston Chronicle* wrote his usual front page column in the sports section of

June 2 under the headline of "Dancing with who brung him." Fowler wrote:

> Fay Vincent came to town, called us media wizards together and chewed us out but good. It is we and the baseball fans of Houston, he said, who are screwing up the sale of the Astros.
>
> We'll get to the fans' transgressions later. We in the media, it develops, beat up poor John J. McMullen relentlessly like so many bullies. If only we'd stop, the ballclub would be sold.
>
> OK, I want to do my part, so I'm going to declare a hiatus on McMullen-bashing — for a few paragraphs, anyway. Instead, I'm going to use that space to propose something constructive. Here's a way baseball could enhance its image dramatically:
>
> Name a member of a minority group commissioner.
>
> Baseball would score a giant victory with those who fault it for dragging its feet on bringing more minorities into management roles, and it would lose nothing in the process. Why? Because if Vincent showed anything on Monday, he demonstrated that the powers-that-be will let any dunce have the job.
>
> What matter the dunce's color?
>
> Vincent, like most ghosts a pale sort, wasted about a half-hour of everyone's time with a stream of pap about how abused McMullen has been and how recalcitrant this city's baseball fans have been, steadfastly refusing to deal in specifics or attempt even a feeble stab at making sense. He was the commissioner from Wonderland.
>
> "This is a fine group of young players," Vincent intoned, "and they, if not John, deserve better, but my view is that John deserves better....I don't think the attitude in this community is fair to baseball, not to mention fair to John."
>
> **We've been very, very bad**
>
> Naturally, we were all on the verge of tears, but we pressed on and asked the ghostly commissioner for a few facts in support of his contention. Since he kept hammering the point that the Astros are composed of exciting young players, including the 1991 National League Rookie of the Year, we noted that these stalwarts lost 97 games last season and occupy last place again. In light of the club's performance on the field, what would he consider an acceptable attendance level?
>
> "There's no weighted average that I feel is the right number," he said.
>
> He then produced a most curious analogy to the Atlanta Braves, who, by Vincent's own words, drew about 3,000 a game when they wallowed for years in the cellar, then sent the turnstiles whirling when they won a pennant last year.

When it was pointed out that Houston has turned out for the Astros when they have won, Vincent countered with a claim that even in 1980, attendance (2.3 million) never hit the 3 million mark. Just as he had ignored the record of those exciting young players of today, he conveniently neglected the fact that 12 seasons ago virtually no club topped the 3 million mark, as the most successful ones do now.

"Houston," he pouted, "has never reached the level of attendance one might have expected."

Vincent also warned darkly of "unattractive decisions" in the future if this city doesn't shape up. When pressed on whether moving the ballclub were a possibility, however, he sniffed, "I don't speak in those terms because baseball doesn't threaten."

Thank goodness.

Keep those owners happy

We do certainly understand that part of the commissioner's job is to do his utmost to maintain the value of each and every franchise, and that if he were seen to do otherwise he would have a host of angry owners to whom to answer. We can even grasp that it would be a most unpleasant experience to have John J. McMullen shrieking in one's ear on a regular basis and that one would go to some lengths to avoid recurrences.

To venture among us and suggest that tepid fans and media people who take weekly nasty shots are thwarting a sale while ignoring McMullen's string of goofs and the current state of the club, though, is to insult the intelligence of everyone in this city.

It was left to McMullen to explain that media criticism of him would scare off prospective buyers because they would be fearful of similarly harsh treatment. Those with sensitive teen-age children would be especially leery, he said.

What bilge wash. Whoever succeeds John J. will enjoy the longest honeymoon since Adam and Eve. He'll be more welcome in the streets than General Patton.

"I'm very pleased and proud of what I've done in Houston," McMullen swore. "I've been a great benefactor to this city."

And, like Tal Smith and Nolan Ryan, the rest of us forgot to thank him.

OK, thanks, John. Best wishes and all that. But when you leave, do us one more favor. Take Fay with you.

Former Astros beat writer Kenny Hand closely followed the McMullen era. Hand had become a lead columnist and wrote his reaction to Vincent's "lecture" in the June 3 *Houston Post*. Under the heading of "Moving tactics won't cut it, Mac," Hand wrote:

Any day now expect Larry King to resurrect the D.C. follies, the tired rumor about the Astros moving to Washington. Or Vermont. Or Iola, Kan. Or *somewhere*.

Dr. John, that eternal pessimist, wouldn't have it any other way.

Why else would he allegedly have whispered to some people in baseball, according to my sources, that potential Astros buyer Drayton McLane is not for real, that McLane only wants the publicity?

Simple. John McMullen must have an agenda. If you believe the Astros owner privately questioned the wherewithal of McLane, it makes sense why Fay Vincent came to McMullen's rescue like a call to 911.

Dr. Mac wants the perception that there *still* is no serious buyer for the Astros, that Houston's fans would stone him if afforded the chance and that, gee, no investor would want to enter this minefield.

He wants it known that he has marketed this club with the Houston Sports Association and its accompanying Astrodome lease for two years and even found a company to take HSA off his hands.

"Not going to happen"

But no takers for the team.

There's only one reason for creating that perception. Despite his published pleas to the contrary, McMullen appears to want the option of moving the Astros if an outsider can meet his price.

So I called several high-ranking baseball officials and asked if the "moving" climate has changed among the owners.

The answer: A resounding no.

"It's not going to happen," said one.

"There are nine franchises for sale and Seattle's the only one that's connected with a move," said another.

"Where would he move?" said a third source. "Washington doesn't have a serious group to buy it and besides, Baltimore would be dead-set against it (because of obvious competition). Orlando? Maybe. But Miami doesn't want that, and what if Tampa-St. Pete gets the Mariners?"

Vincent's veiled threat

Remember, 75 percent approval of the National League's owners (plus a majority vote in the AL) would be required to send the Astros franchise packing. Baseball doesn't make a habit of uprooting clubs. The Washington Senators' move to Texas in 1972 was one of the exceptions.

Vincent, who seemed browbeaten by McMullen, left the implication that if Houston didn't open its arms to McMullen the rest of this summer (and beyond?), there would be "unattractive decisions" involved.

Hey, Fay, you mean the Astros might move if attendance doesn't improve for this team that's on a pace to lose more than 90 games for a second consecutive year? "Baseball doesn't threaten," he replied smugly. Hey, Fay, that *sounds* like a threat.

Drayton McLane is a serious player. He's worth as much as $800 million and some insiders swear he's a billionaire, so enough of this jazz about him being a publicity hound. People who know McLane promise that he is unassuming and that, if anything, was naive about the hornet's nest of media activity he would generate by inquiring about the Astros. *Headline R Us* is not his motto.

McLane still in picture

I'm told that McLane hasn't lost interest over the past six weeks. Quite the contrary. These things take time even when the transaction isn't nearly as complicated as this Astros deal. Do not fear, I am told, McLane will be here eventually as the owner.

In fact, there has been speculation that McLane, the second-leading stockholder in Wal-Mart, might even bring in Wal-Mart's No. 1 guy, David Glass, as a limited partner.

McMullen may figure the more he and the commish can paint Houston as a hopeless situation and ripe for transfer, the quicker McLane may hand him a check.

Deep down, though, can't you picture the often-grumpy McMullen smiling as the Orlando-bound Astros posed for their last team picture here, yelling, "We're moving to Disney World!"

Just what the Dr. ordered.

But only in his dreams.

Vincent left Houston and appeared on the Larry King radio show the next day. A surprise was in store for Vincent, as reported by Jay Frank in the June 4 *Houston Post*. Under a sports section front page headline: "Vincent 'shaken' by Astro fan's wrath," Frank reported:

> Baseball Commissioner Fay Vincent was "visibly shaken" after fielding a barrage of phone calls made from irate Houston baseball fans to a national radio show late Tuesday night.
>
> A day after he came to Houston and told fans they should support the Astros to help the team's sale, Vincent was a guest on radio's *Larry King Show*.
>
> If the baseball chief didn't fully grasp the depth of animosity toward Astros owner John McMullen, he does now. The phone-in portion of Vincent's hourlong appearance was dominated with rancorous calls from Houston.

"He was visibly shaken," King, who considers Vincent "a good friend," said Wednesday by telephone.

"At one point, he looked at me, and the aide who came with him, as if to say, 'This is unbelievable!'"

"People seemed to be saying, 'We hate you (McMullen) so much we'll lose baseball rather than have you make an extra dollar selling this team.' I think Fay was shocked by all their emotion and anger."

During the interview with King — whose show is carried by KTRH-AM (740) — Vincent seemed to backtrack a bit. In his first public comments after the Houston visit, he said he had made only "a modest point that was blown way out of proportion."

The commissioner attempted to soften his stance, although he repeated the gist of his message.

"I said, I think, that it's important for the fans to support this franchise in order for a sale to take place," Vincent reiterated. "To be critical and negative of him (McMullen), and to hold baseball hostage because you don't like an owner, wasn't helpful to getting a sale effected.

"I did not criticize the fans. I was talking about supporting the franchise, precisely so we could have a new owner."

"So, what you were saying is," King replied, "if there's a fan in Houston tonight who wants baseball to remain there, and doesn't like Mr. McMullen as an owner, you should buy a ticket for tomorrow's game."

Vincent: "Well, in a simple-minded way I'm saying that baseball is more important than any particular owner. And if you want baseball in Houston, support baseball while we're in the process of effecting the sale."

King insisted that Vincent is just a soul whose intentions for baseball in Houston are good — even if they don't seem that way.

The CNN and Mutual Radio host said that while Vincent "was issuing a subtle warning" of the possibility the team could move, he believes the commissioner "honestly doesn't want it to happen. He feels there's a lot of potential in Houston, despite all the negative reaction to McMullen."

Vincent indicated as much during the interview. He agreed with King's assessment that Houston "could be a vibrant baseball city," and drew a parallel with Atlanta.

"I was in Atlanta two years ago when there were 3,000 people (in the stands)," he said. "And people were telling me it's a football town and baseball's dead and there's no hope — all the things you hear in Houston.

"Yet a little excitement, the team plays better, and look what happened last year (when the Braves won the pennant)."

King then asked Vincent if McMullen has said he would "sell them (the Astros) to outside interests" if he can't find a Houston-based buyer?

"No, he's never raised that issue with me," Vincent stressed. "We both agree that the best course is to have that sale take place to Houston interests."

"As I said in Houston, he's never asked me for permission to move."

When heard on King's show the words "Astros" and "move" are bound to bring back memories for Houston fans.

In 1986, King started the rumor that the Astros would relocate to Washington, D.C. — where he lives — at the end of the season. He has never revealed his source, although many observers believe it was McMullen.

King didn't rekindle the story Tuesday night, but he ventured close to it. He mentioned he knows investors in Washington and Tampa, Fla., who are eager to buy the Astros and move them out of Houston.

However, King has declined to identify the parties.

King heard from even more Houston fans after Vincent left, during the two-hour "Open Phone America" portion of the program. He said Wednesday he has "a better understanding" of why Vincent left Houston lower on the popularity scale than George Bush and Bill Clinton could ever imagine, with sports talk shows buzzing in the aftermath.

But King firmly believes Vincent was "doing people (in Houston) a favor, however awkwardly" with his remarks.

"As I read it, he's only trying to keep baseball in Houston," King said. "McMullen has probably told him 'I can't take much more of this (ridicule).' Fay figures he has to do something dramatic. So maybe this is it."

The aftermath of the Vincent press conference and the public reaction to it, motivated long-time Houston sports columnist and author Mickey Herskowitz to reflect on the office of the commissioner in his column on the front page of the *Houston Post* sports section on June 5. Under the headline: "Fay latest in long line of grovelers," Herskowitz wrote:

Oy, Fay! What a nice person you are to come to Houston, fling your body in front of John McMullen and take all those arrows for The Good of the Game. But that's why baseball commissioners are paid the big bucks: to grovel for the owners and play their craven little political games.

Actually, it is possible to feel some sympathy for Fay Vincent, who left town just ahead of the mob. Has anyone noticed what a hellish losing streak baseball has been enduring in matters related to his office? The problems began about the time they buried Judge Kenesaw Mountain Landis. Had to, you know. He was dead.

The owners replaced him with a commissioner named Happy, and them embarked on a lifetime search for Dopey, Sleepy, Grumpy, Sneezy, Bashful and Arsenio.

Happy Chandler, a former governor of Kentucky, took the job in 1948 under the impression that he had the power to actually make decisions. As soon as he made a teeny weeny one — he approved the integration of the sport — the owners sent him back to his old Kentucky home.

Ford had no better idea

Ford Frick was a former sportswriter, raising the office to intellectual heights never to be seen again. Frick survived in the job until his retirement by discovering the magic phrase. Whenever a controversy developed, he announced that the problem was "a league matter."

To replace Frick, the owners turned to the ranks of the military, judging correctly that the turbulent times ahead would demand discipline. Some of the owners thought they were hiring Gen. Curtis LeMay, a famed bomber pilot.

By an apparent bookkeeping error, the owners instead elected a general named William D. (Spike) Eckert, who had earned his rank in the quartermaster corps. The news media gleefully reported that the Unknown Soldier had been located. Eckert lasted only a couple of years. He was hired to do nothing, and he did it so well the lords of baseball fired him.

Getting hang of it

At this point, in the mid-1960s, they were dangerously close to defining what the job should be. The new czar was Bowie Kuhn, whose most recent employment had been as legal counsel to the National League. His other qualification for the job was his previous service as a batboy for the Washington Senators.

Those were fun years in the Cuckoo's Nest. Oakland owner Charles O. Finley had to issue a public apology after he called the commissioner "a village idiot." Humbly, Finley declared: "I apologize to all the villages of America. He's the nation's idiot."

After 14 years on the job, the owners pried Kuhn's cold fingers away from the legs of his desk and moved in the dynamic Peter Ueberroth, the man who had organized the 1984 Olympics and turned a profit. Gads, the owners were dazzled by that credential.

Oops, a good choice

The media, the players and the umpires loved Ueberroth, which meant that the owners had made a nightmarish miscalculation. He soon quit to pursue other goals, and his experiences in baseball recently won him a plum job. He is the head of the task force cleaning up Los Angeles after the riots.

His successor seemed the perfect candidate. A. Bartlett Giamatti had been the president of Yale, a lifelong fan. But Giamatti, who had a several-packs-a-day cigarette habit, died in 1990 of a heart attack.

It was hardly surprising to students of the pastime that after experimenting with people named Happy, Ford, Spike, Bowie and Bart, the owners would give the position to a guy named Fay.

One can only hope that this brief history will help you to understand why the Commissioner of Ball would put the knock on Houston's fans. In what he called his "simple-minded way" — Fay, you're too easy on yourself — he suggested that the best hope to liberate the city from McMullen was to start packing the ballpark.

Note to fans: Try not to get flattened by the stampede.

The commissioner of baseball had taken to doing McMullen's bidding. Yet, he seemed amazed at the reaction in Houston to his thinly veiled threats. This reaction seemed characteristic of Vincent — certain he had made the correct decision and surprised at the backlash to his decision from all quarters.

One could not help but wonder if Vincent had become "caught up" in the "power and prestige" of the office of the commissioner. Perhaps he thought of the office as an imperial one, where he could issue edicts and make declarations with seeming impunity. Such a perspective could persuade one to believe that taking inconsistent positions on various matters could be done with impunity.

Ed Fowler reviewed the commissioner's various positions on the status of the Houston franchise during the latter period of McMullen's ownership. In a June 4, 1992, *Houston Chronicle* column entitled "The many faces of Fay Vincent," Fowler began with a quote from Vincent:

> *"I believe that relocating a franchise should be done only in dire circumstances. But I'm convinced that baseball ought to think through this issue. I'm convinced I'm correct about this, but I'm willing to be persuaded otherwise."*
>
> — Fay Vincent
> June 13, 1991

One thing about the commissioner of baseball: Any response anyone might want on a given topic, he probably has delivered it at one point or another.

There's no shortage of examples. Can this be the same Fay Vincent who appeared before us this week, muttering dark threats and chastising the baseball fans of Houston for frustrating the sale of the Astros? The same one who said last October, answering a question from a Canadian reporter who suggested Montreal is a hockey city:

"They told me in Atlanta last year that it was a football city. They tell me in Houston that it's a football town. I don't believe that. When a team does well and becomes competitive, attendance picks up, just like you're seeing in Atlanta this year. I believe Montreal will be a good story.

"I didn't see Atlanta turning around as quickly as it did. But it was one winter, some clever signings, some very good management."

Was that the Vincent who this week indicated Houston fans should turn out in support of the Astros despite their last-place finish in 1991 and current last-place status?

Maybe it was the Vincent who said last July: "It is highly unlikely the Astros will ever relocate."

Follow the bouncing Fay

When the political pundits get through figuring out what Ross Perot is really all about, they ought to tackle this guy if they want a real challenge.

Vincent, last October, on the possibility of John J. McMullen's simultaneous involvement in baseball and horse racing: "He's not interested in challenging me. He's not involved with horse racing at the moment. I would think if he did get involved with it, I would tell him to sell the horse racing.

"It's not going to come to that. The way I feel about horse racing is that if it (a baseball owner's involvement) ever happens, it will be at a time when I'm not involved in baseball. It's not going to happen while I'm in baseball, because he (McMullen) understands my view."

Vincent, two months previous to those remarks: "No one can have direct involvement in a racing or gambling operation and baseball. That's a position I take. I told him (McMullen) a year ago I was opposed to it."

Last November, Richard Levin, Vincent's spokesman, said the commissioner's office was well aware that Rochelle Levy is a partner in the Philadelphia Phillies at the same time her husband, Robert Levy, owns a horse-racing facility in Atlantic City, N.J., and, in fact, is involved with McMullen in a proposed Houston track.

Asked if McMullen could use the same dodge, he said, "That could possibly be so."

Vincent, June 16, 1991, on the relocation of existing franchises: "My position hasn't changed, but I could be persuaded otherwise."

He feels strongly both ways

Vincent, July 27, 1991: "My opposition to franchise transfers remains firm, and despite news reports to the contrary, my position has not changed."

This, we think, is the same Fay Vincent who this week backed up McMullen in his claim that he had never discussed selling the Astros to interests who would move the club to another city.

Louis Susman, an investment banker representing McMullen in the sale, June 1991: "Some people came to a spring-training game in Orlando, and Dr. McMullen told them to get in touch with me. And there were inquiries from practically every expansion city."

Richard DeVos, who was involved in trying to gain a National League expansion franchise for Orlando, June 1991: "The last time I talked to him (McMullen) about it was a month before this thing (expansion) was settled. Basically, he explained to me the situation with the sale. He just wants to find a buyer somehow."

Vincent, December 1991: "What I've said about relocation is that as a general proposition, one has to be skeptical. I never said never. There are circumstances in which franchises might have to move."

Vincent, October 1991: Houston is in "no danger" of losing the Astros.

This week, plans for a racetrack in which McMullen is involved are proceeding apace, and Vincent has issued a veiled threat about "unattractive" alternatives if Houston doesn't do a better job of supporting the Astros.

Many questions arise, obviously, but for starters we'd settle for an answer to this one:

Who is Fay Vincent?

The ultimate Vincent story came out of his forced resignation from the office of commissioner. It is not clear where, when, and from whom the idea to force Vincent from office came. It is clear, though, that Vincent's refusal to sign the owners' version of the Magna Carta in June of 1992 precipitated what ended as a stampede to force him from office.

This "Magna Carta" was a legal document under which "King Vincent" would have relinquished his right to intervene in future labor negotiations under the "best interests of baseball" powers. The owners did not want to worry about a quixotic commissioner scuttling their labor plans by intervening in negotiations in a manner adverse to their interests. While inaccurately portrayed in the media as resolving the 1990 lockout, Vincent's true "sin" in 1990 was his recognition of the folly of Pay For Performance or PFP. His intervention in negotiations in mid-February, which caused the withdrawal of that foolish proposal, alienated some hard-line owners.

Other decisions made by Vincent persuaded a number of owners that their commissioner was a "wild card" not to be trusted to keep the faith or make "good" decisions. His decision on realignment in July 1992, made in contravention of the rules of the National League constitution, and his handling of the Yankee officials in the Howe grievance, served to crystalize opposition to him.

The apparent last straw was his public statements in August that Congress should control the power of the superstations. Given that the Cubs and the Braves each have common ownership with a superstation, and that Tribune Company stations broadcast the games of seven baseball clubs, Vincent was "messing with the lunch" of some of his most powerful constituents.

On August 17 Vincent received a letter from American League President Bobby Brown and National League President Bill White informing the "king" that a meeting would be held on September 3 in Chicago to consider the powers and the term of the commissioner. Vincent's response was to characterize the meeting as unlawful, citing as his authority provisions of the Major League Agreement. The commissioner hired Oliver North's attorney, Brendan Sullivan. Vincent stated definitively that he would never resign.

The embattled commissioner wrote back to the league presidents to say that even "if there is a meeting and a vote to remove me from office or an attempt to limit my powers, all in contravention of the Major League Agreement and my employment agreement, I will not leave." Vincent explained to reporters the reasoning behind his hard-line stance:

> I think about my successor. Suppose my successor is sitting out there and a group of owners comes to him or her and says, "Look, we just pushed Fay out. We really want you to be commissioner."
>
> And he says, "Well, you just pushed Fay out. How do I know you won't push me out? I wonder, says my successor, about the process."

Bowie Kuhn did not go. Fay Vincent is not going to go. I think it would be bad for baseball, bad for the institution. And I actually think it would be bad for the owners trying to do it, because I don't believe they've thought through the consequences of hiring a successor and trying to explain to him why this won't happen again.

Chicago White Sox owner Jerry Reinsdorf was among the group of owners disenchanted with Vincent. It was his desire that the meeting in Chicago be "a frank and open discussion of our problems and the commissioner's performance." Reinsdorf explained, "I know what I feel, but I want to hear what other people think. It's my hope we come out with a clear consensus."

In response to Vincent's defiant proclamation that he would remain as commissioner and resist the efforts to oust him "until such time as the highest court of this land tells me otherwise," Reinsdorf replied, "Every lawyer that I have spoken to has concluded that a commissioner can be removed from office."

As the showdown in the Chicago suburb of Rosemont approached, Alan Truex of the *Houston Chronicle* analyzed the dispute between the owners and the commissioner. Truex wrote in the August 30 *Chronicle*:

Fay Vincent is erudite, amiable and genuinely passionate about baseball. Yet it's doubtful any other commissioner in the sport's history has alienated so many so quickly.

. . .

Vincent often has appeared indecisive. Owners complain semiprivately that he changes his positions so often that they can't trust him.

. . .

When John McMullen sought permission to negotiate a deal that could move the Astros to Florida, Vincent indicated he would oppose such a transfer. But as his own position became tenuous and McMullen's support became more valuable, Vincent began to back off on his stand for baseball in Houston.

He even made a trip here to call one of his rare media conferences so he could criticize Houstonians for not flocking to the Astrodome.

. . .

It surely is no coincidence that Thursday's meeting is being held near Chicago, where Vincent's realignment order was blocked by a court injunction.

It wasn't that most owners faulted Vincent for favoring geographic sanity in a league that has Atlanta playing in the West while Chicago, capital of the Midwest, is lodged in the Eastern Division.

And anyway, the realignment issue is moot — if not mute — until the future location of the San Francisco/St. Petersburg Giants can be established.

Vincent's mistake was in not seeking support of the owners before issuing his executive order on realignment. O'Malley was one of 11 National League owners in favor of realignment, but he was not in favor of the commissioner dictating league matters.

Vincent has been faulted for other high-handed behavior.

He instructed the Hall of Fame to make Pete Rose ineligible for induction, rather than allowing designated experienced baseball writers to make that decision for themselves, as they were empowered to do.

In a more recent controversy, Vincent ended up apologizing for his mishandling of the latest Steve Howe drug inquiry. The commissioner reportedly tried to stifle testimony favorable to the pitcher, summoning Buck Showalter to his office for an upbraiding that caused the Yankees manager to be late for his team's game that day.

So Vincent draws criticism for doing more than he has the right to do, as well as for doing less than he should.

His main failure has been in not grasping the political nature of his office and in not using politics to his advantage. He has not built or maintained lines of support.

At the September 3 meeting, the owners voted 18–9–1 to adopt the following resolution:

> The major league clubs do not have confidence in the ability of the present commissioner, Fay Vincent, to carry out the responsibilities of the office of commissioner, and that under his direction it is impossible for baseball to move forward effectively and constructively.

Vincent was asked to resign immediately. The commissioner refused and issued a statement saying, "I believe strongly that a baseball commissioner should serve a full term as contemplated by the Major League Agreement. Only then can difficult decisions be made impartially and without fear of political repercussions."

Jerry Reinsdorf stated the pragmatism of the owners case: "I think now, for the first time, he can see the numbers against him. Before this, he may very well not have realized there were 18. Now he knows."

Within four days, the defiant commissioner-king fell on his sword and resigned. Ronald Blum of the Associated Press reported Vincent's abrupt resignation.

> Baseball Commissioner Fay Vincent gave up the fight to keep his job and resigned Monday, four days after an overwhelming no-confidence vote by major-league owners.
>
> "I've concluded that resignation — not litigation — should be my final act as commissioner 'in the best interests of baseball,'" Vincent wrote in a three-page letter to owners that he made public.
>
> On Aug. 20, Vincent had vowed "I will not resign — ever." But the teams voted 18-9 with one abstention Thursday urging him to quit, and he decided to resign after a weekend of reflection at his vacation home in Harwich Port, Mass.
>
> Vincent was forced out by owners angry at his refusal to relinquish the commissioner's "best interests" power on collective bargaining, his unilateral order to realign the National League and his stance against superstations.
>
> The group was led by Jerry Reinsdorf of the Chicago White Sox, Bud Selig of Milwaukee, Stanton Cook of the Chicago Cubs and Peter O'Malley of the Los Angeles Dodgers.
>
> Astros owner John McMullen, whose sale of the team to Drayton McLane Jr. is pending, was one of Vincent's backers.
>
> "It would be an even greater disservice to baseball if I were to precipitate a protracted fight over the office of the commissioner," Vincent wrote. "After the vote at the meeting last week, I can no longer justify imposing on baseball, nor should baseball be required to endure, a bitter legal battle — even though I am confident that in the end I would win and thereby establish a judicial precedent that the term and powers of the commissioner cannot be diminished during the remaining months of my term."
>
> Reinsdorf also sounded relieved that a fight was avoided.
>
> "It was the only sensible thing he could do," Reinsdorf said. "It was his best interest and in our best interest. The important thing is that the commissioner made the decision that was right for himself, for baseball and for everybody."
>
> Reinsdorf has said he would like to see the office restructured to make it a chief executive officer reporting to the 28 owners as a board of directors.

"I think the fans knew I was looking out for their interest and (was) keeping the game the way they wanted it," Vincent said. "The commissioner has to look out for the fans, and the owners don't want to hear me speak that idea. I think they'll change the office to a very thin shadow of what it is."

Hal Bodley of *USA Today* spoke to the deposed commissioner. In his column in the September 8 issue, Bodley wrote:

Commissioner Fay Vincent spent his Labor Day weekend with a box of his favorite cigars and a heavy conscience. He had future of our national pastime weighing heavily on his mind.

Should he stay or should he go?

Friends called and offered their support. He discussed his future with them at length.

By Saturday night, most of the cigars in the box were gone. So were most of the reasons why he should continue a battle that was a loser, even if there was a victory on paper.

He had vowed, in his strongly worded five-page letter last week to the 28 men who run baseball, never to resign — until the job was done.

But then last Thursday in Chicago, the vote was 18-9-1 against him. Eighteen owners said they had no confidence in his leadership. They wanted him out. Eighteen of them.

That was the clinching blow.

"At some point Saturday, I think I reached the decision," Vincent said quietly over the phone from his retreat Monday night. "I talked to some good friends, but mostly thought about my own situation. I talked to my family. I think what I'm doing is right for baseball. That has to be the ultimate test."

But what about the letter? Judging from that, it seemed his resolve was cast in concrete.

"That was my view at that time," he said. "A number of things changed. My statement, my letter (of resignation) tried to explain those things. For good or for bad, that's my thinking."

Vincent paused.

"Don't feel sorry for me," he finally said. "I think I did a good job. I gave it the best I could and I think my accomplishments stand on their own."

Ray Buck of the *Houston Post* read all that was said and written on the subject. He wrote in his September 8 column:

Thank you, Fay Vincent.

Thank you for making one good point in your farewell address about the need for baseball to have a strong commissioner, not a yes-man for the owners.

Your idea is valid. Your personality is just all wrong.

You lost respect. You remained self-indulgent to the end, claiming that your resignation is "in the best interests of baseball." That, sir, is not exactly a ringing endorsement for the game. Or you.

When the dust settled, Bud Selig became de facto commissioner by being named chairman of the Executive Council, a group of ten owners granted the authority to manage the affairs of ownership. Said Selig, when asked how long he would be in command, "We have no timetable. I hope it is a relatively short term, but I don't know."

*　　*　　*

Vincent made some cogent points about the importance of an independent commissioner. The owners considered him to be their recalcitrant employee, so they forced him from office. Some owners complained that they needed the commissioner to be their man, comparing the role and power of the commissioner to Don Fehr's role and power within the union.

Those owners miss the point of what the proper role of a commissioner should be. There is nothing wrong with the owners having their own man — that is the role Richard Ravitch plays. Ravitch is the antonym of Don Fehr, not the commissioner.

How should the office of commissioner function, and who should be selected to fill the role, and by whom should he be selected? The following criteria should govern the office and the selection process:

1. The commissioner should be charged with representing the interests of the owners, the players, the fans, and the game of baseball.
2. He should be selected, as is the permanent arbitrator, by joint agreement of ownership and the union.
3. He should serve a four-year term and be eligible to be rehired by the joint agreement of ownership and the union.
4. His four-year term should begin in the middle of a collective bargaining agreement (which is more typically a four-year agreement), so that he can be free of the political pressures of the "reelection process." This should allow him to get directly involved in collective bargaining, if necessary. Who better than an independent commissioner, selected by the

owners and the union, to broker a meaningful partnership that will benefit the owners, the players, the fans, and the game.

5. He should be someone who has experience in baseball, who knows the "inside players," the power structure, the history of baseball, and how the "inside game" is properly played.

6. He should be a lawyer who believes in the application of due process of law in the baseball world.

7. He should understand the economics of all of the parties who contribute to, and are affected by, baseball.

8. He should have common sense, respect for his constituencies, and LOVE BASEBALL.

If ownership is sincere in its stated goal of a true partnership with the players, selecting a commissioner based upon the foregoing criteria would constitute a giant step forward in achieving a meaningful partnership.

Chapter 3

The Clemens Holdout:
Why It Happened
and What It Achieved

Major league baseball players come from diverse backgrounds. They have great athletic ability and well-developed competitive attitudes.

Most young players lack experience in making complex business decisions. At Hendricks Sports Management (HSM), we believe that we should strive to educate and assist our clients in decision making so that in the future they will be able to make those complex decisions for themselves.

One of our goals is that our players "graduate" from our program. No professional athlete performs in his profession indefinitely, so there must be a constant focus on the future, as well as on the present. "Push the present, and plan for the future" is a motto of mine.

In any program, the interaction between the teachers and the students is a dynamic experience, and the teachers often learn from the students. Our program is no exception.

In any school, it is important to attract quality students. We have been fortunate to have attracted a large number of solid citizens who have worked diligently on their postathletic careers. Many have gone back to school to complete their undergraduate degrees, do postgraduate work, or attain professional degrees.

The measure of a good program is the quality of the students' achievements. Our graduates include six lawyers, an oral surgeon, three sports agents, six television broadcasters, a general manager, numerous coaches and scouts in professional baseball and professional football, numerous coaches in college baseball, two bankers, several real estate brokers, a real estate developer, a home builder, several teachers, a travel agent, a production company owner, a health club owner, three restaurant owners, a card show promoter, a food distributor, a horse trainer, an accountant, a manufacturer's representative, an executive assistant to an urban politician, a drug abuse spokesman, a hunting and fishing guide, a commodities broker, a lumber yard owner, a landscape design company owner, a construction company owner, a battery distributor, a computer programmer, four Christian outreach spokesmen, an evangelist, several rental property owners, several insurance brokers, two service station owners, and many other entrepreneurs, businessmen and professionals.

Virtually every professional athlete goes through a mourning period following his retirement from professional sports. It is not easy to make the transition from being a high profile, adrenalin charged competitor to a retired athlete out of the public eye. The retired player often struggles with redefining his identity during the first year or two of his retirement.

A strong bond is created with the athlete-client when one works closely with him, as is done at HSM. We prefer to represent a player for his entire career, and we have represented most of our clients from the moment that they first became a professional, dreaming of success, through their postretirement years.

After our going through the formative minor league years, the highs and lows on the playing field, injuries, contract battles and off-the-field matters, the bonds with our clients usually become complete. Our relationships with our clients can be characterized as "close," "closer," and "closest." I am always pleased when I hear a client tell me, "I met 'Mike' last week. I didn't know he was with us."

This special rapport creates a tremendous advantage for us and our clients during contract negotiations and labor battles. It forges great strength and unity. It makes us a formidable opponent.

George Bell is an example of how the bonding process has worked to create a strong team approach between HSM and a client. From the Dominican Republic, George was twenty-one years old when he signed with us on the advice of Alfredo Griffin. George had just been drafted off of the Phillies minor league roster by Toronto in the December 1980 rule 5(e) draft. Under the provisions of this draft, Toronto was obligated to keep him on its active major league roster during the entire 1981 season. Had the Blue Jays failed to do this, they would have been obligated to return Bell to the Phillies organization.

He was used off of the bench by Toronto in 1981. Bell was injured during most of the 1982 season and spent that year at Syracuse in Triple A. He recovered in 1983, but he played most of that year at Syracuse. The Blue Jays called him up in late August, and he stayed with Toronto through the remainder of the season. In 1984 George Bell started a run of nine straight outstanding seasons in the major leagues.

George Bell has been unquestionably one of the great players of the last decade. My vision of Bell includes a picture of him standing in the batters' box, poised to drive the next pitch. It also includes a picture of a lonely twenty-one-year-old from a foreign country. He is a friend, a fierce competitor, a great jokester, a bright man, and an entrepreneur.

Another such example is Roger Clemens. The story of our relationship and his holdout during spring training of 1987 follows.

*   *   *

Opinion and judgment are so diverse in statistically driven baseball that unanimity is a rare find indeed. No player, for example, has been unanimously elected to the Hall of Fame—not Babe Ruth nor Ted Williams nor Tom Seaver, whose 1992 tally of 98.8 percent is the highest voting percentage attained so far.

Nonetheless, Boston Red Sox hurler Roger Clemens may well have been universally regarded as the best pitcher in baseball over the nine year period through 1992. During that period, Clemens posted a 152–72 record, a .679 winning percentage, which ranked in the top five in major league history.

When the context in which he pitched is taken into account— a league that employs the designated hitter rule and a home stadium, Fenway Park, that is exceptionally friendly to batters — Roger Clemens' earned run average ranked at the top of all pitchers in major league history.

Unfortunately, he suffered nagging groin and elbow injuries in 1993 and posted a very uncharacteristic season — an 11–14 record with a 4.46 earned run average. With a full off-season to rest, Clemens expects to be back "in form" in 1994.

A variety of attributes contributed to Roger reaching the pinnacle of major league success. His 6'4", 220-pound frame makes him look like an NFL linebacker, which gives him an intimidating presence on the mound. He consistently throws the ball above 90 miles per hour, several clicks higher than the major league norm. Thus he comes by his nickname, "The Rocket," honestly.

Roger Clemens has always wanted to be the best, and he has always understood that to become and remain a great pitcher for a long period of time, physical conditioning is essential. In this regard, I call him "The Marine," because he is so fanatical in his dedication to fitness. His precise routine is his own well-kept secret, but it definitely includes a grueling program of running and weight training, year 'round.

Though he possesses great physical prowess, Clemens is also crafty. In fact, he is among the rarest of performers: a power pitcher with excellent command and control of four different types of pitches. Furthermore, he will not hesitate to take the mound with an injury when he believes it is necessary for the success of his team.

In short, Roger Clemens is the ultimate pitching machine.

As in any other field, a major league ball player defines himself largely by the standards of excellence to which he strives. While most players are content to establish their identities at intermediate levels of achievement, the great ones are driven to equal or set the standard in their field. Of course, an extraordinary level of athletic talent is required just to make it to the major leagues. But to reach the highest ranks of the profession, one must also possess the so-called intangibles. These include a competitive and confident attitude, highly focused physical and mental discipline, and maturity. Bob Gibson, Tom Seaver, Steve Carlton, and Nolan Ryan are among the pitchers of the last quarter century who have clearly met all of these criteria of excellence.

The personalities of such players tend to be marked by obsessiveness, a nearly manic intensity, and a realistic, even self-effacing awareness that the goal of preeminence can rarely be achieved.

Roger Clemens is cut from the same cloth. He has always had a maturity about competition well beyond his years. He does not, for example, overreact to his successes and failures from performance to performance. And his daily routine is carefully structured to enable him to peak on the days when he is scheduled to start for the Red Sox. Having represented him for a decade, I know that he is continually focused on the perfect pitch, the perfect game, the perfect season. Though the level of competition he faces necessarily affects his results, it does not alter his standards. Thus, when Roger walks to the mound, he is prepared in every way for the task at hand. As each of his games unfolds, there is seldom doubt in anyone's mind who is in command.

In 1986, Clemens put together one of his finest seasons. But in the aftermath of that stellar performance, he endured a battle in the major league salary arena that no player had endured for twenty years. This struggle would test his mettle off the field. It would also bring into play some of the principal features of baseball's complex process of determining salaries.

The story begins in early 1983, nearly four years before the battle that Roger and I would eventually have to fight at the highest levels of baseball officialdom.

*   *   *

The photograph on the cover on the February 15, 1983, issue of *Baseball America* featured the pitching staff of the University of Texas. *Baseball America*, the only national periodical devoted primarily to minor league and college baseball, had chosen the Texas team as its preseason favorite in the college ranks. That prediction was based largely on the strength of the star pitchers displayed on the cover.

My brother Alan and I reviewed and discussed the talent on that exceptional team, particularly its pitching staff. Having previously represented such star Texas players as Keith Moreland, Richard Wortham, and Jerry Don Gleaton, we had already developed great respect for the baseball program of Longhorn coach Cliff Gustafson. And so we looked forward to following the team during the 1983 season.

Fulfilling its own expectations and those of *Baseball America*, Texas won the national championship over Alabama in a game pitched by Roger Clemens.

Near the end of the season, friend Pris Wright approached me after Sunday services at Cypress Creek Christian Church. Beaming, she said, "Randy, you need to meet my friends James and Betty Capel. James works for an insurance company represented by your old law firm, and Betty teaches with me. Their son, Mike, pitches for Texas. He was the star pitcher on Spring High School's 1980 state championship team."

Because he was one of the cover stars, I knew very well who Mike Capel was. He finished 13–1 in the Longhorns' 1983 campaign. "I'll be glad to meet with them, Pris. Just tell me when."

I met Mike Capel soon after talking to his parents. He had been drafted in the thirteenth round by the Chicago Cubs. Shortly after signing with the Cubs, Capel hired HSM to represent him.

At a subsequent luncheon meeting, he encouraged Alan and me to meet his good friend and teammate, Calvin Schiraldi. Schiraldi had been named the college player of the year by *The Sporting News* and was considered the ace of the Texas staff. He was also MVP at the College World Series. Cal was selected as the twenty-ninth pick in the draft by the New York Mets.

Alan and I were only too pleased to meet with him and his father, Joe. In relatively short order Schiraldi became the second cover star to hire us.

At that luncheon meeting with Capel, I asked him about Roger Clemens: "He's going to be great," I said. "But what kind of person is he?"

"He is very intense, highly competitive, but off the field he is a really nice guy. He has a lot of moods, though," Capel replied.

My kind of guy, I thought. Inspired by his desire for us to represent Schiraldi, I asked, "Well, when do we meet Roger?"

"Let me give him a call and see if he's interested," Capel said.

Roger Clemens was indeed interested. His brother, Randy, had helped him obtain a $121,000 signing bonus from Boston after the 1983 college season, a very solid bonus figure at that time. The odd amount of the bonus was no accident. Twenty-one was Clemens' number, and any time it was available, in any form, he would try to get it. But the Clemens brothers knew that the increasing stakes and complexities of the negotiating process that lay ahead called for representation by an experienced firm.

Alan and I met with the Clemens family. After we passed the mandatory and all-important test of family approval, Roger became the third cover star to hire us.

A short time later, Kirk Killingsworth became our fourth cover star client. At this point, Alan had the *Baseball America* cover photograph framed because everyone at our sports agency had high aspirations for our newest clients—the aces from the 1983 College World Series champions.

I had the very highest expectations for Clemens. There was no doubt in my mind that he would be the standout in the group. I could see it in the way he pitched.

Before the draft and the College World Series, Pat Gillick, the general manager of the Toronto Blue Jays, called to talk about

Clemens. Toronto had the fifth pick in the draft. Gillick asked Alan and me our opinion of Clemens. I told him that I thought Clemens would be great.

"Sounds like he's already your client, Randal," said Pat.

I laughed. "Are you going to draft him?"

He hedged, "I'm afraid to take him and I'm afraid not to take him."

He continued with both his praise for and his concerns about Clemens, who had not pitched as consistently well in 1983 as he had in 1982, though he did finish strongly. We discussed a worry that many team officials share, namely, that ace college pitchers are often overworked.

It was apparent that Gillick was agonizing over Roger Clemens. He and I reviewed many of the great Texas pitchers and how their careers had gone. It's inevitable that players from top-flight college programs are compared to their predecessors, whether or not it is particularly relevant to their own prospects as professionals.

I knew Gillick was probing for information, anything to give him an edge. I told him that I would certainly make Clemens MY first round pick but, naturally, I didn't know everything he did about the other top players.

"There can't be too many players better than Clemens," I concluded. Pat Gillick agreed.

When Boston chose Clemens as the nineteenth pick in the first round of the 1983 draft, I was surprised that he had lasted that long. But I was pleased that he was going to Boston. A team in need of pitching, the Red Sox quickly signed him to a minor league contract.

Roger Clemens was an instant sensation in the minors. He posted a 3–1 won-lost record and a 1.24 earned run average at class A Winter Haven. He was then promoted to AA, where he helped New Britain win the league championship with a record of 4–1 and an earned run average of 1.38.

Clemens appeared to be headed for Boston in 1984. Before he left for spring training, Alan and I met with him over lunch. We wanted to be sure that he would be ready for what lay ahead of him. We figured the worst thing that he could do would be to put too much pressure on himself to make the club and thus pitch poorly in spring training.

Roger responded very well to our advice. He was poised and confident about his future. His self-assurance more closely resembled that of a veteran than a rookie. I concluded the luncheon by telling him that if he made the club, it would likely be as a fifth starter, the last slot in a team's starting rotation.

"The club can keep you or send you down if you are in that role. If they send you down, they'll tell you it's so you can continue in a starting role and be sharp when they go to a five-man rotation. But it also serves the purpose of keeping you short of salary arbitration eligibility. So don't be surprised if you pitch well enough to make the team but don't make the team. Just go down and do your job. Don't let disappointment affect your performance."

Roger nodded in what would eventually become a very familiar gesture, one that indicated "lesson totally absorbed."

That meeting proved prophetic. He pitched well in spring training, was sent down to the minors for a month, and became a member of the Red Sox major league team in May. He racked up a record of 9–4 as a starter in 1984, and his future looked bright.

In 1985, however, Clemens developed a sore shoulder. He was placed on the disabled list twice, missing about 70 days of the season. Despite being hampered, he won 7 games and lost 5. But before the end of the season, the shoulder problem led to an operation performed by famed sports surgeon James Andrews. Roger Clemens' career, we concluded, might be in jeopardy.

*   *   *

One of the primary reasons players and their agents constantly push for the "big bucks" is that they never know how long a player's career will last. This is due more often to concern over the possibility of an injury than concern over the aging process or the possibility of a subpar year. All three factors, though, encourage the salary "push."

One of the little understood things about the most successful baseball agents is that they are good judges of talent. Because the business is so competitive, they really have to be. On the other hand, history demonstrates that performance levels vary from year to year, sometimes drastically. Hence, talent analysts are frequently wrong about players. That's simply the nature of the beast at the big league level. So, the bottom line for an agent-analyst is to have a better record at predicting players' performances than his competitors do.

In addition, an agent needs to know what types of players he can best represent. He, therefore, needs to know the specific makeup and character of his potential clients. The ability to gauge the strengths and weaknesses of major league clubs is also an important asset, for it gives an agent insight into the level of each club's interest in acquiring the player.

To calculate the dollar value of a player, the agent must factor in the specific talents of the player, the availability in the marketplace of players with similar skills, the unique makeup of the player, and the demand for such a player by major league teams. Contract valuation is also affected by such factors as the player's legal rights within the salary system, his current performance level, when he is likely to attain peak value, and his durability, physical condition and injury history. Of equal importance are the agent's judgments about future major league revenue levels and, most importantly, player salary levels. All of these variables affect not only the salary to seek for a player, but also the length of his contract.

In order to stay abreast of current performances and market conditions, I watch more than 250 major league games each year. And I read game stories, box scores, and current baseball events for an average of two hours a day from February through October.

During my twenty-three years as an agent for baseball and football players, one thing has remained constant. While the salaries have grown much larger, player attitudes about salaries have remained constant. Players want to be paid a salary which they believe is consistent with the salaries being paid to comparable players. In this regard, the issue is much more than money. The issue is relative justice, being paid comparable to one's peers. It is a matter of pride.

I have not noticed any difference between the attitudes of players who turned down $50,000 salary offers because they believed $70,000 to be appropriate, and the attitudes of players who turned down $500,000 salary offers because they believed $700,000 to be appropriate. In both cases, the players focused on the existing market and values established for comparable players. It is not a matter of whether the player can "live" on the salary offered. It is a matter of how the player feels, and whether he believes that he is being compensated on a relatively fair basis. No player wants to feel unfairly "rated" relative to comparable players.

Professional athletes are competitive by nature, so it is unrealistic to expect them to be satisfied with a loss, whether on the field or in the bargaining room. Negotiations have everything to do with money, on one hand, and nothing to do with money, on the other hand. While this is a paradox for sure, it is also a truth about compensation for professional athletes.

*   *   *

In 1986, Roger Clemens won his first 14 decisions and finished 24–4. Perhaps the most magical moment of that season came on April 29 when Roger set an all-time record by striking out 20 Seattle Mariners in a nine inning game. At one time in the game, he struck out 8 consecutive hitters. Clemens' 1986 performance resulted in *The Sporting News* naming him as the Major League Player of the Year.

It was clear that the surgery and rehabilitation were behind him. In fact, the Red Sox rode Roger to the World Series, where they lost (4 games to 3) to the New York Mets in a legendary confrontation. Midway through the season, Clemens was named the Most Valuable Player at the All Star game in his hometown of Houston. He later received both the Cy Young Award and the Most Valuable Player award. No other baseball player has ever won all three honors in a single season.

One would think that a season of such unparalleled stature would have led to a hefty multiyear contract for Roger Clemens, but developments on the salary front were throwing up a massive roadblock to his financial aspirations.

The 1985 baseball season had been marked by a two-day strike. The game's new Basic Agreement was ratified after the strike. The agreement included an increase in the service time required for eligibility for salary arbitration. Specifically, a player would now have to accumulate three years of major league service instead of just two before he could submit a disputed contract to an arbitrator. This had been the union's biggest bargaining concession to the owners. Unfortunately, there was no grandfather clause included in the 1985 agreement to cover the seventy or so players who, absent the eligibility change, would have been eligible for salary arbitration at the end of the 1986 season. That group included not only Roger Clemens, but also Kirby Puckett, Joe Carter, Tony Fernandez, Tom Henke, and ten other star players.

The two-day strike was not the only significant off-the-field event in 1985. Collusion commenced later that year. The players' union reacted by filing a grievance over this exercise in "fiscal responsibility" in early 1986. By the fall of 1986, collusion was in full bloom, as the owners flaunted their antitrust exemption and breached the collective bargaining agreement.

In late November of 1986, Roger came to the Hendricks offices at the invitation of Alan and myself. We wanted to discuss strategy on his upcoming 1987 contract. To me, there were two obvious barriers to an appropriate contract—the lack of salary arbitration rights and the looming collusive practices of the clubs.

I cited for Clemens the two reasons why I expected a low-ball offer from the Red Sox. He was shocked and incensed at such a prospect. He asked me why I thought the club would do that to him. After all, every prior contract negotiation for him had gone very smoothly. I told him that I thought that the next step in collusion would be to reduce the raises paid to players ineligible for salary arbitration. He then asked me what I planned to do in such an event.

"Hold out," I said without a moment's hesitation.

Holdouts of any kind, especially successful ones, are hard to find, especially in recent baseball history. In fact, to find a holdout prior to Clemens' that had proved successful, one has to go back to 1966, when Sandy Koufax and Don Drysdale held out in tandem.

The owners had insisted on the inclusion of a collusion clause in the Basic Agreement because they feared that star players might band together in contract negotiations, a la Koufax-Drysdale. Ironically, it was precisely that clause that would later hang the owners in the collusion hearings.

The collusion language contained in the Basic Agreement was simple and straightforward:

> Players shall not act in concert with other Players, and Clubs shall not act in concert with other Clubs.

There were some interesting and, to some degree, successful holdouts in the early years of baseball. Amos Rusie was a very good pitcher for the New York Giants in the 1890s. Rusie sat out the entire 1896 season in protest of the low salary offered to him. He returned in 1897 after being paid for the missed 1896 season. Perhaps encouraged by his prior success, Rusie sat out the entire 1899 season in another salary dispute.

After Babe Ruth revitalized baseball following the Black Sox scandal, holdouts in baseball were infrequent and seldom successful. In his book, *A Whole Different Ball Game*, Marvin Miller reiterated the prevailing view: "Everyone knew that holding out to gain bargaining leverage, even when the holdout was Joe DiMaggio, was notoriously ineffective."

Before Roger Clemens came along, the latest effort to stage a holdout was made by Fernando Valenzuela. In 1981, Valenzuela had been named both the Rookie of the Year and the Cy Young Award winner in the National League. He was also a demonstrably major attendance draw for the Dodgers. He held out briefly in the spring of 1982. But he relented in the middle of spring training. Thus, in the end, Fernando's holdout amounted only to a symbolic protest.

History notwithstanding, the prospect of holding Clemens out was not in the least bit intimidating to me. In the first place, I felt that I was representing the best player in baseball — certainly the one with the best season in 1986. Furthermore, I had engineered a lot of holdouts in football, which meant that the experience would hardly be new to me. Roger readily agreed to the strategy "if that's what it takes."

A holdout is a battle of wills and leverage. It is tough on everyone involved — the player, his family, the agent, the team, even the reporters and the fans. An urgency bordering on a frenzy often develops. And the holdout player's life becomes more frustrating and unstable as the pressure mounts.

It is critical to the success of a holdout that the player believe in his agent. The player must also be strong-willed and be supported by his family. I had all of that going for me in Clemens' case. Possessing an iron will, Roger Clemens thrives on the pressure of competition, both on and off the field. And he had the complete backing of his wife, Debbie, and the rest of his family. With all of that support and given his clear-cut value to his team, I firmly believed that we would ultimately "crack" the Red Sox.

Representing professional football players had fully prepared me for the rigors of holding out. In fact, I believe that for a period of years in the early 1980s I orchestrated more holdouts than any other agent representing NFL football players.

Holdouts were looked down upon by some agents. Other agents were flatly not up to either the task at hand or the pressure that it entails.

While agent Howard Slusher received much publicity for his often acrimonious holdouts, I usually conducted mine in a low key manner. More importantly, each of my holdouts produced a contract which was superior to the last offer made prior to the commencement of the holdout. So, I was absolutely convinced of the value of the holdout as a strategy to be employed when no other bargaining leverage existed.

To understand why football has had a far greater number of successful holdouts than baseball, one need merely focus on the absence of any meaningful free agency in the NFL until just recently. The round in which a football player was drafted was often more determinative of his salary than the talent that he demonstrated on the playing field. After a player was drafted, he had no choice but to sign a series of one-year contracts, almost all of which were not guaranteed. Every team used the series of one-year contracts, primarily to minimize its responsibility to a player in the event of injury. Thus, a player would be bound to a team for years, while the team was bound to the player only from week to week.

In fact, the deck was so stacked against the football players that the only viable remedy to a contract dispute was the radical tactic of the holdout. However, if you chose to play your holdout card, then the player you represented better have had a good dose of talent and mental toughness if you were to achieve significant gains.

I had a number of memorable holdouts that both implemented and affected my negotiating philosophy. Offensive tackle Matt Darwin was drafted out of Texas A&M in the fifth round of the 1984 draft by the Dallas Cowboys. Darwin held out for the entire 1984 season. In 1985, he was drafted in the fourth round by Philadelphia, making him the first player in NFL history to go through the draft twice. Ironically, or perhaps not, Matt held out deep into the 1985 preseason before signing a three-year contract under which he earned a good deal more money than he would have earned under the "final" four-year offer made by Dallas.

His holdout with Dallas was fueled not only by a disagreement over money, but also by unconscionable misrepresentations made to him about waiver documents that he was asked to sign supposedly for "his" benefit. Dallas tried mightily to discredit me, both directly to Darwin's father, Bill, and indirectly to Matt. Bill Darwin was told by Dallas contract negotiator Gil Brandt that his son should sue me for malpractice for wrecking his career. And Matt received a telephone call from an agent who had recruited him, and who said he was "close to Dallas" and could solve the problem if Darwin would just fire me and hire him. Out of frustration, Matt even visited Cowboy owner Bum Bright and told Bright that he had always dreamed of being a Cowboy and would like to see the problem between fellow Aggies solved. Bright had attended Texas A&M and was chairman of the Aggies' Board of Regents. Bright told Darwin that Bright let his football men make the football decisions, and sent Matt away like a little boy.

Veteran offensive guard R. C. Thielemann staged two holdouts. He held out during training camp and the preseason against Atlanta in 1983 and 1985. The last holdout resulted in a trade to Washington. Thielemann immediately became both the highest paid "Hog" and the highest paid offensive lineman in the NFL. And he started on the Redskins' 1988 Super Bowl championship team. Hence, like Darwin's holdout, this holdout resulted in a considerably larger salary and in becoming a member of a distinctly better football team.

Cody Risien held out in the summer of 1987 against Cleveland and vaulted past R. C. to become the highest paid offensive lineman in the NFL. Tony Franklin also held out in 1987 against New England, becoming the highest paid kicker in NFL history.

I conducted yearly holdouts on behalf of numerous Houston Oiler clients, such as Mike Stensrud, George Reihner, David Carter, and John Schuhmacher. The Oilers' General Manager, Ladd Herzeg, seemed to like holdouts as much as I did. As a matter of fact, he often baited players and agents just to see if they could stand up to the pressure of the holdout. Most could not.

Every time, I knew Herzeg would be cheap. And he knew that I would respond by holding out my client. And we both knew that the other would posture and point out the relative strengths of his negotiating positions. We would then argue vociferously over the ability of the player and his importance to the Oilers.

Unlike his caustic relationship with most other agents, Ladd and I reached a casual accommodation about our hardball tactics. We both understood that sooner or later we would "get the deal done." In the meantime, however, we negotiated intently, patiently, and respectfully.

I dealt with Al Davis and his chief lieutenant for player contracts, Steve Ortmayer, on the contracts of Todd Christensen and Lester Hayes. Both Christensen and Hayes were All-Pro players, and their respective holdouts, or threatened holdouts, produced contracts which advanced them to the very top of the salary structure for tight ends and defensive backs, respectively. Negotiating for them against Al Davis was full of constant tension. Like most great players, Todd and Lester are strong-willed, and I need not amplify on Al Davis' legendary strength of will.

Though Davis would get furious that the players were holdouts, he would be unfailingly analytical and pragmatic in dealing with me. He asked much of my clients, and he ultimately paid them well after they produced at the highest level in the game. He simply did not want to pay them the very high salaries that they and I wanted. Those Raider holdouts were always tense and lengthy but, in the end, financially rewarding to the players.

*   *   *

And so in the late fall of 1986, I sat in my office thinking about the prospect of Roger Clemens and me holding out against the Red Sox. I smiled. The two of us, with our collective willpower, would be impenetrable, I concluded.

Roger and I had developed an easy rapport, due in part to our instinctive recognition of the other's willpower. We had inherited our willpower, either genetically or environmentally, from our mothers—Roger from Bess Clemens and I from Edith Anderson Hendricks.

Frankly, I looked forward to the battle. I was fueled in no small part by my anger at collusion. Clients of Hendricks Sports Management, such as Danny Darwin, had been clear victims of the clubs' conspiracy following the 1985 season. By December of 1986, I could see that clients Alan Ashby, Jim Clancy, and Joe Sambito were going to be added to the list of victims.

In that highly charged atmosphere, I felt like a Hollywood gunslinger, the kind who walks into a saloon, guns prominently displayed, just hoping someone wants to challenge him. Of course, the gunslinger always lets the other side draw first, thereby preserving his legal and "moral" defenses. I also thought of Koufax and Drysdale in 1966, a holdout that I had followed while in college. I decided that it might be time to teach some lessons in baseball about the art of the holdout.

As I anticipated the upcoming battle, I thought of how Clemens' 1986 season had represented the ultimate dream of young American baseball players. On sandlots, at little league stadiums, and on high school and college fields, young men fantasized about making it to the big leagues. Ironically, though, prior to the Messersmith-McNally decision the cry, "Only in America!" meant something quite different for baseball players than what it meant for the rest of us where employment rights were concerned.

Free agency had had real meaning for nearly a decade. It had elevated the salaries of top-flight baseball players to a level commensurate with the salaries of others in the entertainment industry. Beginning in late 1985, however, the owners conspired to hollow out that right.

Having long held the view that it was the aggressive realists of the world who win, I felt that it was incumbent on me to evaluate the effects of collusion and to counterattack as best I could. If collusion were to impose an authoritarian, football-like system in baseball, I would bring well-executed football tactics to baseball. Specifically, I vowed that Roger Clemens would be paid appropriately or else a holdout would ensue.

*   *   *

Before the end of 1986, Boston general manager Lou Gorman offered Alan $400,000 for Roger Clemens for 1987. Clemens earned $340,000, including $115,000 in incentives in 1986. Alan called to negotiate with Gorman in mid-January 1987. Alan made a two-year offer. On January 21 Lou indicated that the Red Sox would be willing to pay $500,000 for one year.

From that point forward, the Red Sox put off Alan, time and again, for one reason or another. Finally, the club indicated a desire to meet in spring training, in early March.

Press reports indicated that many young players were being low-balled by their clubs. And free agents, who were also being subjected to collusion, were not being signed at all. Since we had been ignored for two months, I expected little progress at the upcoming meeting. But I was unprepared for the offer that would be made in spring training.

In 1977 Alan and I began traveling to the major league spring training camps of clubs in which we had clients. In short order, we had clients on every single team. Spring training is an ideal time to efficiently meet face-to-face with clients. The meetings not only cover business matters but they also renew friendships, which is fundamental to our way of representing players.

In 1987 we started out in Kissimmee, Florida, the spring training home of the Astros. From that central location we could cover Astros, Twins, Tigers, and Red Sox clients. Several days after our arrival, Lou Gorman called and volunteered that he and club counsel, John Donovan, would come from nearby Winter Haven, the Sox' spring home, to Kissimmee on March 5 to discuss Roger Clemens' contract negotiations with Alan and me.

The meeting commenced with Gorman's acknowledgement of Roger's brilliant 1986 season. He then offered $400,000, a raise of exactly $60,000. The raise offered, we would later find out, was identical to that being offered to Puckett, Carter, Fernandez, Henke, and others in Clemens' seniority group.

Alan and I were shocked. After three months, we were back to the December offer. When I asked how the Red Sox could decrease their offer by $100,000, Gorman indicated that the $500,000 salary that he had discussed with Alan was not really a firm offer. In any case, I was told, this was "the final offer."

I waved off Alan, who started to respond to Lou. I rose and advised Gorman and Donovan, as I walked them to the front door, that they would have our answer the next day.

I phoned Roger in Winter Haven. He was incensed at the Red Sox' offer. Decreasing their figure was the equivalent of pouring gasoline on a smoldering fire. We had previously scheduled a dinner meeting for that night to discuss our plans in the event the meeting with Lou Gorman proved to be unproductive.

At dinner, we agreed that tomorrow would be the day that Roger Clemens would walk out of training camp. And I would tell the press the reasons why.

The next morning, Alan and I met Roger during his workout along the fence paralleling the left field foul line. He said that he had told a few teammates that he intended to hold out. Veteran slugger Jim Rice, Clemens told us, had suggested that maybe he should stay because he hadn't yet "paid his dues."

Taken aback by Rice's recommendation, I thought that he was probably jealous that Clemens was in the process of usurping Rice's top billing among Red Sox players. "Just the advice you need," I told Roger sarcastically.

I mentioned to Clemens that Rice had renegotiated his guaranteed contract, one of the few players who had ever had the gall to even ask for such a patently unfair concession. Our situation was different, I told him. We had not agreed to a salary for the 1987 season; we were merely going to protest an insupportably low offer. Clemens remained undeterred.

Alan and I had requested a final meeting with Red Sox co-owner Haywood Sullivan to find out if Boston was "stuck" at $400,000. We told Roger to stay in left field. We would soon advise him if there had been a change of heart by Boston management. There was not. Minutes later Clemens walked out of camp. Ironically, on the same day the Chicago Cubs accepted the offer of boycotted free agent Andre Dawson to sign a blank contract.

Like a herd of cattle, the press thundered into the parking lot behind the left field wall after they heard that Roger Clemens had left camp. Tape recorders and note pads were whirring and scratching everywhere. I articulated the reasons why Clemens was leaving. "I advised him to leave, and that was also Roger's decision. He won't be back until it's resolved. There won't be any 'No, I'm mad. I'm leaving; I'll be back Monday after I think about it' — which a lot of players do."

It was soon apparent to me, however, that I would be viewed by most of the press as a bad influence over their young hero. Clearly, I was threatening the quality of the Red Sox season, and many of the "reporter-fans," as I think of them, resented this possibility.

I pointed out to the press that day, and many times thereafter, that we were seeking a salary in the range of the salaries paid to Dwight Gooden, Orel Hershiser, and Bret Saberhagen at the same point in major league service. I stated that we were willing to accept a two-year contract for $2,400,000 or a one-year contract for $1,000,000.

Prior to collusion and the change in eligibility for salary arbitration, my proposal would have seemed totally reasonable to the Red Sox for a player with Clemens' achievements and ability. It was unfair, I argued, that he now be offered $400,000, in light of what Gooden, Hershiser, and Saberhagen had been paid at the same point in their careers.

I had my supportive statistics ready and rattled them off. They included most of the information from the following chart, which painted the comparative picture quite clearly:

1987 SALARY PROPOSAL FOR ROGER CLEMENS

Player	Major League Service		W-L Season	Record Career	Prior Salary	Subsequent Salary
GOODEN	2 Yrs	0 Days	24-4	41-13	$450,000	$1,320,000
HERSHISER	2 Yrs	32 Days	19-3	30-11	212,000	1,000,000
SABERHAGEN	2 Yrs	0 Days	20-6	30-17	160,000	925,000
CLEMENS	2 Yrs	142 Days	24-4	40-13	340,000	
					REQUEST	$1,000,000
					CLUB OFFER	400,000

When the reporters went to Gorman for his reaction, his response, as reported in the *Boston Globe*, was typical of what every club was using to justify its treatment of its star young players. "The marketplace is not what it was four or five years ago. It has changed dramatically. A lot of players have not signed and have walked out of camp because of it. The agents don't want to understand it."

That afternoon I was in Port Charlotte, the spring training site of the Texas Rangers. George Grande of ESPN happened to be there, and he interviewed me about Roger Clemens' walkout. I stated over the national airwaves that we wanted 75 percent of what Gooden had made just after he went 24-4 and won the Cy Young Award, 100 percent of what Hershiser had made, and 10 percent above what Saberhagen had made, at the same career service juncture for all four players.

In the televised interview, George Grande asked me if Clemens left in anger. I said, "We had anticipated this possibility. Quite frankly, he was prepared to go. We had been patient for a long time. We considered that he would be made an example of another young player who would not be paid based on his ability."

Grande then asked about Clemens' attitude. I characterized him as "disillusioned, disappointed, and disgusted."

Grande asked, "Where do we go from here."

"We're not prepared for Roger to come back until this situation is resolved. This is not a three day hiatus. It's not an emotional reaction. It's a very calculated response to what we believe is an unconscionably low offer," I said.

George concluded by asking, "When do you see him back?"

My response was, "When the Red Sox realistically respond to what Roger did on the baseball field last year."

A majority of the public in Boston supported the holdout even though a majority of Boston sportswriters, as usual, took the club's party line. Those writers, I am sure, would have supported the team if the Red Sox had offered Clemens the maximum cut.

In contrast, the people in the Houston media were particularly supportive of Roger and me. Perhaps because the Astros' season was not being threatened or because of the local connection, virtually every Houston television, radio, and newspaper sports reporter supported our position. Of course, when one reviewed the numbers in the chart, the fairness of our position was apparent, and the offer by Boston was shown to be unreasonably low.

Not much happened during the first week of the walkout. On March 12 I told Dan Shaughnessy of the *Boston Globe*, "We'll listen to anything they have to propose. But we're certainly not going to be thrown a bone...I still think the best solution is a two-year contract." Shaughnessy wrote in the March 13 *Globe*: "It has been charged that the commissioner's office or the Player Relations Committee might be calling the shots for the Red Sox in this matter, but Gorman said, 'It's totally our decision.'"

I returned home to Houston late in the afternoon of March 11. As soon as I got home, the telephone was ringing. It was Tim Melton from Channel 13 in Houston. ESPN would like to do a live interview that night. I agreed to do it if they would come to my home 35 miles northwest of downtown Houston. He readily agreed.

During the live interview, Gayle Gardner and Larry Burnett asked how long I expected the holdout to continue. I said, "It will take a long time. Roger is now the only young player who has not essentially surrendered to management's efforts to pay young players not on their performance but on their seniority."

I was then asked if I had a plan. To which I responded, "Our plan is to wait until Boston makes us an offer based on what he has done on the field, not based on the fact he can't arbitrate."

Wasn't there a difference, though, since Clemens could not arbitrate? I continued by stating, "Our offer is 75 percent of what Gooden earned when he went 24–4 and won the Cy Young, so our offer considers that Roger cannot arbitrate. We've offered either one or two years, but the Red Sox only want one year."

A couple of days later I agreed to an interview with Steve Mark of Channel 11 in Houston. By then, my reasoning on why Clemens should be paid $1,000,000 was well understood. So, Steve Mark inquired as to the reasons advanced by Boston for their offer.

"They say the market has changed," I replied. I explained the clash as one of ideology, based on arguments of talent versus seniority.

But there was more to it, I advanced: "I believe the league or commissioner's office is running this. If Clemens knuckles under, they have achieved a major victory. If Clemens doesn't knuckle under, they will have problems with their own credibility. If we win, we will have proven somebody can beat them."

He then said, "So, it's the collusion thing."

I responded by saying,

> That's really what's at stake here. They've shut down the free agent market. They don't make any competitive bids. Collusion is real, and it is pervasive. You don't have a radical change in the market suddenly by all twenty-six participants. They didn't quite get religion that quickly. The other side is trying to roll back the system in an unfair fashion, trying to block some of the normal rights players have. It only makes your resolve more firm in terms of

how you must wage war back against them, and that psychologically impacts someone like Roger Clemens.

Overall, I was quite gratified by the analysis of most fans and many members of the media. The holdout showed that the public was becoming more knowledgeable about, and discerning of, the relative value of players. Player salaries were rapidly becoming one more statistic in the baseball world. *USA Today* published charts on player salaries and started a salary arbitration watch, which gave the ardent fan a basis, however superficial, of tracking and evaluating player salaries.

The support we received was also bolstered, I believe, by the fact that I scrupulously avoided, as always, the platitudes and mournful statements often issued by a disgruntled player and his agent: the "I'm doing it for my family" or "It's the principle, not the money" or "I'd rather not play at all than play for this"—statements which not only turn off the fans and press, but turn me off as well.

Our argument was over relative pay, and that would be our campaign theme. As expected, there were certain reporters who took the position that we were wrong. They ignored collusion and the merits of our arguments. They reasoned that Roger Clemens was supposed to take the Red Sox' offer, since $400,000 is a lot of money. In their view, by holding out, Clemens became just one more example of the spoiled ball player in our society, a position beneath the dignity of a young hero.

*   *   *

When I concluded my briefing to the Boston media the day Clemens left camp, they asked where he had gone. I told them I had instructed him to go into hiding. I gave this instruction because I wanted to take the heat that would inevitably ensue. That was my job and, besides, I knew Roger would be in a "can't win" situation if he were trapped by the press.

When Roger Clemens left camp, he went to his condo in Winter Haven. Most of the reporters covering the Red Sox went on an immediate manhunt to find their man. They looked for him at the airport, in Houston, and in Boston. He stayed in Winter Haven, though, for five days. Knowing that Clemens had elected to stay put at his condo, it was amusing watching the media try to find him.

So that we could have some fun during the holdout, I gave Roger the code name "Swordfish." The night before he left camp, Alan, Roger, Debbie Clemens, and I had dinner. Debbie ordered swordfish.

After Alan and I had tried her dish, we asked Roger to take a bite, knowing full well his distaste for all seafood. After the Rocket "declined," I thought of a comic book I had read as a child in which the word "swordfish" had been used as a secret password. Demonstrating the humor and sensitivity of a typical ball player, I immediately stated that Roger's code name would be the "Swordfish" if we had to initiate a holdout. After everyone had finished laughing, I advised Roger that in the morning Alan and I would call on the management of the Red Sox one last time. "Be near the left field line," I told Clemens. "If I yell 'Swordfish,' that means the Red Sox did not budge and the holdout is on."

The next morning, after a futile meeting with Haywood Sullivan and Lou Gorman, I stepped outside the Red Sox offices in Winter Haven, spotted Roger shagging fly balls in left field, and hollered "Swordfish." Without acknowledging me, he immediately headed to the clubhouse, where he changed out of his uniform into his street clothes. The holdout was on.

The Swordfish was not to go out in public or reveal his presence to anyone. If I wanted to talk to him, I would call his house. Just to test our security system, I would say, "Roger Clemens, please," whereupon I would be told, "I'm sorry, he's not here." I would follow with, "The Swordfish, please." And the voice on the other end would laugh and say, "Just a minute." Shortly thereafter, Roger would pick up the phone and answer with his new nickname for me: "Hello, Boss."

My father, Clinton, had used humor in almost everything he did, and the trait passed easily to all six of his children—Carol, Clint, David, Alan, Randy, and Rick. Humor was an important resource for all of us during the holdout. The new nicknames, which served as a source of mutual entertainment, reinforced our bond to succeed.

As the last stop in our early Florida spring training itinerary, Alan and I were scheduled on March 10 to be in Dunedin, the grapefruit league home of the Blue Jays. Coincidentally, that was a day Boston played there. As usual, we arrived early to meet with our clients before their morning workout. Jays player Rance Mulliniks wanted to talk about Clemens' situation and its significance to all players. Two other Blue Jays, Tony Fernandez and Tom Henke, were in the same situation, and both were extremely unhappy. Mulliniks, ever an insightful analyst of the game, told me that every baseball player should be thanking me for what I was doing. He said the owners' collusion was extending into the ranks of the young players and someone had to fight back. He said he was glad it was me.

I was surprised how few people, including players, saw the connection to collusion. During collusion, many players became fatalistic, and one even heard player comments such as "Free agency doesn't mean anything anymore." I shuddered, as did Rance Mulliniks, at how easily many players were discouraged.

For the most part, the press was indifferent during the conspiracy. Most members of the media understood that collusion existed, but the prevailing view was that since baseball players were overpaid, and often uncooperative, they did not deserve any sympathy or support. This was the case in the spring of 1987, while Bob Boone, Tim Raines, Jack Morris, Lance Parrish, and several other quality free agent players went unsigned, and Bob Horner was forced to play in Japan.

When the Red Sox media arrived in Dunedin, they assumed that I was there to grandstand. A bevy of writers cornered me and fired question after question. They told me that Lou Gorman had announced that morning a $1,000 per day fine against Clemens. The reporters wanted my response. I immediately replied that I was increasing our demands by $1,500 per day.

Everyone present laughed, and my response received a lot of play in the national media. So much for the fine as a tactic. Overall, the day was a lot of fun, and some members of the media seemed to enjoy my flippant responses, while others shook their heads in disgust.

At each stop in Florida, everyone wanted to talk about Clemens' situation. In Fort Myers, John Schuerholz, the general manager of the Kansas City Royals, passed Alan and me in the hall at the Royals' spring training headquarters and said with a pensive grin, "You guys have big balls."

The holdout continued as Alan and I traveled to Arizona. We usually left our hotel room at 7:30 A.M. and did not return until midnight. There were typically twenty messages waiting when we returned, roughly fifteen of which were about Clemens. Needing to be up-and-at-'em early the next day, we ignored the calls. Of course, that did not stop some of the reporters, who would call after midnight (past 2:00 A.M. in the East).

One of those resilient reporters was Dan Shaughnessy. The Red Sox had offered to increase the award incentive package for Roger by $100,000. Alan, Roger, and I considered that to be "the bone" we would not accept. Shaughnessy reported our rejection of that token increase and wrote in the March 17 *Boston Globe*, "Hendricks also renewed his charge that the Sox are being steered by baseball's Player Relations Committee."

Shaughnessy then quoted me:

> "It's becoming clear to me that the Boston Red Sox are not
> negotiating. It's Park Avenue and New York City negotiating. They
> (the Red Sox) are always huddling to call us back after a day or
> two. We have reliable information from a number of sources that
> the idea is to hold Roger Clemens' salary down as a means of
> holding down all young players' salaries for the next couple of years.
> What is disturbing is that the Boston Red Sox are not negotiating
> on their own. They are negotiating as a pawn of an industry-wide
> policy. And the people who'll suffer are the Boston Red Sox, their
> fans and Roger Clemens.
>
> If I were a Red Sox fan the question I would ask is, 'Why
> should I get excited about this team when the best the team can
> offer is an increase in the All-Star clause?' The Sox seem to be
> indifferent to what is at stake in the 1987 season. The people in
> New York (PRC) are negotiating, and that is intolerable."

Shaughnessy reported Lou Gorman's response to my charges:

> "They make that assumption because they don't want to accept
> that the marketplace has changed," replied Gorman. "But the
> accusation has no foundation in fact. It is a pure assumption on
> their part."

The Red Sox made a new offer on March 21, but it was only an
increase in a couple of the award clauses. Shaughnessy reported the
state of negotiations in the March 22 *Globe*. "'I turned it down summarily,'" said Hendricks. "'We've been out two weeks and a day, and
all they've done is fool with a couple of incentives.'"

Shaughnessy reported Gorman's frustrations: "'We tell them that
the marketplace today is different from what it was a few years ago,
but they don't want to accept it.'"

My response as reported in the *Globe* was: "'The market doesn't
change until Roger agrees to it. We talked on Wednesday. Then they
waited two days and got back to me with a lot of enthusiasm and not
any money.'"

The Red Sox thought that we would get over our anger in a few
days. In order to let the Red Sox appreciate how serious we were, I
cut off all communication with them from March 22 to March 30.
During that period, Lou Gorman was asked daily by the ever increasing horde of media if there was anything new to report. He issued
unilateral updates of the negotiations rather than appear impotent. I

was amused at the thought of Gorman having to answer all the questions posed by the most competitive sports media in the United States, knowing that there was really nothing new that he could say. The reporters were looking for breaking developments, and Gorman didn't have any. When I later confronted him about the "poetic license" he used on a couple of occasions to characterize the status of negotiations, he sighed and explained how intense the pressure from the media was.

Alan and I returned from Arizona on March 21. The Red Sox offer was now $500,000, plus $450,000 in award incentives; I had reduced our one-year offer to $950,000. The Red Sox continued to reject our two-year offer. It was clear that this battle would continue to be hard fought by all involved.

Michael Madden of the *Boston Globe* had spoken to me in Florida and had followed the "negotiations" during the holdout. He also focused on the unsigned premium free agents, including Red Sox catcher Rich Gedman. Madden wrote in the March 23 *Globe*:

> Only a fool would not recognize a higher force is directing, orchestrating and dictating parameters for contracts this year between individual teams and players. Guidelines clearly have been set and not by the Boston Red Sox.

By late March reporters were clamoring to talk to Clemens; they had heard all they wanted to hear from Gorman and me. They were asking if the stance I had taken was really what Roger wanted. As a result, I called my first and only press conference to-date at the Hendricks offices for March 25. Clemens would be there, the media was advised.

The night before the press conference, Roger came to the office at my request. I had prepared twenty tough questions and answers. I played probing reporter, and he answered. I asked questions such as, "You say that you are a team player. If that is true, why aren't you in camp with your teammates?" The answer would be, "I am a team player. My teammates understand what I am doing and why. They support me, as I would any of them. And when this dispute is over, I will do everything I can to help my teammates and Boston win."

The next day almost every beat reporter from Boston area newspapers, television stations and many radio stations, reporters from ESPN, the Associated Press, every Houston television station, both daily Houston newspapers, and many Houston area radio stations crowded the conference room at our offices. Wires ran every which way. The parking lot was full of trucks with satellite dishes ready to beam live reports and interviews to Boston and the rest of the country.

I announced that Roger Clemens was appearing because so many requests had been made that he personally comment on his contract situation.

In explaining why he was a holdout, Clemens emphatically stated, "I want them to recognize what I did on the field, and right now they're not willing to do that."

I updated the media on the status of the negotiations. I stated that we had reduced our one-year offer to $950,000 and had indicated a willingness to decrease somewhat our two-year offer of $2.4 million. The Red Sox response, I indicated, had been to reject both proposals without making any adjustment in their offer.

I advised the media that the Red Sox did not want to pay Clemens based on what he had done on the field. Instead, I said, the Red Sox offer was "part of an overall plan orchestrated out of New York City designed to hold down salaries of all young players irrespective of their performances. The focal point is Roger Clemens. If Roger can be knuckled under and signed to a relatively low contract, then every young player for the next five years who shows up to negotiate will be told, 'Why should you get a large raise? Roger Clemens didn't, and he won the Cy Young and Most Valuable Player awards.'"

Only two of the twenty preparatory questions were actually asked of Clemens. He responded perfectly. He handled every question thrown at him and, through his answers, reinforced his commitment to and understanding of our position.

After the press conference, George Grande interviewed Roger for ESPN. When asked by Grande if the stance taken was truly his, Clemens replied, "It's my decision. The Hendrickses work for me. We talked it over, and I decided."

Grande pressed Clemens as to what he would do if the situation continued. He responded, "There's gonna be no winners, and that's the way it's gonna be."

When asked how long he would sit out, Clemens said, "If I was planning to play for the Red Sox offer, I'd be in spring training right now." So much for preparatory question number three.

Roger Clemens then interviewed with Bob Allen on Channel 13. When asked how he felt about his situation, he responded:

"I have the best people in the country working for me, the Hendricks. The Red Sox say we have no options, but I do. They thought I'd walk out and come back. They made Alan and Randy wait and didn't have a figure (on a two-year contract)."

When asked if he would sit out the season, Clemens said it's "one option I'll have to consider."

Terry Blount of the *Houston Post* was at the press conference and interviewed us afterwards. Blount wrote in the March 26 *Post*:

Clemens originally asked for $1 million for this season or $2.4 million for two years. He and the Hendricks brothers later lowered their figure to $950,000 for one year.

The Red Sox management countered with a $500,000 base-salary offer and $350,000 in incentives, which they later raised to $450,000.

But the 24-year-old former University of Texas standout doesn't want to accept a contract with incentive clauses.

"The Red Sox keep telling the public they have offered Roger $950,000," Hendricks said. "To have a little truth in advertising, I told them we would be happy to accept $950,000 base salary with no incentives."

To earn all of the incentive money, Clemens would have to be named AL playoff and World Series most valuable player, repeat as AL MVP and Cy Young Award winner and make the all-star team.

But Clemens and his agents have no intention of accepting that proposal.

"This reminds me of Vietnam," Hendricks said. "They feel if they keep bombing us enough eventually, we'll realize we have to surrender."

"We want to see them make some significant movement. We don't feel like they have bargained in good faith."

Hendricks said their proposal is in line with what other top major-league pitchers (Gooden, Hershiser, Saberhagen) who have two years of service.

"But there seems to be a big plan to hold down the salaries of all young players. You know, baseball isn't something where you work 20 years and get a gold watch. The issue is talent, not how long you've played."

"They're trying to use me as an example for all young players," Clemens said. "They keep saying times have changed and the market has changed.

"Well, that's fine, but my numbers haven't changed and the things I've worked for all my life haven't changed. They don't want to recognize what I've done on the field."

If Clemens did sit out the season, he still would be the property of the Red Sox. So he could find himself in the same position next year.

"Everyone asks if Roger is prepared to sit out all season," Hendricks said. "But the question should be asked if the Red Sox are prepared to go all season without Roger Clemens."

After the interviewing period was concluded, several of the Boston reporters expressed to me their disappointment that they had traveled all the way to Houston only to hear Clemens say the exact same things I had been saying.

"What did you expect?" I said. "You asked to talk to Roger, and we accommodated you. Did you think he was going to say something different than what I had been saying?"

As ESPN's roving spring training reporter, George Grande had been following the story intently. Grande's itinerary in spring training had caused him to intersect with Alan and me several times. On each such occasion, George interviewed me to update his viewers. He was at the press conference, and after the interview with Clemens he thanked me for making my client available. He expressed his regret over the circumstances creating the holdout and, without being judgmental, said he hated to see the losses which would soon accrue to all involved.

The day after the press conference, I came into the office and stopped at the desk of my assistant, Sue Stewart, to pick up my messages. "The Today Show," "Good Morning America," Howard Cosell, and many others had called asking Roger and me to appear on their shows. I quipped to Sue that it was sure strange that I was suddenly in such demand.

She laughed and said, "Last night Tom [her husband] and I were at dinner with a couple who are good friends. The husband was real concerned that the pressure on you must be unbearable. I just laughed and said, 'Randy doesn't feel the pressure, he thrives on it!'"

We both laughed heartily as I told her I had no interest in getting up early to do the national television shows, and, besides, I had already said everything I needed to say on the subject.

It became obvious that my campaign was scoring runs. Lou Gorman told the *Boston Globe* that letters to him were running in Roger Clemens' favor by 60–40. Support for Clemens in Houston was overwhelming. Whenever I heard a local sportscast or sports talk show, the commentator could have been reading my litany.

Robert Salmon, a Red Sox fan and former sportswriter from Brighton, Massachusetts, wrote a letter to the editor of the *Houston Chronicle*. His letter appeared in the March 28 *Chronicle*. It read:

"I have sent the enclosed letter to Boston Red Sox General Manger Lou Gorman protesting his treatment of Cy Young Award-winner Roger Clemens.

It's quite obvious that team owners are in collusion to force a reduced salary structure throughout the majors and have chosen Clemens as their prime target.

This is not in the best interests of baseball or the fans, who should be the owners' first concern. We, the fans, pay the freight.

I hope a boycott of Red Sox games will force the Red Sox to treat Clemens the way he should be treated. Your help would be greatly appreciated and may help baseball in general, not just Boston.

I covered the Red Sox for 10 years, from 1954 to 1964, when I worked for United Press International and Associated Press in Boston.

Letter follows:

A former Boston Sportswriter, I am canceling my Red Sox tickets and will initiate a campaign to have other Red Sox fans do the same unless you display some moral and ethical fiber and offer Roger Clemens, without whom the Red Sox will not win the 1987 pennant, a decent salary sans meaningless incentives.

The first responsibility of the Red Sox is to the fans, not the cabal of vulturous, penurious owners trying to forge a new major-league salary structure via Clemens' throat.

I will boycott the Red Sox because of your unbelievable stubbornness, lack of interest in your team's success, and your sad kowtowing to Jean Yawkey and the other colluded baseball owners.

You owe Boston fans much, much more than you have offered this year. You are destroying a great team. You have insulted Clemens twice with your 'incentive' offers and you have insulted loyal Red Sox fans once too often."

On Monday morning March 30, my mood was fatalistic as I left my house for work. I walked to my car, accompanied as usual by my wife, Jill. As I opened the car door, I paused and told Jill, "I just might lose this one. I started this holdout thinking I was fighting one club, but it's real clear I'm fighting all of organized baseball. They are willing to sacrifice the Red Sox for the benefit of both leagues."

Jill asked what I planned to do. I said, "If we go down, the Red Sox are going with us."

She asked what exactly I meant by that. I told her that the threat that Roger would sit out was not an idle one and that neither Roger nor I would ever yield without the Red Sox paying a price as steep as the one Clemens would pay.

That morning I resumed negotiations with Boston. Alan, Roger, and I called the Red Sox from our conference room. We offered to sign for $2 million for two years. Dan Shaughnessy reported Lou Gorman's response to our first communication in nine days in the March 31 *Boston Globe*:

> "The fact that they picked up the phone and called is a positive sign," added Gorman. "And Roger was there in the room with them and I said hello to him. I told them we would weigh it and talk to our people and get back to them. But it's still an outrageous amount of money."

That afternoon George Grande called and told me that he had just interviewed baseball Commissioner Peter Ueberroth and that Ueberroth had expressed concern over Clemens' holdout. Grande told me that he suggested Ueberroth "get involved." Peter responded by saying that I had been talking about him. Grande told Commissioner Ueberroth that he had not heard any specific reference to him. I confirmed to George that my references had not specifically mentioned the commissioner by name.

I had been intentionally vague, although the information I had received clearly implicated the Player Relations Committee. The PRC office is located within the complex of offices on Park Avenue in New York City, which contains both of the league offices and the commissioner's office. George Grande said he would phone Ueberroth with my response and asked if I wanted to talk directly to him. I said that I would.

I had conversed with Peter Ueberroth in depth on several occasions and was fond of talking to him. I found him to be very pragmatic. He made it his business to get to know many people on the labor side. This was quite a contrast to the methods of his predecessor, "Pope Bowie" Kuhn, as he was often called at the union. Kuhn was neither respected nor liked within union, player, or agent circles. I respected Ueberroth for realizing that baseball had lagged in promoting ancillary income and for implementing an aggressive licensing and merchandising program.

The commissioner called later that afternoon, and we talked at length. He said he knew that I was very serious about my goal and asked me several questions. He was concerned about whether or not I had specifically mentioned his name in connection with my allegations about New York influences on Clemens' negotiations. I repeated what I had told Grande. That seemed to satisfy Ueberroth.

The commissioner then asked for my solution to the stalemate. I gave him the one that I had been proposing for quite some time — a guaranteed two-year contract. I pointed out that a two-year contract could have a lower salary the first year, which would appear to favor the Red Sox, and a significantly higher salary the second year, which would favor Clemens. The second year, I reminded Peter, was also the year Roger would first become eligible for salary arbitration, a year in which he would be likely to garner a very hefty raise. Under this scenario, I went on, both parties could claim that they were satisfied with the final contract. I explained that I could not envision a one-year contract acceptable to both parties and told the commissioner that I had no intention of bending on a one-year contract.

Ueberroth asked questions about my motives and Roger's attitude. He also reviewed all of the numbers involved, including my comparison of Clemens to Gooden, Hershiser, and Saberhagen. "If I could be useful and arrange a meeting with Boston management, would you come?" Ueberroth asked.

I said that I could not see the point of meeting with Lou Gorman because he had no power on this matter.

"I plan to invite Haywood Sullivan, and I don't think he will decline my offer," the commissioner said.

I told him to count on Roger and me attending. He told me he would call me back with a time and a meeting place.

So, I called The Swordfish and told him that we would soon be meeting with the commissioner and Haywood. Roger did not want to go to the meeting. He told me that he thought it would look like we were giving in to the Red Sox. I explained that the commissioner was calling the meeting and that if the leagues were in control of his contract negotiations, then surely the commissioner could implement a solution. "Besides," I said, "we have nothing to lose other than time and travel expenses." The Swordfish agreed to go.

Ueberroth called back shortly after I concluded my discussion with Clemens. The meeting would be held at the Sunburst Hotel in

Scottsdale, Arizona. We agreed that no one would disclose that a meeting would be taking place.

At the meeting, the commissioner explained why he had arranged for the four of us to meet. Very simply, he wanted to find a solution and get Roger Clemens playing ball. He complimented Roger not only on his stellar season but also on his character and lifestyle. He said that baseball needed him playing. He told us that Dwight Gooden would enter rehabilitation for substance abuse within a day or two, and it was important that a player of Roger's character be on the field performing for the fans.

The commissioner then asked me if I would like to talk. I reiterated the reasons for the position that I had taken on my client's behalf. I told them that I would fight just as hard if they were my clients. I was doing my job, and there was nothing personal to this dispute. I told them that we all knew Roger Clemens was worth far in excess of $500,000 and that he wasn't signing for that amount, no matter what.

The commissioner asked if I had a solution. I advanced my reasons why a two-year contract would solve the problem and reiterated that I had become flexible on the $2.4 million. I reiterated my latest two-year contract proposal of $2 million, plus incentives. That could solve our mutual problem. A one-year contract, I told Sullivan, was out of the question unless he was prepared to pay $950,000. As Haywood shook his head, I told him that I understood why he couldn't pay that price; no one could afford to lose publicly.

Ueberroth interjected, saying he thought I was correct that a two-year contract was the only solution. He stated that our job at the meeting was to structure a two-year contract acceptable to everyone. He then asked Sullivan to speak.

Sullivan was most cordial and explained to Roger that he, too, was not being personal — that a dispute of this sort was just the nature of the business. The club co-owner told Clemens that he hoped we could reach an agreement, "but not the one Randy has in mind."

It was now Clemens' turn. He said he couldn't understand why Boston would offer him the contract they had. He reminded Sullivan that he had done everything that had been asked of him, both on and off the field. When he joined the Red Sox, the pitchers were second class citizens in their own minds, he explained, and he had worked hard to change that. "I've brought pride to the pitching staff," Clemens said, which was no exaggeration.

The Rocket was particularly incensed, he said, because he had been told that, despite his youth, he should take a leadership role on the pitching staff. He said that he had taken that role and had produced. Now it was time for the team to produce for him. The more Clemens talked, the more intense and animated he became. I was smiling inside. If there was any doubt that we would waver, this would put those doubts to rest. On this evening, I looked downright mellow compared to Roger.

After Clemens concluded his bill of grievances, he injected a comment about Red Sox manager John McNamara, "And another thing, Mac had no business taking me out of Game 6. I had only given up 4 hits in 7 innings. If he leaves me in, we win the World Series!"

Smiles crossed the faces of Ueberroth and Sullivan, as everyone realized we were in the presence of one of professional sports' all-time great competitors.

Peter then suggested that he and I take a walk and let Roger and Haywood talk privately inside the meeting room. As we enjoyed the balmy spring night in the desert, Ueberroth told me he thought I could get a two-year contract and asked what I would settle for. I told him that I had meant it when I said $2 million plus incentives. He told me not to be greedy. He suggested $1.5 million plus incentives. I asked how he would break that down, and he said $.5 million and $1 million. I said that was not enough. I'd always thought $2 million would do the trick at crunch time.

By now, two things were clear. First, Haywood would do whatever the commissioner "suggested." Second, Ueberroth wanted Roger Clemens signed and playing baseball on opening day.

Ueberroth compared our situation with Gooden's. As things then stood, he said, the two premier young pitchers in the game would be on the sidelines come opening day. He expressed his appreciation that my client lived a clean life and was a credit to the game and that baseball needed Clemens on the field.

By the end of the evening, everyone had been paired off, clearly a goal of Peter Ueberroth's. I admired the way the commissioner orchestrated the evening, letting everyone speak, guiding everyone toward a solution, yet remaining confidently in charge. We concluded with his suggesting that Haywood and I meet in the morning to try to work out a two-year contract in order to resolve the impasse. Clemens, Ueberroth, and I then adjourned for a midnight breakfast and were soon joined by National League President and future baseball commissioner Bart Giamatti.

The next day, Sullivan and I met outside by the swimming pool for several hours. We hashed out the general terms of a two-year contract. He told me that he could not go to a flat $2 million but that he could get to that level with incentives.

I said that if we went below $2 million, the incentives would have to take the potential package over $2 million. We generally agreed on $1.7 million plus incentives for placing in the Cy Young and MVP balloting as well as for making the All Star team. I told Haywood that at $1.7 million I had to have an escalator clause. An escalator clause is a provision that adds the amount of incentives earned in the first year of the contract to the guaranteed base salary of the second year of the contract.

Sullivan was most concerned that a final deal not be reached or announced, as such a deal would make the Red Sox look like they had cratered. I didn't view the matter that way, stating that the two-year contract looked like an intelligent resolution to a tough problem. I told Haywood that a two-year contract would look bad only if the team really wanted Roger and me to fold. Besides, I pointed out, the intervention of the commissioner easily explained away the two-year deal.

To accommodate Sullivan, I left the final deal understood but not formally resolved. I agreed that Clemens would go back to camp, even though camp was due to break in three days, so that we would not make the Red Sox look bad. In turn, Haywood agreed that we would consummate the deal formally in less than two weeks, just enough time to get the season well under way and turn the focus of the sportswriters from Roger Clemens' contractual status to the game on the field.

I concurred with this procedure because I understood the nature of an owner's ego. Furthermore, Roger could always leave, again, if Sullivan broke his promise to get the deal done. The deal was basically finished except for the final agreement on the escalator clause. The amount of the incentive clauses were large, but they required Clemens to have a big year. Haywood clearly knew my position on the escalator clause, so I believed that the quid pro quo to reaching the final agreement was my escalator clause in exchange for the media charade likely to take place in Winter Haven.

Roger wasn't sure of what he thought of the results of the

Scottsdale meeting. Like me, he could see that we were close to a deal we could accept, but he was uncomfortable that the deal was not finalized. I told him that the methodology Haywood wanted to follow was essential to reaching a final agreement, because Haywood viewed the two-year contract achieved via a holdout to be a loss by the Red Sox. I also sensed that Roger hankered for the battle; he wanted the Red Sox to surrender. I explained to him that that particular goal would not be achieved overtly without a higher price being paid and that the upcoming appearance during the last day or two of spring training gave the Red Sox something they needed and cost us nothing except, perhaps, a little false pride. We knew what we had achieved, I told him, "so who cares how it plays out publicly. In due course, when the contract terms are known, any intelligent analyst will know we achieved our goal."

We left Phoenix and returned to Houston the evening of April 2. The next evening we flew to Orlando and spent the night at a hotel along Interstate 4. As usual, we discussed what we would say at the press conference the next morning.

I didn't expect the press conference to be any fun. We were expected to say the proper thing about Clemens' commitment to the team being of paramount importance. On the drive over, we practiced our question-and-answer routine and discussed the possibility that someone would ask the "right" question, which was essentially, "Do you have an agreement already in place, so that this press conference is just to save face for the Red Sox?" Our answer would be, "Why don't you ask the Red Sox."

The Red Sox had started the press conference about ten minutes before we arrived. Haywood Sullivan had told the media that Roger would return while the details of a two-year contract were being worked out.

"There was," said Sullivan, "a mutual understanding of trust that we could get this done." The commissioner had brought us together, he continued, and had "escalated the time to get this thing done." The commissioner had played a part because it was in the "best interests of the Red Sox, the player and the game."

The Associated Press reported that our negotiations were:

> ... the first time since 1972, when Bowie Kuhn interceded in the negotiations between the Oakland A's and Vida Blue, that a commissioner became directly involved in a contract stalemate.
>
> Hendricks said he expected to reach a new deal with Boston

in 10 days to two weeks. "Unless it changes, he will have a two-year, guaranteed contract, which is what we were after all along," Hendricks said.

"We have defined the parameters of the final agreement," Hendricks said. "We have narrowed the gap to a small figure, and what remains is not so much determining the amounts, but deciding how they will be categorized."

Sullivan said, either prophetically or with a self-fulfilling prophesy in mind, "Understandings are gonna be tough to consummate. With the trust that Randy and Roger have with us and the trust and faith we have in negotiating a deal with them, then a future date is there."

Roger was asked about the commissioner's intervention, and he replied, "The commissioner came in and helped speed up time. We've got that agreement." He was then asked if he would do it again: "Most definitely. I think a two-year deal is the answer. I want to play in Boston."

During the holdout, Dan Shaughnessy of the *Globe* and Steve Fainiru of the *Hartford Courant* had editorialized that Roger was not wrong to hold out, given the relatively paltry offer of the Red Sox. Both Shaughnessy and Fainiru had tracked me down frequently during the holdout, looking for updates. They knew my firm-minded approach. So, after the press conference they both sought me out.

The disappointed looks on their faces told me a lot. I knew they had taken abuse from Red Sox management and other reporters because of their editorial views. Therefore, I recognized immediately that they viewed Clemens' return, under the circumstances announced at the press conference, to be an act of faith inconsistent with our prior position. Shaughnessy asked if, after all we had gone through, I really would let Clemens return based solely upon the hope that the Red Sox would carry through on a tentative understanding. Dodging his thoughtful challenge, I replied, "Why don't you ask me that question again in ten days."

Alan and I flew to Boston for the second home series of the year. We arrived at Fenway Park early in the morning expecting to meet with Haywood Sullivan. Lou Gorman met us and told us that he and counsel John Donovan would be meeting with us, since Sullivan would be tied up negotiating a television contract extension with NESN, the local cable network. My first thought was that I had made a mistake by not getting a firm agreement in Scottsdale. My second thought was that Haywood was going to regret that fact more than I was.

Lou started the meeting at 10:30 A.M. stating that I should not be concerned that Sullivan was tied up, because he and Donovan could get the deal done. I outlined the deal as I understood it, and Gorman wrote it down. We seemed to be on our way to wrapping up the contract. My fears, I thought, had been misplaced.

We chatted amiably while waiting for a break in Sullivan's meeting. Gorman planned to get Sullivan's final approval, and he finally met with the Red Sox co-owner and returned at 1:00 P.M. with the news.

Lou told us that the final contract would be for $1.7 million plus the incentives, but the total could not exceed $2 million. It was pretty obvious that Gorman had been given his marching orders and was dutifully executing them. I explained that I had an understanding with Haywood Sullivan and that he knew I wanted an escalator clause and that I was not agreeable to a salary cap.

Gorman then left again to consult with Sullivan. Lou returned to report that Sully was firm. I told him that I had to meet with Sullivan. He came back and said that Haywood could not leave the meeting with the NESN people. I said I would wait around for thirty minutes, and he should tell Sullivan that I would then be leaving, "And, by the way, Roger will be going with me."

I had never seen Lou move so fast as he headed to the conference room in which Sullivan was meeting.

I immediately called Roger in the clubhouse and told him to come upstairs to meet with me right away. After Clemens arrived, I explained the situation to him. He concurred that we would either get a deal agreeable to us or we would leave. Roger was feeling betrayed, and rightfully so. I told him to wait in the clubhouse where I could call him. "But," I said, "the Red Sox will likely meet our terms."

Within a few minutes, Haywood barged into the room. He was mad at me for my threat. I accused him of reneging on a deal. He said that he wasn't welching, that he was just sticking to his last position in Scottsdale. I reiterated the position that I had outlined, both in Scottsdale and to Gorman, and suggested that it was rude of him not to conclude our negotiations personally. I told him my threat was not idle and that this walkout would be accompanied by Clemens' saying he would never again play for the Red Sox and by my telling the world the circumstances under which Roger Clemens had returned and why he would now be leaving.

We soon got to work to resolve the matter, and Sullivan was joined by Gorman, John Donovan, and John Harrington. Alan rejoined the negotiations as well. We detailed our differences and floated various solutions back and forth. The mood turned cordial, but with an edge. Within an hour the deal was done. It was structured this way:

ROGER CLEMENS' 1987–88 CONTRACT TERMS

1987 salary — $ 500,000 guaranteed
1988 salary — 1,200,000 guaranteed

Cy Young Award voting:	1st Place	— $150,000
	2nd Place	— 100,000
	3rd Place	— 50,000
Most Valuable Player:	1st Place	— $150,000
	2nd Place	— 100,000
	3rd Place	— 50,000
All Star team selection:		— $ 50,000

NOTES: Any incentive earned in 1987, up to a maximum of $200,000, would be added to the guaranteed salary for 1988. And there would be no ceiling on the total Roger Clemens could earn.

Clemens won the Cy Young Award in 1987, thereby increasing his total compensation to $650,000 for that year. His salary for 1988 escalated to $1,350,000. The Rocket finished second in the Cy Young voting in 1988 and made the All Star team, thus earning $1,500,000 that year. The two-year total of $2,150,000 was a far cry from the one-year $400,000 "final offer" the Red Sox had made at the spring training meeting on March 5. Poetically, Roger's final earnings started with his magic number "21."

Debbie Clemens cooked a dinner for us to celebrate the final contract. The main course was swordfish. Of course, Roger got to eat a steak.

Without the benefit of spring training in 1987, Clemens started the season inconsistently. As the All Star game neared, it became a close call whether Roger deserved to make the team. Boston manager John McNamara would ostensibly make the pitcher selection, but it is common knowledge that the league president, in this instance Dr. Bobby Brown, wields power over those selections. Roger pitched poorly in New York in late June, a factor cited by Brown as to why Clemens was not selected.

Why didn't McNamara fight to choose his ace, as other All Star managers had done? Perhaps his bosses wanted to save some money or exact some revenge. After all, the holdout was still fresh in their minds.

Dan Shaughnessy called and asked if I believed that Roger Clemens was intentionally slighted and if I believed that McNamara was ordered by the Red Sox not to choose him. Having no concrete evidence and figuring that nothing would be gained by griping in public, I quipped, "Tip O'Neil would have chosen Roger," an obvious reference to the well-known fact that O'Neil, then the Speaker of the U.S. House of Representatives, took good care of his Massachusetts constituents. After Blue Jays manager Cito Gaston made his 1993 All Star game selections, I would place him in the same class with O'Neil.

Clemens' final contract was far superior to what the other members of his service group received. In contrast to Roger Clemens' $2,150,000 for 1987–88, in 1987 Joe Carter earned $250,000, Kirby Puckett $465,000, Tony Fernandez $400,000, Tom Henke $331,000, Eric Davis $330,000, Ted Higuera $335,000, John Franco $300,000, Roger McDowell $305,000, Sid Fernandez $308,000, and Rob Deer $225,000.

Over the next few years, in salary arbitration and the collusion hearings, management would characterize Roger Clemens' contract as a special case, one in which he was excepted from the normal bounds applied to players ineligible for salary arbitration.

Indeed, Roger's contract was an exception. For, whether in a collusive or a noncollusive market, baseball players lacking the right to salary arbitration or free agency are "stuck." They are trapped in a system in which a club can dictate a player's salary. And, absent a holdout, the player must stay healthy, must maintain a high level of performance, and must wait until he accumulates the necessary rights before he will be paid a salary truly commensurate with his talents as a baseball player.

Chapter 4

Two Record Contracts and Two Record Hearings

In 1988, Roger Clemens posted an 18–12 record with a 2.93 earned run average. He made the All Star team and finished second to Frank Viola of Minnesota in the Cy Young voting. His season was affected by a pulled muscle in his back, caused while Clemens was moving a carpet from his den to his basement. His son, Koby, jumped in the path where he was about to drop the carpet. Roger lunged to keep a grip on the carpet and in the process pulled the muscle. Nevertheless, Clemens continued to pitch, albeit in pain, throughout the balance of the 1988 season.

Roger's holdout contract was now complete. As a player with over four years of major league service, Clemens was eligible for salary arbitration in early 1989.

As already indicated, the owners altered the tactics of collusion following the 1987 season. The use of a group boycott was replaced with a price fixing scheme executed through an information bank. Not only did clubs "cooperate" by reporting offers to the PRC information bank, but the offers they made to free agents were similar to the salaries the players had previously earned. A player could move from one club to another, but the price for his "freedom" would be to accept a lower salary than what his old club would pay. And unlike normal markets where the values of free agents increase or decrease based upon their previous season's performances, the offers made to players following the 1987 season were tied to their prior salaries.

The primary impact of the collusion years on players eligible for salary arbitration was that the universe of player salaries, to which an arbitration eligible player's salary would be correlated, was artificially depressed. Over time, the residual, chilling effect of collusion continued to affect the salaries paid to free agents after the 1988 season. Collusion had diminished the expectations of players and agents, and resulted in no real increase in the salary structure over a four-year period, even though club revenues had increased significantly.

Having to operate within this collusion-depressed salary structure, I submitted $2,360,000 as Clemens' salary arbitration number in January 1989. The Red Sox submitted $1,900,000. Given our recent history with the Red Sox, negotiations threatened to become testy, especially since the number we submitted was higher than the salary of any pitcher in baseball in 1988.

The salary arbitration season is challenging for many reasons. One reason is that the salaries of players comparable to a client are often not settled when numbers are submitted. This makes salary arbitration a game of moving targets.

Orel Hershiser represented such a "moving target" for Roger Clemens. The Dodgers' ace was 23–8 in 1988 and won the National League Cy Young Award. He pitched 58⅔ consecutive scoreless innings — an all time record — and carried underdog Los Angeles to a World Series championship upset over the favored Oakland A's.

Hershiser was also eligible for salary arbitration and filed $2,425,000 as his number. The Dodgers countered with $2,000,000. Hershiser had been through two salary arbitration hearings, so his negotiations promised to be as tense as Clemens'. Both players had their hearings scheduled for February 16.

Dwight Gooden represented another "moving target." He had posted an 18–9 record in 1988, and his contract was up as well. Clemens, Hershiser, and Gooden represented interdependent moving targets to each other — sort of a Cy Young salary arbitration triangle. What one player signed for would affect the other two.

I had high expectations for what we could do for Clemens. After all, he had finished first twice and second once in the Cy Young Award voting over the prior three years. It was my belief that Roger should be paid at the top of the starting pitcher salary structure, if not at the top of the salary structure for all players.

I recognized, though, that Hershiser had five years of service, a magical 1988 season, and therefore slightly more bargaining leverage than did Clemens. I believed that based upon 1988 performances, Orel had slightly more to sell than Roger. However, based upon career performances, I believed that Clemens had more to sell, for he had been a more consistent pitcher over his career.

Dwight Gooden, like Hershiser, had five years of service. Gooden signed first, a three-year contract for $6.7 million. My immediate reaction was that while "Doc's" contract "fit" within the stagnant salary structure, it did not reflect an increase in the structure that should have started as collusion wound down.

The Red Sox offered Roger $5.25 million for three years on November 29 and raised their offer to $6 million on December 21. I had offered $2.25 million for one year on January 12, and the Red Sox had countered at $2.1 million for one year and $6.3 million for three years.

Our numbers were close on a one-year contract, but Clemens and the Red Sox both wanted a three-year contract. I had offered the Red Sox four different proposals, a one-year, a two-year, a three-year, and a four-year. I told the Red Sox to take their choice. My three-year offer was for $7,800,000, a number the Red Sox were resisting mightily. After Gooden's signing, the Red Sox increased their three-year offer to $7 million on January 24.

I had planned to go to salary arbitration unless we received $7,500,000 for three years. That would have made Roger Clemens the highest salaried player in baseball history. Dan Quisenberry had signed a contract which might have had a higher average value, but "Quiz's" contract was exceptionally difficult to value because it was tied to the future value of several apartment projects in Memphis.

Two days before Clemens' hearing, I continued negotiations via telephone with John Harrington, Haywood Sullivan, and Lou Gorman of the Red Sox. They were willing to go to $7.4 million. I declined their offer, and said I would go to $7.5 million, but that would be the end of the line for us.

The Red Sox triumvirate called the next day. I was impatient, because I had an evening flight to New York for the scheduled hearing. We were close, but "oh so far away." We good naturedly debated our differences. Sullivan said he could not understand why I was so unyielding, since we were only $100,000 apart. I replied that if $100,000 were so inconsequential, he should pay the money instead of debating the issue. The Sox executives excused themselves while I waited "on hold." They then offered $7.45 million, to split the difference, but I told them, "I have $7.5 million on the brain."

The specific language to be contained in a lockout clause also held up the completion of a contract. The clubs were on a mission to obtain this clause in every guaranteed contract in anticipation of the 1990 bargaining sessions. The reason the clubs wanted this clause was obvious. They were preparing for a 1990 lockout, and the clause would excuse the clubs from paying players during a club initiated lockout.

While we debated about the exact language, I offered to forego an All Star clause if the Red Sox would go to $7.5 million. I kiddingly said "for $2.5 million a year, you ought to get an All Star." The Sox officials agreed, and the deal was done at $7.5 million. Roger not only became the highest salaried player in baseball history, but he achieved the $2 million salary level faster than any player in baseball history.

When the deal was announced on February 15, the Associated Press contacted me. I was asked to comment on the record contract, and I stated:

> While it may represent the highest salary per year ever earned in baseball, that's not going to last too long in my opinion. I believe that salaries are going to continue going up.

Clemens ultimately earned $7.7 million under the contract, including award incentives. However, "the record" lasted all of one day. Orel Hershiser signed for $7.9 million the next day. I was hardly surprised. I believed that whoever went last between Clemens and Hershiser would earn the most money, since the last to sign would be able to use the contract of the other player as a new benchmark. The last "moving target" would therefore get the highest contract.

When Clemens signed, Hershiser's hearing was less than fifteen hours away. Orel had won his first salary arbitration case and had lost his second case. He and his agent-attorney, Robert Fraley, were steely minded and were itching for the rubber match. With Clemens' record contract to use as a comparable, they knew they had become the favorite in their case. The Dodgers also recognized that fact, and the Dodgers' ace signed his record contract one hour before his scheduled hearing.

Steve Fainiru had moved to the *Boston Globe*. He called me after the Hershiser contract was announced. He wanted my reaction, figuring that perhaps I would be somewhat disappointed about holding the record for only one day. Steve asked how I felt, and I replied:

I feel like one of those American pole vaulters. I just went 19 feet 11 inches, and Sergei Bubka came along and went 19 feet 11¼ inches.

But there'll be a new meet next year. Maybe Jeff Reardon will be the next pole vaulter. Or it'll be Kirby Puckett vaulting.

Really, if we let this ruin one day, or one week, of our lives, then we're hopeless.

Fainiru asked me if I believed that the Clemens and Hershiser contracts were linked, and if the contract I had negotiated for Roger helped Orel. I quickly responded, "It's like that pass Isiah Thomas made in the NBA All-Star game. Orel Hershiser and Robert Fraley took the ball and stuffed it."

Steve was always a good audience for my humor, and he laughed, as usual. A veteran of the Clemens holdout, Fainiru was familiar with my occasional flippant, metaphorical style of speaking. Nothing I did or said surprised him. "A record is a record," I told him, "even if it lasts only one day."

*   *   *

Roger Clemens went 17–11 with a 3.13 earned run average in 1989, posting his usual workhorse numbers. The 1990 season was in many ways a magical one for Roger — although some of the magic seemed on the darker side. He went 21–6 with a 1.93 earned run average. He considered 1990 to have been his best season, though he finished second in Cy Young balloting to Bob Welch, who won 27 games.

On August 30, the Rocket had 20 wins and the Red Sox were in first place by 6½ games. Because of shoulder soreness, Clemens missed virtually the entire month of September. By September 25, the Red Sox were 1½ games behind Toronto, but rallied to a first place tie with the Blue Jays with only six games remaining in the season.

In a showdown series with the Blue Jays, the Red Sox won the first game, vaulting back into first place. Roger returned the next day and pitched Boston to victory. With the Rocket back in command, the Sox clinched the American League East Division, and prepared to face Oakland, the West Division leader and defending World Series champion.

The 1990 playoffs were a disaster for the Red Sox. Oakland was clearly the superior club and won the first three games. Clemens was the starter in game four in Oakland against Dave Stewart, a formidable playoff pitcher. If the Red Sox were to have a chance, their stopper would have to come through with a big game.

Roger was especially intense and focused that October 10. He wore eye-black under his eyes for effect. He and catcher Tony Pena were concerned that the A's had been stealing their signals, so they worked out a more complex system of signals designed to prevent the Athletics from gaining an edge.

In the bottom of the second inning Clemens walked Willie Randolph. At that point, Roger was concerned with both his pitching mechanics and his signals with Pena. As he stared toward home plate, home plate umpire Terry Cooney interpreted Clemens' stare and body language to be an affront to the umpire. Cooney also thought that Clemens' comments to Pena were directed toward him.

Cooney's report to the American League read:

> When I looked out at the mound, Roger was standing there staring at me shaking his head back and forth as if to say "Boy are you stupid." I ignored it at first, but when it continued I yelled at him without removing my mask: "I hope your not shaking your head at me!"

Within seconds Cooney ejected Clemens, removing from the playoff game one of the greatest pitchers ever to play baseball. While there would later be suggestions that the foundation for the ejection was built on incidents in prior playoff games, Roger had been thrown out of a critical playoff game based in large part upon Cooney's subjective interpretation of body language.

Clemens did not realize that he had been ejected, believing instead that Pena must have said something to Cooney to get himself ejected. Tony walked slowly to the pitching mound, where Roger dispassionately waited to hear Pena's report. When he reported that it was not he, but Clemens, who had been ejected, Roger could not believe what he had heard.

The Rocket went ballistic. His postejection actions were, to put it mildly, provocative and somewhat uncontrolled. His conduct was, though, just what one might expect from a tightly wound competitor in a championship game who had just found out that he had been unjustly ejected.

On November 15, American League President Bobby Brown mailed a letter notifying Clemens that he had been suspended. On November 20, the American League issued a press release announcing Dr. Brown's $10,000 fine and five day suspension of Roger Clemens. It read:

> American League President Dr. Bobby Brown today announced that Boston Red Sox pitcher Roger Clemens has been suspended for the first five (5) games of the 1991 season, and has been fined $10,000.00. The disciplinary action was imposed for Clemens' behavior during Game #4 of the 1990 American League Championship Series. Clemens was ejected from that game.
>
> The disciplinary action by Brown cited "... for making significant physical contact with an umpire (Jim Evans), for threatening Umpire Cooney, for verbally abusing Umpire Cooney with personal obscenities and for not leaving the dugout immediately after the ejection."
>
> Clemens has the right to appeal this action, and should he choose to do so, both the fine and suspension will be held in abeyance pending a result of a hearing on this matter.

In response to the suspension, on November 20 the Red Sox issued a short press release, prepared by counsel John Donovan, but released in the name of Lou Gorman. It read:

> Dr. Brown's statement and subsequent fine and suspension of Roger Clemens speaks for itself. Although we are not in agreement with the severity of the league's action, we are satisfied that the issue has been addressed.

Alan and I went into action immediately. After reading the press releases and the letter advising Clemens of his suspension, we conferred with our client. The next day we issued our own press release:

> The decision by American League President Bobby Brown is disappointing and excessive. No mention is made of the significance of the game, nor is any mention made that umpires, in a position of authority, are supposed to exhibit restraint and maturity in the face of pressure. No warning was issued to Roger. What Roger was muttering was under his breath, not originally directed at Cooney. No mention is made of Cooney's substandard ball-strike calls.
>
> We have concern that the severity of the punishment increases the arrogant power often displayed by umpires, who increasingly think they are part of the game and not arbiters of the game. It is also disappointing to learn that the league office released the announcement of the fine and suspension prior to proper notification of Clemens either directly or through the union.

In the league press release it was pointed out that part of the reason for the harshness of the punishment was because of some of the things said following the ejection. There were, however, many other participants saying various things during this time and no mention has been made of them or their comments.

Roger is greatly disappointed with the lack of support shown for him by the statement issued by the Red Sox.

Needless to say, we instructed the union to file an appeal. The hearing was scheduled for late January 1991.

During the 1990 season, I had talked to John Harrington about Clemens' desire for a contract extension. Roger's one day record contract ran through the 1991 season, and we thought it would be appropriate to extend the contract prior to the end of 1990. My conversation with the head of the Yawkey organization was the first truly extended discussion we had outside of direct contract negotiations. I communicated to Harrington that he should not misinterpret the 1987 holdout or 1989 arbitration brinksmanship to mean that Roger did not want to remain in Boston. To the contrary, I emphasized, Roger was committed to bringing a World Series championship to Boston.

Don't mistake our intensely competitive nature on contract negotiations to be anything other than our taking care of the financial side of the business, I told John. The game off the field was distinct from the game on the field. We were easily able to separate the two, I told him.

Once a contract was signed, that was the end of any discussion about the pay during that period. I had never asked to renegotiate a baseball contract and did not intend to start now, I continued to explain. We discussed the fact that Frank Viola had successfully demanded that Minnesota renegotiate his contract after Orel Hershiser signed. Jim Rice had also successfully renegotiated his contract with Boston a decade earlier.

I stated that, "We want a commitment from the Red Sox. Roger is willing to stay beyond 1991, but you will need to make that commitment before next season, because we will not negotiate during the season. If you choose to wait to negotiate until Roger is a free agent, he will not negotiate, but will simply leave. You decide."

Harrington concluded our conversation by characterizing it as "fascinating." He advised me that the Red Sox wanted to retain Clemens and would take the necessary steps to do so before the end of 1990. We parted on the most cordial of terms. I relayed the thrust of the conversation to Roger, who was very pleased. The Rocket wanted to play for the Red Sox for his entire career.

Harrington postponed discussions of an extension several times during the fall. Whether Clemens' actions in Oakland or the league's subsequent suspension had anything to do with this, I do not know.

Finally, we were scheduled to talk at the winter meetings in early December in Chicago. Near the end of the winter meetings Alan and I met in the Red Sox suite with John Harrington, John Donovan, and Lou Gorman.

Gorman said the club was prepared to sign Roger to a long-term contract extension, and at a salary slightly greater than the salaries of Dave Stewart and Bob Welch, who had won the 1990 Cy Young Award. Since Clemens finished second and Stewart finished third, the Red Sox were clearly trying to "box in" Roger with the two other fine pitchers. Alan and I had other ideas.

The Red Sox offered $14 million for four years, an average of $3.5 million per year. I replied that we expected Clemens to be paid more than Jose Canseco, who had signed the first big postcollusion contract during the summer of 1990, a five-year contract for $23.5 million, an average of $4.7 million per year. I then offered $27.5 million for five years, an average of $5.5 million per year.

Gorman said that the Red Sox did not believe that a pitcher should be paid at the highest salary level. I responded with the fact that while a starting pitcher may play every fourth or fifth day, when he does play he is involved in every pitch, every at bat, every out. His involvement in total "transactions" during one game is equal to the involvement of the typical regular player in four or five games, I said. Besides, I continued, the highest paid player had always alternated between a pitcher and a regular.

We agreed to talk on the telephone over the next few weeks and rendezvous in Boston before the Red Sox annual banquet on January 10. We met on January 7 and agreed on the guarantee language and incentive package. We were still substantially apart on money and years. The Red Sox increased their offer to $16.6 million for four years, and I decreased our offer to $26 million for five years. At the end of the day, the Red Sox were at $16.8 million, and I was at $25 million.

The length of the contract was a stumbling block. The Red Sox were determined to hold the contract to four years, since Clemens was already signed for 1991. A total of five guaranteed years was the maximum exposure Boston wanted to accept.

We met the afternoon of the banquet, and I indicated that I would consider $21.9 million for four years. In that meeting the Red Sox gave the first inkling that they might go to the $5 million level, when their response to my "indication" was to dodge the issue of money and instead focus on Roger's health.

The Red Sox were concerned about the shoulder problems that he had experienced in September, so we agreed that the Red Sox would have to be satisfied with his medical condition. We agreed that club physician Arthur Pappas, a partner in the club and friend of Clemens', would examine him for the Red Sox. We also agreed to have Astros club physician Bill Bryan examine Clemens. Dr. Bryan had operated on members of the various Hendricks families, and we were very comfortable with, and confident in, his objectivity and professionalism.

The plan was for us to reconvene negotiations once we had the medical reports. We expected those reports within two weeks. Roger was confident that he would pass the battery of medical tests.

A few hours before the banquet at the Sheraton Hotel, John Harrington visited with Roger, Alan, and me in my hotel room. Harrington wanted Clemens to know that the Red Sox supported him in his appeal from the suspension and to also let Roger know how much the Red Sox wanted to sign him to a long-term contract. The meeting was short, but important. Clemens was pleased that Harrington made the effort and appreciated the good will implicit in the visit.

Lou Gorman had indicated to the press after the winter meetings that we had talked about a contract extension. Prior to the Boston Baseball Writers' banquet, Roger, Alan and I met with the press, who were eager for an update on the status of contract talks.

David Cataneo of the *Boston Herald* wrote in the January 11 edition of the *Herald*:

> Agent Randy Hendricks yesterday indicated negotiations for a new Roger Clemens contract would likely end on Opening Day, which would leave the Red Sox ace headed for free agency.
>
> "We don't believe it's appropriate to negotiate during the season," said Hendricks, in town for last night's annual Boston Baseball Writers' banquet. "That doesn't mean there aren't exceptions. But it would be unlikely we would negotiate. We believe negotiations should take place during the negotiating season."

"They might talk and we might listen, but it's highly unlikely we would respond. But I don't want to paint myself into a corner. We'll cross that bridge when we come to it."

Hendricks has been in Boston to meet with Red Sox officials about a new pact for Clemens, who is eligible for free agency after his current deal runs out at the end of the upcoming season.

Hendricks reported minimal progress, but appeared cautiously optimistic. "We've agreed what first place is worth and what Cy Young (Award) is worth," said Hendricks. "We're doing a lot better than Iraq and the United States, I'll state that."

Clemens' appeal to Dr. Brown was scheduled for Monday, January 28. He and I flew together from Houston to New York on Sunday morning, January 27, Super Bowl Sunday. We reviewed our position thoroughly on the plane, so by the time we arrived at the Grand Hyatt we were ready to relax. We watched the New York Giants edge Buffalo in Super Bowl XXV, while dining on room service. I ate crab cakes and Roger ate a steak. After the game, we talked to Gene Orza and reviewed the presentation for the hearing scheduled for the next day.

The next morning Roger and I walked to the offices of the American League, a relatively short distance from our hotel. We talked about how we believed the video tapes of the game would prove that he had done nothing to justify his ejection. Lost in the haze of the morning rush hour was the throng of reporters and television cameras awaiting us as we walked onto the block on which the American League offices were located.

Bob Ryan of the *Boston Globe* was one of those reporters. He wrote:

> As he crossed Park Avenue on his way to the American League office, Roger Clemens looked like a Big Little Boy heading to the principal's office. The only catch was that he had requested the meeting himself.
>
> An office is not Roger Clemens' natural habitat. He's much happier out in the open, working up a sweat, and anyway, dress-up clothes do not enhance him. That linebacker's neck was pouring out of his white shirt. The necktie was an alien appendage. Put him in gym shorts and a T-shirt, and of course, a baseball uniform. That's the real Roger Clemens. He is what he is, a hard-working jock. He has no other pretensions. Roger is never going to be on the cover of GQ.
>
> But it won't do to visit the office of the American League president in the same outfit you'd wear to go to the movies. Roger

Clemens played the game he had to play yesterday because he was making a desperate attempt to save $10,000, get back a lost start and, most important of all, clear his name. If it means throwing on a tie and stuffing his astonishing chest into a sportcoat, well, a man's gotta do what a man's gotta do.

We rode the elevator to the American League offices as reporters and cameramen shadowed our every movement. The reporters had to wait in the hallway as we were ushered into a conference room in the American League offices, where the hearing would be held. Gene Orza would present Roger's case, and I would review the history of prior discipline during playoff games. Michael Weiner and Bob Lenaghan of the union were also in attendance in support of Clemens.

John Harrington was there to get the facts first hand and to support his player. The Red Sox were now more responsive than they had been in their knee-jerk reaction to the announcement of the suspension in November. My discussions in Boston with John Harrington and Haywood Sullivan regarding their support had likely played a part in John's visit to Roger's hotel room and his subsequent journey to New York for the hearing.

Marty Springstead, American League supervisor of umpires, was present, as was Richie Phillips, counsel to the umpires' union. Cooney and umpire Jim Evans, who had worked the right field foul line in game four of the playoffs, were already seated. Dr. Brown was seated at the head of the conference table with his new legal counsel, Bill Schweitzer, of the Washington office of Baker & Hostetler.

Rene Lachemann, presently the manager of the Florida Marlins, but then the third base coach of the Athletics, would testify as a witness via telephone.

Phyllis Merhige, director of public relations for the American League, was doing her usual great job of making everyone feel comfortable. Since a television set would be used to show a video replay of the "incident," Phyllis was checking the replay system to verify that it was functioning properly.

I sat at the end of the table opposite from Dr. Brown, where I could observe everyone in the hearing. The television set was directly behind me. As Phyllis fiddled with the set, I turned to her and joked that she had better be sure she had the correct video tape, since it would be embarrassing if a rerun of the "Beverly Hillbillies" were played. Always in an upbeat mood, Phyllis laughed and then told me in hushed tones that I had to be serious. "No, I don't," I said, "Gene's flying the plane today and I'm just the co-pilot."

Since Don Fehr wears two hats, that of executive director and general counsel, Gene Orza's title is associate general counsel of the union. A top flight advocate known for the passion of his arguments, Orza functions in the traditional role of general counsel. He has a great feel for the people in the game and truly loves baseball. He is a baseball trivia expert and a connoisseur of movies, literature, and the stage. He sets high expectations for himself and for all baseball agents. Those who do not uphold those high standards "feel the heat" from Orza. The Clemens ejection greatly troubled him. We had discussed the significance of Boston losing its ace pitcher in a playoff game over an incident imperceptible to the viewer.

The hearing commenced with Dr. Brown reading the umpire reports into the record. We then proceeded to watch the replay of the incident.

After the replay was finished, Orza asked if the two umpires were going to leave the room, since they would later be called to testify as witnesses as to what Roger Clemens said and did. Dr. Brown said that they would be allowed to remain in the room. Gene objected "strenuously" to this ruling, since witnesses to a "trial" are not generally allowed to watch the proceedings. He then asked why Richie Phillips was present at the hearing. Dr. Brown said it was because Phillips represented the two umpires. Orza inquired if Phillips were going to be allowed to participate in the hearing. When the American League president said Phillips was going to be allowed to participate, Orza claimed that allowing the umpires' union to participate was "unprecedented in the history of the relationship" between the players association and the clubs.

A discussion was held as to how many separate tapes of the incident there were, and whether there was a separate camera on Roger the entire time prior to his ejection. Dr. Brown had three separate tapes from CBS, but none were focused on the Rocket the entire time. The American League president advised us that Phoenix Communications, the company that recorded games for Major League Baseball, might have a tape focused on Clemens. All Dr. Brown had seen were the tapes furnished to him by CBS.

Gene proceeded to ask Dr. Brown, the judge in the present hearing, to testify as to his reasoning in reaching the decision to assess a $10,000 fine and suspend Clemens for five games. Bill Schweitzer advised Dr. Brown not to testify, and a somewhat animated exchange followed between Orza and Schweitzer.

After listening to their arguments for a couple of minutes, Dr. Brown asked for a short recess so that he could excuse himself to talk to his legal counsel. In one of the more humorous moments occurring in the "baseball legal system," cardiologist and former major league player Dr. Brown returned within a few minutes to advise us that he would consent to testify. He had obviously overruled his own legal counsel, initiating Schweitzer into the strange world of grievance hearings conducted by the leagues and the commissioner. When Dr. Brown announced his decision, I chuckled out loud while thinking that Schweitzer's background had not prepared him for the proper advice to give to his client, the judge and prosecutor in a kangaroo court.

Orza opened his formal presentation by arguing that Cooney provoked the incident. There was a cancer growing in the game, Orza said, and that cancer was umpires who were intent on becoming personalities in the game and protecting themselves from "being shown up." Umpires were beginning to think that they were bigger than the game, and that attitude had led to Roger Clemens being improperly ejected, the union lawyer intonated.

Upon questioning by Orza, the American League president testified that he did not talk to Commissioner Vincent before reaching his decision. The former Yankee third baseman said he neither did any research nor asked for any research on prior decisions, because he believed he should independently make up his own mind. He was in attendance at the game and personally saw the incident. Further, he had reviewed the tapes furnished to him, the AL president testified.

Orza reviewed the umpire reports with Dr. Brown. The league president testified that he had spoken with the umpires after the game, over the telephone a couple of days before the reports were filed, and after the reports were filed.

Gene and I then reviewed in detail the history of every playoff fine and suspension, and the conduct on which it was based. Orza then pressed Dr. Brown as to how he had reached his decision. The doctor described the situation as an "ugly scene." A number of factors "all went into the mix" to arrive at the fine and suspension. Prior decisions and the discipline imposed were not important, he testified, because "things change" and "one must make proper judgments."

When Gene asked Bobby what he thought had happened when he saw Cooney throw his arm up in the air to eject Clemens, Dr. Brown testified that Clemens must have said something. "I'm guessing," said the American League president. Orza referred to an interview with umpire Don Denkinger, who said Roger had to say something personal about Cooney to get ejected. Dr. Brown said he could not tell what had been said.

Gene pressed Dr. Brown about whether he had suspended or disciplined any umpire in connection with the incident. Dr. Brown refused to disclose what action, if any, he had taken.

Umpire Jim Evans testified next. Like Clemens, he attended the University of Texas. Evans was approximately 150 feet from Roger and at an oblique angle to the pitcher. Evans testified that Roger "appeared to be disgusted at Cooney." Evans said he could see Roger's mouth moving as Roger moved his head. The comments were directed toward home plate, he said. Evans said he could not see any words coming out of the mouths of either Cooney or Pena.

Gene asked Evans how he could be sure of what happened, given his distance from the action. Evans said it was Cooney's step out from home plate and response which led to Evans' conclusion.

It was clear to me that Evans was reaching conclusions based upon what he considered to be the norm, not based upon any specific knowledge of what exactly happened. When asked if it seemed strange that Clemens did not react when he was ejected, Evans said it was not, though when pressed, Evans agreed that most players would have reacted. "Roger stares a lot," Evans said.

Since Rene Lachemann had been told to telephone at a predetermined time, the testimony of Evans was suspended in order to permit Lachemann to testify. A veteran of twenty-six years in baseball, "Latch" identified himself as the Oakland A's third base coach. Lachemann would have been about fifty feet from Clemens, and within an area where what he said would have been audible. Lachemann testified that all he heard was Roger saying, "I'm not talking to you, keep your f____ mask on" and then Cooney ejected Roger.

Phillips was allowed to cross examine Lachemann. He asked the coach whether he had heard Clemens say anything else prior to the ejection. Lachemann said he did not, because he had been talking to the runner at third base.

After Lachemann's testimony was completed, the hearing reconvened with Evans continuing his testimony. He estimated that eight seconds elapsed between the ball four call on Randolph and the ejection. Evans concluded his testimony by saying that while the incident was unfortunate, Clemens was wrong.

Cooney testified next. Gene reviewed an incident in a prior playoff game. Luis Rivera had been called out on a 3–2 pitch on an appeal play to Cooney. Cooney said a lot of Red Sox players and coaches jumped to the front of the dugout to shout their protests of his ruling. He said Clemens and Dwight Evans yelled loudly, as did Marty Barrett, though he did not see Clemens specifically. Cooney stated that the umpire crew all agreed that the call he made was the correct one, and that replay tapes further supported his call.

Orza then took Cooney through his umpire's report, starting with the first paragraph, which stated:

> When Clemens started warming up in the bottom of the 1st innings, I walked to the mound and informed him that T.V. required 2 min. + 25 seconds between each inning, so he could space himself, either stay in the dugout a little longer or take a few more warmup pitches. Not once did he ever acknowledge that I was talking to him, never nodded, never looked my way. Just stared at his catcher and continued to throw warm-up pitches. After a relatively quiet 1st inning, the A's scored in the bottom of the second. On a base hit by Steinbach, the throw from the outfield was off target, hitting either the runner or the bag at 3rd base, allowing Steinbach to advance to 2nd. I walked out and asked Clemens for the ball. At first he ignored me, then glancing my way, he flipped the ball over his shoulder at me, and continued towards the mound.

Orza asked Cooney why he wrote the first paragraph the way he did. Cooney replied that his statements showed Roger's frame of mind. Gene responded quickly, "Or does it show the frame of mind you were in." Cooney replied that Roger was in a strange mood.

Orza continued his review of Cooney's report, focusing on the following portion:

> When I looked out at the mound (after calling ball 4 on Randolph), Roger was standing there staring at me shaking his head back and forth as if to say, "Boy are you stupid." I ignored it at first, but when it continued, I yelled at him, without removing my mask. "I hope your not shaking your head at me!"

He rhetorically asked Cooney if that didn't show Cooney's state of mind, not Clemens'.

After Orza offered our version of what Clemens said, Cooney stuck to the version contained in his report. Orza pointed out that it was odd that CBS did not have a record of Cooney's much more extended version of what supposedly had transpired. When asked how long the exchange took, Cooney said it lasted between thirty and forty seconds.

Richie Phillips then conducted a cross examination of his client. Cooney said Roger taunted umpire John Herschbeck in game two of the playoffs and also Jim Evans for defending Herschbeck. Those incidents, Cooney said, had nothing to do with the ejection. Cooney admitted that he initiated the conversation with Roger because he felt bad when Clemens stared and shook his head at him.

I honestly felt sorry for Cooney at that moment.

Roger testified next. He said his only prior ejection was in 1986 over a "missed first base" call. He was fined either $200 or $300 on that ejection, he said. He continued by saying that Cooney was brusk and authoritative during warm-ups, which was unusual. The Rocket said he had nothing against Cooney going into the game.

Clemens testified that he and Tony Pena had developed special signals for the game, and his concentration on those signals was the reason he was staring so much. Roger said he thought it was Pena, not he, who had been ejected, and he was curious what Tony had done to get himself ejected. That was why he remained on the mound as Pena walked out to him.

The Rocket categorically denied Cooney's version of what Roger had allegedly said. Clemens then stated his version, which took about seven seconds to transpire.

Roger testified that he believed he was ejected for what had taken place in game two, as well as for another incident in game three. With regard to not leaving the dugout, Clemens said he was instructed not to leave the dugout until additional security arrived to escort him to the locker room.

Richie Phillips was allowed by Dr. Brown to cross-examine Roger, even though Orza objected vociferously. At that point, I caught Michael's and Bob's eyes, and rolled my eyes to convey the thought, "Can you believe this?" They responded with looks of incredulousness. I quickly imagined several Doctors of Jurisprudence, dressed in white doctors coats containing elegantly embroidered names across their chests, hovering over a heart monitor connected to a hospitalized patient, somberly deciding whether the patient needed heart surgery.

After Phillips finished, Gene summarized our case and stated that we should be allowed to find out if Phoenix Communications had a tape from a camera focused entirely on Clemens during the incident.

*   *   *

During a recess in the hearing, John Harrington and I met to discuss the status of the contract extension for Roger. I had been doing some research on Roger's achievements during his tenure with the Red Sox, and I shared that information with John.

Before Clemens came to the Red Sox, the club had not contended for some time and attendance had been down. Since Clemens had been a Red Sox, the club had become a perennial contender and ticket sales had been virtually at maximum capacity for the stadium. Television ratings had increased substantially, and the club had signed a lucrative new contract with its cable carrier, NESN.

I asked Harrington if he knew that the Red Sox were one game over .500 without Roger during his career, while his lifetime winning percentage was .695. That difference, I said, was the greatest in baseball history for a pitcher with at least 1,000 innings. Harrington said he was not aware of those statistics.

I pointed out that at 116–51, Roger Clemens had the second highest winning percentage in American League history for a player with at least 100 wins. He had posted at least 17 wins for five straight seasons, a first since Jim Hunter. Clemens was 67–18 after the Red Sox lost, a "stopper" in anyone's book. Harrington said he was aware of some of these latter statistics, since they had been released by the club.

I said, "John, Roger is probably worth $8–10 million a year to the Red Sox. At $5 million a year he is probably a bargain. We aren't going to sign for less than Canseco. If you don't know what you've got, don't blame me if you lose him."

John smiled and replied, "We'll get a deal done. Give me a few days." As I nodded, the door opened and someone told me that I was wanted on the telephone.

I could not imagine who would call me at the American League offices. I was directed to a spare office, where I picked up the phone. It was Paul Beeston, the Blue Jays president. He was laughing as he said, "Randal, how's it going? We are going to miss the Rocket on opening day, aren't we?" I responded quickly, "Don't be so sure. I'm going to appeal just so he can pitch against you." Beeston chuckled and asked if I was serious. I said I was, so he could forget his daydreams of his club missing the Rocket and having an easier opening day. Considering that Clemens was 3–0 with a 1.17 earned run average against Toronto in 1990, no wonder Beeston was interested in the outcome of the hearing.

The love of baseball creates bonds between strange bedfellows. Despite seemingly adversarial roles, I have strong bonds with owners, club presidents, general managers, managers, coaches, scouts, and others involved on the ownership side of baseball. Despite our differing economic interests, the love of the game bonds us as fellow travelers through season after season. We may disagree during the negotiating season, during labor negotiations, or over a grievance, but once the game on the field begins, our common love of baseball prevails.

As is true in all areas of competition, neither labor nor management in baseball has a monopoly on all of the "good guys." There are all types of people in labor and management. I have friends within the union, friends who are agents and friends who are baseball players, although not even clients of HSM. Unsurprisingly, there are people within labor and within management, agents, and baseball players, of whom I do not think too highly.

*   *   *

After the hearing was concluded in midafternoon, Gene, Roger, and I met with the press, who had been kept waiting for most of the day. Bob Ryan of the *Boston Globe* recorded our comments, including Orza's:

> "This is unprecedented discipline in its severity. No player has had such discipline levied upon him in the history of the LCSes. It's a mix between some preejection and some postejection conduct. Far and away, the most important conduct from our standpoint is the preejection conduct, because it did not take place. What happened to Roger, or what Roger did thereafter, tended to be a matter of provocation, as opposed to instigation."

I said, "Roger's side in many respects contradicts the reports of the umpires." Orza and I discussed the videotapes we had viewed from CBS, and the fact that none of the tapes came from cameras focused entirely on Roger during the incident. We said we were going to see if Phoenix Communications had such a tape. We believed it likely that one existed, and we stated unequivocally that if one did, it would verify Roger Clemens' version of the incident.

Ryan observed:

> The Roger Clemens on display yesterday was not the self-proclaimed Possessed Rebel. He was not a full-sized Teenage Mutant Ninja Turtle. He was not a seething, simmering, boiling maniac. He was an eerily calm adult who had a story to tell and who had obvious faith in his advisers and counsel. He said he would have no trouble making peace with Cooney, that he didn't anticipate the case interfering with his spring training concentration.

Mike Shalin of the *Boston Herald* was also present. He tracked down Rene Lachemann. Shalin reported his interview with Lachemann:

> "They asked me what I heard Roger say. And I said I was standing at third base and all I heard was, 'I'm not talking to you. Keep your bleep mask on.' I thought he was yelling at (Mike) Gallego (the Oakland batter at the time)," Lachemann said last night from his Scottsdale, Ariz., home.
>
> Lachemann, who also served as the Sox' third base coach in 1985-86, added that Richie Phillips, the umpires' union lawyer, asked: 'You didn't hear him call him a gutless bleep?' I said, "I didn't hear that."
>
> Lachemann said when he saw Cooney toss out Clemens, he didn't think Roger realized he was out of the game. Lachemann said he made it clear at the hearing that Clemens shouldn't have been ejected under the circumstances.

Peter Gammons wrote an editorial about the incident and its implications for baseball, in the *Boston Globe* a few days later. Gammons wrote:

> The final burden of proof is in the CBS film library. If a secondary camera that was running throughout the fourth game of the American League Championship Series turns up something that the game tapes did not, then fine, Terry Cooney told the truth. But if it doesn't — and CBS people claim what we've seen is all there is — then it is apparent that Roger Clemens told the truth. They ran through the tapes five times at his hearing Monday, and the only curses they found were two four-letter words interjected into what mothers abridge to their daughters as "I'm not talking to you, get back behind the plate."
>
> That is what Rene Lachemann heard from third base. Even crew chief Jim Evans admitted he didn't hear the "gutless (expletive)" tirade until after Clemens had been ejected by Cooney.

Clemens' ejection should have had nothing to do with yelling at Bob Welch, if he did, or waving towels at what he perceived as missed ball/strike calls in Game 2; they should have ejected him from those games, and if Cooney indeed tied the incidents together, then he is guilty of lying in wait, carrying a grudge and acting outside baseball law. If Cooney misinterpreted Clemens' stare in to Tony Pena, that is his overreaction and loss of control.

Clemens was staring in to Pena pretending to go through signs; actually, because they thought the Athletics were stealing their signs, Pena had given Clemens the signs for the entire at-bat before Mike Gallego got to home plate and was going through motions to try to fool Oakland. Cooney's report began with the revelation that Clemens didn't thank him for informing him there was extra time between innings because of the CBS commercials. It doesn't take Susan Dey to strike that as irrelevant. Cooney thought Clemens was showing him up for the borderline calls on Willie Randolph, his throat guard started bobbing, Clemens told him he wasn't talking to him.

If the American League can't find anything else, then Clemens has succeeded in proving what he flew to New York to prove: that after the game, Cooney falsified his report and, in fact, threw him out of that game because Cooney *thought* Clemens was showing him up, for using two curses that did not violate the umpires' code —you can swear, but don't let it be personal—which was no reason to eject him. Clemens never denied that he went bonkers after the ejection (wouldn't Larry Bird or Raymond Bourque have done the same?). He never denied that he waved the towel and mouthed off during Game 2. He never denied that his whole Possessed Rebel routine wasn't without cause. He doesn't care about the $10,000 fine (the Red Sox have told him they'll take care of the missed days' pay), and he doesn't care about the five-day suspension and missing one start except that it would be against the Toronto Blue Jays. But he wanted his chance to set the record straight and question Cooney's integrity—which, although the umpire left the hearing before Clemens could address him, he has done.

What will happen if the final word from CBS is that Clemens is indeed vindicated? Bobby Brown will uphold the decision and back Cooney. Then the Players Association will appeal to commissioner Fay Vincent, and the broad question of umpires' authority will be brought to a head. If a team's best player can be ejected because an umpire thinks he's being shown up, baseball has a problem it had better get cleared up.

·   ·   ·

If what they viewed in that hearing room Monday is all Clemens said, then, indeed, Roger Clemens and the Red Sox got jobbed by Terry Cooney. Not that Clemens and his franchise value are of any small issue to the Boston Red Sox, but the larger issue involves the umpires themselves. First, remove Richie Phillips' hysterical behavior and arguments. Two highly respected members of the Umpires Committee said the exact same thing: "Dr. Brown will uphold the disciplinary action because he has to. It would do terrible damage to the umpires to do otherwise." The members of that committee care about the quality and state of officiating in the game, and anyone who knows AL umpire chief Marty Springstead knows he does, too. But if Terry Cooney falsified his report and was wrong, should he be blindly supported? Should police or teachers be supported no matter what they do to violate their trust? No. Neither should umpires.

In the two days following the Monday hearing, a half-dozen general managers privately praised the Players Association for taking on the broader issue of what they call "the umpire problem." One general manager yesterday said, "I have a lot of disagreements with the Players Association, but I'll guarantee you that 90 percent of the managers and general managers are thankful to them for taking on this issue. It's about time."

The American League office will not address it. Brown upholds the umpires and their reports because he believes to do otherwise would undermine their authority. National League president Bill White did try to address it, but Vincent undermined him, an intervention that has caused a rift between White and Vincent and has left a bitter taste in the mouths of a number of NL owners. White publicly disciplined umpire Joe West. Vincent stepped on White and took the case back to the unwritten law: "Never do anything that might give the public the impression that our officials aren't infallible."

*   *   *

I had grown comfortable about the good faith of John Harrington, so I left New York with the belief that a final agreement on a contract for Roger would be hammered out soon. Salary arbitration season was in full bloom, and I knew that I had to prepare for as many as a dozen cases, not knowing exactly which of those cases I would have to argue and which I would put in a file because the case would settle. I knew that I had to concentrate on our group of four-year starting pitchers — Doug Drabek, Chuck Finley, Greg Swindell, John Smiley, and Eric King — since there was a distinct possibility that these starting pitchers, part of a phenomenal class, might all go through a hearing.

Alan and I talked to Lou Gorman and John Harrington many times over the period from January 30 to February 8. During that period, we resolved our disagreement over a fifth year by agreeing instead to an option year, with a buyout. By February 4, we had agreed on $20 million for the four guaranteed years, but we were stuck on the numbers for the option year. We tried a variety of numbers for the option year in order to bridge our relatively minor differences. Meanwhile, the Red Sox stubbornly held on to their right to trade Roger Clemens, in spite of our request for a no-trade clause.

By February 4, it had become obvious to all involved that we would reach an agreement. Still, it took several days to conclude a final agreement. On Friday, February 8, the deal was finally done. Roger would be guaranteed $21,521,000.

Roger Clemens' latest, record setting contract, would by design contain three lucky "21's," one in the bonus and two in the total guaranteed amount.

The composition of the final contract was as follows:

Signing Bonus	$ 621,000	
1992 Salary	4,400,000	
1993 Salary	4,500,000	
1994 Salary	5,000,000	
1995 Salary	5,500,000	
1996 Option Year Buyout	1,500,000	
1996 Option Year Salary Club Option	5,500,000	from February 8, 1991 to opening day, 1993
	5,800,000	from opening day, 1993, to opening day, 1994
Player Option	6,000,000	from opening day, 1994 through the end of the 1995 World Series, but the option applies only in the event Roger Clemens pitches at least 220 innings in either 1994 or 1995, or finishes in the top three in Cy Young voting during either of those two years.

Clemens' contract contained the first $6 million salary, even though the Red Sox exercised their option for 1996 on March 25, 1993.

Roger had vaulted past Canseco, but both contracts were possible only because collusion had ended. The quantum leaps in the salary structure, represented first by Canseco's contract and then by Clemens' contract, represented the normal salary escalation which would have occurred over the 1986–90 period had collusion not existed.

It was appropriate that Clemens again became the highest paid player in baseball history. Not only was he a tremendous baseball player, but as a young player he had successfully fought against collusion when he held out against an industry dictated raise. The Rocket would now enjoy the greatest benefit of the postcollusion free market.

With free agency once again in full bloom, clubs had to deal with the reality of losing a franchise player. Lou Gorman responded to criticism of the Clemens' contract from officials of other clubs, by saying that he would have been run out of Boston had he let Roger Clemens leave as a free agent.

*   *   *

On April 2, Robert Brown issued his decision on the appeal heard on January 28. Dr. Brown of the judicial branch upheld the decision of Dr. Brown of the executive branch. In his written decision on the appeal, Dr. Brown wrote:

> Every participant in an LCS or World Series understands the importance of the games. The players, managers, and coaches are aware of the absolute necessity of doing nothing that could initiate an ejection. Umpires likewise recognize the significance of removing a player, and the possible effect such an action could have on the outcome of a game and the series. Ejections in post season play, therefore, have been very infrequent. A player simply knows what to say and what not to say, and how to act, if he wishes to remain in the game.

> .   .   .

> The same behavior code applies to all. There is not a special set of rules or regulations for superstars or award winners. Everyone, regardless of ability or importance, must conform to the same set of standards. Exceptions to the rule are not allowed because someone important to a team is playing in an important game.

> As long as a player is on the field, in the dugout, or in the bullpen, he is responsible for his actions. Extreme provocation or perceived unjust circumstances do not absolve the player of subsequent behavior.

> Physical contact between uniformed personnel and the umpire is viewed with great concern by the American League office. Such

a serious offense, if tolerated or minimized, would lead to anarchy and chaos on the field. The ability of the umpire to control the game would disappear and the field would take on the aspects of the jungle. It, therefore, stands to reason that when obvious or blatant physical contact occurs, suspensions and fines have to be levied. This is the only possible deterrent to keeping such incidents from becoming commonplace.

In this instance there was no question about Clemens making contact with Evans. Clemens actually shoved Evans aside as he attempted to get closer to Cooney. I viewed this from the stands and the videotape verified it. It is realized that Evans was not the object of Clemens' ire. But, while the lack of a malicious motive can be recognized in this incident, such is not always the case. Discipline, therefore, for this overt act has to be levied and failure to do so would only encourage increased violence in the future.

When a player, manager, or coach is ejected from the game he knows he is expected to leave the premises immediately. If the ejected player remains on the field or bench he in essence challenges the authority of the umpire and lessens his ability to control the game. Clemens remained on the field during most of the controversy and then retired to the bench. A new Boston pitcher was brought into the game and allowed a full warm-up. After Oakland was retired in the bottom half of the second inning, Umpire Evans noted Clemens was still sitting on the bench. Evans approached the dugout and informed Manager Joe Morgan and Clemens that the game could not proceed until Clemens vacated the dugout. Clemens then proceeded to the clubhouse without incident and the game progressed. Clemens, in his testimony, stated he was told by an employee in an Oakland Coliseum uniform to remain on the bench for security reasons. Umpires Evans and Cooney did not mention in their reports that they had been apprised of this fact.

Both Cooney and Evans reported that Clemens verbally threatened Cooney with future physical violence. Clemens in his testimony confirmed this. Most threats of this nature are issued during times of high emotional tension. Fortunately, in virtually all cases, with the passage of time, reasonableness prevails and little comes of it. Nevertheless, such threats have to be taken seriously as they are directed against authority and are designed to intimidate. Uniformed personnel threatening umpires in the past have been fined.

Evans also reported he heard Clemens direct personal obscenities against Cooney. Clemens admits to using profanity, but denies ever making personal remarks to Cooney. It is always disquieting to hear two people under oath give diametrically opposite testimonies. Umpires routinely eject uniformed personnel that make personal obscene remarks to them. The American League office usually levies fines in such instances, but the ejection itself usually forms the major part of the discipline.

This entire episode was unfortunate and deplorable. It detracted from the entire League Championship Series, and caused an inordinate delay during Game Four. Clemens unquestionably made physical contact of a significant degree with Umpire Evans, delayed leaving the premises, and threatened Umpire Cooney with physical harm. The League simply cannot ignore offenses of this nature. They were meaningful and the discipline must be meaningful. A suspension of a starting pitcher to be effective must deprive him of the opportunity of starting a game (or games). A five-game suspension deprives Clemens of one starting assignment. A suspension involving less games would become insignificant. A fine of $10,000.00 was instituted with the purpose of serving as a deterrent, without being onerous or incurring a hardship. Under the present economics of Baseball, I believe the $10,000.00 fine accomplished that.

The main thrust of Clemens' testimony and defense rested on the assertion that he was ejected for insufficient cause. Clemens denies ever making any personal obscene remarks to Cooney. Clemens, and the Players Association in his defense, accuse both Cooney and Evans of lying and falsifying their reports. They allege that Cooney had a vendetta against Clemens stemming from the latter's actions during a Red Sox protest of a Cooney "checked swing" decision in Game Three. They also allege that Cooney may have ejected Clemens because Cooney thought Clemens was "showing him up" (shaking his head) after issuing a base on balls to Randolph. The quotes of CBS announcer Jim Kaat are listed, describing Cooney as "having a short fuse" and "gets upset easily."

Cooney has had little trouble with players in the past. His ejection rate over the past five years is one of the lowest on the American League staff. He rarely gets into arguments or controversies and is emotionally very stable. His past record does not indicate a tendency to eject players quickly or without reason, harbor grudges or vendettas, or lose self control.

Clemens and the Players Association by utilizing CBS videotapes have attempted to prove that Clemens could not have uttered the obscene personal remarks claimed by Cooney. The regular CBS videotape that provides the "feed" to the viewing public, and a special camera located behind the plate and directed at the pitcher and pitching mound (without sound) are used. Special attention is given to an eight-second period prior to Clemens' ejection and during which Clemens is shouting or talking to Cooney. The camera records in a slow motion time speed and an attempt is made to read Clemens' lips as he mouths the words. It is Clemens' and the Players Association assertion that they can successfully read Clemens' lips and obscene personal remarks are not made.

All of the words spoken by Clemens are not decipherable. The camera may not always be directed at the mound as there are scenes later showing Clemens leaving the dugout and an attractive young lady sitting in the stands. We do not know if everything that has been recorded on tape has been seen by us, or if everything taking place on the mound was recorded. We don't know if the pitcher is followed by the camera when he is off the mound.

It takes only an instant to utter an obscenity. To assume that an operator records every second a pitcher is on the field, that all the recorded tape is kept, that all words spoken (there is no sound) are able to be deciphered by lip reading, remains open to question.

When an accusation of lying and falsifying reports is made against two umpires the proof has to be clear and convincing. I do not believe it is in this case. Attacking the integrity of two umpires is extremely serious. Such charges should neither be made or dismissed lightly.

In this particular case, what Clemens did to prompt his ejection had little bearing on the discipline levied. His actions after being ejected were responsible for his suspension and fine. The player remains accountable for his actions on the field at all times, and the fact that he felt his ejection was not warranted does not absolve him of his subsequent behavior.

The appeal is denied and the five-game suspension starting with the first game of the 1991 season and the $10,000.00 fine remains intact.

Gene Orza and I reviewed Brown's written decision. We believed that our appeal to Commissioner Vincent, filed on April 4, should focus on key sentences in the American League president's decision, including:

We do not know if everything that has been recorded on tape has been seen by us, or if everything taking place on the mound was recorded.

It takes only an instant to utter an obscenity. To assume that an operator records every second a pitcher is on the field, that all the recorded tape is kept, that all words spoken (there is no sound) are able to be deciphered by lip reading, remains open to question.

When an accusation of lying and falsifying reports is made against two umpires the proof has to be clear and convincing. I do not believe it is in this case. Attacking the integrity of two umpires is extremely serious. Such charges should neither be made or dismissed lightly.

In this particular case, what Clemens did to prompt his ejection had little bearing on the discipline levied. His actions after being ejected were responsible for his suspension and fine. The player remains accountable for his actions on the field at all times, and the fact that he felt his ejection was not warranted does not absolve him of his subsequent behavior.

Orza immediately set out to get any tapes that Phoenix Communications had. Bingo! They had a tape from a camera which was fixed on Clemens during the entire incident. We could run the tape in super slow-motion, thus being able to "lip read" every syllable of every word that Roger said while he was on the pitching mound prior to his ejection.

Ever resourceful, Gene's efforts led him to Deborah Copeland of the New York Society for the Deaf. Ms. Copeland, without any prior knowledge of what happened during game four, without anyone telling her any version of the incident, and without anyone suggesting to her what Clemens said, reviewed the tape.

Her report and Roger's version of what he said were virtually identical. The tape confirmed that the entire incident took seven to eight seconds.

While we prepared for the hearing before Vincent on April 19, the Rocket pitched the opening day game against Toronto. He won.

Just prior to the commencement of the season, Dave Nightengale of *The Sporting News* interviewed Cooney, who said:

> I've never contemplated handling the situation any differently because, if I had done so, I would have lost all of my credibility. In my years in the game, I think I've earned respect. I think I have the respect of most of the players and managers. If I had allowed that incident to pass—and everyone on the field knew what was going on— I'd have been known as a person who turned his back. And I couldn't live with that, because I'm a professional.

Unlike the appeal to Dr. Brown, I planned to be an advocate for Roger in the appeal to Vincent. Gene would review the hearing before Dr. Brown, discuss his decision, and put on Deborah Copeland as a witness. He would then review the flaws in Dr. Brown's decision.

Afterwards, I would present, essentially, a closing argument of the case. Following that, Orza would offer his concluding remarks. We did not believe that Vincent could reach any conclusion other than that Roger Clemens had been ejected without good cause.

Gene was at his energetic best, and he did a thoroughly professional and convincing job. The super slow-motion tapes were so "clear" that one could follow Deborah, syllable by syllable, as she spoke for Roger. While Deborah was touching and convincing, one could have lip-synched Roger's testimony of what he said and reached the same conclusion as Deborah had done independently.

Vincent was very alert and cordial during the hearing. He particularly enjoyed Ms. Copeland and appeared quite receptive to our presentation. He had the twinkle in his eye of someone who had been persuaded of something that he had not previously believed to be true. Overall, his reactions convinced me that we had persuaded him that our version of the sequence of events leading up to the moment of the ejection had been proven to be true beyond a reasonable doubt.

Still, the question remained as to how Vincent would handle the postejection conduct. When it was my turn to "pilot the plane," I said:

Commissioner Vincent, I appreciate the fact that you are an attorney and that you understand due process. I thank you for your conduct of this hearing.

I have been representing players for 21 years. I have had numerous disciplinary cases. I've had pitchers throwing at hitters, hitters charging at pitchers, brawls, even client versus client in those brawls.

I've only gone to the Commissioner twice. The first case was on Joaquin Andujar during the 1985 World Series. That discipline was reduced by Commissioner Ueberroth to no fine and from 10 days to 4 days. The other case is the instant case.

This case is different from many others because of its unusual circumstances. This case is different because we've proved that the umpire's report is wrong. My client should not be subjected to excessive discipline when he was ejected without proper provocation and especially when the umpire had a subjective belief, not an objective belief, motivating his decision.

Umpire Cooney came into the game with a grudge. The record shows that Cooney was trying to read Roger's mind. Cooney's report is flat wrong.

The manager, Joe Morgan, carried on. He cursed, but there was no discipline for him because, as stated by Dr. Brown, he was defending his player. If there was no discipline for manager Morgan because he was entitled to defend his player, there should be no discipline for Roger because he is equally entitled to defend himself.

The threshold question is did Roger deserve to be thrown out and was the umpire's report correct. Roger did not deserve to be thrown out. The umpire was wrong. Accordingly, I believe it is inappropriate to uphold the fine and suspension on any basis.

There was no warning, so you have to expect Roger to react. You should consider the following. If Roger was on the field too long, so was his manager, and yet nothing was done about that because he was entitled to defend his player. The bump was accidental. Roger was told to stay in the dugout. The threats could not be taken seriously by any reasonable person. They were made in the heat of battle. Roger is not known as a violent person.

Everything done after the ejection calls for mitigation because it was done in the context of an unjustifiable provocation.

Gene then eloquently concluded the case. The commissioner asked what we recommended he do. I said he should reduce the suspension to, at most, a couple of days, eliminate the fine, and announce that Clemens had agreed to voluntarily make a $10,000 charitable contribution. Roger is a most generous person, and I knew that he would easily agree to make the donation, which without hesitation, he did.

Orza said that any punishment was inappropriate because the ejection was clearly unprovoked and unjustifiable. The decision of Dr. Brown should be reversed in its entirety, he calmly stated.

We left the hearing satisfied. Debbie Clemens had accompanied Roger to the hearing, and both were very pleased with the way the hearing had proceeded. Roger asked what I thought. I told him that we had proven our case, without any doubt. The question, I said, is whether Vincent "is interested in justice or is interested in placating the umpires."

We got the answer to my question on April 26. Commissioner Vincent upheld Dr. Brown's decision. Vincent wrote:

> It is not the Commissioner's responsibility to make determinations with respect to whether on-the-field actions taken (or not taken) by the umpire during the game in question were right or wrong, or to set guidelines for umpires to follow in discharging their duties on the field. Those areas are within the purview of the American League and the National League. The Commissioner's role herein is limited to reviewing the evidence before him and determining

whether the penalty imposed on the player by the American League was for "just cause."

· · ·

Clemens has claimed that there is an inadequate basis for the discipline imposed because there was no justification for his ejection and the events subsequent to the ejection should be viewed in and to some extent excused by that context. I have given careful consideration to this argument.

· · ·

Notwithstanding my findings regarding the events prior to the ejection, I am not persuaded that the discipline imposed should be eliminated or reduced. Regardless of the basis for an ejection — or any other decision, right or wrong, made by an umpire on the field—a player must comport himself during games within accepted norms.

Roger Clemens served a five day suspension and paid the $10,000 fine. The umpires avoided a strike and settled on a new contract just prior to the start of the 1991 season. Terry Cooney umpired during the 1991 and 1992 seasons, as he had done for the prior sixteen years. But when the list of umpires for the 1993 season was published by the American League, Terry Cooney's name was nowhere to be found on the list. When Clemens heard the news, his only comment was "Woo ah."

Chapter 5

The Baseball Economic Study Committee

The Baseball Economic Study Committee was created in the labor agreement forged in 1990. Perhaps because of the "cultural" differences between ownership and players, or perhaps because of the distrust which existed between the leadership on both sides, it was believed that an officially appointed "study committee" might bring a dispassionate review of the economics and structure of baseball. Of course, the fact that the four members of the study committee were appointed evenly — two by ownership and two by the union — only served to fuel skepticism that two pawns of management and two pawns of labor would advocate the party lines of their respective sponsors.

In the Basic Agreement, the study committee was directed to study the following issues:

1) The relationship, if any, between Club revenues and on-field competition;
2) The extent and nature of revenue sharing among the Clubs;
3) The advantages (and/or disadvantages) of compensating players based on a percentage of combined industry revenues;
4) Past and future trends in national and local media markets;
5) The extent, nature and value of Club related party transactions;
6) Franchise value;
7) The number and location of geographical markets (including franchise relocation); and

8) Such other matters as the Committee (or either of the co-chairs thereof) deems appropriate.

The 1990 Basic Agreement stated that the "purpose of the study and the report is to provide the Parties to this Agreement with the basis for a common understanding of the overall economic condition of the industry (including a description of current or impending problems, if any; the cause of such problems; and possible solutions) and to assist in improving the bargaining relationship between the Parties."

Four agents were requested to appear before the committee — myself, Richard Moss, Jim Bronner, and Scott Boras. One could call the roll: Houston, New York, Chicago, and Los Angeles.

Jim Bronner was unable to appear, leaving the job to the rest of us. The three of us dutifully appeared at the Hyatt Gainey Ranch in Scottsdale, Arizona, in late March 1992. Dressed in business suits, which was not our everyday dress of preference, we waited outside the room where the study committee was hearing the offerings of Richard Ravitch, the newly appointed head of the Player Relations Committee.

We had asked to hear Ravitch's speech, but our request was denied, even though Ravitch would hear our presentations. Typical, I thought. Keep us in the dark. Never mind that we collectively represented, including the absent Bronner and his partner, Bob Gilhooley, over 25 percent of all major league players.

Near the appointed hour, Peter Goldmark, one of the owners' appointees to the committee and president of the Rockefeller Foundation, came into the hall where we waited.

"You must be the agents," he said. We nodded our assent as he introduced himself. The inflection with which Goldmark used the words "the agents" indicated his view of our social status, or lack thereof, in this arena. Gee, I thought, another guy deprecating us who is not up to our standards. Amazing, I thought. Too bad this exchange wasn't filmed. It would tell volumes as to why so much tension exists between labor and management in baseball.

After Goldmark returned to the conference room, I asked Dick and Scott if the derogatory manner in which Goldmark greeted us as "the agents" irritated them as much as it had me. Unsurprisingly, it did. I said, "These guys keep motivating us to beat them. Their patronizing manner has always motivated me, hasn't it you?" They quickly agreed. I wondered if Goldmark actually meant to be as derogatory as he sounded. I finally chuckled and said, "We owe that type of guy an assist for continually motivating us to win."

After Ravitch finished, a short recess of the meeting was called, and we entered the room. Present were many familiar faces from management and union circles, as well as the four study committee members. Bud Selig, Chuck O'Connor, Rob Manfred, and Richard Ravitch represented ownership. Don Fehr, Gene Orza, and Lauren Rich from the players association were present. Lauren Rich was and remains assistant counsel at the union, and she has spent most of her time over the past several years on the collusion cases.

The study committee members included Paul Volcker, former head of the Federal Reserve and presently an economic consultant to international business and foreign governments. He would conduct the meeting with a demeanor consistent with that of a man used to a position of power and prestige. I wondered how Volcker would extrapolate his past experiences to the arena of baseball. Because he was a management appointee, I also wondered if he would view his mission as justifying ownership's position in baseball's version of the class struggle.

Peter Goldmark was the other management appointee. A country club man, I thought, or perhaps a yachtsman. During the session, Goldmark would ask the most questions and appear to be the most interested of the four committee members. He would also be interested in the three agents leaving immediately after our presentations were concluded.

The agent presentations were to be followed by the appearance before the committee of a number of major league players, and Goldmark was eager to talk to them. At the conclusion of the discussion which followed our presentations, Goldmark pointedly asked us to leave as the players entered the meeting room. I have become used to grown men fawning over baseball players, but I nevertheless smiled as I reflected on the fact that Goldmark was impatiently ushering out the real players in the arena in which he had been hired to render advice.

The meeting was held in a large, double conference room. We met while seated around a conference table situated in one room. The other room was set up for refreshments following the discussion period, which followed the agent presentations.

As the major league players took seats at the conference table and began their discussion with the members and staff of the study committee, Moss, Boras, and I moseyed over to the refreshment area in the other room. We were soon joined by union and management officials. While we discussed the subjects covered in the agent presentations, the study committee and its staff were unusually preoccupied with the company of the approximately six major league players in attendance.

Chuck O'Connor, counsel to the Player Relations Committee, told me that I had been hard on management in my presentation. I told him that my presentation reflected my convictions. Rob Manfred, like O'Connor an attorney with Morgan, Lewis & Bockius, admitted to me that the ill-fated Pay For Performance (PFP) system proposed by management in collective bargaining in 1990 had been a mistake because it had ignored the role of agents. I smiled as I thought that he must have meant the proposal miscalculated the power of agents and the intelligence of the players and union officials. Far from ignoring us, I said, the system was calculated to replace us. That mistake, I was told, would not be made again.

At the conclusion of their meeting with the players, the study committee members and the staff members milled toward the refreshment area. Goldmark came over to where my group had parked. He expressed surprise that we were still there and said that he thought we were supposed to have left. The shrimp, I told him, were too good to pass up, and besides, I said, "you didn't even notice our presence." If given a choice between social status and talent, I will take talent every time.

The two members of the study committee appointed by the union were Henry Aaron and David Feller. Aaron, while a distinguished economist from the Brookings Institute, was forever having to be distinguished from Henry Aaron, the Hall of Fame slugger with the Braves.

Aaron, who was seated to my right during the agent presentations, doodled in geometric art while Dick Moss and Scott Boras gave their presentations. It was unclear to me how intently Aaron was listening during their speeches, but his doodling stopped within the first minute of my presentation.

David Feller, who was seated to my left, was a professor of law and a retired labor trial lawyer. He had tried and won several major cases for labor before the United States Supreme Court. Feller conducted himself like a professor emeritus. Both he and Aaron seemed intent on finding a solution beneficial to labor and management in order to resolve long standing problems. The questions asked by

Aaron and Feller during the discussion period were sharply focused and showed no signs of a prolabor bias.

During the question and answer period, Goldmark expressed surprise that Dick, Scott, and I did not have uniform beliefs about salary arbitration and free agency. Dick stated that arbitration needed to be preserved as a hedge against future collusion by the owners. I indicated a willingness to trade arbitration years in exchange for earlier, unrestricted free agency.

Scott was most concerned about the recent change in the amateur draft rules, which increased the period over which a club could retain the rights to a drafted player. That change would fall by mid-summer in a grievance initiated by the union. The union successfully argued in that case that the change would impede the movement of major league free agents, and thus constituted a unilateral change in the Basic Agreement.

During the formal presentations, Steve Fehr, Don's brother and consigliare, introduced Moss, Boras and me. As planned, Moss led off. His presentation was essentially a historical view of the labor-management relationship in baseball. He chided the study committee for its failure to invite Marvin Miller to appear before the committee.

Boras followed with his presentation, which focused on both the amateur draft and the limited rights of young major league players and minor league players under the current system.

When it was my turn to speak, I spoke from an outline I had prepared over the prior two days. My presentation not only followed the mandate to the study committee contained in the 1990 Basic Agreement, but covered topics that I believed needed to be addressed.

I had prepared an outline which covered eight broad subjects. I chose to lead off with the responsibilities that the study committee owed to the parties. Somewhat irritated by what I had perceived as a casual attitude toward Moss' and Boras' presentations, I started my speech in an intense manner.

"The study committee's imperative," I began, "should be to strive to be a catalyst to find a basis for common agreement between the parties for a labor pact in order to avoid a disruption in play in 1993 or 1994 due to either a lockout or a strike."

"Therefore," I continued, "the committee should advance a solution or solutions likely to be acceptable to both parties. If this is not done, the committee report will be, at best, propaganda useful to one side or the other, but essentially meaningless in effect."

Having gained their attention with my challenge, I proceeded to cover the subjects I believed appropriate for the committee to consider. The stories and episodes in this book illustrate the points I made in my presentation and will hopefully enlighten the reader on not only this baseball agent's world, but on how the business of baseball has evolved into its present condition.

I continued my presentation by addressing the large-market/small-market issue, which I termed the problem of allocating clubs' revenue. I stated:

> Labor did not create this problem and should not solve this problem. The clubs should bear the responsibility for this. It is unrealistic and inappropriate to expect labor to solve club created problems by relinquishing rights gained through litigation and collective bargaining. The problem is one of revenue allocation, and the clubs need to address this allocation problem by reallocating revenue among themselves.

I next focused on my third topic, the desire of clubs for cost controls:

> Clubs never sought cost controls when they paid 10 percent of their gross income in player salaries in the early 1970's. Clubs should not have rights to controlled costs and guaranteed profits. The owners have never wanted to participate in free market economies. They now seek a contrived economy, not unreminiscent of state controlled economies of Eastern Europe.
>
> The owners PFP proposal in 1990 was ill conceived. It exemplified their desire to have a predicable system under their control. It showed the usual owner arrogance of trying to dictate a system to the players, rather than negotiate a mutually acceptable system. It would have been a disaster to the integrity of the game.

My fourth subject was "the myth that all top players will sign with clubs in New York, Los Angeles, or other top markets:"

> This myth has been advanced since the days of Bowie Kuhn and is empirically inaccurate. Many variables dictate where a player will sign. Players sign where they are comfortable. This exercise of freedom of choice is no different than its exercise by the population as a whole, and explains why top free agents have signed with Kansas City (Mark Davis), Houston (Nolan Ryan), Milwaukee (Sal Bando), Chicago (George Bell), San Francisco (Dave Righetti), Minnesota (Jack Morris), and virtually every other major league city.
>
> Both players and clubs match up supply and demand. Thus, a

player will sign where he can get the best opportunity to perform, but subject to his view of the club's overall talent, his attitude about the club management and ownership, the city itself, and the money offered. A club will not sign a player when that club already has adequate talent at the position the player plays.

The Angels, in a large market, had difficulty signing players this past year. The Yankees had difficulty signing players in the late 80's under the management then in place.

I then spoke of free agency and free markets:

The player viewpoint has been to pursue free agency and free markets — freedom of choice for the players has been a central issue to us. The owners are a cartel who invariably seek to control all aspects of the game. My personal philosophy is that players should have the same freedom of choice to pursue their profession as do others in this country.

I believe that market forces should rule.

The following should determine the outcome of where and for what amount a player signs:

1) The general supply of, and demand for, player talent
2) The quality of talent of a particular player
3) The quality of management talent and the quality of agent talent
4) The prevailing revenue and club and player financial requirements
5) The various intangibles involved in decision making which are peculiar to each situation

If salaries rise or fall due to revenue increases or decreases, that is agreeable to me. I do not want a contrived system which guarantees owners profits, controlled costs and control of the game. No player is guaranteed an intrinsic profit. Players take risks and so should owners.

During the past free agent season, virtually every club cited budgetary constraints as factors in making offers to players, or in shaping the size of the offer, or declining to make an offer. This is how all businesses properly operate — how families operate — it is a *de facto salary cap* within the prerogative of each team. The Clubs have this option available now and do not need an institutionalized salary cap.

Since the elimination of salary arbitration was a goal of the clubs, I made salary arbitration my sixth subject of discussion:

The current system has three classes of players:

1) 0-2+   — these players do not have salary arbitration rights or free agent rights; they receive relatively low pay
2) 2+140 - 5+   — these players are eligible for salary arbitration
3) 6+   — these players are eligible for free agency

A player is required to complete his minor league career and nearly three years of major league service in order to become eligible for salary arbitration. He must show enough ability and consistency to stay in the majors over this period.

Salary arbitration is beneficial to clubs. A club has the opportunity to see a player for three years in the major leagues, and therefore can determine the player's importance to the club. The club can tender a salary arbitration eligible player a contract in December and then pay for only one year of service, therefore placing the primary risk of performance on the player.

A club can elect to not tender a contract in December if it believes the player is not good enough to keep on its roster, or if it believes the player is not worth the salary likely to be payable. Thus, a club can keep a good player for a far smaller financial commitment than the multi-year contract commitment that player would receive as a free agent.

The seventh topic of discussion was "the desire of ownership to control the game." That desire:

is and has been the central issue in all collective bargaining. The owners want control, especially economic control.

Historically, the owners had the reserve system. This fell in the Messersmith-McNally case. The players had to fight to change the perpetual reserve system.

In the 1980-81 labor dispute, the owners sought to reseize control by limiting free agency. The players had to strike for one-third of the 1981 season to preserve free agency.

Collusion followed from the post-1985 season period through the 1989 season. This violation resulted in a $280 million settlement. The players had to resort to arbitration/litigation to defeat this effort by ownership to impede free agency. Collusion was a flagrant abuse and breech of the labor agreement.

The owners followed collusion with their proposal in 1990 — Pay For Performance. This was a plan to allocate a percentage of revenues to the players. This was another effort to fix salaries and control player movement.

The present plan by ownership is a salary cap proposal. This is yet another attempt to control the game and the players.

What happens when players have no rights? They do not receive fair market value for their services. They are not treated with respect. How did I know that collusion existed, at its onset? There was a total change in the attitudes demonstrated by club officials.

I saw an indifference toward player contracts and impending free agency. I saw no rational reason for a club to reject a free agent who would have been of value, contrary to previous years experience. My phone calls were not returned. There was a decrease in respect shown to our side. A cavalier attitude was demonstrated by the clubs. This reminded me of the ownership attitudes I encountered when I first became a sports agent in 1970.

I finally discussed the matchup between the professionals on the players' side and those on the clubs' side. I termed this subject "the quality of talent on the player side compared to that on the ownership side." This needed to be discussed, because

> ... the game of baseball has evolved into a sophisticated system with complex questions involving legal issues, financial and economic issues, bargaining skills and talent evaluation. The player side has done a far better job in these areas. Clubs have been slow to evolve and address these factors with the proper staffing. The clubs should not be entitled to a contrived economic system to correct deficiencies in their operational and management organizations in order to guarantee clubs profits at the expense of rights dearly paid for and achieved by the players.

After my presentation was completed, a short recess was taken. Lauren Rich of the players association headed directly toward me. She had a satisfied look on her face. As she stood next to me, she whispered, "You may have just helped prevent a lockout. You said what needed to be said, and believe me, they paid attention."

Chapter 6

Collusion

The 1985 baseball season ended with the exciting seven game "Interstate 70" World Series between Kansas City and St. Louis. The series was marked by Don Denkinger's controversial call at first base in game six. Many observers believed Denkinger's call cost St. Louis the game and the World Series. Still, judgment calls are a part of baseball.

St. Louis was not only the site of the World Series, it was the site of a meeting of ownership chaired by Commissioner Peter Ueberroth. Also in attendance was the retiring chairman of the Player Relations Committee, Lee McPhail.

To outsiders, it seemed like an ordinary meeting during the World Series. Certainly, no player, player agent, or union official paid any special attention to the meeting, or to the newspaper reports about it.

In fact, though, the meeting was the baseball equivalent of the "Appalachian meeting." Like the Mafia summit which gave a "family" exclusive control over a major city, the collusion meeting gave a club exclusive control over the players on its roster who would become free agents. Thus was collusion officially born on October 22, 1985, although conception undoubtedly occurred sometime earlier in 1985.

While the owners meeting had an official agenda, it was the "off the agenda" matters that were the important topics for discussion.

These matters dealt with clubs becoming "fiscally responsible" and controlling player costs.

During the meeting, Lee McPhail gave a speech detailing the reasons why clubs needed to become fiscally responsible. McPhail urged clubs to stop engaging in "excessive behavior" and to avoid signing players to long-term contracts. Signing free agent players was not good business, McPhail argued, because free agents got hurt more frequently than did the general population of players. The implication was that once such players signed guaranteed contracts, they found it more convenient to avoid playing, either by indulging nagging injuries or prolonging the recovery period from an injury. The not too subtle conclusion was that free agent players, to quote rock musician Steve Miller, "Take the Money and Run."

McPhail did not bother to mention that because free agent players must play at least six years in the major leagues, they are typically older than nonfree-agent players. Due to age and "wear and tear," free agents are more susceptible to injury and slower to rebound from injury. While McPhail's rhetoric reflected a generally held bias within management circles, it was calculated to serve as a smoke screen to cover for collusion.

McPhail also urged the clubs to replace older, expensive major league players with younger, inexpensive players. Don't "give in to the unreasonable demands of experienced marginal players," he urged the owners. In this way, clubs could become more fiscally responsible while sending a message to older players in particular, and all players and player agents in general.

Commissioner Peter Ueberroth attended the annual general managers meeting in Tarpon Springs, Florida, held from November 5 to November 8. The commissioner spoke to the general managers in blunt terms. He told them, "Don't be dumb . . . it is not smart to sign long-term contracts . . . such contracts force other clubs to make similar signings."

The most prominent of the free agents trapped by the reality of the new "fiscal responsibility" were Kirk Gibson, Carlton Fisk, Jack Clark, and Don Sutton. Others affected included Hendricks Sports Management client Danny Darwin.

Darwin was a deceptive 8–18 with Milwaukee in 1985. He started 29 games, pitched 217⅔ innings, gave up 212 hits, and posted a very respectable 3.80 earned run average. All of his statistics, except his won-lost record, were solid statistics for a major league starting pitcher.

A starting pitcher's won-lost record is dependent not only upon his own ability, but upon the run support he receives, the quality of the defense behind him, and the quality of his bullpen. In every major league season, one can find a starter with a superior won-lost record, supported with a lot of runs, a good defense, and a good bullpen. Conversely, in that same season one can find a starter like Darwin with an inferior won-lost record, supported with few runs, a poor defense, or a poor bullpen.

Milwaukee knew that Danny Darwin was a good pitcher, and they wanted him back. No other club made an offer to Danny, so he was forced to return to Milwaukee on a two-year contract at a token raise. Had there been a competitive market, he would have received a much richer pact than the one offered by the Brewers.

Hendricks client Mike Scott was typical of a number of players who, while eligible to elect free agency within the next year, concluded that free agency was no longer a viable option. Scott's career moved up a level in 1985, as he posted a fine 18–8 record. He started 36 games, pitched 221⅔ innings, gave up 194 hits, and posted a 3.29 earned run average.

The day before a salary arbitration hearing in February 1986, Mike accepted the best multiyear, guaranteed contract offered by Houston. While the contract offered was low, even by the standards of collusion, Scott reasoned that there was nothing to be gained by turning down the contract, since there was no assurance that the Astros would offer him more if he had a fine 1986 season.

If he produced in 1986, Mike reasoned, he would still be stuck in Houston. There would be no other market for his services, and no assurance that he would receive a better contract than the one presently being offered. If he suffered through a poor 1986 season, or were injured, Mike reasoned further, he would not be offered a contract by Houston and his market value would plummet. There was thus a large risk if he turned down the Houston offer, but there was not a corresponding reward to him to compensate for the risk if he did produce a big year. So Mike made a pragmatic decision and accepted the Astros' best offer of slightly more than $2 million for a three-year contract.

Other quality players, already signed for 1986, but eligible for free agency following the 1986 season, were confronted with a decision similar to the one faced by Mike Scott. In those situations, the club offered to negotiate a contract extension. The player considered the offer, his role on the club, and his overall satisfaction with the club. If the contract extension offered was substantial, the player faced the same "big risk-no reward" decision Mike Scott faced.

In 1985 Rance Mulliniks produced his best season. It was his third consecutive solid season as a run producing third baseman for Toronto. During spring training of 1986, the Blue Jays offered to extend Mulliniks' contract, which ran through the 1986 season.

Ken Oberkfell had signed a four-year contract with Atlanta in mid-October 1985. His was the last precollusion contract of more than three years in length. Oberkfell, who had become essentially a platoon third baseman, signed for an average of $750,000 per season.

I cited Oberkfell's contract when I negotiated with Toronto on behalf of Rance. While I considered Mulliniks to be a more valuable player, Toronto responded by dismissing Oberkfell's contract. Oberkfell's contract was "overpriced," they said, and anyway, they were not prepared to go four years or even three years. Forget Oberkfell, I was told, because the days of that type of contract were finished.

Rance and I concluded that the final Blue Jays' offer, which was a guaranteed two-year contract extension plus an option year, was the best offer we were going to see from the Blue Jays. The extension covered the 1987-89 seasons and paid approximately $1.75 million. The likelihood of continued collusion in the free agent market at the end of 1986 led Rance to accept the Blue Jays' offer.

Thus, in a matter of six months, the collusive practices of the clubs led to a significant reduction in not only contract values, but in expectations as well. Contracts became shorter in length, players and agents became fatalistic, and the risk-reward ratio for players was suddenly tilted out of whack. The value of free agency, or potential free agency, so heavily prized in the past, plummeted.

The pervasiveness of collusion was so great that the union advised players to accept the best multiyear contracts offered. Jim Sundberg was presented with a "take it or leave it" two-year contract extension in May 1986 after negotiating for several months. Sundberg wasn't sure he liked the contract proposal, but he knew he had to consider it seriously. He called Donald Fehr, who advised him to put little value on the benefit of becoming a free agent after the 1986 season. As a consequence, Jim signed the contract extension with Kansas City.

The predictions of Scott, Mulliniks, Sundberg, and Fehr proved to be accurate, for following the 1986 season collusion got even worse. There were more players and more quality players in the post-1986 season free agent market. This was a natural consequence of the clubs not signing potential free agent players. Flush from their success in the post-1985 season "free agent" market, clubs became more arrogant in their dealings with agents and free agent players in the post-1986 season market.

Some players fought back. They did so by declining all offers made by their former clubs and by retaining their free agent status beyond the January 8, 1987, deadline established pursuant to the 1985 Basic Agreement. Free agent players who did not re-sign with their former clubs by January 8 could not re-sign with their former clubs until after May 1, 1987, well after the commencement of the 1987 regular season.

The problem for these players, whom I dubbed "freedom fighters," was that their former clubs still wanted to re-sign them. Thus, no other club would make them a bona fide offer. So these players became stuck in a limbo, which would cost some of them all of spring training and over three weeks of the regular season.

The freedom fighters included Bob Horner, Bob Boone, Tim Raines, Rich Gedman, and Andre Dawson. Given the black hole of January 9 to May 1, Horner reacted by signing in Japan for the 1987 season, where he soon became a celebrity. Dawson and his agent, Dick Moss, pulled off the "blank contract" gambit with the Chicago Cubs. Dawson showed up at the Cubs' spring training facility and offered, publicly, to sign a blank contract. Put on the spot, the Cubs accepted Dawson's offer and filled in the blank with a salary of $500,000, plus incentives, a substantial decrease from the "Hawk's" prior salary.

The other freedom fighters played catch with their friends while biding their time until after May 1, at which time they signed contracts with their former clubs. The owners surely believed that these players had learned a lesson. That lesson was calculated to discourage any player from challenging the collusive powers of the clubs.

While the freedom fighters were clear front line casualties, there were also secondary casualties. Secondary casualties included Type B free agents, as they were classified under the Elias system used to rank free agents. Type B players had draft choices attached as compensation for their signings, as did the higher ranked Type A free agents like Horner. A club signing a Type A or Type B free agent forfeited a draft choice or choices in the next amateur draft to the player's former club.

During collusion, the compensatory draft choice attached to the signing of a Type B free agent suddenly became too high a price for a new club to pay. This was the case even though the player's former club had not "reserved" the player under the collusion scheme. Thus, players such as Danny Heep, Vern Ruhle, Doug Corbett, and Sammy Stewart were forced into limbo until early June 1987, when the draft choices attached to their signing expired.

In the case of Danny Heep, as soon as the draft choice expired, he signed with the Dodgers and, despite the long layoff, was soon in the major leagues. Like the freedom fighters, Heep had to play catch on the side, only his exile was for an extra five weeks. The lesson being taught by collusion was that Type B free agents should think twice before declaring free agency, lest they be forced to sit out of baseball until early June of the year following their declaration.

There were a myriad of other ways that free agents were victimized. Charlie Lea started the 1984 All Star game and was the ace of the Montreal pitching staff that year. Lea developed shoulder problems the following year, which eventually led to surgery. After extensive rehabilitation during 1986, he appeared ready to pitch again at the major league level in 1987.

Charlie had signed a three-year guaranteed contract covering the 1984–86 seasons, with a club option at $950,000 for the 1987 season. Thus, at the end of the 1986 season, the Expos could have exercised the option or allowed Lea to become eligible for free agency. The Expos wanted him back and dispatched general manager Murray Cook to visit Lea's home in Memphis. Cook made it very clear that the Expos wanted him to return, even though Cook informed Lea that the Expos would decline to exercise their option in his contract. The Expos' strong interest in keeping Charlie was reiterated to Alan Hendricks by Expos executive Bill Stoneman.

The Expos offered Charlie the major league minimum of $62,500, plus incentives. Their reasoning was that since he had missed time due to injury, he owed it to the Expos to re-sign for the minimum salary. Charlie rejected that "generous" offer and elected free agency. The Expos pursued him intently but refused to increase their offer.

During the free agent season, a number of other clubs expressed token interest in Charlie. This was typical of how "the other clubs" played the free agent game during collusion. There was talk, but no offers were made when the old club wanted the player to return.

While one could sympathize with the Expos' argument that Charlie owed the Expos special consideration, it did not follow that he owed the Expos an obligation to sign for a salary substantially below fair market value. Collusion was used to deny him the right to ascertain his value in a free market.

Starting pitchers Joe Magrane, Pete Vuckovich, Brian Holman, Jose Guzman, and Danny Cox all missed significant time during their careers due to injuries, surgery, and rehabilitation. Despite being in various stages of their comebacks, all five pitchers received salaries significantly in excess of the major league minimum because they negotiated their contracts in collusion free markets.

Collusion forced Charlie to re-sign with the Expos at the major league minimum. Though not a high profile player at that time, his situation nevertheless represented an example of how collusion worked against all major league free agent players who were "reserved" by their former clubs.

Alan Ashby was the primary catcher of the Houston Astros over an eight year period through 1986. He was a key player on the Astros during their run to the 1986 National League Western Division championship. When Ashby caught, the club record was 59–27, a winning percentage of .686. When other catchers caught, the club record was 37–39, a winning percentage of .487.

After the 1986 season, Ashby became a free agent. Despite the fact that there were a number of quality catchers on the free agent market, and thus a number of clubs in need of front line catching, he did not receive an offer from any club other than the Astros. Unsurprisingly, neither did any of the other free agent catchers, except for Lance Parrish, who changed clubs after strange negotiations with Philadelphia and his old club, Detroit.

Dick Wagner, the Astros general manager, was a veteran practitioner of hardball tactics in negotiations. Collusion served to inspire Wagner to new heights. The result was that Ashby was forced to return to Houston at essentially the same salary that he received in 1983. Despite the fact that salaries rose substantially from the 1983 season to the 1986 season, Wagner offered no salary increase and forced Ashby to re-sign with the Astros for the smallest increase of any collusion impacted free agent in the post-1986 season free agent market.

At least one club could not help itself and strayed from the agreement not to offer a contract to a free agent whose old club sought to retain him. The Phillies signed Lance Parrish after he crossed the January deadline, which prevented him from returning to Detroit until May. Philadelphia offered Parrish a contract even though Phillies owner Bill Giles received telephone calls from Jerry Reinsdorf and Bud Selig reminding Giles to "keep his fiscal responsibilities in mind." During the Collusion II case, attorneys for the owners attempted to use the Parrish episode to prove that collusion did not exist. Instead, Parrish's entire experience helped prove the existence of collusion. That experience included a heavy-handed attempt by the Phillies to obtain a waiver from Parrish and the union to prevent them from using the Parrish negotiations to show the existence of collusion.

Larry Andersen received the same treatment from Houston as did Ashby. Larry posted solid seasons in 1984 and 1985 with Philadelphia. The Phillies started slowly in 1986, and the club decided to shake up the players by making a roster move. The roster move was the release of Larry, a move the Phillies would regret for years. Larry quickly signed with Houston and became an important member of its pitching staff during the 1986 Astros cinderella season.

Andersen elected free agency after the 1986 season. Despite appearing in 38 games, pitching 64⅔ innings, allowing 64 hits, and posting a 2.78 earned run average for the Astros, no other club offered him a contract, including the Phillies. While admitting that waiving Andersen was a mistake, the Phillies still made no offer. Andersen returned to the Astros in 1987 at the same salary he earned in 1986. Dick Wagner's negotiating position, reinforced by collusion era leverage, was that since Larry had been released by the Phillies, he did not deserve a raise.

Larry Andersen played with the Astros into the 1990 season, when the Astros traded him to Boston for Jeff Bagwell. Pursuant to George Nicolau's ruling in Collusion III in July 1990, Andersen was made a "new look" free agent following the 1990 season. He signed a two-year, guaranteed contract with San Diego for over $2,000,000 per year. Ironically, the Phillies actively pursued and signed Larry when he again became a free agent following the 1992 season. Playing at age forty in 1993, Larry was an effective set-up man on a pitching staff which helped the Phillies dramatically improve from a last place club in 1992 to a World Series club in 1993.

While collusion affected free agent players and players who

would soon become eligible for free agency, it also affected salary arbitration eligible players. Denny Walling was such a player. He was a nine-year veteran who was eligible because he was subject to the repeater rights provision of the Basic Agreement. "Repeater rights" restricted a player's right to elect free agency to once every five years. If the player's contract was shorter than five years, upon its expiration the player would become eligible for salary arbitration until he was again eligible to elect free agency.

Over the 1984 through 1986 seasons, Denny Walling's playing time increased as a platoon third baseman for Houston. Ray Knight had been Houston's primary third baseman in 1984, although Phil Garner and Walling also played third that year. In late August, Knight was traded to the Mets. Garner became the primary third baseman in the platoon, backed ably by Walling. Both players continued in those roles through the 1985 season. In 1986 Walling assumed the role of primary third baseman, backed up by Garner.

The 1986 season was a good one for Denny Walling. In 382 at bats over 130 games, he hit .312, hit 13 home runs, scored 54 runs, and drove in 58 runs. He was the third most productive offensive player for Houston that year.

Denny proceeded to a salary arbitration hearing, and I won his case. The arbitrator chose our salary request of $595,000, rather than the Astros' salary request of $450,000. Dick Wagner had offered $522,500 to settle the case, but we rejected his offer.

The most comparable players to Denny at the end of 1986 were Rance Mulliniks and Ray Knight. Phil Garner was also relevant.

In early 1987, on the date for filing Walling's salary arbitration number, the salaries of these three comparable players were as follows:

	1987 Salary	Average Salary of Contract
Mulliniks	475,000	583,000
Knight	unsigned	unsigned
Garner	450,000	450,000

During Walling's hearing, the comparability of Mulliniks and Garner were much discussed.

Knight was particularly relevant because he was the primary third baseman for the National League Eastern Division champion Mets, while Walling was the primary third baseman for the National League Western Division champion Astros. However, Knight was not discussed in the hearing because he was an unsigned free agent. After Walling's case, Knight signed with Baltimore for $600,000.

In ruling for Walling, the arbitrator clearly found that Denny was worth more than Garner. He also found that Denny's value in 1987 was approximately equal to the average annual value of Mulliniks' three-year contract. This made Walling's value in 1987 at least $100,000 greater than the salary Mulliniks would receive in 1987.

It is enlightening to review the collusion-free salaries that the union recommended for Mulliniks, Garner, and Knight. These are the salaries that the union concluded the players would have received "but for collusion."

	Actual 1987 Salary	MLBPA Collusion Adjusted 1987 Salary	Average Salary of Collusion Adjusted Contract
Knight	$600,000	$1,000,000	$1,000,000
Mulliniks	475,000	575,000	675,000
Garner	450,000	550,000	550,000

The impact of collusion depressed the salaries of comparable players, which directly affected the numbers filed in the Walling case. Had the recommended salaries been actual salaries at the time Denny Walling filed for salary arbitration, we probably would have filed a number around $850,000. The Astros probably would have filed a number between $550,000 and $625,000.

It is inescapable, therefore, that Denny was a victim of collusion, just as were Knight, Mulliniks, and Garner. Unlike these players, who were damaged as either a free agent or as a prospective free agent, Denny Walling was damaged as a salary arbitration eligible player. On February 14, 1994, arbitrator Tom Roberts awarded Denny a 1987 collusion adjusted salary of $665,000. Roberts also increased the 1987 collusion adjusted salary of Rance Mulliniks to $600,000.

Prior to admissions made to me by some club officials that the information bank existed after the 1987 season, I knew that the market had been rigged once again. The primary reason I knew was because the offers made to players tracked their prior salary histories. In a noncollusive free agent market, clubs value players on a prospective basis, and the most recent performance of a player is given the greatest weight in making that evaluation. Thus, clubs sign a player based upon their judgment of what he will do in the future, not what he did in the two or three preceding seasons.

The contract signed by Darren Daulton after the 1990 season, when he was a prospective free agent in a noncollusive market, was a classic example of how a club signs a player based upon the club's projection of the player's future performance. The Phillies believed that Daulton had a good future and paid him handsomely, rather than risk losing him in the free agent market. Daulton's new contract was well in excess of his value as measured by prior years' performances. The Phillies' projection proved to be accurate, for Daulton played so well that he "out performed" the very contract that was considered by many observers to have been well in excess of his "value."

In noncollusive free agent markets, solid players who come off of career years, or who rebound strongly from injuries, or who assume and perform well in more important roles, usually receive very significant salary increases. During the post-1987 free agent market, though, offers to free agents generally represented token raises over the players' prior salaries.

For example, suppose player A earned $750,000 in 1987 and posted an average year. He might have been offered $825,000 for 1988 by his old club and $775,000 and $800,000 by two other clubs. Suppose player B earned $500,000 in 1987 and posted a season superior to player A. He might have been offered $650,000 for 1988 by his old club and $600,000 and $625,000 by two other clubs. In a noncollusive free agent market, player B would have been offered far more than player A. Since I represented players very similar to players A and B, the price fixing aspect of the post-1987 season free agent market soon became obvious to me.

By January of 1988, I was discouraged by the third consecutive year of collusion. I was down, but far from out. As had become a recent habit, I flew to New York City the first week of January to use the union computer system for my upcoming salary arbitration cases.

Prior to my trip, I telephoned Peter Ueberroth, and we arranged to meet for breakfast one morning. I had grown personally fond of the commissioner, even though I suspected that he was the architect of collusion. I had represented players before him in several grievance hearings. I had also met with him to resolve the Clemens holdout, and we talked on the telephone on several occasions. This commissioner had made it his business to get to know the leading agents — quite a contrast from his predecessor, Bowie Kuhn.

At breakfast we talked about a great many things. As our meeting neared an end, I mentioned, almost as an afterthought, that I was sad because my hometown team was about to "take a hit." The Astros and Hendricks free agent clients Dave Smith, Danny Darwin, and Larry Andersen were on a collision course. All three players intended to go past the January 8 deadline, which would disqualify them from re-signing with Houston until after May 1.

Ueberroth seemed genuinely concerned about the situation and inquired as to the reasons why these three important Astros pitchers would not re-sign with Houston. I told him that the Astros' offers were ridiculously low and that I was not going to let the Astros pull off low-ball offers to my free agent clients two years in a row.

"Maybe I can be of help to you," Ueberroth said. "Would you meet with John McMullen if I arranged a meeting? If you and John McMullen sit down in the same room, maybe you can get something resolved." The deadline was only a few days away. I told the commissioner I would think about his offer and call him with my answer.

That afternoon I conferred with my brother Alan and called all three clients. Everyone agreed that we had nothing to lose by meeting with McMullen. I telephoned Ueberroth and left word with his secretary that I was agreeable to a meeting. She asked where the commissioner could find me, and I replied that I was working in the union offices.

Within an hour, Peter telephoned and told me that he had arranged a meeting with McMullen for the next morning. I thanked the commissioner for his intervention. I then phoned Alan and all three clients and told them to be on standby.

The next morning I rode the subway in New York City for the first time, going from the Grand Hyatt hotel on 42nd Street to McMullen's offices in the World Trade Center in lower Manhattan. I frequently walk in the cities to which I travel, and I also like to ride the local rapid transit system. While a veteran of many New York walks and cab rides, I thought that a subway trip down Manhattan during the morning rush hour had to be safe, so I started the day with a new adventure.

When I arrived in McMullen's reception area, I was asked to sign the visitors' register. As I signed my name, I noticed that the signature directly above mine was Bill Wood's, the general manager of the Astros. This will be a serious meeting, I thought, if McMullen had Bill Wood fly from Houston to New York on about three hours notice.

McMullen walked into the reception area and greeted me warmly, my second clue that the day would prove to be productive. We candidly discussed our relationship, which had not been on the warmest of terms. The Astros owner stated that perhaps he had not worked hard enough to get to know me. That was my third clue.

We left the reception area and went into the owner's private office, where Bill Wood was waiting. If Smith, Darwin, and Andersen were going to sign before the deadline, it was "now or never."

It became apparent immediately that both the Astros owner and the general manager wanted to sign all three players that day. It was also apparent that they would be tough negotiators, though not nearly as tough as Dick Wagner had been the year before. In the reception area, McMullen told me that he liked the way Wagner had negotiated for him. I replied that Wagner's style ran off players and would have run off McMullen's players if not for collusion. He waved his hand and told me all that was in the past. Wagner or collusion, I wondered.

While McMullen and Wood knew that they had an incredible ally in the form of Collusion III, they did loosen the purse strings considerably. They substantially increased their offers as we discussed each player, one by one, starting with Andersen. We ordered in lunch, and I used the occasion to consume a New York hot pastrami sandwich.

At the appropriate juncture in each player's negotiations, John and Bill would leave the room. I initially used the owner's private line to report to the player and to Alan. I did not use a line through the switchboard, because I figured that my calls could be monitored. I changed phones several times, just to be on the safe side. When I talked to each player, I explained that I was in McMullen's private office. I reported the offer and told the player to call Alan. I advised Alan of the particulars of each situation and requested that he discuss in detail with each player the Astros' offer and our position on that offer and then call me back. I talked to Alan in both cryptic and general terms, or "code words," a form of communication we had developed over the years.

After several hours of negotiations and telephone calls, the meeting progressed to the point where it was fun for everybody. Andersen, Darwin and Smith, though, could not believe that after months of protracted negotiations, with little progress having been made, that their contract status might be resolved within a matter of hours.

Alan was more than up to the task of being a world class air traffic controller, working several phones simultaneously, talking to everyone. While our code words did not require Alan to say, "Vector 90 right," he did say, "One and a tenth will do Smyth." I instantly knew that Dave Smith would sign for $1,100,000.

Contracts were finally agreed to on behalf of Smith, Darwin, and Andersen. Smith's contract had been especially difficult to consummate, but as soon as it had been completed, I brought up Denny Walling's name. I asked McMullen and Wood if they preferred for me to beat them again in salary arbitration or work out a deal for Denny. Although I said this with a big grin on my face, Bill, who was by then very familiar with Hendricks humor, could not suppress a groan.

"What's your problem?" I said, still smiling. He told me it was the Walling decision the prior year. I said, "You know why we won, don't you?" a reference on my part to the complex way in which I had proved the merits of Walling's case. Wood replied, "Yeah, I know why you won." "Tell me why," I said, curious to know which part of my case he considered to be the most persuasive.

"Because you're such a good talker," he replied. I burst into laughter. It always seems that a club believes I win on "advocacy" and not on "merit," while I believe the opposite to be the case.

Within the next two hours, we finished a two-year contract for Walling and proceeded to finalize a one-year contract extension for Mike Scott. McMullen had always been fond of Joaquin Andujar, and we finalized a one-year contract to return Andujar to the Astros.

In the course of one day, six players had been signed. Before the day began, the future of the Astros looked bleak. At the end of the day, it looked great. Considering the reality of collusion, and their contract status before the meeting, all six players were exceedingly happy.

Alan and I spoke after all six contracts were concluded. This time we did not have to speak in code words. "The people in Houston won't believe it when they open their morning newspaper," Alan said. I agreed. The next day, the front page of the sports section of the *Houston Chronicle* blared: "Astros finally armed for 1988 season." The *Houston Post* ran its story on the front page. The headline read: "Reliever Smith among 6 signing Astros deals."

John McMullen was in a festive mood, and instead of ending the day with an angry glare at me as he had done at our last meeting in Houston, he invited me to dinner. On the drive to the restaurant, we discussed the navy. McMullen is a graduate of the Naval Academy and is very proud of his military heritage. I told him that my father, Clinton, had been in the Navy twice — the second time as a volunteer during World War II. I shared stories of our family "dutifully" watching the annual Army-Navy football game — cheering for Navy, of course.

"My dad also loved watching the football games of Texas A&M

to see the cadets stand the entire game," I said. "Little did I realize at that time that one day I would have a daughter [Kristin] graduate from A&M." We traded stories and enjoyed each other's company as McMullen drove us to Gerrino's, an Italian restaurant in Hoboken, where we were met by John's wife, Jackie, and Lou Lamoriello, the general manager of the New Jersey Devils (the NHL hockey team McMullen owns).

As we walked across the street to the restaurant, snowflakes were falling gently. I thought for a minute that I was in *It's A Wonderful Life*, and I looked around to see if Jimmy Stewart was joining us for dinner.

The food was the best Italian food I've ever eaten, and since I love Italian food, that restaurant has a special place in my memory bank. Without taking anything away from the food, though, perhaps that day had something to do with how well I enjoyed dinner.

McMullen drove me back to the Grand Hyatt, and as I walked into my room at about 11:00 P.M., the phone was ringing. It was Neil Hohlfeld of the *Houston Chronicle*. The Astros had announced the contract signings in time to make the early morning papers. As soon as I hung up, the phone rang again. It was Ivy McLemore of the *Houston Post*. The phone would continue to ring, or flash its blinking red light, for the next several hours.

*   *   *

From 1984 through 1986, George Bell averaged 28 home runs, 91 runs scored, 97 runs batted in, and a batting average of .292. In 1987 he took his game to a new level. He hit .308, scored 111 runs, hit 47 home runs, and drove in 134 runs. For his achievements in 1987, George Bell was named the American League Most Valuable Player and *The Sporting News* Player of the Year.

Bell had completed more than five years of major league service at the end of 1987, so he was eligible for salary arbitration. He was also one year away from free agency. Had collusion not existed, the Blue Jays would have "gulped" at the thought of what it would have taken to sign Bell. Instead, the Blue Jays engaged in brinksmanship negotiations during the salary arbitration process.

Beginning in February 1986, the Blue Jays and the Hendricks arbitration team started a tradition of settling George Bell's pending salary arbitration case at the last conceivable minute. The 1986 case, which covered the 1985 season, was scheduled to be heard at the

Hyatt Regency O'Hare in Chicago. I still smile at the mental picture of Tal Smith coming up the escalator from the level of the hearing rooms, motioning for my client and me to "come on" and engage him in battle. George was uncertain of whether to accept the final Blue Jay proposal made to us fifteen minutes before the hearing was scheduled to start.

Pat Gillick, the Blue Jays general manager, had clarified a question on the distinction between being "elected" or "selected" to the All Star team, and he proceeded to the hearing room about five minutes before the scheduled start of the case. George and I debated the merits of the proposal for so long that Tal had come to get us. After a few more minutes, we proceeded to the hearing room, where we announced that George would accept the proposal.

In February 1987, Bell's case was scheduled in New York City. Everyone stayed at the Grand Hyatt hotel, so, as expected, negotiations reconvened in the lobby of the hotel the evening before the hearing. No progress was made, though, and everyone went to bed expectant that the case would proceed the next morning.

At 7:00 A.M., I received a call from Gillick, wanting to continue negotiations. I hollered at Pat that the time for negotiating was past. At 8:15, I left the room, briefcase in hand, ready to try Bell's case. When I got off the elevator, there stood Pat Gillick, Paul Beeston and Gord Ash, Blue Jays assistant general manager. Beeston was dressed in a suit, with no socks, as usual. He had a cigar in hand and a big grin on his face.

I had on my game face, but looking at Beeston cracked me up. With reporters from Toronto milling around, I said in a stage voice "The case is at the Triple A, not in the lobby of this hotel." Beeston laughed uproariously, Ash grinned, and Gillick looked glum.

The three Toronto executives approached, and Gillick made a slightly modified proposal. I rejected the proposal immediately, and "the Beest" laughed heartily. I asked him what was so funny, and he told me that he had just won a bet that I would say "no." I stood there, shaking my head, enjoying the moment yet going slightly more crazy. I thought, "These guys don't understand I have to get mentally ready for this case." Then I immediately thought, "Maybe they do understand, so that is why they torture me."

Beeston and Ash motioned for me to walk away with them, since our mirth had encouraged the reporters to move in on us. Paul became serious and said, "Gord has one last proposal for you." Gord then made a new offer, which constituted a bona fide effort to bridge our differences.

I looked at them both, but said nothing. My face probably said it all. Where had this offer been, and why was I getting it at 8:30 the day of a 9:00 case?

"You guys are amazing," I said. "Okay, we've got a deal." Beeston howled and, of course, I had to ask him why. "Because I won another bet," he said.

At that moment, George Bell got off the elevator. I told him that we had a deal. He was happy with the settlement, but disappointed that we were not going to try the case. Unlike the prior year, in which the arbitration process was relatively new to him, George was now a veteran and eager for the contest, especially because we had not been close to a settlement until that moment.

Within minutes everyone was talking of where we would eat lunch to celebrate the signing. I suggested a new restaurant I had read about, Le Bernadin. After a quick discussion, we had reservations for both the Hendricks group and Blue Jays group. The luncheon was a total contrast to the events of the prior month. A casual observer would have concluded that we were all good friends working for the same company. Of course, in many ways, we were.

By February 1988, I had grown tired of the repetitive game over George Bell's contract. I solemnly told Beeston and Gillick that either we reached an agreement before traveling to New York, or we would try the case. They agreed. If I get on the airplane, I thought, I will try the case.

Three days before the scheduled hearing, we had both rejected the other side's last proposal. Our number for the salary arbitration hearing was $2,105,000, and the Blue Jays' number was $1,725,000. Our best offer to settle was $2,000,000, and the Blue Jays' was $1,850,000. So, everyone went to New York.

Steve Mann had just joined our salary arbitration team after many years of working with Tal Smith's salary arbitration team. When Mann first called me after the 1986 season, I listened to him politely, but considered the possibility that he was a management spy seeking to infiltrate our organization. While I knew that he possessed considerable talent, most of my questions were designed to find out why he had "switched sides."

Since Bill James had worked as part of our salary arbitration team since the 1979 season, I was unsure whether we should or could use Mann's services. I had decided not to use him for cases covering the 1986 season. However, after talking to Steve over the course of the next year, I decided to add him to our salary arbitration team for 1987 season cases. From our discussions, I had concluded that Steve Mann was strong willed, very competitive, and blunt. None of those traits bothered me. Rather, I considered them assets. I did not know how he would blend into our team, how he would affect our "chemistry."

The night before George Bell's scheduled hearing, our team assembled at the Grand Hyatt. Those in attendance were my brothers Alan and David, Mann, Bell, and myself. Bill James would join us later. Alfredo Griffin was not in the room, or the United States for that matter, but his presence was felt. We kidded George that Alfredo was his real agent.

This was Mann's first strategy session with a baseball player, as opposed to a club, in a salary arbitration case. It was also his first strategy session involving the Hendricks gang and a client. The mood was lighthearted, with jokes flowing back and forth. The discussion about Bell's contract situation, however, was deadly serious.

Finally, George looked at me and said, "Randy, what do you think? Do you think we should go through arbitration?"

Andre Dawson had just lost his salary arbitration case and would be paid $1,850,000 instead of his requested $2,000,000. Since Dawson was the National League Most Valuable Player, the union lawyers were pessimistic about our chances of winning.

I remained upbeat, because of my client's four consecutive superior seasons. Injuries had adversely affected Dawson's production and consistency over the same period. At my request, the union had sent to the hotel the Cubs case against Dawson. The Cubs had rated George Bell ahead of Andre Dawson on the basis of consistency and productivity over the prior four seasons. Bingo. Many of the arguments advanced by the Cubs against Dawson supported my case for Bell. I considered using part of the Cubs case as an exhibit for our case.

I had anticipated a possible Dawson defeat and prepared a chart in my case entitled: "Why Andre Dawson Should Have Lost His Salary Arbitration Case and Why George Bell Should Win His Salary Arbitration Case." The chart did not denigrate the great ability of Andre Dawson. Rather, it demonstrated through an analysis of the salary arbitration criteria and recent player signings that Bell's 1987 season performance *and* his performance over the prior four seasons should put him at a higher salary level than Dawson.

I responded to my client's penetrating question.

George, while Dawson just lost, I am not too concerned about that hurting our chances. I'm ready and am prepared to go, as usual. You've been offered $1,850,000 to settle your case, the same salary as Dawson just received. We've offered $2,000,000 to settle. I think their offer is too low. We're $150,000 apart. If we go, we risk $125,000 to chase $380,000. I'll take that risk and play that game if you want.

Bell then asked, "What do you think of the multiyear offer?" The Blue Jays had also offered $5,500,000 for a three-year contract, with the first two years being guaranteed and the third year being an option year. Without hesitation, I replied, "Way too low. The minimum for you should be $6,000,000, and $6,300,000 is more appropriate, and that's considering the fact that collusion is still going on."

He then said, "Alfredo says that there is no point in going through free agency. He says I'll just be back in Toronto. He told me to get the most guaranteed money I can and sign." I replied, "Alfredo is probably right about free agency, but you have to draw the line at where you fight and where you settle."

My client was clearly agonizing. On one hand, he was tired of the annual game with the Blue Jays, where we settled "on the courthouse steps" after the Blue Jays increased their final offer just enough to produce a settlement. On the other hand, he wanted a multiyear contract, although not at the Blue Jays' last offer. George was searching to see if someone had a strong opinion.

Steve Mann had been quiet throughout the entire discussion. After a moment's silence, he said, "Why are you hesitant to go to arbitration, George? I've read Randy's case. You have a great case. You're a great player. What's wrong? You should be ready to fight."

Alan, David, and I looked at each other, stunned. George Bell, a black belt in karate, fierce competitor and notorious hothead on the field, strong willed off the field, hesitant to fight? What a joke. We wanted to be sure that he wanted to fight for logical reasons, not emotional ones. And here came the new kid on the block, obviously relishing the thought of battle, egging on our client whom he had just met.

George was as shocked as we were. I read the look on his face, a look that meant, "Who are you to say that to me," but also a look that meant, "You may be right." He then returned to the multiyear offer. I concluded that Bell wanted to follow Alfredo's advice, advice pragmatically crafted due to the reality of collusion. The question was whether the Blue Jays would increase their offer significantly.

As the meeting pressed on towards 11:00 P.M., my client concluded the discussion by asking me again if I was ready. I knew that by "ready" he meant, "Do you think you will win?" I told him I was ready.

Bell then advised us that he would not accept $1,850,000 for one year or $3,700,000 for two years, or $5,500,000 for three years. He then left for his room, prepared to go ahead with the case scheduled at 9:00 A.M. the next morning.

After George and David left, Alan and I talked to Mann, who had sensed that perhaps he had gone overboard. I said to him, "I don't think that you should have said what you did." Alan then uttered what is now considered a classic line in our office. He said, "I respect what you said, but not your right to say it." We all laughed at the irony of Alan's humor, which had surely hit the mark. They then adjourned for bed. As was usual for me the night before a case, I stayed up for several more hours, annotating the case to facilitate my presentation the next day.

The next morning our team assembled in the lobby and cabbed over to the offices of the American Arbitration Association, where salary arbitration cases are heard in New York City. When we got off the elevator, the Blue Jay management team of Beeston, Gillick, and Ash were waiting for us. Tal Smith's team, which would present the Blue Jays case against George Bell, was ready to go.

I kidded the Blue Jays executives that we were finally going to do a case on Bell. Paul Beeston laughed and said, "Not so fast" and motioned for me to come over to him to talk. We decided to talk further and adjourned to a vacant hearing room, designated as the George Meany room.

It was ten minutes before the case was scheduled to start, and there we were discussing numbers again. Paul is one of the most practical negotiators with whom I have ever dealt. He stated that we owed it to everyone involved to try one more time to bridge the gap. I told him that I agreed with the spirit of his comments, but I was sick and tired of these last minute deals. He chuckled and rolled his eyes, his way of saying, "Who isn't?"

Beeston then asked if the Dawson loss bothered me. I said, "Heck no" and told him about my exhibit which showed that George should win and Andre should have lost. The "Beest" sat back in his chair and roared with delight, enjoying the moment. "Randal," he said, "I'll bet you're serious."

"You know I am," I replied. Despite my attempts to keep a straight face, I started laughing. His laugh is contagious. Three people —my daughter Kristin, my brother Alan and Paul Beeston—can get me laughing just by hearing them laugh.

Just then someone knocked on the door. I yelled, "Who is it? Come in!" I was irritated that someone was interrupting our good time. It was Alan and Gord Ash. They both looked solemn. "The arbitrator is waiting. The case is supposed to start right now," Alan pronounced. Beeston just chuckled, enjoying the irony of the moment. After vowing no more last minute settlements, there we were laughing like kids at recess while everyone else waited somberly.

I waved off Alan and Ash and said, "Give us some time. We might still work out a deal." They left to pass the word. To Beeston I said, "You're probably the only person in the world who can do this to me and have me laughing while you get away with it."

Getting mentally ready to try a salary arbitration case and negotiating a settlement of that case are, to me, mutually exclusive psychologies. To try a case, I get laser focused, mentally intense, and competitively ready. Imagine a race horse in the starting gate, and you will get the picture.

When negotiating a contract, my frame of mind is very open. I am a transmitter and receiver of data, of both the objective and subjective kinds. I evaluate inflections of speech, body language, and other nonverbal forms of communication. I analyze the import of the words used to express my counterpart's position. When negotiating, I am generally relaxed.

So what the Blue Jays did for three straight years was torture me. I was supposed to be ready to try the case and be ready to negotiate, simultaneously.

Paul Beeston and I sat in the Meany room for the next ten minutes, firing numbers back and forth. We made progress on the multi-year contract, but reached no agreement. This time Alan did not knock, but rather barged in with Gord Ash. Alan said everyone was starting to get very impatient. They wanted to know whether we were going to try the case or settle the case? I calmly said, "Give us a few more minutes. Tell everyone they'll have our answer then."

I walked to the door and looked down the hall. There stood the union lawyers, Tal Smith's team, and the reporters from Toronto — Dave Perkins, Bob Elliott, and Larry Millson. All eyes were on me. The arbitrator looked right at me. He was not smiling.

I shut the door and resumed my discussion. "Well, are you going to give in so we can get this done?" The Beest laughed, "No." "Good," I said, "it's time we did one. Let's see, we're about $50,000 apart on a one-year deal and $150,000 apart on a three-year deal. That means we're apart by about 2.5 percent. Since this time of year is so crazy, we might as well show we are, too, and arbitrate over a 2.5 percent difference."

He agreed that the arbitration season made everyone crazy. He then proposed we split the difference on the multiyear contract. I told him I would do it if my client would agree. I opened the door and called to George, who was busy talking to David. They both came to the door. I explained the situation and asked George what he wanted to do.

Bell looked at David. David then looked at me. I said, "It's up to George. In some ways, I'm past caring what we do. I'll settle or I'll try the case. I just want George happy." George asked David what he recommended. David said, "George, don't you really want a multi-year contract?" George said, "Yes, because what good will becoming a free agent do when the owners don't play fair?"

"So it's the multi-year contract," I said. George looked at David and David said "Yes." I said, "Hold on, I'll get it done."

I went back into the Meany room, and twenty-five minutes after the case was scheduled to start, sealed the deal with Paul Beeston. It was a three-year deal which paid George $5,970,000.

After conducting all the obligatory interviews with the Toronto reporters over the course of the next hour, Alan and the Blue Jays executives were ready to adjourn for what was by then our annual luncheon to celebrate the deal. Everyone else was upbeat and happy, as always. I felt like I had gone through a wringer, again.

I was pleased that my client was satisfied. I enjoyed the company of the Blue Jays executives. The food was invariably good in the restaurants we picked to celebrate. Despite all this, I felt like a horse who was in the starting gate only to be backed out and led back to the paddock because the race was cancelled. If I get into the starting gate, I want to run, if for no other reason than I am ready to run.

But I knew that I had done my job.

The fact that George Bell was satisfied was understandable only in the context of the reality of a collusive market. The collusive market had dictated the settlement. Instead of the nearly $6,000,000 for three years which Bell received, in a noncollusive market he likely would have signed a five-year guaranteed contract for between $12,500,000 and $15,000,000. Such was the impact of collusion on arguably baseball's best player in 1987.

Salaries for top players actually decreased or plateaued during collusion, instead of increasing with the revenues in the game. George Bell's $2,000,000 salary and Don Mattingly's $2,000,000 salary were top salaries for players signed during collusion, even though Dan Quisenberry, Mike Schmidt, Eddie Murray, Bruce Sutter, and Jim Rice had signed five-year contracts for salaries approaching $2,500,000 per year several years earlier. The history of George Bell's contract negotiations illustrates how leverage shifted in favor of the clubs in every contract negotiation during collusion.

*   *   *

Once the three collusion cases were settled for $280 million on December 21, 1990, the focus of the union lawyers and player agents shifted from an effort to secure damages on behalf of all affected players to an analysis of how, and to what extent, each affected player was damaged. A unified, joint effort to defeat the owners was replaced with a painstakingly meticulous review of every player impacted by collusion. The possibility that the union and player representatives would disagree over how, and to what extent, some players were damaged, would challenge long-standing relationships.

Damage claims were filed on behalf of over 800 players by the May 31, 1991, deadline. The union then began the process of evaluating each claim. The union collusion evaluation team reviewed the merits of each claim, guided by the criteria set forth in the Framework established for the evaluation of individual claims. The union team had to be mindful that its aggregate damage findings fit within the dollar amounts allocated by the Framework for each subgroup of claimants.

Like other player representatives, I prepared damage claims for our clients who were adversely affected by collusion. Unlike the union, I did not focus on allocating damages among a large group of claimants. My focus was on recovering appropriate damages for each affected client.

Suddenly, my friends and allies at the union were cast as possible opponents. If they viewed a client's claim differently than I, we would soon become good faith opponents in the appeals process created by the Framework. If I filed a formal objection to one of their findings, we would be cast, for the first time, as adversaries in the hearing held on the objection. This possibility gave me an uncomfortable feeling.

In order to fairly divide the $280 million settlement fund among the claimants, a framework was adopted to govern the evaluation of each individual claim. The Framework is the "Constitution" which sets forth the criteria under which individual claims are to be evaluated. It sets forth procedures under which claims were filed, as well as guidelines and principles to be followed in analyzing how collusion affected players. The Framework anticipates that the union will issue partial distribution plans covering parts of the collusion period. A procedure to cover objections by players to the union's awards on their claims is set forth. The Framework also provides for hearings to be held on objections and for the filing of posthearing briefs on those objections.

The Framework sets forth general principles which are to be "taken into account in formulating any Distribution Plan. These principles . . . are derived from the arbitrators' rulings and the record evidence in the collusion cases." As stated by the Framework, the initial impact of collusion was felt by its "prime victims, . . . players who became free agents at the end of the 1985, 1986 and 1987 seasons."

Also hurt were players who were one year away from free agency, whether repeat free agent players or players with five years of major league service. Players with three or four years of major league service, and who therefore were eligible only for salary arbitration, "were initially less adversely affected because the salary arbitration process initially insulated them somewhat from the effects of collusion."

"Beginning with the period following the end of the 1989 season, the market for free agent players essentially returned." Free agents were no longer directly injured, and players with five years of major league service saw most of their bargaining leverage return, but "the salaries for 3+ and 4+ players . . . were the last to rebound because . . . collusion-tainted salaries were still generally depressing the new contracts for these classes of players."

The Framework adopts a general rule that damages to a player are to be measured by the difference between the salary the player would have received, but for collusion, and the actual salary paid to the player during collusion.

The Framework sets forth criteria to be used to evaluate each player's claim. The criteria are:

a) The player's status, e.g., elected free agent; released free agent; non-tendered free agent; salary arbitration eligible
b) The player's Major League Service
c) The player's performance
d) The player's history of compensation
e) The salaries (and collusion claims, if applicable) of comparable players
f) Collusion-free patterns of multi-year contracting, if applicable
g) The player's experience as a "new look" free agent, if applicable
h) The Guidelines Regarding Allocation of the Settlement Amount
i) The General Principles
j) Any other factor which would normally apply in the determination of a player's salary and other benefits in a collusion-free market, including but not limited to, those factors set forth in Article VI of the Basic Agreement (which deals with player salaries)

The Framework sets forth damage allocations for each affected group of players for each year of collusion's impact. The allocations were a starting point and a constraint for the union in reaching its recommendations, although no one expected any partial distribution plan to conform exactly to the suggested allocations. The damage allocations were based upon the economic models of expert witnesses in the collusion cases. The following chart is a general summary of the damages allocated for each group of players for each year of collusion's impact.

Year	6+ Players	5+ Players	4+ Players	3+ Players	Total
1986	$ 5,196,000	$ 2,895,500	$1,251,227	$ 696,250	$ 10,038,977
1987	24,710,000	4,984,326	6,143,327	1,721,000	37,558,653
1988	40,110,000	13,518,122	6,642,122	6,065,122	66,335,366
1989	53,366,000	4,507,000	3,838,593	10,599,593	72,311,186
1990	28,690,000	620,430	5,016,429	4,294,000	38,620,859
1991 on	17,866,020	0	0	0	17,866,020
					$242,731,061

Out of the $280,000,000 settlement, $37,268,939 was allocated to presettlement interest.

The $280,000,000 settlement was considered very satisfactory when it was announced. The settlement conformed to the average damages calculated under several econometric models submitted by expert witnesses in the collusion cases. Perhaps influenced by postcollusion salary levels, some observers not privy to all of the evidence on damages have opined that the real losses suffered by players due to collusion may have approached $400,000,000. If such were the case, then exceptional "discipline" is required of the union to arrive at aggregate damage awards within the range of each damage allocation. I call this process cramming a size ten foot into a size seven shoe.

Players damaged by collusion fall within one or more of four groups of claimants. These groups are:

Group 1: 1986 Salary Shortfall Claimants
These are players who claim salary shortfalls from Collusion I for the 1986 season.

Group 2: Salary Shortfall Claimants for 1987 or Later Seasons
These are players who claim salary shortfalls from Collusion I, II, or III.

Group 3: Lost Extensions
These are players who claim they lost contract extensions, but for collusion, from Collusion I, II, or III.

Group 4: Lost Job Claimants
These are players who claim that due to the boycotts of Collusion I and II, they lost jobs or "were prematurely retired."

In analyzing player claims, the union has sought to apply the criteria even-handedly. It has focused on the status of each player and considered that each player has a unique story to tell about how collusion affected him.

Once the union completed its analysis of the lost salary claims for the 1986 and 1987 seasons, in accordance with the Framework it issued a partial distribution plan on December 8, 1992. That partial distribution plan covered 415 different players and 633 different claims. The partial distribution plan set forth the union's recommended salaries and recommended consequential damage awards.

The magnitude of the task faced by the union in assessing claims is shown by the following chart, which contrasts the aggregate amount of claims to the funds allocated and the union's recommendations.

Year	Claims	Amount of Claims	Funds Allocated	Union Recommendations
1986	247	$ 42,137,143	$10,038,977	$10,047,476
1987	386	111,729,470	37,558,653	33,343,708

The following chart shows the additional damages sought by the forty-nine individual objectors (one objector had a claim for 1986 only; eleven objectors had claims for 1986 and 1987; thirty-seven objectors had claims for 1987 only), as well as the additional damages awarded on February 14, 1994, by arbitrator Roberts.

Year	Claims	Objections	Additional Damages Sought	Additional Damages Awarded
1986	247	12	$ 2,384,967	$ 65,000
1987	386	48	15,389,133	2,361,344

Over 800 players filed claims covering all of the collusion years. A few claimants were former players who did not play in the major leagues during the collusion period. Their claims are predicated upon "unusual" logic and will not result in any damage award.

A partial distribution plan covering the 1988 and 1989 seasons will be issued in 1994 or 1995, depending upon the amount of time collective bargaining in 1994 requires of the union. It may take until 1996 to complete all procedures established by the Framework for determining damages for all years through 1991.

A claimant has the right to object to the union's recommended damage award to him in a partial distribution plan. The objecting player is required to deposit $2,500 to cover the cost of the hearing held on his objection. The $2,500 additionally ensures that the player has a belief in the merits of his objection. If the player's objection is found by the arbitrator to be "substantially successful," the player will be refunded the $2,500 deposit.

Each objector is required to state in his objection the reasons why he believes that "the criteria set forth" in the Framework "have not been properly applied in the determination of his damage award." The player is also required to set forth his position on a proper damage award. The objecting player has the right to oral argument at a hearing scheduled by the arbitrator.

A total of forty-nine players filed objections to the December 8, 1992, Partial Distribution Plan. Out of this group, forty-eight requested oral argument. Their hearings were held in April and May of 1993. I represented nine objecting players and argued the merits of their objections. I submitted trial briefs and evidence at those hearings.

The two-month period of those hearings was every bit as exhausting as a salary arbitration season. It was nonstop adrenaline and Diet Cokes. Because it was a new process, there was a certain amount of improvisation as I proceeded through the preparation and trial of each objection. My teammate was the ever dependable Steve Mann. We were assisted by June Higgins. This was a skeleton team compared to a salary arbitration season team. There was, though, one psychological advantage over preparing for a salary arbitration case. I knew with certainty that I would try the case, rather than face the possibility of settling it, as is often done during the salary arbitration season.

I represented forty-three of the 415 players covered in the December 8, 1992, Partial Distribution Plan, so thirty-four players I represented elected not to file objections. I did represent eleven of the thirty-five players who filed Comments to Objections. Comments are a procedure whereby a player can "hitch" his claim to the claim of an objecting player. A player filing a comment essentially argues that if the objecting player to whom he believes he is comparable is successful in his objection, then the player filing the comment should have his recommended salary and consequential damage award increased as well.

Players filing comments are not entitled to oral argument, but instead they are required to confine their arguments to the written word. Comments filed pursuant to the arbitrator's guidelines on the December 8, 1992, Partial Distribution Plan ranged from brief, letter length statements to full fledged legal briefs.

The procedure for the hearings held for the objectors generally tracked the procedures for salary arbitration cases. Prior to the commencement of the first hearing, the union filed a "Statement" which summarized its analysis of each objector's claim, and how it reached the recommended salary and damage award for that objecting player. The union Statement included the status of the objecting player, his unique story as understood by the union, a statistical analysis of the player's career, and an analysis of the player's claim.

A salary arbitration hearing is a trial by ambush. That is, neither side submits anything to the other side prior to the commencement of the case. Of course, negotiations prior to the salary arbitration case and experience in arbitration provide each side with a good idea about how the other side will present its case.

The hearings on objections filed to the December 8, 1992, Partial Distribution Plan proceeded more like a normal trial. The player had submitted a claim, so the union had an opportunity to review the player's position. There was an opportunity for dialogue with the union between the filing of a claim and the issuance of the Partial Distribution Plan. The union then filed its Statement prior to the hearing. Thus, a player representative was able to prepare for an objection hearing based upon the union's summary of how it reached its findings.

At the hearing, the player representative goes first and has one hour to present the player's case. The player representative can use the entire hour in his initial presentation, or he can "reserve time" to respond to the union. I reserved time in all of my hearings. Because the union previously filed a statement of its position, it has only thirty minutes to respond to the player's case. The union usually needs less than its allotted thirty minutes. If the player representative reserves time, the hearing concludes at the expiration of the reserved time.

Player representatives frequently file trial briefs at the hearings. The objecting player often appears and testifies. I had all nine of my objecting clients appear, and all testified extensively. Both the union and the player representative are permitted to file an "initial post-oral argument brief" and a "reply brief" to the other side's initial post-oral argument brief. For the December 8, 1992 Partial Distribution Plan, those briefs were due in mid-July and late July 1993, respectively.

The arbitrator is Tom Roberts, who decided the Collusion I case. Roberts is a veteran of many salary arbitration cases, having heard thirty-six cases in the 1970s, 1980s, and 1990s. His experience qualifies Roberts to deal with the intricacies presented by the Framework and the collusion claim objection process.

The arbitrator was granted significant responsibility and authority by the Framework. He is a one-man supreme court, since his decisions are final on all matters. Given the allocation of funds, though, his job is quite demanding and difficult.

The arbitrator reviews the Partial Distribution Plan, all objections, all comments, the union Statement, presides over the objection hearings, reviews the evidence presented at the hearings and the transcripts from each hearing, and reviews legal briefs filed during and after each hearing. After careful consideration over a period of several months, if the arbitrator "determines that the approved Framework and the criteria set forth therein have not been properly applied with respect to any portion of a proposed Distribution Plan, he shall have the authority to modify or amend the Distribution Plan to the extent necessary, in his judgment, to cure the defect. IN DOING SO, THE ARBITRATOR MAY RAISE OR LOWER THE DAMAGE ALLOCATION . . . TO ANY PLAYER OR PLAYERS."

The authority granted to the arbitrator means that he can award any amount to an objector that he believes to be appropriate. Since the arbitrator's award can be anywhere between the player's request and the union's award, the tension in the hearings is considerably less than found in a typical salary arbitration hearing. Still, there are some salvos fired by both sides in the hearings. That is inevitable when lawyers assemble to argue the merits of their cases.

Unlike salary arbitration hearings, where the decisions are rendered within forty-eight hours, in the collusion objection hearings the arbitrator reserves judgment on each objection until he has heard all objections, read all briefs filed, reviewed the comments, and reviewed the entire partial distribution plan from which the objections were filed. That process required six months before arbitrator Roberts rendered his decision on the December 8, 1992, Partial Distribution Plan on February 14, 1994.

The claim and objection filed by Charlie Lea illustrates the complex task the union faced in evaluating the myriad of individual claims. The union's conclusion regarding Lea's claim illustrates why I filed a number of objections.

The facts of Lea's unique story have been detailed previously in this chapter. The union and I agreed that he clearly fell within the definition of collusion's prime victims, as established by the arbitrators and defined within the Framework. We also agreed that the evidence proved that Montreal clearly wanted Charlie Lea to return to the Expos.

The union concluded, however, that it was his injury and the nearly two years out of major league baseball, not collusion, which caused Lea to be paid only the minimum major league salary in 1987. I disagreed with this conclusion and filed an objection which asserted that while my client would not have received the option price of $950,000 contained in his prior contract, in a noncollusive market he would have received a salary of $350,000, rather than the major league minimum salary of $62,500, plus incentives, paid by the Expos.

I cited as evidence in support of my assertion the salaries paid in noncollusive markets to starting pitchers Joe Magrane, Pete Vuckovich, Jose Guzman, Brian Holman, and Danny Cox. All five pitchers missed considerable time due to injury and rehabilitation, yet received salaries substantially in excess of the major league minimum.

During the hearing held on Lea's objection, a "healthy" debate ensued regarding the comparability of his "story" to the "stories" of Magrane, Vuckovich, Guzman, Holman, and Cox. While the union defended its conclusion, it acknowledged that Charlie Lea's claim was not an easy case to resolve.

I argued that it was collusion, rather than Lea's prior injury, which caused him to be paid the minimum salary. None of us were physicians, I stated, nor could any of us easily calculate the precise interplay between the impact of the prior injury and the impact of collusion on my client's 1987 salary. What we could examine, though, was the evidence of how other quality starting pitchers had been treated in noncollusive markets. In my judgment, that evidence clearly supported my request for a $350,000 recommended salary.

During my reserved time, I argued that it was uncontroverted that Charlie was a prime victim of collusion. I had demonstrated considerable evidence of how comparable, quality starting pitchers had been treated in noncollusive markets. The union had not disagreed with my evidence, I said, but rather had disagreed with the comparability of Lea to those five pitchers. It would be patently unfair for the arbitrator to sustain the union's position, I concluded, because my client had clearly been denied an opportunity to test his market value in a noncollusive free agent market. To sustain the union's position would be to conclude that Charlie Lea was a collusion victim, albeit one with no damages.

In his February 14 decision, arbitrator Roberts awarded Charlie a 1987 collusion adjusted salary of $250,000.

The hearing held on Lea's objection demonstrated that:

1. The union, the player and the player representative, former and future allies, are pitted against each other, however "cordial" the collusion claims process may be.
2. Arguments become more fully developed as the objection process proceeds.
3. Of utmost importance is evidence of the treatment of "comparable" players in noncollusive markets.
4. It is not easy to conclude which player or players are the most comparable to an objecting player. Not only will different players be selected as "comparable," but different conclusions can be drawn even when there is agreement on a "comparable" player.

5. In attempting to construct what likely would have happened, "but for collusion," different, reasonable conclusions can be reached from the available facts.

6. The objection process, which includes the hearing and the filing of posthearing briefs, serves a very useful purpose by having the arbitrator decide "close calls" and correct "mistakes" in judgments made by the union. The objecting player has the satisfaction of knowing that he has had his "day in court."

7. The collusion objection process is based upon the principles of due process, and the arbitrator does not render a decision until all parties involved in the process have had an opportunity to appear before him.

Some of my most satisfying moments have come from working with the lawyers at the baseball players association. When I first dealt extensively with the baseball players' union, Dick Moss was in the process of leaving as its able general counsel to become a player agent. Moss was instrumental in the union achieving many of its legal victories. Don Fehr, who worked as an outside lawyer on the Messersmith-McNally case, replaced Dick Moss.

I have worked with the baseball union on a wide variety of subjects, from the global issue — collective bargaining — to the narrow issue — an individual player grievance. At every juncture I have found the lawyers at the baseball union to be talented, energetic, and dedicated. Most of them love baseball, and all of them respect the game.

The collusion cases required a tremendous amount of effort from everyone on the players' side. Tremendous attention was paid to strategy, to evidence, to testimony, and to a review of files. It took a high level of energy to sustain such a massive effort over such an extended period of time. Resolving to whom to distribute the settlement proceeds has been like one extended salary arbitration season — only one with periodic digressions into other urgent matters.

Working with the union attorneys in New York City suits my style. It is a high energy lifestyle, and long work days are the norm, not the exception. Getting the job done right is paramount. I feel at home in that environment.

Before the union developed individual computer disks for each agent to use in his office to prepare for salary arbitration, I traveled to New York City in early January each year to use the union's computer system. I went during the first week of January to beat the rush of agents, who would show up one to two weeks later. In this way, I usually could have the system to myself. After "normal" office hours, I often had five different computer terminals operating at once as I did my research. My night owl style was the source of much humor within the union offices.

Because of my late hours at the union offices, and the fax requests which I would send to the union in the middle of the night upon my return to Houston, Arthur Schack nicknamed me "The Count." His return fax to me, complete with the numerous computer runs which I had requested of him, would be addressed solely to "The Count" at the offices of Hendricks Sports Management. For my part, I explained my nocturnal habits as a function of my always operating on Hawaiian standard time. Unsurprisingly, much of this book was written on Hawaiian standard time.

I have discovered that most people interested in baseball, outside of major league players, have misconceptions about the professionals who work for the union. While the personalities of Don Fehr and Gene Orza have hopefully shone through in the pages of this book, a glimpse into the personalities of the other professionals with whom I have worked extensively at the union is in order.

Mark Belanger is special assistant. He is the former defensive standout at shortstop for the Orioles. Quick to laugh, Mark is a great organizer. His organizational skills range from the macro — player unity on labor issues, to the micro — organizing and updating the computer system for salary arbitration. Ever meticulous, he has given me his blessing to run the computer system, because he knows that I will not crash the system or trash the office.

Somehow, calling Assistant Counsel Lauren Rich the "mother of collusion" seems inappropriately appropriate. She calls herself the "Quollusion Queen." These labels provoke laughter from her, something that is done rather easily. She has tirelessly devoted her career to all three collusion cases and their aftermath. She has dealt with the implementation of the Framework, player claim analyses, and the partial distribution plans. Lauren is a trooper and is viewed like a sister by agents, players, and union officials.

Arthur Schack is counsel, and administers salary data and processes grievances. When an agent consummates a player contract, he calls Arthur Schack immediately. If he does not, Arthur will track him down. Salary arbitration season is high season for Arthur, and no agent can function without him, because he can always be counted on to have the latest in salary information. He is very popular with agents.

Michael Weiner is assistant counsel and has worked coopera-
tively with Lauren Rich on the collusion cases and claims process.
He also represents the union in salary arbitration hearings. Mike is a
good example of how the union has maintained its high standards by
hiring the right people. He is presently alternating between being a
big city union lawyer and a small town lawyer near his residence
several hours outside of New York City.

Doyle Pryor recently joined the union legal team after years of
being outside counsel during salary arbitration season and during
the collusion cases. Doyle is one of the many people involved on the
players' side in baseball who is from Kansas City. He and I have
shared some "fun" moments in salary arbitration cases.

Judy Heeter is another Kansas City lawyer. She represents the
union in licensing matters. She has "shaped up" a number of compa-
nies who have violated player rights. With the help of Allyne Price
and Tina Morris, who are in charge of the licensing program at the
union, Judy has protected and enhanced player income from licensing.

Special mention should be made of Skip McGuire, who as outside counsel headed the successful Collusion I legal team. He was
assisted by Alan Michaels.

Steve Fehr, Don's brother, was outside counsel and headed the
successful legal team on Collusion II and Collusion III. Unsurprisingly based in Kansas City, Steve also represents players. His representation of David Cone has been some of his best work.

"But for" the tireless work and abilities of all the lawyers, agents,
and players involved in the collusion cases, the owners might have
succeeded in their collusive efforts, and the phrase "but for collusion" would not now be a part of the working vocabulary of all of us
who still live with the effects of collusion as we process and advocate
each player's claim.

Chapter 7

Salary Arbitration

No subject in baseball is more misreported and misunderstood than salary arbitration. Year in and year out one hears from both club officials and members of the media that players "win" in salary arbitration, whether they win, lose, or settle their cases. As John Schuerholz, general manager of the Atlanta Braves says, players get either a "BIG W" or a "Little w" in salary arbitration. Notwithstanding Schuerholz' capabilities in baseball administration, his viewpoint on this subject is a limited one shared by most of the management participants in this particular battleground of the baseball wars. This typical management perspective on salary arbitration reflects the usual "loss of control" neurosis so prevalent in club circles.

Agents and club officials do share one common complaint — too many decisions are incorrect. The fear of injustice drives a lot of the participants to settle cases. Many criticized decisions can be adequately explained by how the cases were prepared or argued. In other instances, the critics simply lack in-depth knowledge of the particular case, so the criticism is, at best, generalized, or, at worst, off target.

However, there are some decisions that are simply inexplicable other than through the explanation that the arbitrator reached the wrong decision. There is a school of thought that such decisions serve the purpose of reminding the parties that the salary arbitration process is primarily designed to induce the parties to settle cases by agreement, rather than through an arbitration hearing.

That viewpoint is not persuasive to those of us who play the salary arbitration game. We want "justice" and a well-reasoned decision. If one loses a case, but could read a well-reasoned decision of the case written by the arbitrator, the loss could become both instructive and even acceptable. On the other hand, if one loses a case and reads a decision which misweighs the criteria and contains a contorted analysis of the case, then it would be clear that the arbitrator in that case should be fired. Unfortunately, under the present system, one never knows which of the two foregoing scenarios determines the outcome of a case, because the arbitrators are not required to give any reasons for, or write even a brief summary of, their decisions.

There are many misunderstandings and misperceptions about salary arbitration cases. Many fans believe that if a player is "good," he will win in salary arbitration. In reality, salary arbitration cases are "numbers" games. The side which proves its number to be closer to what the arbitrator believes is an appropriate salary is supposed to win. Notice I said "supposed to." I believe that many arbitrators, consciously or otherwise, put "the burden of proof" on the player to prove that his salary request is proper. In such cases, doubts are resolved in favor of the more conservative number (i.e. the club number). Arbitrators who do this may be lacking in courage and may be afraid that they will appear foolish if they award a player too high a salary. There is no burden of proof in the criteria; hence cases should be resolved based strictly on whether the player's salary or club's salary is closer to the arbitrator's assessment of a proper salary. Expressed differently, each case has a midpoint salary exactly one-half of the way between the player's salary and the club's salary. The decision for the arbitrator should be whether the player is worth more or less than the midpoint salary.

As the amount at stake in each case has increased dramatically over the past ten years, so has the quality of preparation and presentation from player representatives and club representatives alike. Unfortunately, the quality of the arbitrators has decreased, as many veteran arbitrators who understand both the intricacies of the games of baseball and salary arbitration have been fired and replaced by unseasoned arbitrators who lack the requisite understanding of both games.

Those veteran arbitrators who were fired were terminated by either the PRC or the MLBPA because of a particular decision or a series of decisions. Invariably, one hears about the incorrect decision in the case of player "X" as the reason why a particular arbitrator was fired. The other often cited reason for firing an arbitrator is that he ruled too many times in favor of the other side. When an arbitrator rules a disproportionate number of times in favor of clubs or players, the record of that arbitrator is often interpreted to mean that he has a bias towards the side with the most victories. This may be true, even though it is logically possible that the arbitrator was assigned cases which, if properly decided, would justifiably give an aggregate advantage to one side.

The participants are also concerned that some arbitrators may split decisions in order to stay within the good graces of both the union and management. When this concern exists, the side with the winning record under such an arbitrator considers itself the underdog going into the next case.

The salary arbitration system is an adversarial system which results in a trial if the parties do not reach a voluntary settlement. In this general way, the salary arbitration system resembles litigation. And like the world of litigation, the salary arbitration world has its recognizable characters and characteristics.

Some clubs and agents are not reluctant to try salary arbitration cases. Others avoid the hearing room at all costs. Still others will try a case from time to time to keep the other side honest. The "players" in the salary arbitration game know who fits into which category.

Some of the most capable agents in baseball have losing records in salary arbitration. They are usually good advocates, and they are not afraid to try tough cases. Others in the industry file "weak" numbers and then rack up cheap victories.

Insiders know that for a comparable player a superior agent can settle a case for a higher salary than a weaker agent. Agents are judged by insiders for their settlements as well as for their arbitration record. Given a choice, a good agent will take nine good settlements and go 0–1 in salary arbitration, rather than take five good settlements, two fair settlements, two poor settlements and go 1–0 in salary arbitration.

A disturbing trend over the past few years has been the ever increasing number of cases which settle at the midpoint. This is not due to an increased ability of the participants to shrewdly select numbers which are equidistant from "justice." Rather, it is due to two phenomena.

The first is that a midpoint settlement is perceived to save face for all involved. The settlement represents a tie, so one cannot be accused of being weak and giving in to the other side — a criticism that stings many who play the salary arbitration game. Of course, some midpoint settlements are cave-ins, but they do not appear to be so to the nondiscerning person.

The second reason cases are settled at the midpoint is that the participants have developed an increasing distrust in the ability to obtain justice from a salary arbitrator. This increasing distrust manifests itself, in mathematical terms, like a coin toss; hence, if cases start to resemble a coin toss, a 50/50 or midpoint settlement appears appropriate.

For years, I have given thought to the percentage of cases which are improperly decided. The problem with such an analysis is that it is subject to limited knowledge about the merits of the cases presented.

In some instances, I am intimately familiar with the player and the merits of his number, and hence, his best case. In other cases, I have only a general notion of the merits of the case for each side. To further complicate matters, no matter how in-depth my knowledge might be, I am neither privy to how each side argued its case, nor to the quality and quantity of evidence presented in the case. Being absent from the hearing room is undoubtedly a disadvantage in evaluating whether a case has been properly decided.

Nevertheless, there are some good cross references. I frequently speak to agents, union lawyers, club officials, and advocates for clubs to obtain their views on how they evaluated a case. If they were present at the hearing, I solicit their views on how the case "went over" in arbitration. This fills in a lot of the gaps.

I have reached the conclusion that about 75 percent to 80 percent of all salary arbitration cases are properly decided. Others involved in the process have opinions that range from 66 percent to 90 percent.

The foregoing means that, on average, an advocate has one chance in four of "winning" his case and yet "losing" the case based upon the arbitrator making an incorrect decision. He who forgets this truth is headed for a lesson on the subject, sooner or later.

The spread between player and club submissions has increased steadily over the years, so much more money is now at stake in a hearing than was the case a decade ago. The cases presented by agents and clubs have become much more sophisticated as the stakes have increased. Unfortunately, the sophistication of the cases often overwhelms some arbitrators. Many rookie arbitrators react favorably to a simple case, in keeping with their level of sophistication on salary arbitration and baseball. While such arbitrators are generally very able and intelligent people, their knowledge of baseball comports with the views of the typical fan.

For example, batting average has been a widely worshipped statistic over the years, with player batting averages posted daily throughout the baseball season. Yet, many who earn a living within the baseball world regard on-base percentage as a more important measure of a player's worth to a club. Imagine, therefore, the problem which results when arguing before an unsophisticated arbitrator that a player with a .275 batting average and a .390 on-base percentage is more valuable than a player with a .300 batting average and a .350 on-base percentage.

Imagine, further, that adjustments are made based upon the home ball parks in which the two players play. For example, assume that the first player plays for the Astros and that the second player plays for the Cubs. If the value of hitting is getting on base, then the player who gets on base more frequently is a more valuable hitter, even if the other player is better at hitting.

Over 90 percent of all those involved in baseball would conclude that the first player is the more valuable offensive player. However, an arbitrator convicted with the notion that batting average is the most important statistic for a hitter would conclude that the second player is the more valuable offensive player.

I have suggested for several years that the remedy to real, or perceived, problems with arbitrators is to change the process as follows. Appoint three permanent salary arbitrators, who would hear all cases. The majority would decide each case, and a written synopsis of the rationale for the decision in a case would be required. The synopsis would be no more than three pages in length and would be essentially an outline summary of the rationale for the decision, rather than a lengthy opinion. As with judicial decisions, there might be concurring or dissenting opinions filed. At the end of a salary arbitration season, the union and management could each replace one arbitrator.

Over time, a sense of *stare decises* would develop from the decisions in the cases, and a general sense of predictability would emerge, which would allow agents, players, clubs, the union, and management to reach more enlightened decisions on whether to settle a particular case, and at what salary figure, or to try that case before the panel of arbitrators.

*   *   *

Major league baseball players are grouped into three distinct classes when it comes to salary arbitration rights. The first class is composed of "junior" players, or those players who possess less than the two years and approximately 130 days of major league service time (there are 172 service days in a full season) necessary to qualify for salary arbitration.

Clubs exert nearly total, though often enlightened, control over the salaries of this group of players. Notwithstanding the considerable talent or outstanding performance of a junior player, at this stage of his career his salary is ultimately determined by his club. His salary will invariably fall far short of the salary he would receive were he eligible for salary arbitration or a free agent.

Many clubs do exercise a type of relative good faith in negotiating the salaries of players within this group. In a typical case, a club will conduct its own salary arbitration type of analysis to determine exactly where the club believes the player fits within the salary structure for his service group. Of course, the "arbitrator" is the general manager of the club, and thus the club "feels in control," to a large degree, over the salary of the junior player.

Few members of the media and very few fans have any empathy for the fact that a professional baseball player must play his entire minor league career and almost three full seasons in the major leagues before he becomes eligible for salary arbitration. Many players drop by the wayside before reaching this plateau. A player must demonstrate sufficient ability and consistency to reach and remain in the major leagues to qualify for salary arbitration. Thus, most salary arbitration eligible players are both good major league baseball players and survivors.

The second class of major league players is comprised of the salary arbitration eligible players. These players have accumulated at least two years and approximately 130 days of major league service, but less than six years of major league service. Additionally, players with over six years of major league service, who are subject to repeater rights restrictions, are also eligible for salary arbitration.

The third class of players are those with at least six years of major league service, who are eligible to declare free agency. The players in this group who elect free agency can accept salary arbitration if it is offered to them by their former club in early December of their free agent year.

Clubs resent two fundamental things about salary arbitration. First, they resent the fact that they must start paying the player a salary which more closely reflects his true economic value than did the salary he was paid prior to his becoming eligible for salary arbitration. Second, clubs resent the fact that a neutral party, Heaven forbid, rather than the club, might determine a player's salary.

It is their loss of control over directly determining a player's salary that most club officials resent. Their perspective is warped by the favorable economic benefit they have reaped from that player's services for the prior three years. The resentment over the fact that they can no longer perpetuate their "good deal" and control the player's salary leads to the loud condemnation of the salary arbitration process by club officials.

As indicated, there are a number of improvements which can and should be made to the salary arbitration process. However, the majority of club officials who condemn salary arbitration as being bad for clubs, and who seek to eliminate salary arbitration from the next labor agreement, are misguided.

The system is far more beneficial to clubs than would be free agency for players at the same service interval. To understand why, one must first recognize that clubs have had the opportunity to evaluate a player for three years at the major league level, and therefore, are in a position to determine the importance of that player to the club.

On each December 20 a club can retain a salary arbitration eligible player on its roster, in exchange for a commitment of only one additional year of service, by tendering the player a one-year contract. This places the risk of performance for the upcoming year squarely on the shoulders of the player.

Alternatively, in December a club may elect to "nontender" a contract (i.e. elect not to offer a contract) to a salary arbitration eligible player. This occurs when the club believes that either the player is not good enough to keep on its major league roster or that the player is not worth the salary likely to be paid to him under the salary arbitration system.

Therefore, the club has the option to keep on its roster a good player for a far smaller financial commitment than the multiyear contract commitment the club would have to make were the player a free agent.

* * *

In the early 1970s when I first began negotiating contracts for professional athletes, the salary structure was based primarily on seniority, or service time. A talented young player was told to wait his turn and put in his time before he could receive a high salary. Some clubs had de facto pay scales based upon performance within service time categories. For example, a talented young player who sustained a strong level of performance might have been paid $15,000 as a rookie, followed, on a season-by-season basis, by salaries of $30,000, $45,000, $60,000, $75,000, and $90,000. Of course, variations would occur depending upon the quality of performance by the player in a particular year. To earn the majestic salary of $100,000 represented a crowning achievement.

Once a player achieved a high salary, he usually maintained his salary at that high level, even after his performance declined. The player's salary remained high in deference to his seniority and status in the game.

As a young buck in the business of representing players, especially young buck players, I was determined that those players would be paid based more upon talent than upon seniority. I lacked the respect usually accorded to the traditional system, and I was not bashful in demonstrating that disrespect. This did not particularly endear me to the generation of general managers and owners who ran clubs in the 1970s.

Once free agency came into baseball, clubs started paying both free agent players and players who would soon become eligible for free agency, salaries based more upon talent, or a combination of talent and potential, than upon seniority. Thus, seniority in the salary structure applied primarily to players with less than six years of service. Still, clubs continued to "honor" seniority when they signed older, average players.

As clubs lost players to free agency, they began to sign key players with five, and sometimes four, years of service to multiyear contracts extending beyond the year in which the player would otherwise become eligible for free agency. At this point, the clubs should have recognized that the system of determining salaries had forever changed. They should have greatly diminished the significance of seniority in determining salaries, especially for older players. But old habits die slowly.

The result was that clubs allowed themselves to be caught in a triple squeeze play. Their one safety valve, diminishing the salaries of

senior players with declining performances, was not essentially utilized until 1992, when budgetary constraints forced the clubs to
change those old habits.

Besides the ever increasing revenues generated by the game,
which allowed for the payment of larger salaries to the players, the
following three factors created the phenomenal increase in salaries
over the period 1977–94.

1. Free Agency: Clubs had to bid for player talent without artificial constraints. Thus, free agent players received market
   driven salaries.
2. Salary Arbitration: Because the salary arbitration criteria
   include categories of player talent and performance, a superior salary arbitration eligible player was able to cite the multiyear contracts of superior free agents and the multiyear contracts of superior 3+, 4+, and 5+ players to secure a high
   one-year salary in a salary arbitration hearing. Those multiyear
   contracts frequently contained level salaries, rather than
   escalating salaries; the salary arbitration eligible player was
   able to "target" the average value of the contract, rather than
   the first year salary of the contract.
3. Seniority: Clubs seldom cut player salaries, or nontendered
   players. The result was that salaries stayed relatively high for
   below average players with seniority, thus helping comparable players achieve relatively high salaries.

All three factors pushed salaries upward. Had clubs focused on
talent as the predominant factor for determining salaries, they would
have had a mechanism to force salaries down for players who suffered an off year. Instead, their reverence for seniority proved adverse
to their interests in the new salary system.

Another mistake clubs made was in failing to recognize that if
they nontendered salary arbitration eligible players who were unlikely
to be worth the salary they would be paid through the salary arbitration process, the free agent pool of marginal players would increase.
The National Football League has recognized for decades that the
bottom one-third of every team's roster is interchangeable. NFL clubs
are not reluctant to "cut" players. NFL general managers realize that
they can sign NFL caliber players, albeit marginal ones, from the
pool of players "on the street." Players of this caliber play for their
market value irrespective of their seniority. In one respect, players
within this group were the first true free agents. The fact that cur-

rent players within this group are replaceable keeps their salaries very reasonable, so no NFL club fears making such a player a free agent.

For over fifteen years I have reflected upon the opposite courses taken by football and baseball on the subject of interchangeable players. I believe there are several reasons why baseball clubs were extraordinarily slow to change their tradition of keeping interchangeable players until recent necessity forced them to change:

1. An NFL team acquires its players from college programs, and thus does not have any developmental costs for those players. If a player is not sufficiently productive, the team is not reluctant to cut the player, even if the player might have some value to another NFL team. Mistakes are made, of course, but NFL teams appear resigned to this fact. They take comfort in the knowledge that the inevitable mistakes of other teams will later balance the ledger.

   Baseball clubs, on the other hand, spend so much time and money developing players that they find it distasteful to waive a replaceable major league player in which they have invested a lot of development money. Baseball clubs have large minor league departments and budgets. The people in those departments are proud when one of their minor league players makes it to the "Bigs." That pride is shared by the major league front office. There is a reluctance to cut loose a player who may later succeed in the major leagues and therefore embarrass the official who made the decision to waive the player. This reluctance is only intensified by the well-publicized lists of successful major league players who previously played in another major league organization.

2. NFL teams recognize that there will always be a pool of available talent to sign as needed. This reality makes it easier to terminate marginal players, because replacements are readily available, including, in many cases, the very player who was previously terminated.

   Because baseball clubs historically hoarded players, often irrespective of the cost and benefit, there was not a pool of available, marginal major league players. This encouraged clubs to hang onto a marginal, overpaid player because the club was unsure of where it could find a replacement for the player. This vicious cycle continued in baseball until the end of the 1991 season, when necessity forced a number of clubs to change long standing habits.

3. Baseball clubs were "managed" in many cases by individuals who were not trained in financial management and who did not correlate the ability of a player to his cost to the club. Too often, a general manager, whose background and training consisted of a career in baseball, would ask a manager if he wanted to keep a marginal player. The manager, of course, would inevitably elect to keep the marginal player with whom he was familiar, even if the financial cost was excessive to the club. Rather than evaluate the "value" of a player and make a prudent financial judgment, the general manager would ratify the manager's decision and keep the overpriced veteran-in-decline. And to exacerbate matters, the overpricing was a result of the clubs' emphasis on seniority in the salary structure.

Owners, apparently, had no overall sense of player value, because they retained the very individuals who repeated these types of mistakes in positions of power. Apparently, the business of baseball was so profitable that these types of mistakes went unnoticed except by the very discerning.

The overall effect was to keep seniority alive and well in baseball far beyond its usefulness to clubs. Not surprisingly, union officials and veteran agents recognized these "errors of the way" by management. These errors were discussed "in hushed tones" for over a decade, lest the "enemy" come to its senses.

The push by agents and players to overturn the preeminence of seniority in favor of talent came about for several reasons. One of the major reasons was agents competing for clients. The competition in baseball for clients is usually very professional, but intense, nevertheless. The talented young baseball player has a relatively large number of agents ready and willing to represent him during his career. Those agents come from every geographic region of the United States. Thus, when a player selects an agent to represent him, he is, in theory, selecting the best available agent from the entire agent pool.

The player is confident that he has selected the best agent. The agent, in turn, recognizes that he has been selected because the player believes in him. The less than subtle implication is that the player expects the agent to perform at the highest possible level. The agent understands that he must deliver for the player if he is to fulfill the expectations of his new client and maintain their relationship. This, in effect, drives the demand for high salaries.

The typical, talented young player does not care to pay homage to the platitudes that he must "pay his dues" and "wait his turn" to receive a high salary. He can clearly identify that his ability and achievements as a player place him near the top of his profession, although the impatient young player often fails to appreciate the value of a consistent, repeated excellent performance. So, a young player who has achieved one or two outstanding seasons will often view himself as being comparable to a player who has achieved five or six outstanding seasons.

All of these forces pressure the agent to deliver a superior contract for the talented young player, seniority considerations notwithstanding. In my earliest days in baseball, I made my mark "fighting" for top young players such as Joe Sambito, Len Barker, Chris Knapp, and others. I refined my technique and later fought some major battles in the mid- to late-1980s for young baseball players such as Roger Clemens, Doug Drabek, John Smiley, and Greg Swindell. My unwavering philosophy was to prove that I was committed to these players and would fight for their interests. This both discharged professional responsibilities and created bonds.

It was only natural, therefore, that there would be a clash between aggressive agents representing talented young players and management over the clubs' preference for a seniority driven system.

In the 1970s, a "cynic" might have concluded that one reason management preferred its seniority system was because only a small percentage of young players survived injury or the aging process to climb the seniority ladder to the highest salary level.

In the late 1970s and early 1980s, there were many contract disputes over the issue of talent versus seniority. Many of those disputes resulted in salary arbitration cases. Slowly, but surely, the talent factor was given more credence for young players, while seniority was maintained as an important consideration for older players.

To understand how this happened and appreciate how salary arbitration cases are tried, one must examine the criteria for salary arbitration set forth in the Basic Agreement. The criteria by which an arbitrator is bound are as follows:

A. The Quality of Player's Contribution to Club During the Past Season (including but not limited to his overall performance, special qualities of leadership and public appeal);

B. The Length and Consistency of Player's Career Contribution;
    Note: Except for a player with five or more years of

Major League Service, particular attention is paid to players in the same service group or the service group immediately preceding the service group of the player whose case is being tried. This is subject to the special accomplishments exception. This is a post-1985 season addition to the criteria.

C. The Record of Player's Past Compensation;

D. Comparative Baseball Salaries;

E. Existence of Any Mental or Physical Defects on the Part of Player;

F. Recent Performance of Club, Including League Standing and Attendance.

The following type of evidence is included:

... Any evidence may be submitted which is relevant to the above criteria, and the arbitrator shall assign such weight to the evidence as shall to him appear appropriate under the circumstances. The arbitrator shall, except for a Player with five or more years of Major League service, give particular attention, for comparative salary purposes, to the contracts of Players with Major League service not exceeding one annual service group above the Player's annual service group. This shall not limit the ability of a Player or his representative, because of special accomplishment, to argue the equal relevance of salaries of Players without regard to service, and the arbitrator shall give whatever weight to such argument as he deems appropriate.

Evidence of the following shall not be admissible:

(i) The financial position of the Player and the Club;

(ii) Press comments, testimonials or similar material bearing on the performance of either the Player or the Club, except that recognized annual Player awards for playing excellence shall not be excluded;

(iii) Offers made by either Player or Club prior to arbitration;

(iv) The cost to the parties of their representatives, attorneys, etc.;

(v) Salaries in other sports or occupations.

Through the 1993 season, the players have won 166 cases and the owners have won 209 cases. The year-by-year record of salary arbitration decisions follows.

YEARLY RESULTS OF BASEBALL SALARY ARBITRATION CASES

Year	Season	Player Wins	Club Wins
1974	1973	13	16
1975	1974	6	10
1978	1977	2	7
1979	1978	8	5
1980	1979	15	11
1981	1980	11	10
1982	1981	8	14
1983	1982	13	17
1984	1983	4	6
1985	1984	6	7
1986	1985	15	20
1987	1986	10	16
1988	1987	7	11
1989	1988	7	5
1990	1989	14	10
1991	1990	6	11
1992	1991	9	11
1993	1992	6	12
1994	1993	6	10
		166	209
		44.27%	55.73%

*   *   *

My analysis of a case is driven by the "numbers." As the hearing date for the case of a client approaches, I estimate his current market value. Player signings occur as the schedule of cases progresses. These signings give me more comparables to use in arriving at my estimated value. Since I will have completed my preparation of the case for the client, my conviction about his market value will then be very strong. My estimated value will guide me in evaluating the odds of winning and whether to settle or try the case.

I consider whether my estimated value lies above or below the midpoint. The higher above the midpoint, the greater the odds I figure the player will win. The face-saving component of a midpoint settlement has no meaning to me.

I also consider the player's relationship with the club, as well as the history of the club in contract negotiations with the clients of our firm. Some clubs strive to work out equitable settlements. They will redress a relative "wrong" the next year. With such clubs, a settlement is always preferable to a hearing. A settlement avoids an extreme result and goes a long way toward maintaining a cordial relationship between the player and the club. With such enlightened clubs, justice will almost always prevail in the long run, and both the player and the club are much happier. That's important, because they live with each other for over seven months a year.

Enlightened clubs do end up in salary arbitration when they are forced to hold the line against unreasonable settlement demands, just as enlightened agents do when they refuse to accept unfairly low settlement offers. Sometimes, though, an agent and a club will sharply disagree about the value of a player, and a hearing will occur not because of acrimony, but because "reasonable men can disagree."

If I am offered a modest settlement, I will go to a hearing unless I believe my client is worth the offer. After all, if I expect a club to "play in my zone" when the market shapes up in my favor, then I ought to "play in their zone" when the market shapes up in their favor. I have settled many cases, above and below the midpoint, on this basis.

I have never gone to a salary arbitration hearing on a case where I was offered more than the midpoint. In those cases, the club settlement offers were in line with my estimation of the player's value and the risks of arbitration. Once both parties in a salary arbitration case commit to reaching a proper settlement, the search for the "correct" number guides them, not the search for a face saving midpoint settlement.

Of the cases I have tried, two were cases where I was offered a midpoint settlement. I won both cases. In the other cases, I was offered settlements ranging from nothing (I won that case) to just below the midpoint.

The settlement offers made to me on the other cases indicated that the clubs considered themselves to be the favorite, often prohibitively so. Against that backdrop, my record of winning two-thirds of the time looks as if it has been forged on upset victories. And I have gained a reputation for such. Of course, my record could mean that I have evaluated cases better than my opponents. If just winning cases were paramount to me, I would have tried a lot more cases, even when the club settlement offers indicated a belief that I was the favorite.

*   *   *

The second Doug Drabek salary arbitration case, which followed his 1990 Cy Young Award winning season, represents the second landmark salary arbitration case for major league players. The first landmark case was the Bruce Sutter case won by Jim Bronner eleven years earlier. The second Drabek case established that a 4+ player could effectively use the route of special accomplishments to break the restrictions of seniority established by the criterion that the arbitrator "give particular attention" to service groupings of players with less than five years of service. That criterion was added to the 1985 Basic Agreement. Despite the special accomplishments exception, no 4+ player had ever penetrated, through salary arbitration, the highest salary level then in existence in baseball.

Ownership was concerned that arbitrators would pay 2+, 3+, and 4+ players free agent salaries, so the "particular attention" provision was added to the criteria in the 1985 Basic Agreement. It was designed to keep a player within a salary structure of his service group and the service group with one more year of service. The union countered, however, with the caveat that "particular attention" to a player's service group should not "limit the ability of a Player or his representative, because of special accomplishment, to argue the equal relevance of salaries of Players without regard to service."

The practical effect of this amendment to the salary arbitration criteria was to give additional credence to seniority within two-year service groups, while preserving the right of a great young player to argue that his special accomplishments made service time, or seniority, irrelevant to him. From my perspective, this was the best of both worlds. Average 2+, 3+, and 4+ players would be paid salaries within the ranges established for their respective service groups and the service group one year ahead. Great young salary arbitration eligible players could "break out" from the constraints of a salary structure driven by seniority to be paid at a much higher salary level, including free agent salary levels.

This provision could slowly but surely be used to push salaries upward, I believed. In late 1989, as collusion ended, I set out on a mission to push salaries upward in those service groups in which I had fine young players.

To his credit, club arbitration advocate Tal Smith recognized what I was doing. In three salary arbitration cases, he argued that this was what I was trying to achieve. His arguments were to no avail, though, as I won all three cases.

I let Tal Smith's arguments go unanswered in those cases, though I was appreciative of the fact that he had deduced my plan to push salaries upward. Of course, the "numbers" I filed in those cases were rather revealing, but to my knowledge no other management commentator or member of the media made that point publicly. In winning all three cases, I succeeded in "pushing the envelope" of the salary structure applicable to those clients and their peers.

The group in which I took the most delight in "pushing the envelope" was the starting pitcher class with three years of service after the 1989 season. That distinguished group included many of the outstanding young pitchers in the game, though none had achieved meaningful special accomplishments by the end of the 1989 season. In all of my years in baseball, I had not seen a stronger class of starting pitchers, so it was only natural to push this group.

The group included Hendricks' clients Drabek, Smiley, Swindell, and Chuck Finley. Other prominent members of the group included Greg Maddux and David Cone. Other fine starting pitchers included Chris Bosio, and the erratic Bobby Witt. Quality starters in this group who suffered from injury woes were Scott Bankhead, Kelly Downs, Mike Bielecki, Billy Swift, and Hendricks client Eric King.

At the end of the 1989 season, the top salary for a 3+ starting pitcher was $512,500. By the end of February 1990, the salary level for this special group had soared to new heights, as seven pitchers in the group secured 1990 salaries between $755,000 and $1,300,000. Drabek won in salary arbitration at $1,100,000, Cone won at $1,300,000, and Smiley won at $840,000.

The top salary for 4+ starting pitchers at the end of the 1990 season was $1,087,500 — less than what Drabek and Cone earned as 3+ starting pitchers during the same season. I had a large hand in pushing the 1991 salaries of the top six of the group to between $2,025,000 and $3,350,000. Drabek won in salary arbitration at $3,350,000, and Swindell won at $2,025,000.

The top salary for 5+ starting pitchers at the end of the 1991 season was $2,500,000. I represented three of the five in the group who saw their salaries rise to record levels. The top five in this group were paid between $3,440,000 and $4,625,000, with Chuck Finley becoming the highest paid member of the group.

The Drabek case following the 1990 season, in which he went 22–6 and won the Cy Young Award, established that a player of his caliber and seniority could utilize the special accomplishment provision to break totally free of service group constraints on salary. The salary paid to Drabek in salary arbitration took him to the top level of the salary structure in existence for starting pitchers in baseball when I selected $3,350,000 in January of 1991. The Drabek victory served as a springboard for Jack McDowell's victory at $4,000,000 as a 4+ starting pitcher following the 1992 season.

What follows are exhibits from the Drabek 1990 season case. Preceding some exhibits are comments which indicate what the exhibit was designed to prove and how it fits within the criteria of salary arbitration.

Because salary arbitration cases are private hearings, the media and public know very little about how cases are tried. The result is that most impressions about salary arbitration are formed not from the evidence offered, or arguments made in specific cases, but from the posthearing statements of the participants. Thus, I believe it is instructive to "go inside" a case in order to understand how cases are argued and what type of evidence is presented.

P-1

DOUG DRABEK
CAREER RECORD AND INTRODUCTION

NAME:	Doug Drabek
POSITION:	Starting Pitcher
PITCHES:	Right-Handed
DATE OF BIRTH:	July 25, 1962
AGE:	28
TIME IN SERVICE:	4 years, 132 days

Year	TEAM	G	GS	IP	W	L	Pct.	H	SO	BB	ERA
1986	New York (A)	27	21	131.2	7	8	.467	126	76	50	4.10
1987	Pittsburgh	29	28	176.1	11	12	.478	165	120	46	3.88
1988	Pittsburgh	33	32	219.1	15	7	.682	194	127	50	3.08
1989	Pittsburgh	35	34	244.1	14	12	.538	215	123	69	2.80
1990	Pittsburgh	33	33	231.1	22	6	.786	190	131	56	2.76
5 years		157	148	1003	69	45	.605	890	577	271	3.21

LEAGUE Totals	G	GS	IP	W	L	Pct.	H	SO	BB	ERA
American — 1 yr	27	21	131.2	7	8	.467	126	76	50	4.10
National — 4 yrs	130	121	871.1	62	37	.626	764	501	221	3.03
Major — 5 yrs	157	148	1003	69	45	.605	890	577	271	3.21

CHAMPIONSHIP SERIES RECORD

Year	Club	League	G	IP	W	L	Pct.	H	SO	BB	ERA
1990	Pittsburgh	N.L.	2	16.1	1	1	.500	12	4	3	1.65

The categories of this record are Games Pitched (G), Games Started (GS), Innings Pitched (IP), Wins (W), Losses (L), Winning Percentage (Pct.), Strikeouts (SO), Walks (BB; BB stands for Bases on Balls), and Earned Run Average (ERA).

The most relevant criteria for evaluating a starting pitcher are wins, losses and ERA.

Note that although Doug Drabek is a four-plus player, he has been a major league starting pitcher for five years.

Doug Drabek has **very good control** and has allowed **less than one hit per inning** every season of his career.

His earned run average has improved every season.

P-3

DOUG DRABEK
STATUS AMONG NATIONAL LEAGUE LEADERS IN 1990

DOUG DRABEK in 1990 was among the National League leaders in many or most of the important pitching categories.

1. DRABEK won 22 games. This ranked him first in the National League.

2. DRABEK had a winning percentage of .786. This ranked him first in the National League.

3. DRABEK posted a 2.76 earned run average. This ranked him sixth in the National League.

4. DRABEK held opposing hitters to a .225 batting average. This ranked him fourth in the National League among starting pitchers.

5. DRABEK pitched 9 complete games. This ranked him tied for second in the National League.

6. DRABEK pitched 3 shutouts. This ranked him tied for third in the National League.

7. DRABEK started 33 games. This ranked him tied for seventh in the National League.

8. DRABEK pitched 233 and one-third innings. This ranked him fifth in the National League, with two of the four pitchers who were ahead of him being only two or less innings ahead.

DOUG DRABEK was an almost unanimous selection for the Cy Young award in the National League, receiving 23 of 24 first place votes.

Exhibit P-5 covers the criterion which deals with club performance, as measured by club standing and club attendance. This exhibit shows that Pittsburgh won the National League Eastern Division in 1990, posting the best won-lost record in the National League.

Pittsburgh drew 2,049,908 fans, an all-time attendance record for the Pirates.

1990 FINAL NATIONAL LEAGUE STANDINGS
(Compiled by the MLB-IBM Baseball Information System)

Eastern Div.	W	L	PCT.	GB	VS. EASTERN DIVISION						VS. WESTERN DIVISION					
					PIT	NY	MON	PHI	CHI	STL	CIN	LA	SF	SD	HOU	ATL
Pittsburgh	95	67	.586	—	—	8	5	12	14	10	6	8	8	10	7	7
New York	91	71	.562	4.0	10	—	10	10	9	12	6	7	7	5	7	8
Montreal	85	77	.525	10.0	13	8	—	10	7	11	3	6	7	7	7	6
Philadelphia	77	85	.475	18.0	6	8	8	—	7	10	5	4	8	7	7	7
Chicago	77	85	.475	18.0	4	9	11	11	—	8	4	3	7	8	6	6
St. Louis	70	92	.432	25.0	8	6	7	8	10	—	3	5	3	9	6	5

Western Div.	W	L	PCT.	GD	VS. EASTERN DIVISION						VS. WESTERN DIVISION					
					PIT	NY	MON	PHI	CHI	STL	CIN	LA	SF	SD	HOU	ATL
Cincinnati	91	71	.562	-	6	6	9	7	8	9	—	9	7	9	11	10
Los Angeles	86	76	.531	5.0	4	5	6	8	9	7	9	—	8	9	9	12
San Francisco	85	77	.525	6.0	4	5	5	4	5	9	11	10	—	11	8	13
San Diego	75	87	.463	16.0	2	7	5	5	4	3	9	9	7	—	14	10
Houston	75	87	.463	16.0	5	5	5	5	6	6	7	9	10	4	—	13
Atlanta	65	97	.401	26.0	5	4	6	5	6	7	8	6	5	8	5	—

Pittsburgh had the best Won-Lost record in the National League in 1990.

NATIONAL LEAGUE ATTENDANCE

The National League surpassed the 24 million mark in attendance for the fourth consecutive year in 1990. Last year's record of 25,323,834 was not reached, but there were 19 rained out games in 1990 and some teams lost openings due to the lockout. However, every team played their full schedule of 162 games, maintaining the integrity of the season. 972 games were played over 949 dates.

The Pittsburgh Pirates set a club attendance mark of 2,049,908, the first time they have eclipsed the 2 million mark. The Los Angeles Dodgers passed the 3 million mark for the eighth time in their history. Five clubs passed the 2 million mark at home (New York, Pittsburgh, Chicago, St. Louis and Cincinnati) and six clubs surpassed the 2 million mark on the road (New York, Pittsburgh, Chicago, Cincinnati, Los Angeles and San Francisco).

Eastern Division clubs drew a total of 12,965,249 fans to their games and the Western Division clubs drew 11,526,268 fans.

Club	Home Games/Dates	Attendance	Club	Road Games/Dates	Attendance
Atlanta	81/77	960,129	Atlanta	81/78	1,851,517
Chicago	81/77	2,243,791	Chicago	81/80	2,160,568
Cincinnati	81/78	2,400,892	Cincinnati	81/78	2,174,093
Houston	81/81	1,310,927	Houston	81/78	1,831,131
Los Angeles	81/81	3,002,396	Los Angeles	81/80	2,113,630
Montreal	81/81	1,373,087	Montreal	81/80	1,941,918
New York	81/78	2,732,745	New York	81/78	2,349,021
Philadelphia	81/77	1,992,484	Philadelphia	81/80	1,965,844
Pittsburgh	81/78	2,049,908*	Pittsburgh	81/79	2,033,535
St. Louis	81/81	2,573,225	St. Louis	81/80	1,906,633
San Diego	81/79	1,856,396	San Diego	81/78	1,911,315
San Francisco	81/81	1,975,528	San Francisco	81/80	2,230,303
TOTALS	972/949	24,491,508	TOTALS	972/949	24,491,508

*Club record

Pittsburgh set an all-time club attendance record in 1990.

P-6

PITTSBURGH STARTING PITCHERS
1990

In winning the divisional title in 1990, the Pittsburgh Pirates used twelve different pitchers to start a game:

Pitcher	G	GS	IP	W	L	Pct.	SO	BB	ERA
Doug DRABEK	33	33	231.1	22	6	.786	131	56	2.76
Neal Heaton	30	24	146	12	9	.571	68	38	3.45
John Smiley	26	25	149.1	9	10	.474	86	36	4.64
Bob Patterson	55	5	94.2	8	5	.615	70	21	2.95
Bob Walk	26	24	129.2	7	5	.583	73	36	3.75
Zane Smith*	11	10	76	6	2	.750	50	9	1.30
Bob Kipper	41	1	62.2	5	2	.714	35	26	3.02
Randy Tomlin	12	12	77.2	4	4	.500	42	12	2.55
Rick Reed	13	8	53.2	2	3	.400	27	12	4.36
Walt Terrell*	16	16	82.2	2	7	.222	34	33	5.88
Mike York	4	1	12.2	1	1	.500	4	5	2.84
Jerry Reuss	4	1	7.2	0	0	.000	1	3	3.52

*Smith and Terrell also pitched with other teams; the records given are their records while with the Pirates.

The Pirates opened 1990 with a five-man starting rotation of Doug Drabek, Neal Heaton, John Smiley, Bob Walk and Walt Terrell. As you can see from the chart above, none of the other four pitchers was consistently effective, and none remained in the starting rotation throughout the year.

The Pirates were required to re-build their pitching rotation throughout the summer, experimenting with young players, relievers, and veterans acquired from other teams. The standard for eligibility for league leadership in pitching categories is 162 innings pitched. Doug Drabek was the only pitcher to pitch 162 innings for the Pirates in 1990.

Doug Drabek led the Pittsburgh staff in every meaningful category. Drabek was sixteen games over .500 (sixteen more wins than losses); the rest of the staff, as a whole, was twelve games over .500. This makes a total of +28, which was the best in the National League.

P-8

Exhibit P-8 details the impact on salaries of the collusion settlement and the increases in the salary structure which followed the 1990 season.

This exhibit details salaries, during the collusion years, of the best starting pitchers in baseball, in order to put those salaries in context and to set the floor from which salaries rose for the group of the best starting pitchers in baseball.

This exhibit also made adjustments in salaries in accordance with Joint Exhibit 2 between the PRC and MLBPA. Joint Exhibit 2 adjusted salaries during the collusion years according to a formula agreed to between the parties. The sole purpose of Joint Exhibit 2 was to adjust those salaries for salary arbitration purposes commencing with the 1991 season. The intent and effect was to "stop" the continuing effect of collusion on the salary structure, effective with the 1991 season.

Exhibit P-8 continued with a discussion of recent signings and projected signings. Specifically, the record contract of Roger Clemens was set out to show that entirely new levels would be reached for the group of the best starting pitchers in baseball.

IMPACT ON SALARIES OF COLLUSION SETTLEMENT
AND
POST 1990 SEASON SALARY INCREASES

Prior to the 1989 season, the four best starting pitchers in baseball were Dwight Gooden, Roger Clemens, Orel Hershiser and Frank Viola. Prior to the 1989 season each signed a lucrative multi-year contract, commencing with Dwight Gooden in early February, 1989. Gooden's contract with the New York Mets made him the highest paid major league player, calling for salaries of $2,250,000 in 1989, $1,700,000 in 1990, and $2,250,000 in 1991 plus a $500,000 signing bonus. The average annual value (AAV) of the contract is $2,233,000.

Within two weeks thereafter, Roger Clemens broke Gooden's record by signing a three-year, $7.5 million contract with the Boston Red Sox. Roger received a $300,000 signing bonus and salaries of $2,200,000, $2,500,000 and $2,500,000. The average annual value (AAV) was $2,500,000.

Days later, Orel Hershiser and the L. A. Dodgers agreed to a three-year, $7.9 million contract, again breaking the record and making Hershiser the highest paid player. Orel received a 1,100,000 signing bonus and salaries of $2,400,000, $1,600,000 and $2,800,000. The AAV of the Hershiser pact is $2,633,000.

Not to be outdone, Frank Viola and the Minnesota Twins announced an agreement a week into the 1989 season. Viola's deal matched Hershiser's.

Thus was the salary structure for the top starting pitchers prior to the 1989 season and prior to the collusion settlement.

In April, 1990, Greg Maddux of the Chicago Cubs signed a one-year contract extension for 1991 for $2.4 million.

Set forth below is a chart of these players' salaries, adjusted per the collusion settlement.

Player	Yrs.	Total Value	AAV	Collusion Adj Salary
Dwight Gooden	3	$6.7M	$2,233,000	$2,501,000
Roger Clemens	3	$7.5M	$2,500,000	$2,800,000
Orel Hershiser	3	$7.9M	$2,633,000	$2,950,000
Frank Viola	3	$7.9M	$2,633,000	$2,950,000
Greg Maddux	1	$2.4M	$2,400,000	$2,662,000

The salaries of Gooden, Clemens, Hershiser and Viola were adjusted upwards by 12% and the salary of Maddux was adjusted upwards by 10.9% to reflect the collusion adjustment on a percentage basis. The collusion adjusted salaries of these five players will be frequently used in other charts to reflect their 1991 salaries.

After the collusion settlement and subsequent to the 1990 season, the salary level in baseball increased rapidly. Proof of the new salary levels is found at nearly every level of the salary structure.

Dramatic proof is found in the recent contract of Roger Clemens, who signed a guaranteed four year contract for $21,521,000, with an option for a 5th year. The average annual value of $5,380,250 is the highest in the history of baseball.

Since the contracts of Dwight Gooden and Frank Viola expire at the end of the 1991 season, both should command salaries between $4,500,000 and $5,000,000 per year.

Orel Hershiser pitched in only four games in 1990, undergoing complex shoulder surgery. He has not pitched since the operation and his career is still in doubt. Therefore, until Hershiser's health is resolved, he is unlikely to sign a new contract.

Since the conclusion of the 1990 season, and the collusion settlement, there has thus been a dramatic increase in the salary level of major league players. The new contract of many players, but especially Roger Clemens' new contract for $5,380,250 per season, evidences this fact. Accordingly, the 1991 salaries of Clemens, Viola, Gooden and Hershiser must be considered in the context of the salary levels which existed during collusion and prior to the salary levels currently in existence.

It is apparent that there has been a dramatic increase in salaries since the collusion settlement.

P-10

Exhibit P-10 shows the distinguished company which Doug Drabek had joined. This list of eight pitchers with over a .600 lifetime winning percentage (1000 or more innings pitched) gave additional support to the proposition that Doug Drabek was one of baseball's best starting pitchers.

PITCHERS WITH CAREER WINNING PERCENTAGES OF .600 OR BETTER (1000 OR MORE INNINGS PITCHED)

PITCHER	W	L	PCT	1991	1992
GOODEN, DWIGHT	119	46	.722	2501*	
CLEMENS, ROGER	116	51	.695	2800*	5380
HIGUERA, TEDDY	89	54	.622	3250	3250
WELCH, BOB	176	109	.618	3450	3450
KEY, JIMMY	87	56	.608	2016*	2548 option*
DRABEK, DOUG	69	45	.605	3350/2300	
BROWNING, TOM	93	61	.6039	3121	3121
HERSHISER, OREL	99	65	.6037	2950*	

* collusion adjusted salary

To be 100 or more points above the .500 level in baseball is quite
a feat. In terms of team performance, a .600 record is the equivalent
of 97 wins and 65 losses, usually good enough to win a division title
(3 of 4 in 1990). Thus it is not surprising that only nine active pitchers with more than 1000 innings under their belts have been able to
sustain .600+ records throughout their careers. Doug Drabek ranks
sixth in this very special category.

Only 70 pitchers in the entire history of baseball have career
winning percentages of .600 or better in 1000 or more innings pitched.

P-12

Exhibit P-12 is a list of the eleven pitchers who pitched 675
innings or more over 1988-1990. In order to average the 225 innings
per season necessary to make this list, a starting pitcher has to be
consistently effective, as well as stay healthy. This group of durable
and effective starters also would earn in 1991 or 1992 a salary supportive of our position in Drabek's case.

PITCHERS WITH 675 INNINGS OR MORE
1988–1990
(3-year totals in ascending ERA order)

PITCHER	G	GS	W	L	PCT	IP	ERA	*1991*	*1992*
1 CLEMENS, ROGER	101	101	56	29	.659	745.2	2.69	2,800*	5,380
2 DRABEK, DOUG	101	99	51	25	.671	695.0	2.87	3350/2300	
3 MARTINEZ, DENNIS	100	99	41	31	.569	693.1	2.95	3,166	3,166
4 VIOLA, FRANK	106	106	57	36	.613	766.0	3.00	2,950*	
5 STEWART, DAVE	109	109	64	32	.667	800.1	3.04	3,500	3,500
6 HURST, BRUCE	99	98	44	26	.629	685.0	3.14	1,960*	3,200
7 MADDUX, GREG	104	104	52	35	.598	724.1	3.19	2,662*	
8 WELCH, BOB	104	104	61	23	.726	692.1	3.21	3,450	3,450
9 LANGSTON, MARK	102	102	41	42	.494	734.1	3.46	3,200	3,200
10 BROWNING, TOM	108	108	48	26	.649	728.0	3.52	3,121	3,121
11 BODDICKER, MIKE	104	103	45	34	.570	675.2	3.57	3,083	3,083

Using a standard of 675 or more innings pitched over the past
three years, only eleven pitchers make this iron-man list of starting
pitchers. Doug Drabek ranks 7th in the innings pitched category.
His quality ranking in earned run average is second.

Notice that there are no pitchers on this list with ERAs higher
than 4.00. In fact, there are only two pitchers with ERAs above 3.50,
and both of them are within just 7 points of that very respectable

3.50 mark. This is not a matter of coincidence. In order for a pitcher to accumulate 225 or more innings in a season, he typically must be consistently effective in the 32 to 36 starts that he makes in the course of a season. In other words, he has to last an average of about 7 innings per start to amass considerably more than 200 innings by season's end. This exceptional degree of effectiveness is reflected in the earned run average; generally, the higher the ERA, the greater the number of subpar outings a pitcher has had, the sooner and more frequently he has been lifted for relief pitchers, and the fewer innings he has pitched. Among the exceptions are injury-plagued pitchers whose quality of performance is high but who simply haven't made enough starts to reach the 225-inning level.

And so, the above group consists entirely of pitchers who are durable and effective and healthy — precisely the combination of attributes that every club seeks to get from a pitcher.

* collusion adjusted salary

P-15

LENGTH OF SERVICE
AS A
SALARY ARBITRATION FACTOR

The influence of "Length of Service" on player salaries is different for four basic "Length of Service" groups. These groups are:

a. Players with 0+ years, 1+ years and 2 years and up to 127 days of service — these players are ineligible for salary arbitration and because of these limited rights, their salaries are restricted.
b. Players with 2 years, 128 days of service and less than 3 years of service — the salaries of this group of players are grouped with the salaries of 3+ years of service players.
c. Players with 3+ years of service — the salaries of this group of players are grouped with the salaries of 4+ years of service players.
d. Players with 4+ years of service—the salaries of this group of players are grouped with the salaries of 5+ years of service players.

Notwithstanding arbitration rights, 2 and 128+, 3+ and 4+ players are impacted by the arbitration criteria which provides:

The arbitrator shall, except for a Player with five or more years of Major League service, give particular attention, for comparative salary purposes, to contracts of Players with Major League service not exceeding one annual service group above the Player's annual service group. This shall not limit the ability of a Player or his representative because of special accomplishments, to argue the equal relevance of salaries of Players without regard to service, and the arbitrator shall give whatever weight to such argument as he deems appropriate.

This criterion, therefore, tends to group the salaries of 4+ players with the salaries of 4+ and 5+ players, except for a showing of special accomplishments.

Therefore, it is instructive to compare DOUG DRABEK to the performance and salary levels of other 4+ and 5+ pitchers, but considered in the context of DOUG DRABEK's special accomplishment of winning the 1990 Cy Young award. When DOUG DRABEK's performance as a pitcher is carefully considered, it is clear that a salary of $3,350,000 is appropriate. A salary of $2,300,000 is simply too low, and would place DOUG DRABEK at the wrong place in the salary structure in existence for 1991 for baseball's best starting pitchers.

P-16

Exhibit P-16 reviews career performance data of all 4+ and 5+ starting pitchers. This chart is used to "prove up" Exhibit P-15 and to clearly show Drabek's superiority to all other 4+ and 5+ starting pitchers.

CAREER PERFORMANCE
4+ AND 5+ STARTING PITCHERS

Pitcher	Service Yr.Days	G	IP	W-L	Pct.	SO	BB	ERA
Tom Candiotti	5.138	179	1167	71-65	.522	711	388	3.69
Doug Drabek	**4.132**	**157**	**1003**	**69-45**	**.605**	**577**	**271**	**3.21**
Kirk McCaskill	5.159	162	1043	68-55	.553	643	382	3.80
Greg Maddux	4.021	140	911	60-53	.531	540	319	3.68
Jim Deshaies	5.041	155	948	56-48	.538	638	358	3.50
Bobby Witt	4.125	143	891	56-52	.519	869	608	4.48
David Cone	4.058	132	785	53-27	.663	725	276	3.14
Jose Rijo	5.118	193	872	53-52	.505	753	399	3.60
Greg Swindell	4.046	120	805	51-39	.567	587	195	3.88
Chuck Finley	4.134	152	767	48-41	.539	544	311	3.22

John Cerutti	5.007	191	772	46-37	.554	369	254	3.87
Eric King	4.104	161	633	42-28	.600	355	261	3.67
John Smiley	4.035	163	646	40-34	.541	405	185	3.73
Scott Bankhead	4.138	109	629	38-34	.528	441	182	4.18
Mike Bielecki	4.068	143	673	38-37	.507	414	293	4.12
Bruce Ruffin	4.064	167	770	38-51	.427	394	321	4.22
Chris Bosio	4.064	147	754	37-46	.446	512	187	3.94
Jeff Robinson	4.000	96	522	36-26	.581	328	260	4.65
Kelly Downs	4.070	113	588	36-32	.529	399	190	3.55
Bill Wegman	5.012	123	721	36-44	.450	321	176	4.63
Jamie Moyer	4.114	133	669	34-49	.410	415	266	4.51
Floyd Youmans	5.014	94	539	30-34	.469	424	280	3.74
Roy Smith	4.017	119	538	25-27	.481	295	178	4.45
Mike Jeffcoat	4.026	175	398	20-22	.476	192	119	4.14
Pete Filson	4.138	148	392	15-18	.455	187	150	4.18

The chart above compares Doug Drabek's career records to those of other 4+ and 5+ starting pitchers.

As the chart clearly shows, Drabek has more career wins and more innings than any other 4+ pitcher, and almost any 5+ pitcher. He is superior to almost all of the other 4+ and 5+ starting pitchers in winning percentage, ERA, strikeout/walk ratio and all other measures of effectiveness.

Thus, any comparison of Drabek to other 4+ and 5+ starting pitchers can only show that Drabek should be paid more than the other 4+ and 5+ starting pitchers.

P-21

DOUG DRABEK COMPARED
TO JIM DESHAIES

In the Doug Drabek arbitration case one year ago, we argued that the most comparable pitcher to Doug Drabek at that time was Jim Deshaies of the Houston Astros. These were their 1989 records, and their career records through 1989:

1989 Records

	G	IP	W	L	Pct.	SO	BB	ERA
Drabek	35	244	14	12	.538	123	69	2.80
Deshaies	34	226	15	10	.600	153	79	2.91

Career Records

	G	IP	W	L	Pct.	SO	BB	ERA
Drabek	124	772	47	39	.547	446	215	3.35
Deshaies	121	739	49	36	.576	519	274	3.42

The arbitrator apparently accepted the validity of this comparison, and awarded Drabek a salary of $1,100,000, two percent more than Deshaies' salary of $1,075,000.

In 1990, however, Drabek and Deshaies had completely <u>different</u> seasons. Drabek had his best major league season; Deshaies had his worst.

<u>1990 Records</u>

	G	IP	W	L	Pct.	SO	BB	ERA
Drabek	33	231	22	6	.786	131	56	2.76
Deshaies	34	209	7	12	.368	119	84	3.78

Based upon a 7-12 record over 34 starts in 209.1 innings, with a 3.78 e.r.a. for the 5th placed Astros, Jim Deshaies received a raise of $1,025,000 to a salary of $2,100,000. For going 22-6 for the division champion Pirates, who set a record for attendance and winning the Cy Young award as the best pitcher in the National League, Pittsburgh proposes to pay DRABEK a raise of $1,200,000 to $2,300,000. Such a result would be clearly inequitable, as it would imply that the difference between a 22-6 Cy Young season and a 7-12 season is a minor thing. DOUG's brilliant 1990 season compels him to be paid significantly more than Deshaies. A salary of $3,350,000 is clearly the more appropriate salary.

==

P-25

Exhibit P-25 was designed to zone in on the salary request of $3,350,000 made for Drabek. The group on this list was starting pitchers who will earn $2,950,000 or more in 1991 or 1992, and covered the 1987-1990 seasons. Fifteen starting pitchers were in this group, and Doug was compared to them all in several categories.

Over the four year period, Doug trailed only Clemens, Stewart, Welch, Hershiser, and Viola. Two pitchers were found to be comparable to Doug — Dennis Martinez and Bret Saberhagen. Doug was superior to the rest of the group. This chart, and clones of it covering shorter periods, clearly established that Doug belonged with this group.

The chart for the 1990 season (Exhibit P-28) showed that only Bob Welch and Roger Clemens posted seasons which could be considered superior to Doug's. Thus, charts covering the criteria of career and past season were used as evidence in support of Doug's salary request.

ALL STARTING PITCHERS WHO WILL EARN $2,950,000
OR MORE IN 1991 OR 1992
1987 – 1990
(descending 1991 salary order)

Pitcher	1991 Salary	G	GS	W	L	PCT	IP	ERA	1992 Salary
Stewart, Dave	3,500,000	146	146	84	45	.651	1061.2	3.20	3,500,000
Welch, Bob	3,450,000	139	139	76	32	.704	944.0	3.21	3,450,000
Ryan, Nolan	3,300,000	129	129	49	46	.516	875.0	3.23	—
Higuera, Teddy	3,250,000	115	115	54	35	.607	794.1	3.37	3,250,000
Langston, Mark	3,200,000	137	137	60	55	.522	1006.1	3.56	3,200,000
Martinez, Dennis	3,167,000	122	121	52	35	.598	838.0	3.01	3,167,000
Browning, Tom	3,121,000	140	139	58	39	.598	911.0	3.82	3,121,000
Boddicker, Mike	3,083,000	137	136	55	46	.545	901.2	3.72	3,083,000
Morris, Jack	3,000,000	128	128	54	56	.491	921.0	3.13	—
Saberhagen, Bret	2,967,000	124	123	60	41	.594	915.0	3.13	2,967,000
Darwin, Danny	2,950,000	193	67	39	31	.557	672.1	3.11	2,950,000
Hershiser, Orel	2,950,000*	111	106	55	40	.579	813.2	2.60	—
Viola, Frank	2,950,000*	142	142	74	46	.617	1017.2	2.97	—
Clemens, Roger	2,800,000*	137	137	76	38	.667	1027.1	2.77	5,380,250
Hurst, Bruce	1,960,000*	132	132	59	39	.602	921.0	3.48	3,200,000
Drabek, Doug	3,350/2,300	130	127	62	37	.626	871.1	3.08	
Doug's Ranks Among Above Group:		10	11	5	6	5	12	5	

There are 16 pitchers in this group.

The only pitchers who have outperformed Doug Drabek over the last four years are Clemens, Stewart, Welch, Hershiser, and Viola. Three of these five men, Clemens, Stewart, and Welch, will earn more than we are seeking in this case. The remaining two, Viola and Hershiser, are special cases: both pitchers signed their contracts in April of 1989 and therefore have not benefited from the recent escalation of major league salaries; Hershiser's career is in jeopardy following the shoulder surgery that he underwent in April, 1990.

The only other pitchers in the group who are comparable to Doug for the four-year period are Martinez and Saberhagen. As the chart indicates, we are asking for $183,000 more than Martinez will earn this year, a difference of 5%. As for Saberhagen, he entered into his contract 15 months ago, thereby missing out on the recent escalation. Furthermore, his 1990 season was severely disrupted by an injury, a fact that will be quite evident in the 1990 statistics which will be presented in exhibit P-28.

*Collusion adjusted salary

STARTING PITCHERS
WHO WILL EARN $2,950,000 OR MORE IN 1991 OR 1992
(descending salary order)
1990 SEASON

Pitcher	1991 Salary	G	GS	W	L	PCT	IP	ERA	Salary 92
Stewart, Dave	3,500,000	36	36	22	11	.667	267.0	2.56	3,500
Welch, Bob	3,450,000	35	35	27	6	.818	238.0	2.95	3,450
Ryan, Nolan	3,300,000	30	30	13	9	.591	204.0	3.44	—
Higuera, Teddy	3,250,000	27	27	11	10	.524	170.0	3.76	3,250
Langston, Mark	3,200,000	33	33	10	17	.370	223.0	4.40	3,200
Martinez, Dennis	3,167,000	32	32	10	11	.476	226.0	2.95	3,167
Browning, Tom	3,121,000	35	35	15	9	.625	227.2	3.79	3,121
Boddicker, Mike	3,083,000	34	34	17	8	.680	228.0	3.36	3,083
Morris, Jack	3,000,000	36	36	15	18	.455	249.2	4.51	—
Saberhagen, Bret	2,967,000	20	20	5	9	.357	135.0	3.27	2,967
Viola, Frank	2,950,000*	35	35	20	12	.625	249.2	2.67	—
Darwin, Danny	2,950,000	48	17	11	4	.733	162.2	2.21	2,950
Hershiser, Orel	2,950,000*	4	4	1	1	.500	25.1	4.26	—
Clemens, Roger	2,800,000*	31	31	21	6	.778	228.1	1.93	5,380
Hurst, Bruce	1,960,000*	33	33	11	9	.550	223.2	3.14	3,200
DRABEK, DOUG	3,350/2,300	33	33	22	6	.786	231.1	2.76	
DOUG'S RANK AMONG ABOVE GROUP:		9	8	2	3	2	6	5	

* collusion adjusted salary

There are 16 pitchers in this group.

For the 1990 season, Doug Drabek's rankings among the $3,000,000+ pitchers are even higher than in the four-year comparisons. Close inspection of these ratings reveals that Roger Clemens and Bob Welch are the only pitchers in the group who had a better season than Doug. Of the rest, only Stewart and Viola turned in performances close to Doug's.

When the arbitration criteria of the performance for the past season is applied, it is another reason why Doug Drabek should be paid in the $3,000,000+ range with baseball's best starting pitchers.

Exhibit P-27 was designed to zone in on the salary request of $2,300,000 made by the Pirates. In a fashion analogous to Exhibit P-25, Doug was shown to be superior to all pitchers on this list for the period 1987-1990 (as well as for the 1990 season in Exhibit P-29).

Only Dwight Gooden, who had a collusion influenced salary (and who would soon sign a contract for approximately $5,000,000 per year) was comparable to Doug. Thus, a clear pattern of evidence had emerged to support Doug's salary request and to prove the inappropriateness of the Pirate's salary request.

ALL STARTING PITCHERS WHO WILL EARN
BETWEEN $2,000,000 AND $2,750,000 IN 1991 OR 1992
1987-1990 (descending salary order)

Pitcher	1991 Salary	G	GS	W	L	PCT	IP	ERA	1992 Salary
Liebrandt, Char.	2,667,000	127	121	43	45	.489	806.2	3.64	2,667,000
Maddux, Greg	2,662,000*	134	131	58	49	.542	880.0	3.62	
Smith, Zane	2,650,000	140	106	33	42	.440	744.2	3.57	2,650,000
Jackson, Danny	2,625,000	113	110	44	43	.506	717.2	3.74	2,625,000
Valenzuela, Fern.	2,550,000	121	120	42	48	.467	794.0	4.05	—
Gooden, Dwight	2,501,000*	112	110	61	27	.693	779.0	3.34	—
Black, Bud	2,500,000	127	88	37	32	.536	632.1	3.69	2,500,000
Gubicza, Mark	2,450,000	122	122	52	44	.542	860.1	3.36	2,450,000
Witt, Bobby	2,433,000	112	110	45	43	.511	733.2	4.27	2,433,000
Witt, Mike	2,400,000	129	119	43	54	.443	833.2	4.19	2,400,000
Sutcliffe, Rick	2,352,000*	106	105	47	37	.560	713.2	3.80	—
Sanderson, Scott	2,250,000	114	79	37	31	.544	512.2	4.06	2,250,000
DeLeon, Jose	2,167,000	135	133	47	53	.470	858.2	3.74	2,167,000
Gross, Kevin	2,133,000	129	123	41	54	.432	797.0	4.21	2,133,000
Young, Matt	2,133,000	107	37	14	30	.318	317.0	4.00	2,133,000
McCaskill, Kirk	2,100,000	98	97	39	33	.542	607.1	3.69	—
Garrelts, Scott	2,067,000	190	60	42	32	.568	579.2	3.26	2,067,000
Fernandez, Sid	2,017,000	124	120	47	37	.560	741.2	3.24	2,017,000
Key, Jimmy	2,016,000*	117	117	55	34	.618	763.0	3.47	2,548,000*
Davis, Storm	2,000,000	111	99	45	32	.584	576.0	4.34	2,000,000
Smith, Bryn	2,000,000	117	115	41	38	.519	705.1	3.50	2,000,000
Deshaies, Jim	2,000,000	125	124	44	42	.512	794.0	3.49	—
Drabek, Doug	3,350/2,300	130	127	62	37	.626	871.1	3.08	

DOUG'S RANKS
AMONG ABOVE GROUP: 5 4 1 6 2 3 1

* Collusion adjusted salary

Outside of the fact that a few pitchers have had more starting assignments and pitched a few more innings than Doug, only Dwight Gooden's four-year performance stacks up to Doug's. After all, Doug ranks 1st in two of the three bottom-line qualitative measures of pitching performance: wins and earned run average, and is second in winning percentage to Gooden.

When Gooden signed his current contract in 1989, it made him the highest paid player in baseball. As stated in P-8, Gooden's salary was negotiated prior to the substantial salary increases following the

1990 season and prior to the collusion settlement. It is likely that Dwight Gooden's next contract will call for a salary in the $4 million to $5 million range.

With Gooden's context understood, it is appropriate that Doug receive a higher salary than all of the other pitchers whose names appear on this chart.

Given Doug's clear superiority to this group of starting pitchers, it would be totally unjust for Doug to be paid $2,300,000 in 1991, a salary which, after the adjustment for collusion, would make Doug 12th out of the 22 pitchers on the list.

P-29

STARTING PITCHERS WHO WILL EARN
BETWEEN $2,000,000 AND $2,750,000 IN 1991 OR 1992
1990 SEASON (descending salary order)

Pitcher	*1991 Salary*	G	GS	W	L	PCT	IP	ERA	*1992 Salary*
Liebrandt, Charl.	2,667,000	24	24	9	11	.450	162.1	3.16	2667
Maddux, Greg	2,662,000*	35	35	15	15	.500	237.0	3.46	—
Smith, Zane	2,650,000	33	31	12	9	.571	215.1	2.55	2650
Jackson, Danny	2,625,000	22	21	6	6	.500	117.1	3.61	2625
Valenzuela, Fern.	2,550,000	33	33	13	13	.500	204.0	4.59	—
Gooden, Dwight	2,501,000*	34	34	19	7	.731	232.2	3.83	—
Black, Bud	2,500,000	32	31	13	11	.542	206.2	3.57	2500
Gubicza, Mark	2,467,000	16	16	4	7	.364	94.0	4.50	2450
Witt, Bobby	2,433,000	33	32	17	10	.630	222.0	3.36	2433
Witt, Mike	2,400,000	26	16	5	9	.357	117.0	4.00	2400
Sutcliffe, Rick	2,352,000*	5	5	0	2	.000	21.1	5.91	—
Sanderson, Scott	2,125,000	34	34	17	11	.607	206.1	3.88	2125
DeLeon, Jose	2,167,000	32	32	7	19	.269	182.2	4.43	2167
Gross, Kevin	2,133,000	31	26	9	12	.429	163.1	4.57	2133
Young, Matt	2,133,000	34	33	8	18	.308	225.1	3.51	2133
Deshaies, Jim	2,100,000	34	34	7	12	.368	209.1	3.78	2100
Garrelts, Scott	2,067,000	31	31	12	11	.522	182.0	4.15	2067
Fernandez, Sid	2,017,000	30	30	9	14	.391	179.1	3.46	2017
Davis, Storm	2,000,000	21	20	7	10	.412	112.0	4.74	2000
Key, Jimmy	2,016,000*	27	27	13	7	.650	154.2	4.25	2548 *opt
Smith, Bryn	2,000,000	26	25	9	8	.529	141.1	4.27	2000
Drabek, Doug	3,350/2,300	33	33	22	6	.786	231.1	2.76	
DOUG'S RANKS									
AMONG ABOVE GROUP:		4	4	1	2	1	3	2	
			(tie)						

* collusion adjusted salary

Doug's rank of first in wins and winning percentage, 2nd in earned run average, and high ranking in other categories demonstrate that Doug was superior in 1990 to the starting pitchers in the $2 million to $2.75 million range.

P-30

SALARIES AND RAISES EARNED BY
OTHER CY YOUNG AWARD WINNERS IN 1989 AND 1990

	Salary	*Next Season*
1989 NL Mark Davis	$ 600	$3250
1989 AL Bret Saberhagen	$1300	FIXED *
1990 NL **Doug Drabek**	$1100	$3350/$2300 ARB
1990 AL Bob Welch	$1358	$3450

Salaries listed on this chart have not been adjusted for the effects of collusion on Davis and Saberhagen.

The points we are making:

1) It is normal for Cy Young Award winners to receive very large raises, and

2) In recent years it has become normal for Cy Young winners to receive in excess of $3 million a year.

No recent Cy Young Award winner has signed a contract for less than the mid-point of this case.

* Bret Saberhagen's 1990 salary, after his Cy Young season, was fixed by a prior contract signed in February, 1988. However, he did sign a contract extension following the 1989 season. He will be paid $2.97 million per season over the period of the extension (1991-1993), plus incentive bonuses.

P-31

Exhibit P-31 showed that Doug was clearly superior to recently signed Pittsburgh starting pitcher Zane Smith. The Exhibit was designed to show that it would be unjust for Pittsburgh to pay Doug less than the Pirates had recently agreed to pay Smith.

SALARY OF ZANE SMITH

The Pirates will pay $2,650,000 per season to Zane Smith. Let us examine the contract of Zane Smith.

Zane Smith was 12-9 in 1990 and is 51 - 68 lifetime. He signed a contract calling for:

* a signing bonus of $500,000;
* $2,100,000 in 1991;
* $2,400,000 in 1992;

* * \$2,600,000 in 1993;
* * \$3,000,000 in 1994;
* * For a total of \$10,600,000 guaranteed for 4 years; (an average of \$2,650,000 per year)
* * \$235,000 in "award bonuses";
* * Single room

Zane Smith helped the Pirates over the final third of the season. However, DOUG DRABEK won the Cy Young award while Zane Smith did not receive a single vote. Yet, the Pirates propose to pay DOUG DRABEK less in 1991 than the average of Zane Smith's four year, guaranteed contract.

P-33F

Exhibit P-33F was a summary of the case designed to show that our number best addressed Doug's value in the context of the post-collusion salary structure and the criteria of salary arbitration. Much was again made of the issue of special accomplishments, because that was the one critical hurdle we needed to jump to get Doug far beyond his seniority group, and away from the applicability of the phrase "particular attention" to service groups.

THE KEY ELEMENTS OF THE DOUG DRABEK CASE: A SUMMARY

1. THE COURSE OF SALARY ESCALATION SINCE THE END OF THE 1989 SEASON

We have seen abundant evidence throughout the salary comparisons made in this hearing that players' salaries have been escalating rapidly over the last 15 months. This has been the case for all three of the general salary categories of players: those with less than 2 years and 128 days of service, none of whom is eligible for arbitration or free agency; those with 2+128 but less than 6 years of service, all of whom are eligible for arbitration; and those with 6 or more years of service, all of whom are part of a completely unfettered free-market salary system. It is the latter two groups that concern us in this case.

History will record that two events are largely responsible for the trend of escalation. The first event is the resolution of the past collusive practices of the clubs by way of a new Basic Agreement between the clubs and the players. This has enabled the market for free agents to become fully free once again and it has begun to correct the artificial depression of the salaries of younger players, in part through the principles and terms of Joint Exhibit 2. The second event is the sale of national television rights to the CBS and ESPN networks, which preceded the writing of the new Basic Agreement and which has undeniably altered the clubs' collective sense of the affordability of player contracts.

It will take some time to fully assess the effects on salaries of these two watershed events. In the meantime, however, there are some effects which can be traced rather precisely and which have direct relevance to Doug Drabek's salary. We are speaking, first, of the trend in top baseball salaries that has unfolded since November, 1989.

On the 17th of November, 1989, Kansas City Royals starting pitcher Bret Saberhagen signed a 3-year contract with an average annual value of $2,966,667. That contract made Saberhagen the game's highest paid player on an annual average basis. The glow of that distinction, however, would shine on Saberhagen for only 5 days, for it was on November 22nd that outfielder Kirby Puckett of the Twins signed a 3-year contract averaging $3,000,000 per year. Just six days later, Rickey Henderson of the A's joined Puckett atop the salary list by entering into a 4-year deal with a $3 million annual average value. On December 1st, before the ink was dry on that pact, starting pitcher Mark Langston signed on with the California Angels for an average of $3.2 million per year. Moreover, this was a 5-year deal, which has helped to reestablish an old pre-collusion practice with respect to contract length. Over the next seven weeks, three more players would nudge their way to the top of the salary mountain.

The following chart is the chronology of top-salaried players and their successors from November 17, 1989 through January 22, 1990:

Player	Club	Lg.	Signing Date	Position	Term of Contract	Average Annual Value
Saberhagen, Bret	KC	A	11/17/89	Starting P	1991-93	$2,966,667
Puckett, Kirby	MIN	A	11/22/89	Outfielder	1990-92	3,000,000
Henderson, Rickey	OAK	A	11/28/89	Outfielder	1990-93	3,000,000
Langston, Mark	CAL	A	12/01/89	Starting P	1990-94	3,200,000
Davis, Mark	KC	A	12/11/89	Relief P	1990-93	3,250,000
Stewart, Dave	OAK	A	1/17/90	Starting P	1991-92	3,500,000
Clark, Will	SF	N	1/22/90	1st Baseman	1990-93	3,750,000

Of particular importance is the Will Clark contract, the last one on the list, for it demonstrated that a player with less than 6 years of service could lay legitimate claim to the top salary slot.

We need to bear in mind, too, that the official emancipation of the players had not yet occurred. In fact, as we all no doubt remember, there would be a lockout of the players that would last for two months after the Will Clark signing. Thus all of the salary escalation to this point was based merely in the anticipation of a new salary regime. Nothing had yet been officially settled.

Tacit approval of the new Basic Agreement came in late March of 1990. Very soon thereafter, a new king assumed his position on the salary throne. On this occasion it was first baseman Don Mattingly of the Yankees, whose contract called for an average salary of $3,860,000 for five years' duration.

At about that same time, in April of 1990, the Chicago Cubs decided to reassess the contract of their top young starting pitcher, Greg Maddux. Maddux was coming off a fine 1989 season (19W-12L, 2.95 ERA, 238.1 IP) and the Cubs, one can reasonably infer, wanted to lock Maddux up for the 1991 season—before the rate of salary inflation would accelerate even further. There was an element of risk for the club in that they could not know for certain whether or not Maddux would continue to pitch as well as he had in the previous two years. On the other hand, the Cubs knew very well that if Maddux did turn in another solid season on the mound, they would be getting his services at a bargain rate by signing him a year in advance. So, the Cubs entered into a one-year $2.4 million contract with Maddux for 1991.

Thus the Maddux contract was a future-oriented deal. More to the point of today's proceeding, it was a contract made with a 3+ starting pitcher and it was based on just 674 career innings pitched and only two full years of play at the major league level. Both parties, we must assume, knew what they were getting into. We must also assume that they were pleased with the result.

What that contract represented with respect to Greg Maddux's peers was more than a doubling of the 1990 contracts. Specifically, the top two starting pitchers with 3 or 4 years of service at the time, Doug Drabek (3+) and David Cone (3+), were being paid $1.1 million and $1.3 million, respectively, for 1990. The only other starting pitchers who had cracked the $1 million barrier were Jim Deshaies ($1,075,000) and Tom Candiotti ($1,062,500), both of whom were

4+ players and neither of whom stacked up to Drabek or Cone in performance terms. What the Maddux contract signaled was that a Drabek or a Cone, if he continued to excel in the 1990 season, could already look forward to a contract of more than $2.4 million — and this was only April! With salaries on the constant rise, Maddux would almost certainly be surpassed and possibly by a wide margin.

And so the 1990 season began with a fundamentally different major league salary structure than had existed the year before.

It would take less than three months into the 1990 season for yet another new salary standard to be set. This time it was Oakland outfielder Jose Canseco who revised the major league salary structure. On June 27th, Canseco and the A's agreed to a contract that would guarantee the rightfielder $4,700,000 per year from 1991 through 1995. And there were more signings to come. Once the 1990 season ended, a new rash of inflation began, this time affecting primarily the non-stars, people like Zane Smith ($2.65 million), Danny Jackson ($2.625 million), and Bud Black ($2.5 million), just to name a few. These are starting pitchers who clearly do not measure up to Doug Drabek in terms of the quality or the consistency of pitching performance.

Then, in January of this year, another major signal was emitted to the negotiators for the clubs and the players. In this instance, it was the 3-year contract signed by relief pitcher Bobby Thigpen of the Chicago White Sox, which called for $3 million per year. Thigpen had set a record for saves in 1990 with 57, which had helped him to place fourth in the Cy Young voting in the American League. The distinctive feature of this signing, however, was that it involved a player with just 4 years and 21 days of service and just 382.1 innings of work under his belt. In other words, it established a new top figure for pitchers with less than 5 years of service.

When the clubs and the players filed their arbitration submissions on January 18th, yet another barrier came down. That is, nine players with less than 6 years of service submitted figures greater than $3 million, ranging from starting pitcher Tom Candiotti's request of $3,050,000 to first baseman Glenn Davis's submission of $3,650,000. Prior to this year, no player had ever sought $3 million via the arbitration process. If Thigpen had not consummated his contract before the filing deadline, the total would have been ten this time around.

While all of this was transpiring, it was becoming more and more obvious that a new peak would soon shoot through the top of the salary structure, for Roger Clemens and Dwight Gooden were approaching the final year of their contracts and it was time for them to meet with their clubs and settle on terms for 1992 and beyond. Probably no interested observer, from management or labor or the press, doubted that both Clemens and Gooden would make a run at, or even exceed, Canseco's level.

Sure enough, Roger Clemens, popularly known as "The Rocket," shot through the salary roof on February 8th. His new contract, with its annual price tag of $5,380,250, has once again redefined the major league pay scale. Dwight Gooden's contract, one can safely conclude, will not be far behind, in any sense. The pay scale that has now developed for the pitchers who have entered into contracts since the close of the 1989 season appears in the following chart (service time for those with less than 6 years is indicated in parentheses):

			Arbitration (plyr/club)
$5 million	—	Clemens Gooden (?)	
$4 million	—		
$3.5 million	—	Stewart, Welch	
$3 million	—	Langston, Ryan, Higuera, Martinez, Browning, Morris, M. Davis Darwin, Saberhagen, Boddicker, Thigpen (4)	*Arbitration (plyr/club)* Drabek (3.35/2.30) Candiotti (3.05/2.15) Rijo (2.90/1.60) Finley (2.80/1.75)
$2.5 million	—	Z. Smith, D. Jackson Valenzuela, Black, B. Witt, Garrelts, Maddux (4), S. Davis, DeLeon, Gross, M. Young, Deshaies (5), McCaskill (5)	Cone (2.45/1.95)
$2 million	—		

2. THE ISSUE OF SPECIAL ACCOMPLISHMENT

By any definition one might choose to invoke, Doug Drabek must be regarded as a player of special accomplishment. Here are the main reasons for this claim:

A. HE HAS OUTPERFORMED ALL OTHER PITCHERS WITH LESS THAN 6 YEARS OF SERVICE. The only pitchers with 4 or 5 years of service who are within any kind of reach of Drabek are Thigpen and Finley. But Thigpen, as accomplished as he is, is a relief pitcher, who cannot have the

overall positive impact on a club that a starter such as Drabek can have. And Finley has been on a par with Drabek for only the last two of their five years on the mound, thereby falling tangibly short of Drabek on "length and consistency" grounds.

B. DOUG IS THE ONLY STARTING PITCHER WITH 4 OR MORE YEARS OF SERVICE WHO HAS PERFORMED ABOVE THE LEVEL OF HIS LEAGUE, AS MEASURED BY THE EARNED RUN AVERAGE, SINCE HIS FIRST MAJOR LEAGUE SEASON AND WHO HAS SIGNIFICANTLY IMPROVED ON THAT MARGIN IN EVERY SUBSEQUENT YEAR. This unique achievement gives Doug as strong a performance profile and therefore as much current and future value as a club could hope for, short of having Roger Clemens on its roster.

C. DOUG IS ONE OF ONLY 12 ACTIVE PLAYERS WITH A CY YOUNG AWARD TO HIS CREDIT. Cy Young votes are often mixed and occasionally controversial. In Doug Drabek's case, there was no ambiguity, no doubt. He received every first place vote but one, and that writer placed Doug second. There have been just 12 unanimous selections in the 35-year history of this most prestigious pitching award. That represents 20.3% of the 59 awards that have been bestowed since 1956. The only active pitchers who have been selected unanimously are Rick Sutcliffe (1984), Dwight Gooden (1985), Roger Clemens (1986), and Orel Hershiser (1988). This puts Doug in very special company, indeed.

If the "special accomplishment" clause had been intended to refer only to the clear-cut best player or pitcher in the game, then it would apply only to Roger Clemens and perhaps Rickey Henderson or Jose Canseco. But if that had been the intent, then it would have been labeled the "unique accomplishment" clause or the "most valuable player/pitcher" clause. Unfortunately, though, the clause provides no guidelines whatsoever as to what constitutes special accomplishment.

As we see it, if it requires that one stand out among his service peers, then Doug Drabek qualifies. If it requires that one have a good rookie season and that he get better and better every year thereafter, then Doug Drabek qualifies. If it requires that one receive the highest form of recognition for the work that he has done, then Doug Drabek qualifies. If it requires that one help lead his club to a championship, then Doug Drabek qualifies. And if it requires that one be a model teammate and citizen, with intense mental discipline, good physical work habits, and undeniable devotion to his profession and to the success of his team, then Doug Drabek qualifies. But if it requires that one pitch a no-hitter, then Doug Drabek fails—by one batter in the bottom of the ninth with two out.

Assuming, as we do, that Doug is specially accomplished, the question becomes how to apply that elite status to the determination of his salary.

The explicit rules of procedure state that any arbitration candidate with less than 6 years of service may be compared to any group or subgroup, regardless of the issue of service time, but that "the arbitrator shall...give particular attention, for comparative salary purposes, to contracts of Players with Major League service not exceeding one annual service group above the Player's annual service group."

The rules go on to say that "this shall not limit the ability of a Player or his representative, because of special accomplishments, to argue the equal relevance of salaries of Players without regard to service, and the arbitrator shall give whatever weight to such argument as he deems appropriate."

On the one hand, these provisions clearly set a "special" player apart from his peers insofar as salary comparisons are concerned. On the other hand, they neither compel an arbitrator to disregard nor preclude an arbitrator from disregarding the matter of service time in arriving at a "special" player's salary. How far the arbitrator chooses to go, in either direction, within these loosely defined parameters is the arbitrator's sole prerogative.

What does all of this mean for Doug Drabek? Well, we would not presume to say how you ought to think or behave within the aforementioned bounds, Mr. Goetz. We would, however, like to tell you exactly how we see the matter. Indeed, we regard this as our central responsibility in this hearing.

3. THE 5 KEY ELEMENTS OF DOUG DRABEK'S CASE

A. DRABEK IS SUPERIOR TO DESHAIES AND McCASKILL

The Pirates' offer of $2.3 million places Doug Drabek in a salary class with Jim Deshaies and Kirk McCaskill, both of whom will earn $2.1 million this year. McCaskill, a California Angel, is with a club that wound up in fourth place last year and that hasn't made a serious run at the A.L. West flag since it won the division championship in 1986. Deshaies plays for a Houston club whose recent records are middling and whose attendance is near the bottom of the major league heap. Pittsburgh's N.L. East trophy from last season and its all-time attendance mark, though still short of the Angels' level, are factors that we believe offset the 9.5% gap between $2.3 million and $2.1 million, making those figures virtually the same. On the basis of their performances, Drabek should be well ahead of Candiotti and McCaskill in salary terms.

B. PENDING ARBITRATION RESULTS FOR INFERIOR PEERS

Then there is the matter of Candiotti, Rijo, Finley, and Cone, all of whom are within one year of Doug's service class and all of whom, as we have demonstrated, Doug has outperformed on a career basis and in 1990. All four of these pitchers stand an excellent chance of earning more than $2.3 million. In fact, the first three could earn $3.05 million, $2.9 million, and $2.8 million, respectively. Consequently, one has to conclude that the Pirates' submission is low and, pending the outcomes for this subgroup, perhaps extremely low.

C. THE MADDUX CONTRACT

The club's $2.3 million figure would place Doug distinctly behind Greg Maddux. The literal value of Maddux's contract is $2.4 million. To that amount, Joint Exhibit 2 directs us to add a post-collusion adjustment. Then there is the matter of the undervaluation of Maddux's contract because it was signed before the second and third tidal waves of post-1989 salary escalation. We have addressed these points, and our view is that the true current value of the contract is in excess of $2.65 million. We have also shown that Greg Maddux is a player to whom Doug is plainly superior in all respects.

D. THE THIGPEN CONTRACT

In addition, there is Bobby Thigpen to consider. A $2.3 million salary would put Doug at a level $700,000 behind Bobby Thigpen's $3,000,000 salary. We firmly believe that a top-flight starter such as Doug Drabek, who contributes 225 innings of outstanding work in a season, has substantially more overall value than Thigpen—a reliever who pitches 90 innings per season, who does not demonstrate the same degree of consistency as Drabek over the last five seasons, and who spent a good chunk of time in the minor leagues as recently as 1987.

The first 7, 8 or 9 innings in a game are every bit as important as the last inning or part of an inning, particularly when those initial innings are provided by a pitcher as effective as Doug Drabek. And then there is the matter of the 135-inning annual gap between Drabek and Thigpen. That represents nearly ten percent of a club's total innings pitched, a gaping hole which the reliever cannot fill but which the club is required to fill.

On these grounds, we believe that Doug Drabek is a distinctly greater asset to a club than Bobby Thigpen and that Doug is therefore entitled to more than the $3 million that Thigpen will be paid in 1991.

And so, even if there were no special accomplishment clause and if we were consequently confined to comparisons with players of similar service, we would argue that our submission of $3.35 million is more consistent with Doug's performance to date than is the club's.

E. $3,350,000 IS NOT TOO HIGH A FIGURE

The next question, then, is whether our figure would place Doug too high on the totem pole. More specifically, are there any veterans out there whose post-1989 salaries are lower than $3.35 million who have outperformed Doug. The answer, very simply, is "No."

We honestly believe that, as we speak, Doug Drabek is the third most valuable starting pitcher in baseball behind Roger Clemens and Dwight Gooden. However, arguments could be made for Dave Stewart and Bob Welch of the Oakland A's. It was in specific deference to Stewart and Welch that we selected a figure lower than their salaries. Therefore, we do not feel that we have pushed our submission to, nor certainly beyond, its outer limit. To the contrary, we believe that $3.35 million is exactly the right salary for Doug Drabek in today's market.

So, whether it's a question of where to place Doug relative to his peers or where to allow his special accomplishments to place him relative to those with more service time, the answer is the same—distinctly above $3 million but not more than 10% or so above Bobby Thigpen.

In effect, then, there is really no need to invoke the special accomplishment clause, even though it appears to be well warranted, because a straight competition with his service peers gets Doug to our submission. If, on the other hand, you deem it appropriate to compare Doug's salary straight up with the salaries of other pitchers — regardless of service time — you will find that much more support for our submission.

Several interesting exchanges occurred in the Drabek case. Tal Smith's arbitration team, which represented the Pirates, argued that Doug Drabek was subject to the Cy Young jinx. They introduced a chart which showed that in recent years virtually every pitcher except Roger Clemens had suffered a decline in performance in the year subsequent to his Cy Young year. The Smith team clearly intended to place doubt in the mind of arbitrator Raymond Goetz.

The argument was an offshoot of a favorite club tactic — to create the feeling in the arbitrator's mind that he will look like a fool if he rules for the player. One could also term their argument the regression to the mean.

In connection with the Cy Young jinx argument, the Smith team argued that salary arbitration eligible players do not receive salary cuts. While the arguments were clever, I was very pleased that they used those arguments. I knew that Goetz had decided Bret Saberhagen's salary arbitration case in favor of the player. This followed the 1985 season in which Saberhagen won the Cy Young Award and led the Kansas City Royals to the World Series. The next year, Saberhagen had an off year and voluntarily took the maximum 20 percent pay cut. I reasoned that since Goetz lived in Kansas, he had to know that Saberhagen took a cut following the 1986 season.

I also knew that Goetz had ruled for the Dodgers and had given Orel Hershiser a salary cut in a salary arbitration case following the 1986 season. Hershiser had posted a 19-3 record in 1985, and he won a salary arbitration case, which granted him a raise to $1,000,000 from his prior salary of $212,000. In 1986, though, after Hershiser was 14-14, the Dodgers filed at $800,000—a 20 percent salary cut.

I had a ready response to both arguments of the Smith team. I noted that Drabek did not appear on their Cy Young jinx chart because his 1992 performance remained to be seen. "We are here," I said, "to determine Doug's salary based upon his past performance, not upon conjecture about his future performance." Besides, I pointed out, if Doug Drabek suffered from the Cy Young jinx, he would take a salary cut the next year, just as had Bret Saberhagen and Orel Hershiser.

Following the conclusion of my surrebuttal argument, and aware that the Smith team had unwittingly reinforced my position, I experienced perhaps my most serendipitous moment in salary arbitration.

The history of exhibit P-33F is noteworthy for several reasons. Many Hendricks cases have "skipped numbers" in the exhibits or have exhibits with letters attached to the numbers. The reasons for this are that the cases expand and contract as new data is received and as the hearing date approaches.

As the Hendricks salary arbitration team assembles for a hearing, we review the case and play "devil's advocate." It is our goal to predict the club's case, and we are usually right on target.

I know that Steve Mann and Bill James will show up with some last-minute exhibits which belong in the case. We also create new exhibits on our portable computers within hours of the scheduled hearing. The case expands and contracts, too late to renumber the dozen copies of the "final" case which left Houston with me.

I prepared most of the Drabek case, from its strategy to its exhibits. Bill James and Steve Mann each contributed several important exhibits, which I incorporated into my theme. As we reviewed and discussed the case the night before the hearing, we were confident it would be a winner.

We knew what we would hear from the Pirates—several different attacks on why our number was too high, or "overreaching." Tal Smith's team was too experienced to try to make Drabek look bad, an impossible task anyway.

As we adjourned our meeting at 1:30 A.M., Steve Mann said: "The only thing missing is a summary. We need one so the arbitrator will have no doubt that we should win. I'll work on it." Thus, was Exhibit P-33F born in the middle of the night before the Drabek case.

٭   ٭   ٭

The preparation and trial of a salary arbitration case by the Hendricks team involves a tremendous amount of teamwork. Over the past several years, our team has included both Bill James and Steve Mann. As noted, Bill started working with us after the 1979 baseball season and has worked with us ever since. We first noticed him when we saw an advertisement for his home-produced book, which analyzed the performances of major league players. After reading his book, we telephoned to ask if he would like to work with us on salary arbitration cases. He jumped at the chance.

In those early days, we "holed up" at my house and prepared charts by hand, using calculators. It would often take two to three hours to prepare a chart. Sometimes the chart "did not work" and the effort seemed wasted, except for the knowledge gained that either the theory being tried did not work, did not fit the case, or yielded a totally different result than anticipated.

Today, thanks to the availability of complex statistical performance data and computer programs written specifically to aid in the preparation for salary arbitration, we can generally prepare a chart in two to three minutes. While finalizing a chart for use in a case requires a lot of polishing, the preparation of a chart for case evaluation is no longer the laborious task it once was.

During Steve Trout's salary arbitration hearing before arbitrator Steve Goldberg following the 1981 baseball season, I introduced a Bill James chart which was designed to prove that Trout's record of 9–16 with the White Sox in 1980 was a function of poor offensive and defensive support, and was not a proper measure of Trout's pitching performance that season. We asserted that with average run support and average defense, Steve's record would have been 13–12 or 14–11.

In those days, the club's rebuttal preceded the player's rebuttal. During the White Sox rebuttal, then assistant general manager and now Florida Marlins general manager, Dave Dombrowski, questioned the exhibit and scoffingly said, "Who is Bill James?" During my rebuttal, I introduced another "James exhibit." That exhibit covered every starting pitcher in the American League Western Division and clearly supported the methodology used in reconstructing Trout's won-lost record.

Those exhibits represented Bill James at his best — producing a specific exhibit to prove an important point in a case. I call those exhibits "pearls," and I often ask Bill to put on his deep sea divers' suit and find me some pearls. He always obliges.

It was not long before people stopped asking, "Who is Bill James?" As his published works drew greater attention, his fame in the world of baseball analysis increased until he assumed celebrity status. His annual *Baseball Abstract* combined wit and wisdom, though it took its toll on him over the years as it became more of an obligation than a labor of love.

As Bill James became more and more involved in the publication of various books and articles, his availability to us was reduced to the type of "open window" NASA uses to launch space flights. He would be available to us, but only at the end of January, just as he exhaustedly completed another book.

Happily for HSM, Steve Mann offered his services to us in 1987, before James' availability became somewhat curtailed. Steve Mann came aboard in January of the 1988 arbitration season. That inaugural journey had its moments, including the "famous" George Bell meeting. There was no question, though, that Steve brought an added dimension to our team.

Mann had worked for the Tal Smith team, so he had a well-developed perspective on how management typically viewed a case. He also designed the computer system for the Smith team. That system was important, because the Smith team often had to prepare twenty or more final cases each year, never knowing, like us, which cases they would have to try. The Smith team's problem was much more acute than was ours, because in any year they might have had between forty and fifty cases scheduled in mid-January.

While Bill James is a laconic, humorous analyst, Steve Mann is a hard-driving, tough-minded competitor, who thrives on mental combat. Steve still plays competitive baseball in his forties, and reminds me that the competitive softball I play in my late forties is a far cry from real baseball. Of course, I remind him that I prefer to "play" a hit-and-field game than "watch" a pitcher-catcher game. And I am also not reluctant to remind him that the team I play for, the Grey Sox, won the Texas state championship in the masters division in 1992.

Our "rivalry" is extraordinarily good-natured and keeps us both razor sharp. Steve is a great teammate, and he works as tirelessly as do I. His reliability is second to none.

The 1992 salary arbitration season covering the 1991 baseball season produced an exhilarating and exhausting test of the Hendricks team. While I try to avoid having more than one case set for trial per day, that year I was "doubled-up" on the Jay Buhner and Bob Milacki cases. I was scheduled to try the Buhner case in the morning and the Milacki case in the afternoon of the same day.

Since most cases settle, I was not overly concerned when the schedule was announced in mid-January. Nor was I overly concerned that Brian Holman's case was scheduled for the morning after Milacki's case.

As usual, I had picked the numbers submitted for each player, subject to the client's approval. While I solicit input and recommendations on each number from our team, the final call is mine. The number selected is very important, because it is irrevocable. It is also important to try to predict the number the club will file, as well as to predict future signings of comparable players, since those signings help shape the market for the player in arbitration.

Since the advent of computer programs for use in salary arbitration preparation, our numbers have been selected after careful research and case analysis. In the "old" days, our numbers were sometimes a product of "wishful thinking." It is difficult to overemphasize the importance of the number selected. Texas Rangers general manager Tom Grieve has said, "The number is everything."

Once the numbers of the player and the club are announced, the hard case preparation begins. A good case, to quote Michael Pare in *Eddie and the Cruisers*, combines "words and music." In the salary arbitration world, those components are "statistics and legal arguments."

The first case I worked on in 1992 was Brian Holman's. Holman had completed three seasons as a starting pitcher but had suffered a severe shoulder injury in late September. He underwent what is now known as "Orel Hershiser surgery" (a reconstructed rotator cuff) at the end of the 1991 season. It appeared that Brian Holman would miss most of the 1992 season.

One of the criterion of salary arbitration is the existence of any physical defects. Other criteria include the quality of the player's performance during the prior season and over his career. Our number of $1,180,000 reflected an approximate 15 percent discount from my judgment of Holman's value as a healthy player. Seattle filed at $425,000, or 36 percent of our number. The one and only way Seattle could have defended its number was by arguing that Holman's "physical defect" outweighed all other criteria. I was prepared to argue that salary arbitration involves, essentially, a retrospective analysis, not a prospective one. Thus, I would have argued that what my client had done over the prior three seasons, not speculation on what the next season might hold, should have been dispositive of the case. The Holman case would have been largely a legalistic one, since each number supported a different theory of the proper application of the criteria, rather than a different interpretation of Brian's statistical performance.

After my preparation of the Holman case was completed, I turned my attention to Bob Milacki's case. Because the Buhner case was scheduled for the same day, Steve Mann focused on it.

While other cases were also being "worked on" by members of our team, I wrote a draft of the Milacki case while Steve wrote a draft of the Buhner case. Meanwhile, Bill James worked on finding "pearls" to put in both cases. Alan, Joe Sambito, and recent team addition, June Higgins, were taking special requests from me on the other cases.

While I built Bob Milacki's case on his comparability to the other 3+ starting pitchers, Steve Mann built Jay Buhner's case on the correlation of salary to slugging percentage. When we were finished with our drafts, we each "shipped" them via modem to the other for review. Meanwhile, Bill James prepared charts for our review and for possible inclusion in the cases we had drafted.

As the salary arbitration season progressed, a number of our cases settled. However, large differences remained between the settlement proposals in the Buhner, Milacki, and Holman cases. With all three cases scheduled within a twenty-eight hour period, and the trial dates rapidly approaching, our team headed for Chicago, the site of the hearings. Alan, Joe, June and I left from Houston. Steve flew out of Philadelphia, while Bill left from Kansas City. Since Bill's hometown of Winchester, Kansas, is about 40 miles northwest of Kansas City, one could almost make him another member of the Kansas City baseball connection.

Just before we left for the airport, we received news that Jay Bell had lost his case before arbitrator Gil Vernon. Bell, like Buhner, was a 3+ player. Bell's number was $1,450,000, and the Pirates' number was $875,000. Buhner's numbers were $1,445,000 and $750,000 and his case was scheduled before arbitrator Vernon the next morning.

The first thing I did when I arrived at the Hyatt Regency in Rosemont was to telephone Michael Weiner and Doyle Pryor to request that they send me a copy of both Jay Bell's and the Pirates' case. The prevailing view of the union lawyers was that the Bell decision did not bode well for Buhner. Seattle obviously shared this view, as club negotiator Norm Gurwitz told Alan that the Bell decision reinforced their determination to hold tight at its $1,000,000 settlement offer. "Besides," Norm told Alan, "this is our chance to stop the Hendricks winning steak," a reference to the fact that we had not lost a case in six years. We told the Mariners that we were not interested in their offer.

After I read the club and player briefs in the Bell case, I considered it unimportant to Buhner for several reasons. First, I concluded that I would have argued Bell's case on a very different theory than the one primarily advanced on his behalf. Second, shortstop Bell and right fielder Buhner played different positions. Third, our premise in the Buhner case would be totally different from the one used in Bell's case. Fourth, we would not rely on any of the evidence presented by either side in the Bell case.

Bill had brought his exhibits for all three cases. He was somewhat concerned with Buhner's case, and wanted to read the "final" draft, since he had previously read only the first draft.

In the face of Bill's concern, Steve remained supremely confident in our Buhner case. The final case represented a fine tuning of his draft, with several important exhibits added by Bill and me.

It is often a mistake to oversimplify the theories presented in a case, but I believed that the Buhner case would become a contest between the relative importance of slugging percentage, home runs, and RBI and the relative importance of batting average and full-time playing status. While Jay Buhner's case may have represented a classic example of "too high" versus "too low," I believed the balance lay in our favor.

I was very satisfied with the final Milacki case before I left Houston. I knew that Baltimore was not convinced that Bob Milacki had permanently arrived as a major league starting pitcher. Their opinion, I believed, could not be backed by compelling statistical evidence.

The Milacki case was a good example of how a player can be viewed differently by his agent and by his club. I advised Alan that we were 2 to 1 favorites, and since Baltimore had offered only 31 percent of the $480,000 spread ($1,180,000 versus $700,000), I recommended that Bob decline the Orioles' settlement offer. When each side in a case believes that it is a 2 to 1 favorite, then that case should be tried.

As I lay in bed the night before the Buhner case, I thought of how ironic it was that the arbitration schedule had produced a triple header for me. I preferred to stagger cases every other day, and now I would "pitch" back-to-back-to-back "games."

The Buhner case was worth $695,000 to the winner, and it was scheduled from 9:00 A.M. to 12:30 P.M. The Milacki case was worth $480,000 to the winner and was scheduled from 1:30 P.M. to 5:00 P.M. The Holman case was worth $755,000 to the winner, and would commence at 9:00 A.M. the following day.

The next morning brought no movement, so the Buhner case was a "go." At the beginning of each case, during "housekeeping," briefs are exchanged. As usual, I presented the direct case, or case-in-chief, while Mann and James reviewed the Mariners' brief. Their immediate review gave us extra time to prepare for our rebuttal. Since the player is allotted only a fifteen minute break between the conclusion of the club's direct presentation and the commencement of the player's rebuttal, every extra minute to analyze the opponent's attack counts.

During a club's presentation, I take notes for use in rebuttal. At the conclusion of the club's direct case, Mann, James, and I huddle and quickly divide the responsibilities for our rebuttal. Our biggest problem is cramming all of our comments and counterattacks into the thirty minutes alloted for a rebuttal. A typical rebuttal involves fifteen minutes from me, ten minutes from Steve, and five minutes from Bill. I require more time in order to counterattack the music, or legal arguments of the other side.

Rebuttal is a "fun" time for us, for I do not believe that a more formidable arbitration team exists. Our overlapping skills and differing perspectives enable us to thoroughly analyze our opponent's case.

After the Buhner case was completed, everyone on the Hendricks team went to lunch, except me. I went to our "war room" to rehearse for the Milacki case. While there, I fielded a call from Orioles general manager Roland Hemond, who was calling to express his disappointment that we had not settled Bob Milacki's case.

Even though I had known the always polite general manager for many years, I barked at him after he suggested that Milacki should not be "put through" the arbitration process. The call was a signal that the Orioles planned to attack Bob. I was unmoved, since I had prepared Milacki for what the club would likely say.

Both the Buhner and Milacki cases were argued very well by all involved. Leonard Levine of Los Angeles argued the Buhner case for Seattle, while Lon Babby of Williams & Connelly of Washington,

D.C., argued the Milacki case for Baltimore. After arbitrator Anthony Sinicropi heard the Milacki case, our team retired to the war room to discuss both the Buhner and Milacki cases prior to continuing our preparation for the Holman case. As usual, we voted on whom each of us thought had won.

The voting was not unanimous in either case. However, Steve, Bill, and I voted that we had won both cases. I kidded everyone that our three votes were the only ones that counted. Alan responded by saying that Steve would say we had won no matter what had happened in the hearing—a tribute to Steve's ultra-competitive nature. As everyone laughed, Steve demurred, saying he called them as he saw them.

We continued kidding each other with what remained of our nervous energy. During the Milacki case, June Higgins made the "mistake" of whispering to Joe Sambito that I sounded tired. She said that I was much better in the Buhner case, because I had been highly energetic during that case.

Poor June! After Joe innocently repeated her comment, I screamed at her, saying that she had been in too many moot court cases and not in enough real ones. I stared at her as I said I had "got in all of my evidence and proved up my case and that's what counts, not style points." When I wasn't looking, I think she threw a punch, or at least a glare, at Joe for his indiscretion.

As the evening progressed, we continued tinkering with the Holman case. Alan was on the phone talking to Seattle. The Mariners were no longer as self-assured as they were before the Buhner case. They had seen their "unbeatable" case severely challenged and knew that the following day would bring more of the same.

Alan and I had discussed a very complex two-year proposal for Brian Holman. We considered all sorts of solutions, including a two-year contract loaded with incentives to cover days on the active roster (i.e. health), games started, and innings pitched.

Alan and Gurwitz traded offers as the evening progressed. After midnight, Alan approached me with a revised two-year proposal from the Mariners. "What do you think?" he asked. "I don't think anymore," I said. "I'm somewhere between brain-dead and running on empty. Call Brian and ask him. I have to be ready in the morning."

Holman was in the hotel. He and Alan discussed the proposal and worked up a counteroffer. Finally, after much back-and-forth negotiating with Seattle, a two-year contract was consummated before 2:00 in the morning.

Brian and his wife, Jami, came to the war room to express their appreciation. Their middle of the night visit was very much appreciated by everyone on our team. I gave Jami two extra copies of the case and told her that she could use them for Brian's version of "This Is Your Life," since otherwise those copies would be filed in our office.

I was happy, tired, and frustrated all at the same time. The Holmans' gratitude was uplifting, yet, once again, I had put much effort into a case, only to see all of my work go into a file cabinet.

I was glad, though, for a good night's sleep. Just before noon, I was awakened by Alan, who had received a phone call from Arthur Schack. We had won the Buhner case. That "woke me up." Before our team had time to come back down to earth, the phone rang. It was Arthur again. I read Alan's face before he spoke. We had also won Milacki's case.

Chapter 8

The Pirates: A Study in How to Assemble and Dismantle a Great Club

The Messersmith-McNally decision of December 1975 and the resulting Collective Bargaining Agreement of August 1976, sounded the death knell of the perpetual reserve system in baseball. Prior to the passing of this era, clubs needed a good scouting program and a good player development program in the minor leagues in order to establish a winning major league club.

Beginning in 1977, clubs were able to add players to their major league rosters through the acquisition of free agents. Clubs were also subject to losing major league players through the same free agent system. This new reality required increased management skills of front office executives.

During the initial years of free agency, aggregate player salaries were relatively low. Clubs continued focusing mostly on whether they wanted a player on the club, rather than on the player's "value," or the correlation of a player's ability to his salary.

This is not to say that clubs did not have budgets, because they did. Nor is it to suggest that management personnel had no sense of value. Some club executives did "value" players, but the aggregate economics of the game did not enforce a disciplined approach to monetarily "valuing" players.

As a rule, management personnel generally had an overwrought attitude regarding player salaries and value. This type of attitude was evidenced by the constant complaints that players were "overpaid." These were actually complaints about an increasing salary structure, not criticism based upon the correlation of a player's ability to his salary.

The proof that clubs did not generally measure value was found in the fact that they did not "non tender" players based upon their potential salaries being higher than their value. Rather, they released players when they believed a player could no longer adequately perform at a major league level of skill.

Winning baseball clubs are built around a nucleus of outstanding players. Enlightened club management has always recognized this fact. As the system in baseball changed, it became more important to "value" players. Intangibles had to be added into the mix of variables used to determine value.

It thus became very important for a club to decide which players to sign to long-term contracts and when to sign them. It became critical to sign the players who would likely form the nucleus of a club. These players carry a club because of their abilities, and because they help establish the necessary "chemistry" found on championship clubs.

The Los Angeles Dodgers reacted to the reality of the new free agent system by signing their outstanding infield of Steve Garvey, Davey Lopes, Bill Russell, and Ron Cey to long-term contracts. This insured the continuity of their winning tradition, which had been maintained, in large part, by the play of this outstanding infield, which hit the field together in 1973.

A more recent example of a club signing a young franchise player to a long term contract was in October 1993, when the Chicago White Sox signed Frank Thomas. Even though he had accumulated only three years of major league service, the White Sox signed the American League Most Valuable Player through the year 2000. In November 1993, the Detroit Tigers signed 3+ shortstop Travis Fryman to a five-year contract. Both players were handsomely paid, and their contracts reflected a greater appreciation of their outstanding ability than of their service time. Their contracts also reflected commitments made by enlightened clubs to build a championship team around a franchise player.

As player salaries continued to escalate and profit margins were squeezed in the 1990s, club management was forced to evaluate players based upon value. For players who had acquired salary arbitration rights, or free agent rights, clubs became as interested in the player's precise salary as in his precise ability. If the player was not "worth" his likely salary, based upon the criterion of seniority, clubs were no longer reluctant to cut the player's salary. As management, players, and agents accepted this trend, it became a part of the mechanism for determining player salaries. The result was that clubs finally started offering veteran players a salary decrease if their production was not up to their prior performance level.

Today, one hears complaints about the difficulties involved in running a modern major league club. However, club officials have always complained in public about how difficult their job is—whether it's closing a trade, signing a player, turning a profit, or dealing with the union. While sports reporters have dutifully reported this somewhat gratuitous whining, they have generally neglected their journalistic duty to raise the question of whether these whining officials were simply overmatched by agents, the union, or the system. As the game has grown more complex, increased skills are required to manage a club. Individuals with versatile skills are therefore a necessity for a "modern" club.

During the collusion era of 1986-1989, clubs were in the unique position of controlling key players without fear of losing them in the free agent market. The quality of management required to manage a club thus regressed to prefree agency times. Player salaries were repressed during the collusion period, and player movement was minimal.

By the end of the collusion era, the Pittsburgh Pirates had established the nucleus of a great club. Most of their key players were salary arbitration eligible players who needed several more years to become eligible for free agency. All of those fine young players were more than willing to sign long-term contracts and commit their futures to a Pirates club managed by Jim Leyland, one of baseball's very best managers.

The failure of Pittsburgh management to sign those players to long-term contracts after either the 1989 or 1990 season is one of the most glaring examples in modern baseball history of a flawed management strategy. Furthermore, the failure to sign those players constituted a breach of faith with Pirates fans. Amazingly, this misguided strategy and its failure have gone largely unreported in the national press. Instead, the press largely accepts the explanations offered by Pirates' management that the club lost its star players because it was a small-market club unable to afford to sign them.

Pittsburgh sportswriter Bob Hertzel was among a few commentators who reported that the Pirates were the victim of self-inflicted wounds. Their hardball management tactics failed to recognize that their emerging star players were key employees who were instrumental to the club's future success — not replaceable labor unionists to be hardballed during contract negotiations. The real story is not that a small-market club lost its star players over economic circumstances, but rather that the management of that club failed to capitalize on the opportunity to sign *all* of those players when they were both affordable and eager to sign long-term contracts.

The Pittsburgh Pirates were one of the most successful baseball clubs on the field during the 1970s, finishing first in the National League's Eastern Division six times, second three times, and third once. The Pirates won division titles in 1970, 1971, 1972, 1974, 1975, and 1979. They finished second in 1976, 1977, and 1978. They finished third in 1973. The Pirates capped off the club's best ever decade with a dramatic comeback from a 3–1 deficit to defeat the Baltimore Orioles in the 1979 World Series.

The 1980s saw the Pirates' fortunes on the field decline. They finished third in 1980, fifth in 1981, fourth in 1982, and second in 1983. These Pirates clubs were competitive, as evidenced by the winning records posted in 1980, 1982, and 1983, but none made a serious run for the division flag.

The 1984 season represented the beginning of a significant decline for Pittsburgh. The club finished last, a position the Pirates would repeat in 1985 and 1986. The club hit bottom in 1985, when they lost 104 games. The 1986 season was not much better, as the club lost 98 games.

The free fall in the standings during 1984-86 represented an embarrassing decline for a franchise which had not finished more than 9 games behind the division champion since 1969. The 1984 club finished 21½ games out of first, the 1985 club ended the season 43½ games out of first, and the 1986 club finished 44 games out of first.

Prior to the 1986 season, the Galbreath family sold the franchise to a group of local, corporate dominated owners. The 1986 *Sporting News Baseball Guide* referred to "a commitment to youth" by the new owners to turn around the fortunes of a franchise that had hit rock bottom.

New front office employees Syd Thrift and Larry Doughty quickly demonstrated a superior ability to identify the talent necessary to rebuild the Pirates. As a result, the Pirates started amassing a nucleus of outstanding young players. Just as importantly, the Pirates shrewdly hired Jim Leyland, who would later distinguish himself as one of baseball's best managers. After the disastrous 1986 season, few outside observers would have predicted that the Pirates would become a dominant club within a few seasons.

The Pirates had the sixth pick in the first round of the 1985 draft and used that pick to select multitalented outfielder Barry Bonds, a future most valuable player. Third baseman Bobby Bonilla became a Pirate for the second time when the Pirates traded Jose DeLeon to the White Sox for Bonilla in July 1986. The Pirates had originally signed Bonilla as a free agent in 1981, but lost him to the White Sox in December 1985 in the rule 5(e) draft between major league clubs.

Pitcher John Smiley was called up from class A baseball to the Pirates major league club in September 1986. A twelfth round selection in the 1983 draft, Smiley's future performance in Pittsburgh would justify the Pirates' bold move to vault him past Double A and Triple A directly to the major leagues.

On November 26, 1986, the Pirates traded pitchers Rick Rhoden, Cecelio Guante, and Pat Clements to the New York Yankees for three young pitchers: Logan Easley, Brian Fisher, and Doug Drabek. The addition of future ace Drabek to the starting rotation would bolster the Pirates' pitching for years to come.

On April 1, 1987, the Pirates traded catcher Tony Pena to St. Louis for outfielder Andy Van Slyke, catcher Mike LaValliere, and pitcher Mike Dunne. Notwithstanding the loss of Pena's ability, the trade would yield large dividends to the Pirates for years to come. Dunne became the rookie pitcher of the year in 1987, before fading primarily due to injuries. Van Slyke became a perennial gold glove center fielder and club leader. LaValliere replaced Pena and won a gold glove himself.

Jose Lind was signed by Pittsburgh as a free agent in 1982. He made the Pirates major league club for the first time in 1987 and became a fixture at second base for years to come.

In August of 1987, the Pirates claimed pitcher Jim Gott off of waivers from the San Francisco Giants. Gott had missed most of the 1986 season due to injuries. He became a reliable closer for Pittsburgh.

In an amazingly short time, the Pirates were transformed, for

Bonds, Bonilla, Smiley, Drabek, Van Slyke, LaValliere, Lind, and Gott would form the nucleus of a division championship club within a few seasons.

The results on the field were immediate and dramatic. Pittsburgh won 80 games in 1987, a 16 game improvement over the disastrous 1986 season. This placed the Pirates in a fourth place tie with the Philadelphia Phillies.

The 1988 season represented the first full season together for the newly-assembled core players. Drabek, Smiley, and Gott were the mainstays of a pitching staff that decreased its earned run average from 4.20 to 3.47 — an outstanding 73-point improvement in one season. Van Slyke, Bonds, and Bonilla had their best years at the plate. As a result the Pirates finished 85–75, earning second place. Attendance rose to 1,866,713, an all-time Pittsburgh record. The future looked very good for this dynamic young club.

As the 1989 season approached, the Pittsburgh faithful were optimistic that the Pirates would finally catch the New York Mets. The 1986 World Champions had just lost to the Los Angeles Dodgers in the 1988 league championship series. The Mets were a very good club, but they lost to a hot Dodgers club, led by ace Orel Hershiser. The Dodgers would go on to upset the heavily favored Oakland A's in the World Series.

The avoidance of injuries plays a large part in the success of a club, and injuries would "help" torpedo the Pirates' 1989 season. Jim Gott was lost for the season in early April after only two-thirds of an inning. Mike LaValliere became injured and missed two-thirds of the season. Andy Van Slyke, then the leading offensive player on the club, was injured. Though he missed only 32 games, Van Slyke was severely hampered for most of the season and played at a level below his norm. First baseman Sid Bream missed the entire year. The result was that the Pirates finished fifth with a record of 74-88. Attendance dropped to 1,374,141.

There were still individual bright spots. Doug Drabek posted a 2.80 earned run average, sixth best in the National League. He pitched 244⅓ innings, allowing opponents only a .238 batting average. Due to poor run support, Doug finished only 14–12. Drabek clearly needed his 5 shutouts to post a winning record.

The Pirates franchise was at a crossroad. The expectations for the 1989 season had not been met, primarily due to injuries, and attendance declined. At the same time, the core group of fine young players were all eligible for salary arbitration.

Club management had several options. It could have dismissed the 1989 season as a product of injuries and projected a continuation of the progress from the 1988 season into the 1990 season, barring the recurrence of injuries. Under such a scenario, the club would have signed its core group of players to long-term contracts at collusion depressed salaries. Those salaries would have been very reasonable indeed.

The Pirates front office believed strongly in the ability of its core players. Had the club signed those players, it would have followed the lead of the Dodgers in the 1970s, mirrored the strategy of the Indians over the past two years, and followed the pattern of numerous other successful clubs over the past fifteen years. The club would have demonstrated to both the players and fans alike that the Pirates were committed to winning for years to come through the leadership and ability of those all-star caliber players.

Club management had another option. The Pirates could have signed one-year contracts with its core group of players. Such a strategy could have been justified on the hope that the club would rebound in 1990. The members of the core group were either two or three years away from becoming eligible for free agency. The Pirates could have easily justified this strategy to the players and their agents by stating that the club needed one more year to evaluate its results both on and off the field.

The players and their agents could have been told that if the 1990 season proved successful, the club would offer multiyear contracts to the players who had maintained or improved their performances. This strategy would have been readily understood, and all involved would have been focused intently on producing a great 1990 season for Pittsburgh. A sense of unity would have been created, even with the players recognizing that their long-term rewards would be "on the come."

The club had a third option. It could have concluded that its fortunes on the field and at the box office would not improve. Under this assumption, a logical step would have been to adopt strict controls on player costs. The next step in the progression would have been for the club to play "hardball" with its players in contract negotiations.

History recorded that Pirates management, led by Douglas Danforth, adopted the third option. One of the "costs" of this approach was the alienation of its key players.

So, the Pirates adopted a confrontational style in contract negotiations following the 1989 season. Pittsburgh management declared
publicly and privately that the club would make its best offer to each
player through the number it filed in salary arbitration. Thus, if contract negotiations were not concluded by the date for submitting
irrevocable numbers for salary arbitration, it was most likely that
contract negotiations would be resolved through salary arbitration
hearings.

By adopting such a position, the Pirates were effectively declaring themselves exempt from the effects of new player signings as the
salary arbitration season progressed. Pittsburgh management demonstrated no interest in an extended dialogue calculated to lead to a
mutually agreeable resolution of the contract negotiations. The
Pirates believed that the salary arbitration process could be used to
control player costs, and upper management gave little consideration to the long term impact of this policy on its relationship with
its core players. This policy was not embraced by Pirates general
manager Larry Doughty, who was appropriately apologetic for the
nonnegotiating policy of the club.

The Pirates got their wish and went to salary arbitration with
eight players following the 1989 season. The following summary of
those salary arbitration cases reveals the financial effects of the club's
policy.

Player	Player Salary	Club Salary	Arbitration Salary	Midpoint Salary
Doug Drabek	$1,100,000	$ 750,000	$1,100,000	$ 925,000
John Smiley	840,000	630,000	840,000	735,000
Billy Hatcher	690,000	525,000	690,000	607,500
Bob Kipper	525,000	380,000	525,000	452,500
Rafael Belliard	380,000	235,000	380,000	307,500
Bobby Bonilla	1,700,000	1,250,000	1,250,000	1,475,000
Barry Bonds	1,600,000	850,000	850,000	1,225,000
R. J. Reynolds	785,000	535,000	535,000	660,000
			$6,170,000	$6,387,500

The eight cases exceeded the number of cases a typical club has
in five years. The Pirates saved a total of $217,500, or $27,187.50 per
player, compared to settling all eight cases at the midpoint. Compared to midpoint settlements, the Pirates saved approximately 3.5
percent by going through arbitration. However, if it cost the Pirates
from $20,000 to $30,000 to try each case, then Pittsburgh did not
save any money.

The Pirates were publicly pleased after their first three cases. Club president Carl Barger defended the club's policy of arbitrating instead of seriously negotiating with the eight players, even though Pittsburgh had gone to salary arbitration only three times between 1974 and 1989. After the Pirates defeated agent Dennis Gilbert's salary arbitration team in the Bonilla and Reynolds cases, Barger's comments about the Pirates victories and his defense of the club's negotiating policy were reported in the February 19 *Sporting News*:

> We don't gloat and get elated when we win in arbitration, and we don't sulk when we lose. The system doesn't permit happiness. But did we do the right thing? Yes.

I tried the Drabek and Smiley cases. The decisions to decline the Pirates' settlement offers were easily made. The Pirates offered Drabek $785,000 to settle his case. That offer represented 10 percent of the $350,000 difference between the numbers filed by the player and the club. Smiley was offered $651,000 to settle his case. That offer also represented 10 percent of the $210,000 difference in his case.

Drabek had no compunction about declining the Pirates offer. Alan and I kidded him that he was betting a BMW to win a house.

Alan and Smiley had the following exchange when Alan phoned John with the Pirates' best and final offer:

Alan: "What do you think about their offer?"

John: "I don't like it. Why are they doing this?"

Alan: "It's a test; they want to see if you're a man or if you're a mouse, and I don't want to hear any squeaking out of you."

John: "Don't worry buddy."

I put it to Smiley another way the night before his case: "They would rather prove how tough they are instead of how smart they are."

The paltry settlement offers made to Drabek and Smiley were typical of the settlement offers made to the other players. Rather than communicate to its players that the club preferred a negotiated resolution, the Pirates implied that they preferred a policy of confrontation.

The Pirates' negotiating strategy following the 1989 season produced no significant monetary savings. The cost of the strategy was a tremendous amount of ill-will generated between the club and its players, especially Bonilla and Bonds.

The March 12, 1990, *Sporting News* reported that the eight Pirates cases exceeded the number of salary arbitration cases done by the entire American League. Next to Pittsburgh, the most cases tried by a club was two. Pittsburgh *Sporting News* correspondent John Mehno reported the reaction of the Bonds' camp after the Pittsburgh left fielder lost his case:

> "Barry would prefer they just trade him," said Rod Wright, Bonds' agent. "As far as the Pirates' players, coaches and manager, he enjoys them and thinks it's a great team to play with. But he hasn't been dealt with fairly."
>
> "This doesn't have to do with winning or losing arbitration. You can take losing if you feel you've been treated fairly."
>
> . . .
>
> "I've been representing players since 1978, and I've never seen it. The Pirates did that with all of their players. Rather than negotiate, they decided they'd take their chances in arbitration. That doesn't build morale. What goes around comes around."

Mehno wrote that when Bonds reported to spring training, he tried to smooth over the things his agent had said. Still, Mehno suggested, that "hard feelings lingered" with Bonds.

Bobby Bonilla was more direct about his loss in salary arbitration. "I am hurt" by the club's policy of refusing to negotiate in good faith, he told Bob Hertzel. Hertzel wrote in the April 9, 1990 *Sporting News*:

> The relationship between a baseball player and management is fragile at best. The player is an employee, but he is also the product and, as such, sometimes needs handling that is not found in any corporate handbook.

Collusion had severely depressed the salary structure in baseball through the 1989 season. If Pittsburgh had the vision to capitalize on this market condition and sign its key players to long-term contracts, they would have been able to do so at prices which would have represented bargains for years to come.

*   *   *

The most appropriate time for a club to sign a key young player to a long-term contract is after the player has accumulated four years of major league service. After four major league seasons, the club will usually have a firm opinion of whether the player is a key player and figures in its future plans. Since a four-year player needs two more years of service until he is eligible for free agency, the prospect of a multiyear, guaranteed contract is quite alluring at that point in his career.

When a club signs its key players to long-term contracts, it sends a strong signal to its community that the club intends to try to win. Commitment to winning is a strong marketing tool. Fans respond when they have hope that the club can win. When a club is genuinely able to sell "hope," its attendance reflects that "fact." Additionally, because the players on the club recognize that a sincere effort is being made to win, their motivation and collective effort also improve.

Conversely, when a club signals that it is not serious about winning, attendance suffers. In 1993 San Diego jettisoned all of its highly paid players, except for Tony Gwynn. The fans reacted negatively, as one might have expected, when their hope for a good season was taken from them. The situation in San Diego was most egregious, because the club reneged on a preseason commitment not to trade its highly salaried players. Unsurprisingly, ticket sales dropped from 1,953,462 in 1992 to 1,375,432 in 1993 (official National League "attendance" in 1993 represented ticket sales, whereas it previously represented fans in attendance).

The 1993 Houston Astros are a recent example of the importance of the creation of "hope." The 1992 Astros drew 1,211,412 fans, primarily because the community recognized that John McMullen wanted the lowest possible payroll while he attempted to sell the club. The Astros let their free agents move on in the early 1990s and were inactive in the free agent market, except for some shrewd signings of players trying to re-establish their careers.

The 1992 Astros turned their season around in August of that year, and they went on to finish fourth with a record of 81–81. Following the 1992 season, Drayton McLane, Jr., purchased the Astros from John McMullen. McLane immediately demonstrated a commitment to the fans. He made changes at the Dome, including upgrading the food quality and establishing family nights.

More importantly, he signed free agent Texans Doug Drabek and Greg Swindell. Drabek, from the town of Victoria, 120 miles southwest of Houston, played baseball at the University of Houston. Swindell had helped lead Houston's Sharpstown High School to the state championship. He was also a stellar pitcher for the University of Texas. Not only were two local pitching heroes signed to help anchor the starting pitching staff, but Chris James, from Houston's Stratford High School, and former Astro Kevin Bass were signed for outfield depth.

Fan interest and hope for the 1993 season rose immediately. Not since the 1986 Astros club, which lost a heartbreaking playoff series to the Mets, or the 1980–81 Astros, who lost equally dramatic playoff series to the Phillies and the Dodgers, had the Astros roster generated so much fan enthusiasm. Fans and media talked about the Astros challenging the Braves in the NL West.

In February 1993, Houston signed key four-year players Ken Caminiti, Craig Biggio, and Steve Finley to multiyear, guaranteed contracts. In one dramatic off-season, the Astros management regenerated hope and solidified its roster for the long term. The club was aware of the importance of these players to its future. It was also mindful that a club can trade a quality player under a multiyear contract.

The 1993 Astros fell somewhat short of expectations, finishing third with an 85–77 record, an improvement of only 4 games over the 1992 club. Most observers considered the 1993 club to have been a good bit better than the 1992 club. The 1992 Astros were outscored by their opponents 668 to 608, while the 1993 Astros outscored opponents 716 to 630. The 1992 Astros were 32–21 in one-run games, while the '93 Astros were 19–24 in one-run games.

Excluding the difference in one-run victories, the biggest fall off from 1992 to 1993 was in the performance of the bullpen, especially the performance of closer Doug Jones. Jones had signed as a free agent in 1992 and had reestablished himself by saving 36 games while posting an 11–4 record. He was named the Astros most valuable player in recognition of that outstanding season. Jones was 4–10 in 1993 with 26 saves. His 4.54 earned run average and 102 hits allowed in 85⅓ innings underscored his inconsistency. In December 1993, Houston traded Jones to Philadelphia for closer Mitch Williams.

Ironically, Drabek and Swindell did not lead the starting pitching staff in 1993. Darryl Kile, Pete Harnisch, and Mark Portugal all exceeded expectations and ranked among the best starting pitchers in the National League. Still, Drabek and Swindell assumed the pressure that goes with being the one-two starters on a good staff.

Hope, more than on-field performance, resulted in ticket sales of 2,084,618 for the Astros in 1993, an increase of 28 percent over the 1,626,020 tickets sold in 1992. Hope for a better club in 1994 should cause the 1994 Astros to draw even better.

Cleveland is another team which has demonstrated the importance of creating hope among fans. The Indians, trying to reverse forty years of losing and below average attendance, started signing its key young players to multiyear contracts in 1992 and 1993. General Manager John Hart convinced club ownership that it had to establish a strong club identity centered around players to whom the club had made a commitment. The strategy was designed to change the image that good young players would pass through Cleveland, but would not stay. The strategy also targeted the 1994 season, in which the Indians would play their games in a new, state of the art stadium in downtown Cleveland.

The 1992 Indians finished 76–86, and the club drew 1,224,274 fans. The 1993 club also finished 76-86, but drew 2,177,908 fans. The 1993 club suffered a devastating loss in spring training, as pitchers Steve Olin and Tim Crews were killed and pitcher Bob Ojeda was severely injured in a boating accident. Hart demonstrated exceptional sensitivity and leadership during very trying times. Manager Mike Hargrove helped keep his club focused during a season made difficult by the loss of these key performers.

Tim Crews had signed as a free agent for the 1993 season, yet the Indians treated his family as one of their own. He was a client of ours and an outstanding person. He made friends easily everywhere he went.

Through the character demonstrated during the adversity of 1993, the commitment to key players, the prospects of a new stadium, and the leadership of its management, the Indians regenerated hope in the community. The result was a dramatic increase in attendance in 1993.

And to its core group of good young players, the Indians added free agents Dennis Martinez and Eddie Murray in December 1993. While time will tell if Martinez and Murray were the "right" players for the Indians, the strategy of management was the "right" one.

*   *   *

At a time when Pittsburgh should have been building bridges with its key players, it was burning them. The Pirates should have signed Bobby Bonilla to a long-term contract after the 1989 season. Instead, they forced him into salary arbitration by making a low-ball

settlement offer. Their low-ball settlement offer could only be interpreted by Bonilla as a challenge to go to salary arbitration.

When a player elects to go through a salary arbitration hearing
because he believes that he has a better case than the club, or because
he believes that the club's offer to settle is inadequate, the player and
his agent recognize that they have had the option "to settle or to
go." While a loss creates disappointment, the player also recognizes
that he and the club drew the battle lines together. Under such a
circumstance, it is easier to accept the loss and get on with the season.

Bobby Bonilla, though, felt forced into salary arbitration. As is
the case in virtually every salary arbitration hearing, the player's ability
was criticized. This "stung," as did the loss in salary arbitration. The
stage was thus set for difficult negotiations the next year.

At the end of 1989, the top salary in baseball was the $3,250,000
salary I had negotiated for Cy Young Award winning, free agent Mark
Davis. With the Davis contract creating a ceiling, and considering
Bonilla's four years of major league service and his salary arbitration
request of $1.7 million, it was reasonable to presume that Bonilla
would have signed a five-year guaranteed contract for between $10
million and $12 million. Had the Pirates been willing to make such a
commitment, the contract would have averaged between $2 million
and $2.4 million per year.

It is possible that Bonilla would have signed for around $9 mil-
lion, given the security such an offer represented. Whether $9, 10,
11 or 12 million, the Pirates would have secured Bonilla's services
though the 1994 season.

The Pirates became a very good club in 1990. They won the
National League Eastern Division championship, but lost the
National League title to eventual World Series champion Cincinnati.
The Pirates were led by Barry Bonds, the National League Most Valu-
able Player, Bobby Bonilla the runner-up in MVP voting, and Doug
Drabek, a Cy Young Award winner. Pittsburgh had arrived as a club.

Storm clouds were forming on the horizon. Despite winning
the division title, the Pirates were back in salary arbitration with four
of their key players. Because John Smiley broke his hand during the
1990 season, his contract was resolved without the need for a salary
arbitration hearing. However, second baseman Jose Lind replaced
Smiley as one of four key Pirates who would go through a salary
arbitration hearing.

Bobby Bonilla was now a player with five years of major league service. The Pirates tried to sign him to a multiyear contract. No effort was made, though, to sign four-year players Drabek and Bonds.

Bonilla was definitely signable as 1991 began. As reported in the January 7, 1991, *Sporting News*, the Pirates star right fielder said, "I love Pittsburgh, but I will not be penalized to play there." If the Pirates star was hoping for a quick, agreeable contract negotiation, he would soon be disappointed. His negotiations were filled with acrimony which had carried over from the 1990 salary arbitration hearing. The Pirates offered Bonilla approximately $16 million for four years, but he wanted more money for four years, and approximately $20 million for five years.

Negotiations continued without a resolution, and both parties appeared to be headed for a second straight salary arbitration case. Bonilla filed a number of $3.475 million, while the Pirates filed at $2.4 million.

I had just completed negotiations on an $11 million three year, guaranteed contract for third baseman Kelly Gruber of the Toronto Blue Jays, a five-year veteran. Gruber had finished fourth in the 1990 American League Most Valuable Player voting. Kelly Gruber and Bobby Bonilla were comparable players. Both were primarily third basemen, although Bonilla had been shifted to right field by the 1990 season. Gruber was an outstanding defensive player, while Bonilla's move to right field was caused by his erratic play as a third baseman.

Bonilla played significantly more than did Gruber in 1986 and 1987. While Gruber became a full-time player in 1988, Bonilla had amassed larger career statistics through 1990. Still, given their strong 1990 season performances and high placement in the Most Valuable Player voting, both players remained the most comparable player to the other. The 1990 season statistics for Bonilla and Gruber demonstrated that comparability:

	G	AB	R	H	2B	3B	HR	RBI	AVG	OBP	SLG
Bonilla	160	625	112	175	39	7	32	120	.280	.322	.518
Gruber	150	592	92	162	36	6	31	118	.274	.330	.512

The career statistics through the 1990 season reflected Bonilla's greater playing time:

	G	AB	R	H	2B	3B	HR	RBI	AVG	OBP	SLG
Bonilla	761	2717	408	757	157	31	98	426	.279	.350	.467
Gruber	688	2219	321	590	111	19	83	326	.266	.313	.445

Gruber's contract averaged $3.667 million per season and was consummated a week before Bonilla's scheduled hearing. The Pirates offered Bonilla $3.1 million to settle his salary arbitration case. This represented 65 percent of the difference between the salary arbitration numbers of the Pirates and Bonilla. The Pirates were obviously trying hard to sign their right fielder. In ordinary times, the Pirates offer to settle the case would have been sufficient.

The Pirates multiyear contract offer was reasonable, given Gruber's contract. But even though the Pirates and Bonilla were roughly 6 percent apart on a multiyear contract, neither party would agree to the other's offer. The smoldering feelings from the previous year were rekindled, and Bonilla rejected the one-year settlement offer. The case proceeded to a salary arbitration hearing.

I had tried the Drabek case the day before Bonilla's case was to be heard. The decision in Drabek's case was rendered the morning of Bonilla's case. The Drabek victory at $3.35 million represented the largest victory in salary arbitration history. His raise of $2.25 million represented the largest raise ever received through this process. In fact, the raise Doug received was larger than the highest salary previously awarded in salary arbitration.

Buoyed by our victory, Bonilla and his representatives proceeded optimistically to his hearing. Incredibly, Bonilla lost. He was now a two-time loser in salary arbitration and would play in 1991 for $2.4 million.

For all practical purposes, the Pirates could now forget about signing Bonilla, a very affable player who would become obsessed with money and his impending free agency during the 1991 season. The Pirates had won two battles, but they would lose the war. And they had not really saved any money in the process.

This situation could have been avoided had the Pirates signed Bonilla for approximately $2.2 million per year on a five-year contract following the 1989 season. Following the 1990 season, they would pay Bonilla $2.4 million after defeating him in salary arbitration.

As it turned out, the Pirates paid Bonilla $3.65 million for 1990 and 1991, an average of $1.825 million per year, after defeating him twice in salary arbitration. The club could have signed Bonilla to a two-year contract for that amount following the 1989 season and had a satisfied player, not a disgruntled one. Had Bonilla signed a two-year contract, negotiations for a multiyear contract extension probably would have proceeded cordially. It would have been highly unlikely that the 6 percent difference between the numbers of the Pirates and Bonilla would have scuttled a long-term contract, as actually occurred in early 1991.

Because the salary structure was in a rapid, postcollusion ascent, the Pirates could not sign Bobby Bonilla to a four-year contract at $4 million per season. Despite the largess of their offer to Bonilla, the Pirates inflexible policy continued as the club elected not to offer multiyear contracts to players with four years of service. Accordingly, the Pirates made no effort to sign either Barry Bonds, the National League Most Valuable Player, or Doug Drabek, the Cy Young Award winner, to a multiyear contract prior to a salary arbitration hearing. Bonds was not very pleased with the club's policy. Amazingly, instead of trying to sign Bonds, the Pirates considered trading him.

Carl Barger was quoted in the January 21, 1991, *Sporting News* concerning the possibility that the Pirates might trade Bonds: "There's a difference of opinion within our organization about whether or not this is the time to trade Barry Bonds. A lot of the difference of opinion comes when you analyze what he can bring."

A year later, Bonds was still incensed about a comparison the Tal Smith team had made in support of the Pirates in the prior year's salary arbitration hearing. When the Pirates compared Bond's RBI total as a leadoff hitter to the totals of cleanup hitters Jose Canseco and Kevin Mitchell, Bonds responded, as reported in the February 11, 1991, *Sporting News*, "I didn't want to put on a Pirates uniform again." When asked about the current year's impending case, Bonds said, "I'll get 'em. You better believe I'll get 'em." Carl Barger was nonplussed. The same story reported his response: "I believe the best thing that ever happened to (Bonds) was he got so mad (at losing) at us at taking him to arbitration that he had a great year."

The Pirates had a golden opportunity to sign Bonds in 1991, and, by his own words, he indicated that he would have signed a long-term contract at $4 million per season. Whether at $4 million per season, or $3.5 million per season, the Pirates could have signed the Most Valuable Player to a five-year contract through the 1995 season.

Bob Hertzel wrote of Bond's frustrations in his N.L. Beat column in the February 11, 1991, *Sporting News*:

Barry Bonds either wants to be with the Pittsburgh Pirates for a long time or not at all. Bonds told the Pittsburgh Post-Gazette that he wants a long-term contract now. He said that if he doesn't get one, no amount of money will keep him in Pittsburgh when he's eligible for free agency after the 1992 season. "I don't care if they offer me $100 million. I'm gone," he said. The Pirates have no plans to offer Bonds more than a one-year contract.

"I'm tired of this, sick and tired," the 26-year-old left fielder said. "Any other club in baseball would be trying to sign me to a multiyear contract at $4 million a year without blinking an eye." . . .

Bonds, who said he won't settle (his case) for less than $3 million, doesn't figure to strike a compromise before next week's hearing. . . .

"You can't touch what I did. I will not lose," (said Bonds). . . .

The Pirates, who have said on more than one occasion that Bonds will not be offered a long-term contract this winter, have considered trading him.

As the cases for Drabek, Bonilla, and Bonds headed for repeat hearings, the Pirates did make bona fide efforts to settle each case. Barger stated the club's revised policy toward settlement in the February 4, 1991, *Sporting News*:

"We have some room (for settlements) in our figures. Not immense room, but some. A lot depends on the agents. I wish the spread wasn't as large in some cases, but I think our figures make a lot of sense."

None of the Pirates' settlement offers were sufficient to induce the players to accept them.

Bonds' salary arbitration hearing was scheduled for the day after Bonilla's. Bonds filed at $3.25 million, and the Pirates filed at $2.3 million. Those numbers were slightly below the numbers filed in the Bonilla case. Both players were outfielders and played for the same club. They finished at the top in MVP voting.

At the time of Bonds' hearing, the Drabek decision had been announced. The Bonilla decision was pending. After the Bonds hearing was completed, the Bonilla loss was announced. It is very likely that the Bonilla decision sunk Bonds.

Most observers believe that it is a stretch to compare a pitcher to a regular player. Thus, it is quite likely that the arbitrators in the Bonilla and Bonds cases ignored the Drabek decision and concentrated on the comparability of other regular players to the two Pirate outfielders. In light of the Gruber contract, the Bonilla decision remains inexplicable. Once Bonilla lost, though, it became relatively easy for the arbitrator in the Bonds case to give the Bonilla decision precedential weight.

Like Bonilla, Bonds became a two-time loser in salary arbitration. The Pirates' best chance to sign Bonds had come and gone.

We had asked the Pirates for a multiyear contract for Drabek. Doug was happy with his teammates, manager Jim Leyland, pitching coach Ray Miller, and the city. Like Bonds, we were rebuffed.

Prior to Drabek's hearing, we offered to settle the case at $3 million, which was two-thirds of the difference between our number of $3.35 million and the Pirates' number of $2.3 million. The Pirates offered to settle the case at the midpoint salary of $2.825 million. Doug and Kristy Drabek told me that I should decide whether to accept or reject the Pirates' offer. When I protested and said that I did not believe I should make that decision, Kristy laughed and said that my victory the previous year had earned me the right to decide. Besides, she told me, "We can live just as well on $2.3 million." Doug smilingly nodded his assent.

Satisfied that the Drabeks would accept victory or defeat with equanimity, I notified the Pirates that their offer was unacceptable. I reiterated our settlement offer, but the Pirates were not interested. With a $175,000 difference in the final settlement offers, I made travel arrangements for the trip to Chicago, where the Drabek case would be heard. With cases also scheduled for Chuck Finley, Greg Swindell and Eric King, I had hotel rooms booked for our entire salary arbitration team for a solid week. The cases would be heard at the O'Hare Hilton. Using the underground tunnel from the airport terminal to the hotel, I spent seven days in Chicago that February without ever going outside. From my hotel room window I saw the weather change from overcast, to near blizzard conditions, to sunny skies. My life was totally unaffected by this weather, as my commitments kept me indoors and focused on the four cases scheduled to be tried that week.

I rejected the Pirates' settlement offer because I believed that my case was a winner. Several hours after the case was finished, Alan and I met with Larry Doughty. I reiterated my offer to settle the case for $3 million, figuring that the Pirates would be more interested in that offer after they had heard my case. I also reiterated Doug's desire for a multiyear contract.

My posthearing settlement offer was met with some amusement by the affable Doughty, who dutifully communicated my offer to Carl Barger. The Pirates believed they had won the case, Doughty advised us, but they would settle at $2.825 million, their prior offer. Larry, Alan, and I laughed at the irony of each side believing that it had won the case, yet reiterating prehearing settlement offers. We agreed that the high esteem in which Doug Drabek was held had led to the continued settlement discussions.

The Pirates had no multiyear offer for us, Larry Doughty said, but he advised us that the club would make one during spring training. As Alan and I left Doughty's hotel room, I said to Alan, "Isn't it funny how many times both sides think they've won a salary arbitration case. The Pirates don't know that they just got beat." Alan agreed, but he suggested that since no one ever truly knows what an arbitrator will do, the more amazing thing was that the Pirates had not made a multiyear offer to their Cy Young Award winner.

Alan, Joe Sambito, a former client who has been a colleague since his retirement from baseball, and I had an informal bet on what the Pirates would offer Drabek in spring training. If our bets had been placed on the "Price Is Right" show, the buzzer would have sounded, for we all guessed well over the Pirates' four-year offer of $14 million, which included the current year. Though Doug had just won $3.35 million for 1991, the Pirates offered, essentially, a flat contract of four years at $3.5 million per season.

We offered $18 million for four additional years, but our offer was summarily rejected by Larry Doughty. When I asked why his offer was so low, he replied that his offer was all he had been authorized to make. He could not disagree when I said that the Pirates' offer did not represent a bona fide effort to sign Drabek to a long-term contract. I told Doughty that the Pirates appeared to have a club policy of being "a day late and a dollar short." Rather than getting upset with me at the flippancy of my comment, he indicated that his hands were tied, a statement I found rather easy to accept.

Prior to Doug Drabek's salary arbitration hearing, the Pirates could have signed him to a five-year contract for between $16 million and $17.5 million. Such a contract would have averaged between $3.2 and $3.5 million per year. The Pirates would then have had one of their key players signed through the 1995 season. After the salary arbitration hearing, the Pirates would pay Drabek $3.35 million for 1991.

Bonilla, Drabek, and Bonds could have been an integral part of the Pirates' team through at least the 1994 season at an annual cost of approximately $9.2 million. Instead, none of the three players wears a Pirates' uniform, and they presently earn approximately $17.8 million in annual salaries.

The $8.6 million annual difference between the salaries these three players earn and what they would have signed for with Pittsburgh, contrasts starkly with the average of $168,750 per player saved by the Pirates in salary arbitration in February 1991 (when the club won three cases — Bonilla, Bonds, and Lind, and lost the Drabek case). Carl Barger's defense of the Pirates' strategy in salary arbitration was modified, again, after the four cases were decided. As reported in the March 4, 1991, *Sporting News*, he said, "You never really win in arbitration. It's a terrible process. I'm not gloating."

In contrast to Bonilla, Drabek and Bonds, the Pirates signed Andy Van Slyke and Mike LaValliere to long-term contracts. It is notable that neither of these two players ever went to salary arbitration to resolve a contract negotiation. After Bonilla rejected the Pirates' multiyear offer in February 1991, the ever witty Van Slyke set the stage for his own contract extension by publicly stating that he would sign an extension "in blood" if the Pirates made him the same offer they had made to Bonilla.

By the end of March, Van Slyke had signed a three-year contract extension "in ink" for $12.65 million, or $4.216 million per year. He was and is a defensive standout and a far better defensive player than Bonilla. The rapid signing of Van Slyke occurred despite the fact that he had been overshadowed recently as an offensive player by Bonilla. The following chart reveals the extent of that offensive superiority:

1990 Season

Player	G	AB	R	H	2B	3B	HR	RBI	AVG	OBP	SLG
Bonilla	160	625	112	175	39	7	32	120	.280	.322	.518
Van Slyke	136	493	67	140	26	6	17	77	.284	.367	.465

It is noteworthy that Van Slyke was able to achieve a superior contract within a few weeks, while Bonilla could not achieve one in over two years.

Mike LaValliere became a free agent after the 1991 season, yet re-signed with the Pirates for three additional years. During the Pirates' obsession with going to salary arbitration, our client LaValliere was able to resolve his contract negotiations without resorting to salary arbitration.

Part of the reason was that both the Pirates and our firm recognized that LaValliere's contract situation was an unusual one. There were no proper comparables in his service group. He was a defensive standout at catcher. The pitchers on Pittsburgh liked to pitch to "Spanky" because of the way he called a game. It is difficult to quantify the defensive attributes of a catcher, so we resolved each of LaValliere's contracts based upon extended dialogue with Larry Doughty about the unique situation. Not unsurprisingly, we were able to continue this dialogue and re-sign LaValliere with the Pirates rather easily even after he became a free agent.

Van Slyke, LaValliere, Smiley, Drabek, Bonilla, Bonds, and Lind all wanted to remain in Pittsburgh and play for Jim Leyland. This core group of Pirates players was so good that the Pirates won the National League East Division three straight seasons during 1990–92. Had the Pirates treated all of these players as key employees, resolved contract disagreements firmly but amicably, and had the initiative and foresight to sign all of these players to multiyear contracts, the Pirates would have remained a juggernaut for years to come. Instead, they fell into mediocrity in 1993, with only Van Slyke still on the club.

The Pirates developed an acute case of "financial myopia" during the 1989–92 period. Rhetoric about impending doom was the party line. Rather than signing its key players to multiyear contracts, the Pirates' brass publicly complained about the unfairness of life.

Pittsburgh writer Bob Hertzel was not fooled. Writing in *The Sporting News* on February 25, 1991, after the completion of the arbitration season, Hertzel editorialized:

> When the Pittsburgh Pirates captured last season's National League's East championship with a talent-laden lineup that included the league's Most Valuable Player (Barry Bonds), the runner-up in the MVP voting (Bobby Bonilla) and the Cy Young Award winner (Doug Drabek), cries of "break up the Pirates" could be heard gathering in the distance.
>
> Those cries may be answered sooner than anyone expected, because the Pirates' management is seriously considering dealing at least one of its star players in an effort to make ends meet. Such is the situation today in what some refer to as the rich team-poor team baseball environment.
>
> Pirates President Carl Barger has become baseball's self-appointed inflation fighter, preaching doom and gloom for

franchises in smaller markets if what he perceives as the fiscal madness that has gripped baseball is not controlled.

But the louder he roars, the more the spending increases. When the Red Sox gave Roger Clemens a contract extension that made him the game's first $5 million man, Barger lashed out at Red Sox General Manager Lou Gorman, as much for the timing of the extension — a week before the Pirates took Bonds, Bonilla and Drabek to arbitration — as for reaching a new salary plateau.

"We have been trying to sign Clemens for five months," Gorman said, "What am I supposed to do? Call Pittsburgh and find out what would be a good time?"

But Barger's anger can be understood, because his team [is] in a vulnerable position.

"Wouldn't it be tragic if it reached the point where you couldn't afford to win?" he asked, aware that a glance at the Pittsburgh financial statement showed that his team lost $7 million in 1990 despite a championship season and record attendance.

Drabek was awarded $3.35 million in arbitration, but Bonilla lost his case and will have to settle for a 1991 salary of $2.4 million. Bonds also lost his hearing and will be paid $2.3 million instead of the $3.3 million he was seeking.

Drabek's award is the largest ever granted in arbitration. In fact, Drabek, who earned $1.1 million in 1990, received a larger raise than the total salary any player had ever earned in arbitration.

After Clemens signed his extension, the Pirates figured they might be looking at a possible 1991 payroll of $25 million. In some ways, the Pirates' protests were unfounded. The bulk of the $7 million that is claimed as an operating loss remains in the Pirates' treasury, the loss being the result of the collusion judgment and of an obligation to pay released pitcher Walt Terrell $2.1 million.

The Pirates wrote off $8 million in collusion payments for 1990, yet those payments are to be made in installments over the next two years, thus lessening the impact on their cash reserve. And the Pirates admit they can borrow the money and pay it back in even smaller installments. Further, the Pirates have no one to blame but themselves for Terrell's contract. No one in baseball understood the rationale behind giving him a three-year, guaranteed contract in the first place.

Besides, a $25 million payroll for a championship team is not out of line in today's inflationary marketplace. The Dodgers, for example, gave free agents Darryl Strawberry, Brett Butler and Kevin Gross a total of $35.5 million to sign with them this year. To put that figure in perspective, consider that is twice what Dodger Stadium cost to build.

Twins General Manager Andy MacPhail figures that if he had kept his 1987 world championship team together, the club's 1991 payroll would be about $32 million. The Twins' payroll is around $20 million, and the club has tumbled from first to second to fifth to seventh in the American League West standings. There has been a matching decline in attendance.

What happened in Minnesota should teach a lesson to the Pirates and other teams that play in smaller markets. To draw fans, you must win. To win, you must have championship- caliber players. To get those players, you must spend money.

There is growing concern for the future of major league baseball in Pittsburgh. One of the 12 partners in the Pirates' ownership group, Eugene Litman, has said that adding partners is out of the question because the current owners "don't want to dilute our partnership."

If the picture is as bleak as Barger has painted it, one would think there would be a move to dilute, perhaps even dissolve, the partnership.

The gap between management and the players continues to grow. The Pirates were unable to sign Bonilla to a long-term deal, and he can become a free agent after this season. Bonds has threatened to depart after the 1992 campaign.

"We seriously have to consider trading at least one of them," Barger said.

But is that cutting costs or cutting your throat?

Hertzel was on to the Pirates' creative accounting. The Pirates "wrote off" their share of collusion damages, $10.8 million, even though they did not pay those damages in 1990. The Pirates would later "publicly write off" the collusion payments when they actually made them. All of Terrell's contract was "written off" in 1990, because Terrell was released that year. Yet, he was paid over the 1990–92 period. Presumably, the Pirates wrote off, publicly or through their accounting treatment, Terrell's 1991 and 1992 salaries as they were paid. Simple math shows that the Pirates "made" over $5 million in 1990.

The complaint about the timing of the new Roger Clemens contract was a bogus one. In other interviews, Barger suggested that the Pirates lost the Drabek case because of the new Clemens contract.

The parameters of the Clemens contract were broadly outlined by our firm and the Red Sox in early January. Negotiations were put on hold until the results of two physical examinations, completed in late January, were received. Had we planned to use Clemens' new contract to manipulate salary arbitration contracts, as was suggested in Drabek's case, we would have rushed to consummate the Clemens contract before salary arbitration numbers were filed, not after the hearings were 40 percent complete. Had the Pirates accepted our settlement offer in the Drabek case, which was $175,000 higher than their settlement offer, a hearing would have been unnecessary.

I considered it amazing that Barger could blame the Drabek loss on the Clemens contract, when Barger was not present during the Drabek hearing. The contract Zane Smith signed with the Pirates was more instrumental to Drabek's victory than was the Clemens contract. The Drabek case was far more complex, sophisticated, and persuasive than yelling the name "Roger Clemens" at every juncture in the hearing, as Barger led the public and press to believe.

*   *   *

Bonilla signed with the New York Mets as a free agent following the 1991 season. He received $29 million on a five-year guaranteed contract. From a financial perspective, Bonilla ultimately benefited from the Pirates' parsimonious policy, just as the Pirates suffered from that policy.

Carl Barger joined the expansion Florida Marlins as club president. Barger was united with good friend and client Wayne Huizenga, the Marlins owner and entrepreneurial force behind the Blockbuster Entertainment empire.

Mark Sauer moved from the St. Louis Cardinals to Pittsburgh and replaced Barger. Sauer hired quixotic Ted Simmons, also from the Cardinals, in late January 1992, to serve as the Pirates general manager. Two constants remained in Pittsburgh, though. Douglas Danforth still ran the Pirates off-the-field, and Jim Leyland ran them on-the-field.

Barry Bonds, by then embittered at the Pirates, declared publicly that he would leave Pittsburgh after the 1992 season, when he would become eligible for free agency. Bonds filed at $5 million in salary arbitration, while the Pirates filed at $4 million. Within a short time after the filing deadline, the Pirates reversed two years of hardball negotiations with Bonds, commenced to "roll over," and agreed to pay Bonds a settlement of $4.7 million, plus incentive bonuses. The 70 percent settlement, plus incentives, included a provision stating that the Pirates would pay for a hotel suite for Bonds every time the Pirates played in Los Angeles. When the 1992 season was over, Bonds had cashed in on his incentives, earning $5.15 million for the season

— more than he would have received through a victory in salary arbitration.

Had this contract been granted as part of a multiyear contract to keep the league's best player in Pittsburgh, the Pirates' approach would have been readily understandable. Instead, the club rolled over for a player who had announced his imminent departure. The Pirates were now three for three in mishandling the Bonds negotiations.

John Smiley had recovered nicely from his broken hand in 1990 and had won 20 games in 1991. Both he and Drabek wanted to remain with the Pirates, so Alan and I notified the new club president, Mark Sauer, and new general manager, Ted Simmons.

We filed Drabek in salary arbitration at $4.9 million, while the Pirates filed at $3.685 million. Less than forty-eight hours before the hearing on a third consecutive salary arbitration case, we settled with the Pirates at $4.5 million, plus award bonuses.

The decision to settle was a difficult one. I was convinced that we would win again, especially because of my belief that the Pirates' "number" was too low. A couple of days before Doug Drabek's case was scheduled to be heard, he called and asked if I would be angry at him if he accepted the Pirates' $4.5 million settlement offer. Doug was very sensitive to all of the effort expended by the Hendricks team in preparing his cases. He also knew that I considered us to be the favorite in his case.

"Would you be mad if I accepted the Pirates offer?" he asked. I laughed and asked why he wanted to accept the offer, other than the fact that it represented 67 percent of the difference between the numbers. While a player would be imprudent not to seriously consider such a settlement, I figured we were headed for a repeat of the prior years' showdowns. "Because I've never signed a contract with any award bonuses," said the 1990 Cy Young Award winner. "It would be nice to sign a contract like that for a change."

I told Doug not to be concerned about offending me. "We work for you, not the other way around," I told him, appreciative of his sensitivity to our efforts and commitment to him. He accepted the $4.5 million offer, which included bonuses for placing in the Cy Young Award voting, All Star selection, the Clemente Award, and other playoff awards.

Drabek's desire for award clauses, typical of the wishes of most players, seemed unimportant in February. Ted Simmons reluctantly agreed to those clauses, though he clearly made his dislike for such clauses known to Alan and me. The different perspectives on award clauses, seemingly of no great moment in February, would prove critical as negotiations for a long-term contract for Doug Drabek progressed.

John Smiley earned $1.425 million in 1991 — $25,000 more than the $1.4 million number we had filed in salary arbitration in deference to the broken hand he suffered in 1990. Like Bonds, Smiley exceeded his salary arbitration number by earning incentive bonuses.

"Smiles" was due a large raise for his outstanding 1991 season. We filed at $4.1 million, and the Pirates filed at $2.7 million. Smiley settled for $3.44 million, or 53 percent of the difference between the numbers.

Pittsburgh continued its tradition of arbitrating cases in 1992. The Pirates lost in the Jose Lind case and won in the Jay Bell case. Bell filed at $1.45 million, and the Pirates filed at $875,000. Ironically, the Pirates offered Bell $1.25 million, or 60 percent of the spread, to settle. The offer reflected Simmons' view that the Pirates were the underdog. Bell's refusal to accept the offer reflected his and his agent's judgment that they were a clear favorite. After hearing the case, the arbitrator took a different view and handed Tal Smith's team a win for Pittsburgh and agent Scott Boras' team a loss for Bell.

Jose Lind filed at $2 million and the Pirates at $1 million. Simmons believed that Pittsburgh was the favorite in this case, primarily because he believed Lind's number to be too high. The Reich brothers avenged their loss to the Pirates in 1991, as Lind won. Simmons came away from both cases believing that salary arbitration was nothing but a dice roll.

The Pirates went to salary arbitration fourteen times over the 1990–92 arbitration seasons (covering the 1989-91 playing seasons). The number of cases declined from 8 in 1990, to 4 in 1991, to 2 in 1992. The Pirates, represented by Tal Smith, finished 7–7. The Hendricks finished 3–0 (Drabek, Smiley, Drabek), Sam and Tom Reich finished 2–1 (Belliard, Lind, Lind), Rex Gary and Jim Turner finished 1–0 (Hatcher), Tom Selakovich finished 1–0 (Kipper), Scott Boras finished 0–1 (Bell), Rod Wright finished 0–2 (Bonds, Bonds), and Dennis Gilbert and Steve Schneider finished 0–3 (Bonilla, Reynolds, Bonilla).

Overall, the Pirates saved $1.36 million, or about $97,000 per case, before expenses. The Pirates' savings were reduced by the cost of trying the cases. The net savings to the club amounted to one victory in 1991 over Bonilla or over Bonds. All of the players involved in the fourteen cases left Pittsburgh, one way or another, except for Jay Bell.

Ted Simmons recognized the importance of signing a quality four-year player to a multiyear contract, and he signed four-year player Bell to a multiyear contract prior to the 1993 season. Apparently, Pittsburgh management learned a lesson, because new general manager Cam Bonifay, with the blessing of upper management, proceeded to negotiate a multiyear contract with four-year HSM client Jeff King during the early 1994 season.

*   *   *

Alan and I met with Simmons in spring training of 1992 to discuss long-term contracts for five-year veteran starting pitchers Drabek and Smiley. We were told by Simmons that the Pirates could afford to sign only one of the two pitchers, and they preferred to sign Drabek. "What about Smiley?" Alan and I asked. There would be no offer made to Smiley, we were told. Within weeks, Smiley was traded to Minnesota for Denny Naegle and Midre Cummings. Smiley proceeded to win 16 games for the Twins in 1992.

The contract negotiations for Drabek during spring training and into the early part of the 1992 season went largely unnoticed and unreported outside of Pittsburgh. Not all of the negotiations were reported, though, even in the "Steel City." Ted Simmons and I reached an agreement on a three-year contract on April 11, 1992. Drabek approved the agreement that afternoon. The three-year agreement would have kept him with the Pirates through the 1994 season.

Unfortunately, the agreement was rejected by Mark Sauer, who, according to Simmons, believed that a lockout would occur in 1994. Simmons reported that the club president believed that the structure of the contract would require the Pirates to pay too much in 1992 and 1993 if there were a lockout in 1994.

The April 11 "agreement" was the culmination of negotiations that began in early March. I had offered to sign Drabek with the Pirates for $25 million on a five-year contract, plus the award bonus incentive clauses contained in his 1992 contract. "Simba" (Simmons) responded by offering his ace pitcher $18.3 million for four years, plus the award bonus clauses. We rejected that offer and countered with $20 million for four years, plus the award bonuses. Simmons rejected that offer.

On April 3 Simmons offered $19 million for four years, but this new offer excluded the award bonus clauses. When I asked, "What is wrong with our offer of $20 million?" Simmons indicated that $20 million was a magic number, and the top brass of the Pirates "could not get there."

I called the former Cardinals and Brewers catcher at his home in St. Louis several days later and asked him if he would be interested in a three-year contract. He said he would be, but was surprised that Drabek or I would accept only three years. I replied that my client wanted to stay in Pittsburgh, and I believed that he should sign a contract averaging $5 million per year. I pointed out that the shorter the length of the contract, the less risk the club would take financially. This was my way of attempting to bridge our differences in order to finalize an agreement. Simmons agreed with my reasoning, and our discussions turned to the subject of a limited no-trade provision.

Simmons respected the "10 and 5" rights earned by a player under the Basic Agreement. The "10 and 5" provision allows a player with ten or more years of major league service, the last five of which have been with the same club, to veto a trade. In essence, a club cannot trade such a player without his permission. Ted did not believe that any player should be able to veto a trade until he had earned 10 and 5 rights.

I responded that Drabek would be making a commitment to Pittsburgh, and, therefore, he wanted assurances that he would remain a Pirate and not be traded. I modified the no-trade request and replaced it with a request that Doug be able to name fourteen clubs to which he would not consent to be traded. After concluding our spirited but friendly discussion, I advised the Pirates general manager that I would soon be calling him with an offer.

My formal offer to the Pirates was for a three-year contract at $15.5 million, plus award bonuses, plus a limited no-trade provision. The specific composition of my offer was as follows:

Signing Bonus — $3,000,000, payable $500,000 upon signing and $2,500,000 on July 1, 1994

1992 Salary — $4,500,000 (the same salary Doug was receiving under his one-year 1992 contract)

1993 Salary — $5,500,000

1994 Salary — $2,500,000

Ted accepted the financial terms, but rejected the award bonuses and the limited no-trade provision. We agreed on the guarantee language, as well as on a single room for Drabek on all club road trips, a fairly common benefit extended to players playing under long-term contracts.

With only the award bonus clauses and the limited no-trade provision holding up a final contract, I told Simmons that I would ask my client if he were prepared to drop those requests in order to consummate a deal. Even though Drabek was scheduled to pitch that day, I called him to advise him of where we stood. After a short discussion, he gave his consent to consummate a contract without the additional requests. I then telephoned Alan, who concurred with the deal. Within hours, I was back to Ted Simmons with our acceptance. He was ecstatic. We agreed to celebrate by watching Doug win the game that Saturday night.

Almost as an afterthought, Simmons told me that Mark Sauer needed to bless the deal. I told him that I understood and asked him to get back to me as soon as possible. He told me that it might be as late as Monday before he had an answer.

Simmons and I both understood that the contract was structured to minimize the effects of a possible lockout in 1994. Simmons was willing to accept the risk; Sauer was not. Sauer was treating the possibility of a lockout in 1994 as a virtual certainty.

Angered at the Pirates president's veto of our deal, I hollered at Simmons that the decision was irresponsible. Sauer risked losing Drabek through free agency and receiving only a draft choice in return, over the "possibility" of a lockout. Simmons calmly defended Sauer's right to make that judgment call. I reminded him that we had taken a risk by reducing our monetary demands. "I hear you," Simmons replied, a phrase that had come to mean in our discussions, "I understand."

Since Douglas Danforth was a member of the PRC, I considered the rejection of the Drabek contract to be an early warning sign of the owners' intent to initiate a lockout in 1994. In the case of Danforth, the word "owner" should be cautiously applied, since he plays the role of autocratic owner quite well, but without the capital investment required to play the role with authenticity.

On April 15, 1992, Simmons crafted a new offer. He offered $19 million for four years, plus award bonuses. The joker was that Drabek could only earn a maximum of $500,000 in award bonuses over the four-year term. I told Simmons that, as usual, I would discuss his offer with my client.

On April 21, I countered the Pirates with the following two offers. I told Simmons that he could take his choice. The offers were:

Signing Bonus	—	$ 2,000,000	payable $500,000 upon signing and $1,500,000 on July 1, 1994
1992 Salary	—	4,500,000	
1993 Salary	—	5,500,000	
1994 Salary	—	3,500,000	
		$15,500,000	for three years

plus the following award bonuses

Cy Young: first	—	$150,000
second or third	—	50,000
All Star: midseason		
or postseason	—	50,000
Clemente Award	—	50,000

or

Signing Bonus	—	$ 1,000,000
1992 Salary	—	5,000,000
1993 Salary	—	5,250,000
1994 Salary	—	3,500,000
1995 Salary	—	5,250,000
		$20,000,000

plus the following award bonuses,
not to exceed $1,000,000 over the life of the contract

Cy Young: first	—	$250,000
second or third	—	150,000
fourth or fifth	—	50,000
All Star: midseason		
or postseason	—	100,000
Clemente Award	—	100,000
League Championship Series Most Valuable Player	—	100,000
World Series Most Valuable Player	—	250,000

Simmons did not accept either offer. Instead, he offered the following contract on April 28:

Signing Bonus	—	$ 500,000
1992 Salary	—	5,000,000
1993 Salary	—	5,000,000
1994 Salary	—	3,750,000
1995 Salary	—	5,250,000
		$19,500,000

plus the following award bonuses,
not to exceed $1,000,000 over the life of the contract

Cy Young: first	—	$150,000
second	—	50,000
All Star: midseason or postseason	—	50,000
Clemente Award	—	50,000
League Championship Series Most Valuable Player	—	100,000
World Series Most Valuable Player	—	150,000

We were absurdly close. Drabek and I wanted $20 million. For the same reason, Simmons wanted to stay under $20 million. We were apart by $125,000 per year, a difference of 2.5 percent.

"What about $20 million and your incentives?" I asked. "Man, you have my best offer," Simmons said, "I can't touch $20 million." Shortly thereafter, I offered a compromise contract:

Signing Bonus	—	$ 1,000,000
1992 Salary	—	5,000,000
1993 Salary	—	5,250,000
1994 Salary	—	3,250,000
1995 Salary	—	5,250,000
		$19,750,000

plus the following award bonuses,
not to exceed $1,250,000 over the life of the contract

Cy Young: first	—	$250,000
second or third	—	150,000
All Star: midseason or postseason	—	100,000
Clemente Award	—	100,000
League Championship Series Most Valuable Player	—	100,000
World Series Most Valuable Player	—	250,000

Incredibly, my offer was rejected. I did not understand why. I still do not understand why. We were under the magic $20 million number.

My client could earn too much, Simmons told me. "We are apart by $62,500 per year or 1.25 percent," I said. Simmons said that he understood the difference. I replied, "You are prepared to lose Doug Drabek through free agency over a 1.25 percent difference, or over the amount he can earn through incentives." The Pirates general manager made it clear that he understood the score.

Drabek was stunned. He wanted to stay in Pittsburgh. We had gone through two salary arbitration hearings and had resolved the third one the day before it was scheduled to be heard. We had reached an agreement on a three-year contract, only to have it vetoed over the possibility of a lockout that ultimately did not occur. We were told that the Pirates could not get to $20 million, so, reluctantly, we dropped below that magic number in order to make a deal. Now, our offer had been rejected, irrationally in my judgment, when we were apart by 1.25 percent.

"Doug will ultimately get his $19 or $20 million," I told Simmons. "But you stand to lose a great player over a 1.25 percent difference. How can you defend not paying the extra 1.25 percent compared to the cost of losing a great player?" He said it was his problem, and he would explain the loss of Drabek if it came to that. Little did I know at the time that after Drabek signed with Houston, reports would emanate from Pittsburgh suggesting that he never really wanted to sign with the Pirates.

Negotiations with Pittsburgh basically stopped in May, even though press reports indicated that an agreement was forthcoming. Those reports, which emanated from the Pirates' front office, probably did more harm than good. Doug and I believed that we had fired our best shots and had been rebuffed. The Pirates' game of hardball had become tiresome to both of us.

There was another important reason to suspend negotiations, though. I do not like to negotiate a contract during the regular season, unless a contract can be concluded quickly. I believe that in-season negotiations distract the player. He thinks about his contract when he should be thinking only about baseball. Every pitch or every at bat is magnified. If a pitcher wins a game, or a hitter goes 2 for 4, he will think he has gained leverage in contract negotiations. Conversely, if a pitcher loses a game, or a hitter strikes out in the clutch, he will think he has lost leverage in those negotiations.

So I called a halt to negotiations. I told Simmons that our offers stood for the near future, and that he could accept any one of them at any time, but that I was not going to negotiate further. He said he understood my position. He said that he was surprised I had continued negotiations for so long, since I had familiarized him with my general policy of no in-season contract negotiations. I responded by saying that I had continued negotiations because we both had believed that a deal was imminent. He agreed that he, too, thought we would get a deal concluded. We agreed to talk further at the end of the season.

Doug Drabek's record was 15–11 in 1992. He started 34 games, pitched 256⅔ innings, gave up 218 hits, and posted an earned run average of 2.77. He was the Pirates' ace, again, as Pittsburgh won another National League Eastern Division championship. Drabek was only a couple of outs and an error away from winning the seventh and deciding game of the league championship series against Atlanta.

Drabek declared free agency after the World Series. Simmons asked me if the Pirates still had a chance to sign Drabek. I told him that they did, since Doug wanted to stay in Pittsburgh and play for Leyland and pitching coach Ray Miller.

After we were allowed to negotiate financial terms with other clubs, Simmons phoned to find out if we had received any offers over $20 million, as I had predicted we would. I advised the Pirates general manager that we had received an offer well in excess of $20 million. He reminded me that he had never doubted that we would receive such an offer once Drabek became a free agent.

Simmons said, "I guess we're out of it. We can't compete with an offer over $20 million." The offer was for $23.5 million, I told him, and I reminded him that the highest offer would not necessarily sway Drabek. "Make me an offer," I told him.

On November 23, Ted Simmons made an offer. It was $15 million for three years. After I asked about a four-year offer, he said he would try to sell upper management on a $20 million offer for four years. He advised me that he did not believe that upper management would agree to such an offer. "Why only three years now, when you were prepared to go four years in May?" I said. "Because Doug is a year older," Simmons replied.

In addition to Pittsburgh, Drabek wanted to play for Houston. These were his clear-cut top choices. The Yankees were offering a lot of money and would undoubtedly react favorably if we countered their offer. While the Braves were playing their cards close to the vest, they would ultimately make a too-late run at Drabek.

I called Bill Wood, the Astros general manager, the next day. I explained where Houston stood on Doug's priority list. I offered to sign Drabek with the Astros for $21 million, plus award bonuses, on a four-year contract. I told Wood that I had a higher offer and advised him of my belief that the market would continue to go up for the star-caliber player. He listened carefully and promised to get back to me.

On November 25, 1992, the Astros rejected my offer and countered with an offer of $18.5 million, plus award bonuses, for four years. I summarily rejected that offer.

In my discussions with Wood over the next two days, I suggested that we might consider a contract of $23.5 million for five years, of which $19.5 million would be guaranteed. Since Drabek had earned $4.5 million in 1992, such a proposal would garner $24 million, guaranteed, for the period 1992–96.

Drabek agreed with my "suggestion" because he no longer would have the duplicate housing expenses necessitated by maintaining homes in both Houston and Pittsburgh, and he would no longer have to pay Pennsylvania a large nonresident state income tax. He would save a considerable amount of money by playing for the Astros in Texas, a state without a state income tax. I calculated that $19.5 million from the Astros was the equivalent of $20.2 million from the Pirates.

I wanted to find out if the Pirates would go to four years, so I telephoned Ted Simmons on November 27. I was unprepared for what I heard. He cryptically told me that the Pirates were withdrawing their offer of $15 million for three years. "What about the possible $20 million four-year offer?" I asked. "It's not there," Simmons said. "We're out of it."

I was incredulous. I said, "You're quitting. I can't believe it. You want me to tell Doug Drabek that you don't want him back at any price?" Simmons' response was to tell me that he knew Drabek would sign for a price outside of the Pirates' range, so what would be the point in the Pirates continuing to negotiate.

I told him that the Pirates had made a big mistake. "You're not going to take $15 million for three years," he said. "Don't be so sure. Doug might from the Pirates. Why won't you go to $20 million?" I responded. "Like I said," Ted replied, "he's a year older. Anyway, we're out of it." With that, the negotiations with the Pirates ended.

Doug was certainly surprised at the Pirates' response. He was more stunned than I, if that were possible. We quickly recovered, though, and agreed that little of what the Pirates had done in contract negotiations over the past several years had made sense.

I told the Drabeks that I believed that I could get a contract for between $28.5 and $30 million for five years, if they would go to the highest bidder. They said they now preferred to play for Houston, and if nothing could be worked out with the Astros, then I should pursue the highest bidder. I thus focused my entire attention on the Astros.

Alan contacted the Yankees and told them that we would not respond to their offer until negotiations were concluded with Houston. Other clubs were told that we were trying to finalize a deal, although we did not reveal with whom we were negotiating.

Astros general manager Bill Wood wanted the best deal he could squeeze out of me and kept offering less money than my "suggestion." On November 28, I lost my patience and barked that I was sick and tired of him chiseling on me when he knew that he was already getting the best deal any club could get for Doug. Wood chuckled at my flash of anger, a sign that he was testing my limits. I then knew that he was probing to see how high he would have to go to sign Drabek.

Bill was under the pressure of reporting to a new owner and reconciling his views on signing Doug with those of his scouts. His scouts had a slight preference for Jose Guzman over Drabek, but Wood knew the value of signing a "hometown" player with the Astros. I believed Bill preferred Drabek on the basis of talent and geography, but the Astros general manager wanted to build a consensus for his decision. Wood had been negotiating with Guzman and had offered him a contract. For his part, Guzman had offers from seven clubs, and he was in a hurry to sign. Such is life during the free agent market.

On November 30, Bill finally agreed to my "suggestion." Doug Drabek was introduced as an Astro at a press conference held on December 1 at the Astrohall. The December 2 *Houston Post* blared "Astros deem Drabek a perfect fit," while the *Houston Chronicle* headline read "Drabek fills Astros' top need."

By signing Drabek, new Astros owner Drayton McLane, Jr., demonstrated that he intended to compete and would spend the money to do so. By signing with Houston, Doug demonstrated a willingness to accept considerably less than his optimum market value.

I have often wondered what would have happened had Pittsburgh continued negotiations. Jim Leyland obviously wonders also. In the September 23, 1993, *Houston Chronicle* his response was printed to the question of whether or not he missed Barry Bonds:

"We miss Drabek even more than Bonds." Had Pittsburgh and Houston made equivalent offers, I would have seen a visibly tortured Doug Drabek. In any event, Pittsburgh's loss became Houston's gain.

One should not believe that Drabek pitched poorly in 1993 merely because his won-loss record was 9–18. A starting pitcher's won-loss record is highly dependent upon his offensive and defensive support, as well as the bullpen. While he certainly did not pitch as well in 1993 as he did in his 1990 Cy Young Award season, he pitched much better than his deceptive won-loss record would indicate. It is enlightening to compare Drabek's 1993 season performance to that of Jack McDowell, the 1993 American League Cy Young Award winner. Such a comparison follows:

	GS	W	L	IP	H	SO	BB	ERA	CG	SHO	BA	OBP	SLG
Drabek	34	9	18	237.2	242	157	60	3.79	7	2	.267	.312	.381
McDowell	34	22	10	256.2	261	158	69	3.37	10	4	.266	.314	.379

Rank in League

	GS	W	IP	Strikeouts	Shutouts	Complete Games
Drabek	7	37	5	9	3	2
McDowell	6	1	2	13	1	3

The importance of run support cannot be overestimated. In Drabek's 18 losses, his club scored 31 runs. In McDowell's 10 losses, his club scored 15 runs. In McDowell's 22 wins, his run support averaged over 8 runs per game.

Drabek threw 2 shutouts and 6 one-run games, yet could earn only 9 wins for the entire season. Similar hard-luck pitchers in 1993 were Tom Candiotti, who was 8–10 for the Dodgers and Mike Morgan, who was 10–15 for the Cubs. In contrast, John Smoltz of Atlanta was 15–11.

Smoltz had a solid 3.62 earned run average, but received 4.94 runs per game. Candiotti posted a 3.12 earned run average and received 2.94 runs per game. Morgan's earned run average was 4.03, and he received 3.31 runs per game. Drabek's 3.79 earned run average was backed by only 3.21 runs per game, among the lowest run support in the National League.

Given his consistent performances over the prior seven seasons, Drabek is likely to post far better won-loss numbers for Houston in 1994. Like Bonilla, Bonds, Smiley and Lind, Drabek could be playing for a Pittsburgh club which would have been a contender in 1994, instead of the mediocre club it will likely be.

Chapter 9

Andre Thornton

Today agents are considered a normal part of the landscape in baseball. The rights of players are well established, if not respected. The situation was quite different when I entered the field of professional athlete representation. The presence of agents was openly resented by club officials. Clubs routinely displayed a patronizing attitude toward agents and players alike, and they frequently employed hardball tactics.

The first baseball club on which Alan and I had major league clients was the Cleveland Indians. At that time the Indians were run in this old-style manner.

Andre Thornton played for the Indians from 1977 through 1987. The story of his career with Cleveland is replete with irony and illustrates how these old-style tactics were used against the best of players.

Thornton grew up in Phoenixville, Pennsylvania, near Philadelphia. He was one week shy of his eighteenth birthday when he signed with the Phillies in 1967 as an undrafted player. He served in the military reserves for portions of the 1968 through 1972 seasons. During this period, he played in Huron, Eugene, Spartanburg, Peninsula, Reading, and Richmond.

In 1972 Thornton moved up to Triple A, playing for Eugene until Philadelphia traded him to the Atlanta Braves organization. He played in Triple A at Richmond for the balance of 1972 and the first part of 1973. The Braves traded Andre to the Chicago Cubs organization for Joe Pepitone in May 1973. Chicago then assigned Thornton to Wichita in Triple A.

The Cubs brought Andre Thornton to the show in 1973. While he had only "a cup of coffee" in 1973, that taste (7 hits in 35 at bats in 17 games) was all Andre needed, for he never saw the minor leagues again. He had arrived in the "Bigs" at age twenty-four.

Andre played for the Cubs into the 1976 season. He was traded to Montreal in May for Steve Renko and Larry Biittner. In December, the Expos traded him to Cleveland for Jackie Brown.

The 1977 season started slowly for Thornton, but he moved his career into high gear that year. He hit 28 home runs, scored 77 runs, and drove in 70 runs. His career as a respected power hitter for a below average club was beginning. Tragedy, however, lay just around the corner.

In October 1977, driving from Cleveland to West Chester, Pennsylvania, a powerful gust of wind caused his van to crash on a treacherous road. His wife, Gertrude, and his daughter, Theresa, were killed. Despite the enormity of his personal loss, this man of Christ ministered to those in attendance at the funeral of his wife and daughter. Andre Thornton spoke to the congregation:

> There are tears in my eyes, but my heart is comforted. The reason I'm standing here now is because you knew Gert and Theresa and you know what our lives represented. You know how we tried to live our lives for the Lord. We thank God for giving us a chance to touch as many lives as He made possible.
>
> Today, these tears you see are not for me. These tears are for you, and I pray that before one of your lives is stolen away, before another person here passes away, each of you would ask Jesus Christ into your life and would know Him as your Savior.

Andre was an inspiration to many. In June 1979, Phil Pepe of the *New York Daily News* wrote a column which expressed the feelings of many who had been influenced by the life and convictions of Thornton.

> It was raining when I woke yesterday morning and I thought of Andre Thornton. I thought of him because a week ago in Cleveland, while they were waiting for the rain to stop so the baseball game could go on, I spent an hour talking with him; a most remarkable hour. I have thought of him often since then. I have been touched by Andre Thornton.

I had never talked with him before, not really. I knew him as a powerfully built athlete who could crunch a baseball, and my conversations with him were the typical questions asked of a star whose home run has just won a game.

"What pitch did you hit? Have you always had good success against Catfish Hunter? Is this the biggest home run of your career?"

But I had never talked with Andre Thornton before. I knew about the tragedy in his life. I had read about how he and his family had been driving on a rain-slicked highway when the accident occurred. His wife and two-year-old daughter were killed. Andre and his four-year-old son survived. My heart went out to him in his grief and I said a quick, silent prayer that he could find peace and understanding in his bereavement, and I subsequently read that he had picked up the pieces of his life and I admired him for it.

I wondered how he had found the strength to carry on, but how do you find the right words to ask a man to discuss how he repaired the broken pieces in his life? Andre Thornton made it easy.

He was sitting in front of his locker, reading a newspaper and waiting for the rain to stop. The paper had been filled with tragedy, reports of the DC-10 crash in Chicago, another story about an Ohio man who had played Russian roulette with his four- year-old son, putting a gun to the child's head and pulling the trigger, killing his son.

"So many people don't realize the brevity of life," he said. "Those 272 people on that airplane might have had two minutes during which they knew they were going to die. We're going to have to answer that question. What is life all about? Where am I going? Am I going to have to stand before God?"

He was speaking softly, with great feeling, and I got the inescapable feeling that I was in the presence of a very special human being.

"When my wife and daughter were killed," he said, "I knew I couldn't possibly understand the reasons for such a tragedy. There was nothing humanly anyone could do to heal the severed lives that were picked up that day."

"My faith in Christ brought me through this thing. I couldn't have found the strength without having faith and knowing this is God's will. Gert (his wife) and I had known the Lord all our married years. I can remember her saying God uses our lives and she wondered how He was going to use her. Now she knows how God has used her life."

I was enraptured as he spoke, with deep emotion, at peace. "I never experienced more pain, nor would I ever experience more pain," he said. "I'm just thankful I knew God, to be able to trust in

Him. I believe my beliefs and I suspect my doubts. I certainly could pray, and that's what I did . . . .

"I look at these games as a job," he says. "Put next to the things that are eternal, it doesn't mean much. If it meant that God wants me to leave this game, I would. I'm just an average ball player. I'm not looking to be in the Hall of Fame. This is where God has chosen to use me, and I put as much effort and as much love as I can in what I do."

"I'm serving the Lord by playing baseball. It allows me to reach more people. I believe that God does things to strengthen us and to test us. The tragedy in my life was meant to do that, and as a result I received thousands of letters from people who have been touched and affected by my tragedy. It humbled me."

When I left Andre Thornton, knowing I had been touched by this man and that I would never be the same, he said to me: "I will pray for you."

I have been associating with athletes for more than 20 years. Not one of them has ever said that to me before.

The man of faith had an exceptional year on the baseball field in 1978. He hit 33 home runs, scored 97 runs, and drove in 105 runs. He hit for the cycle that year, a feat as rare as pitching a no-hitter.

Andre was recognized off the field as well. He received the Danny Thompson Award given by Baseball Chapel to the player who demonstrated exemplary Christian spirit in baseball. The Cleveland Baseball Writers voted him their Cleveland Man of the Year.

In early 1979, Andre was named the winner of the Roberto Clemente Award. The award is based upon sportsmanship, character, community involvement, humanitarianism, playing ability, contribution to team, and contribution to baseball. Thornton's acceptance speech was published in the Cleveland newspaper:

> It's indeed a humbling and very gratifying and wonderful experience to be standing here before you as recipient of this great award, when I think of the people who have received the award and when I think of the man for whom this award is given.
>
> I only met Roberto Clemente once in my life. I had the opportunity to see him play on the field at various times, and certainly as a ball player I could never reach the goals that this man attained. His ability was awesome, and not in my wildest dreams could I possibly say that I could fill his shoes on a ball field. But I am thankful that this man's life to us was something more than just the things he was able to do on a baseball field.

I won't remember Roberto Clemente for the fact that he was probably one of the greatest players that will ever play this game. I will remember that he gave his life giving, and helping, and serving other people.

I think of my own life in the same terms, considering the things that are really important. I have been gifted with the ability to play baseball, and I am thankful that I have been able to do it at times well—thankful that I have had the opportunity to play here before you in Cleveland, and hopefully be representative of you and this community.

And as I think about the things that I could possibly do in my life that would let you know how much I care for you, the only thing that I could possibly have to give you is not what I could do for you on the baseball field, but to give you my life. When I think of giving you my life, I think of sharing what Christ has done for me. The people I talk to, the people that question me, the people that want to know, "Andre, how can you make it? What gives you the strength to go on?" very seldom ask me how many home runs I hit last year.

It's almost forgotten in their minds simply because there's a problem much deeper than the one baseball can answer. The people who come to me are the people who are hurting, people who want to know if there is any hope, people that want to know, "How can I stand?" "Can this life offer me any enjoyment?" "Is there a purpose for this life?" I want to be able to share with people that there is hope; to encourage people that there is a purpose to this life; to encourage people in a time that, as the commissioner said, is very sinister. I think it is imperative that I not only be the best baseball player I can possibly be for you—because that is my job —but that I also be the man that God wants me to be, because that's what He demands. If I could ever do anything in this life for the Lord, it is to live in obedience to His Word. For there is nothing that brings a greater joy, and there is nothing that gives greater understanding.

Andre Thornton was a great competitor. He played linebacker in high school, and on several occasions we discussed the possibility that he would have made a very good linebacker in the NFL. Andy is a fan of professional football and follows the NFL season closely. He is still trying to figure out, though, how to get even with me for the dinner I won when he picked Denver and I picked the New York Giants in the 1987 Super Bowl. The winner got to pick the restaurant, and I picked the Tack Room in Tucson during spring training that year. I have to admit I was most ungracious as I gloated all evening over how obvious a pick the Giants were.

A game I attended where Cleveland played the Texas Rangers, in Arlington, exemplified Thornton's competitive spirit and determination to win. He was on second base when a Cleveland batter hit a line drive single up the middle into centerfield. In one continuous motion, the center fielder scooped up the ball and threw to home as the third base coach waved Thornton home. Jim Sundberg was the Rangers catcher and a huge favorite of the home town fans. "Sunny" set up for the throw with his left foot firmly planted on the third base line, his shoulder hovering directly above the middle of home plate.

Thornton charged toward the plate, looking the part of the linebacker we had envisioned zeroing in on a runner. The throw to home, while on line, was a one-hopper. As Sundberg leaned towards the ball in anticipation of catching it, Andre reached the dish a fraction of a second ahead of the ball.

He did not slide, nor did he break stride. His left shoulder collided with Jim Sundberg's left shoulder, and Sundberg went reeling, like a ballet dancer doing a pirouette. Andre scored standing up as the ball bounced past Sundberg to the backstop.

The crowd rose to boo the Indians slugger vociferously for his contact with their local hero. Neither of these gentlemen competitors overreacted to the event. Sunny went after the ball, the batter went to second, and Andy loped back to the visitor's dugout. The crowd continued to boo for at least a minute, but play continued uneventfully.

During the rest of the game, every time Andre Thornton came up to hit, the crowd booed loudly. He was impassive to the boos and concentrated on his hitting.

After the game, we had dinner at the Steak and Ale next to the stadium, a local hangout for Rangers and visiting players. With some mirth in my voice, I reviewed both how Sundberg had set up to field the throw and the resulting collision at the plate. I asked him how it felt to be booed so loudly by the fans.

He did not blink nor hesitate. With no smile on his face, he replied, "Randy, the basepath is mine."

Prior to the 1979 season, Andre Thornton signed a five-year contract extension with the Indians, covering the 1980–1984 seasons, at $370,000 per season. That was essentially the salary the Los Angeles Dodgers were paying Steve Garvey, and Andre believed that salary to be appropriate for him. While he knew that Garvey's contract was a couple of years old, he considered that the Indians ownership was forever pleading poverty. By agreeing to this contract, rather than demanding more money or testing the free agent market, Andre was committing himself to the City of Cleveland and the Indians organization.

Andre Thornton produced another top notch season in 1979. He hit 26 home runs, scored 89 runs, and drove in 93 runs. After producing three consecutive outstanding seasons, Thornton seemed certain to continue his streak in 1980.

Unfortunately, he wrenched his knee in spring training in 1980. It was soon clear that he would need an operation, and an orthopedic surgeon in San Diego operated on Andre's knee in March. The Indians placed him on the disabled list at the end of spring training.

Thornton rehabilitated his knee with the hope of returning to the Indians as soon as possible. He was taken off the disabled list on June 9. It soon became apparent, though, that the operation had not solved all of the problems with his knee. He was disabled again on June 19, and a second operation was scheduled; this one was to be performed by team physician Earl Brightman of Cleveland. The second operation effectively ended the 1980 season for Andre Thornton. The season was a total washout, and under Thornton's Baseball Register record for 1980 is this entry: "(Did not play)."

After the second operation, Thornton rehabilitated his knee at Kent State University. Kent State was closer to his home in Chagrin Falls than was Municipal Stadium. The university had superior weight equipment and workout facilities than the Indians had at Municipal Stadium in downtown Cleveland. I accompanied Andy to one of his workouts at Kent State, and I saw first hand how hard he worked. The staff at Kent State was most accommodating, and, they greeted Thornton warmly the day I visited.

I remember that visit particularly well, because it was my first time on the campus where the Ohio National Guard fired on student protesters during the Vietnam War. As I walked on the campus, the music of Crosby, Stills, Nash & Young danced in my head. I thought of how Jack Lambert (the Steelers great linebacker) and the tragedy of the National Guard shootings, had put Kent State indelibly on the map.

Enjoying my time on the campus on a warm summer day, I thought of how it made sense for Thornton to do his "rehab" at

Kent State. There was no rush-hour traffic to fight going back and forth to workouts. Andre told me that the Indians preferred that he rehabilitate at Municipal Stadium, but I thought nothing of it at the time.

Two knee operations in one year were not to be his only test in 1980. On August 26, Dr. Brightman wrote Phil Seghi, the Cleveland general manager, regarding Brightman's examination of Thornton's knee on August 25:

> Andre Thornton was examined by me again today on August 25, 1980. He now shows further improvement. He has regained flexibility of the knee. He states that he is still fatigues easily. His range of motion is now normal from 0 to 125 degrees. His muscle strength has improved to 54% of normal. There is no effusion of the knee. He is able to lift 87 pounds on Nautilus machine at 90 degrees. He is jogging at the present time. He is ready to begin running figure of eights but he is not ready for sprinting. He will not be ready for sprinting until he measure 80% of normal strength by Cybex. He should be able to begin batting practice early in September.
>
> It was anticipated that he would be able to play by August 15, 1980. This was delayed because of loss of muscle strength to virtually zero following his arthroscopic surgery. He was fully rehabilitated prior to his arthroscopic surgery and it was felt that he would maintain his muscle strength after that surgery.
>
> The profound loss of muscle strength was probably due to fear and pain and the inability or loss of desire to exercise following arthroscopic surgery. This slowed his rehabilitation.
>
> I will keep you further informed of his progress.

On September 5, Phil Seghi "wrote" Andre a letter. While Seghi signed the letter, there is little doubt in my mind that it was drafted by the Indians' attorney, most likely at the behest of club president Gabe Paul. The letter was as follows:

> I am writing this letter to you in order to bring to your attention certain facts and to advise you of the position of the Cleveland Indians in connection with your contract with the club. Among other things, I am somewhat disturbed by a recent report which I received from Dr. Brightman regarding your recovery from knee surgery and the present status of your rehabilitation.
>
> Dr. Brightman seems to feel that you have suffered a profound loss of muscle strength, probably due to fear and pain and the inability or loss of desire to exercise following arthroscopic surgery.

I think, based on his findings, that there must be an intense effort on your part to do whatever is necessary in order to effect a complete recovery from the surgery. To that end, I am going to request that you follow a strict program of exercise and rehabilitation which will be furnished to you and I will expect you to follow that program rigorously.

It has also been called to my attention that you have failed to cooperate with the club in its efforts to publicize its product in that you have been very uncooperative in signing autographs, making appearances and the like. I am told that you recently even refused to autograph a picture while stating that "I don't sign autographs". May I call to your attention Paragraph 9 of your agreement which states in part as follows:

> "...in the event that the player is injured in the course of performing his baseball duties... to the extent that player is temporarily or permanently unable to actively perform as a baseball player for the club, the player agrees to use his best efforts to perform such baseball-related activities (including public relations activities on behalf of the club) during the term of the Contract as the club may reasonably request from time to time . . ."

That paragraph goes into detail as to what your specific duties are in connection with the above language. It is the club's intention to have you perform such duties and you will be given a program of such duties to be performed by you in the near future.

Finally, the club is considering the possibility of placing you on the active list so that you may wear a uniform and sit on the bench during the course of the remaining ball games so as to help build the morale of the club. We are fully aware of the fact that you have been unable to play because of an injury relating to your performance as a baseball player. However, the club has to date fulfilled all of its financial obligations to you which consist of paying you a large sum of money during the course of your disability. We do not think it is too much to ask of you that you perform whatever functions are necessary to further the best interests of the club and, more particularly, to live up to your obligations under your agreement.

To say that Thornton was stunned to receive "Phil's letter" would be a mild understatement. He responded with his own letter to Phil dated September 8:

> I am writing this letter in regard to the letter which I received from you on September 5. I was deeply hurt and insulted by the

false accusations and misleading statements that I take as a personal attack on my integrity as a man and professional baseball player.

You will be receiving a letter from my lawyer, agent and the Players Association in reply to these erroneous accusations and statements.

On September 17, the Indians, under Seghi's signature, fired back:

On September 5, 1980 I wrote you a letter which, among other things, contained a reference to Paragraph 9 of the Addendum and Special Covenants portion of your contract with the Cleveland Indians. This paragraph deals with your obligation to use your "best efforts" to perform such baseball-related activities, including "public relations activities on behalf of the Club," as the Club may reasonably request, during the period of your disability. This paragraph also requires that the Club must give you ten days notice of the activity which the Club requests you to perform.

On September 8, 1980 you were informed in writing by Pete Spudich that the Indians had arranged for you to appear at four functions on the dates and at the places named in that written communication.

On September 11, 1980 you called me, Pete Spudich and Bob DiBiasio and told each of us much the same thing, that is, that the Indians did not have the authority to decide where you would go; that the Club could give you ten days notice and then you would decide whether you would go; that the Club could not tell you to go after the season is over, etc. May I call to your attention that Paragraph 9 does not refer to the performance of these activities during the season. It does say, however, that these activities shall be requested during a maximum of eight months of any calendar year.

Finally, I was informed today that you have arbitrarily cancelled all four speaking engagements which had been arranged for you by the Indians in accordance with the provisions of Paragraph 9.

All of the developments which I have outlined above, and especially your refusal to honor the obligations which you voluntarily undertook, are most distressing to me and injurious to the best interests of the Club.

Andre, I very much want to avoid a serious confrontation with you. Our Club has lived up to every one of its obligations to you under the terms of your contract. I don't think it's too much to ask that you live up to your obligations.

I have given instructions that in the event the Club wishes you to appear at certain functions in its behalf, in accordance with

Paragraph 9, that you are to be notified in writing and you will be expected to make those appearances. If, for some reason, it is impossible for you to appear on the requested date, we will expect you to notify us promptly.

Regretfully, I must inform you that in the event you persist in your refusal to fulfill your obligations under Paragraph 9, the Club will consider such action a material breach of your contract and I intend to recommend that the Club take whatever legal action is necessary in order to protect its rights.

Prior to these attacks, I had been an advocate of a player making a written commitment to his club to promote and assist the club in the event that his career was interrupted by injury.

I agreed to paragraph 9 in Andre Thornton's contract because I believed it to be fair and reasonable. Given the way paragraph 9 was being used as a weapon against Thornton, I resolved that in the future no such clause would appear in one of my contracts. His contract was the last to have such a clause, which is a shame because the intent of the clause is good.

I investigated the circumstances surrounding the Indians' allegations, counseled with Andre, and collected my thoughts before responding to the Indians on November 5:

> This letter is being sent to you in reply to your letters of September 5, 1980, and September 17, 1980, to this firm's client, Andre Thornton. Because of the ominous tone of those letters, I am sending a copy of this letter to Marvin Miller and Donald Fehr, so that they are fully aware of all correspondence, allegations and statements of facts and positions of both the Club and Player.
>
> Your letter of September 5, 1980, states that Andre has not properly rehabilitated his knee due to a lack of a concerted rehabilitation effort by Andre and due to an unwarranted reaction to pain by Andre. Certainly, Dr. Brightman's letter implies this position. Also, your letter of September 5, 1980, states that Andre has not cooperated in fulfilling the public relations obligation contained in his contract.
>
> Your letter of September 17, 1980, repeats the assertion of Andre's lack of cooperation in fulfilling his public relations obligation, and states that your Club will enforce its rights under the contract in the event of a breach by Andre.
>
> Before dealing directly with the implications of the charges made in your letters, it is necessary for all relevant facts to be reviewed. Andre strongly disagrees with the alleged facts contained

in your letters, and therefore strongly disagrees with your conclusions and positions.

I do not believe that you would disagree with the position that Andre has a very positive public image, both on the field and off the field. Both this positive image and Andre's public Christian stance have reflected favorably on your Club.

Many times Andre has gone out of his way to help promote the Club. I am sure you and Gabe recall that at the time of negotiations over Andre's current contract, as well as at the formal signing thereof, Andre stated privately and publicly that he was happy with the City of Cleveland and with the Club's organization, and that he was not interested in attempting to squeeze out of the Club the last available dollar.

Andre advises me that during past years he has substituted several times for you or Gabe at speaking engagements which you were unable to attend.

It would be hard for me to accept any other conclusion than that Andre has strongly helped promote the public image of the Club during his four years in Cleveland. If Andre had not been so helpful, or if Andre had been a negative force on your Club, or had a negative public image, then I could understand the aggressive nature of your letters (in light of Dr. Brightman's letter to you); however, I believe that Andre's integrity, public image and credibility entitle him to much more consideration than your letters show. I believe Andre is entitled to much more of a presumption of honesty in his statements than is shown in your letters (especially your second letter).

Dr. Brightman's letter and your first letter certainly raise some interesting points with respect to the two knee operations and Andre's rehabilitation from his knee injury. The gratuitous statements contained in Dr. Brightman's letter that Andre's muscle strength loss was due to fear and pain, rather than the knee injury itself and the inadequacy and incompleteness of the first knee operation is a serious charge. This charge is unwarranted by the facts, and Andre strongly disagrees with this charge. Andre did all of the prescribed therapy and rehabilitation. The letter of Russell Weinman, Dr. Brightman's associate, indicates how rigorously Andre has followed his rehabilitation program. Jack Halbach, of the Kent State Sports Medicine Center, states in his letter how impressed he was at Andre's dedication and desire to return to competition. Of course there was pain involved. The nature of the injury, two surgeries and the rehabilitation necessarily involve pain. However, to imply that Andre can't take pain so he is not properly rehabilitating his knee is unwarranted by the facts and common sense.

I am concerned that Andre had to undergo two operations for the same knee problem. This certainly raises a legitimate question as to the competency of the medical services Andre received.

The first operation was obviously not successful. While Andre thereafter had almost normal quad strength, there was a very limited range of motion and flexibility of Andre's knee because of the remaining torn cartilage. Andre could not flex more than 120 degrees without experiencing a great deal of pain and physical inability to go beyond that point.

After the second operation, and prior to the time it would be appropriate for Andre to commence a rehabilitation program, Andre lost all muscle strength. Brightman charges that Andre's muscle strength loss was due to fear, pain and the inability or unwillingness of Andre to exercise during his rehabilitation. This is a grave charge, and is controverted by Andre's having followed the prescribed rehabilitation program. It is even controverted by Brightman's own associate. Andre was, needless to say, shocked by these charges. When Andre directly confronted Brightman over these charges, Brightman "backed way off" these charges and stated to Andre that Brightman had not meant for his letter "to be taken" the way it was.

It is understandable that you would be upset if you believed that a player (let alone one under a long term, guaranteed contract) was not properly rehabilitating himself. And Brightman's letter certainly would seem to indicate that. However, I regret that you did not check directly with Andre, for you would have been able to verify the underlying facts and would have discovered that Andre faithfully followed his rehabilitation program. You would also have discovered that Brightman was not present during Andre's workouts, and that those persons who were would have verified Andre's intense rehabilitation efforts and his dedication to the prescribed rehabilitation program.

With respect to Andre's obligation to do public relations work for the Club during the period of an injury, I am sure that you will recall that:

(1) Andre is obligated to do activities under the governing paragraph during any injury (and this is part of Andre's contractual obligation)

(2) Andre is obligated to use his best efforts to perform baseball-related activities (including public relations)

(3) The Club must be reasonable in its request

(4) The Club can make its requests during a maximum of eight months

(5) The Club must give ten days advance notice of any request

(6) The Club should give Andre sufficient background information in order that Andre be able to perform adequately

(7) The Club's request must be in keeping with Andre's stature as a professional athlete, and cannot be clerical or require Andre to be in the Club's offices on a regular basis

(8) The Club must reimburse Andre for his expenses.

Andre believes that he has fulfilled both the letter and spirit of his agreement with the Club.

I do not believe that requesting Andre to speak at churches is covered by his contract. The contract states that the requests are to be for baseball-related activities. Certainly, the subject of baseball is likely to come up, and a strong public Christian image, such as Andre possesses, helps the Club. But I do not believe that the Club can require Andre to speak before church groups where Andre will inevitably speak about Christ far more than about baseball.

The speaking engagements confirmed for Andre without his prior knowledge or consent were made for church group appearances. Because of the inappropriate manner in which these four appearances were handled, Andre cancelled these proposed appearances.

Finally, Andre is curious as to whether or not the whole course of events surrounding your two letters was an intentional effort on the Club's part to alienate Andre from the Indians.

I received the Indians response in a letter signed by Phil Seghi, dated November 11, 1980:

I have your letter of November 5, 1980 which I received on November 10th. I see no point in answering, paragraph by paragraph, your four-page letter plus enclosures. It would simply serve no good purpose because I have no intention of engaging in a series of lengthy correspondence. I think I can state the club's position very briefly and simply. The club has a contract with Andre which it has honored and will continue to honor in both its letter and its spirit. It has no intention of not honoring the contract, nor does it have any intention of putting forth any effort "to alienate Andre from the Indians" as you assert.

By the same token, the club has every right to demand that Andre live up to all of his obligations as set forth in the contract. Although it was not anticipated by anyone at the time the contract was signed, Andre did experience an entire season of disability which prevented him from playing ball. Paragraph 9 of the contract specifically covers that situation. The terms and provisions of that paragraph were agreed to in good faith by both parties. It is not unreasonable for the club to insist that Andre live up to his obligations under the contract and particularly under Paragraph 9. It is the club's opinion that Andre has not lived up to either the letter or the spirit of Paragraph 9.

Accordingly, I must reiterate to you what I have already advised Andre and that is, in the event Andre fails to live up to his obligations under his agreement with our club, I will have no alternative but to recommend to the club that it take whatever legal action is necessary in order to protect its interests.

Ultimately, nothing came of the dispute. I believed that Gabe Paul wanted to "send a message" because Andre Thornton did not use a club physician for the first operation, did not recover quickly from either operation, and was rehabilitating outside of daily supervision by the club trainer.

I was shocked that Thornton, who had done so much for the Indians from 1977 though 1979, was having his integrity and commitment to the club questioned. Even he was not above the line of players who could be manipulated and patronized by their club.

I was, and still am, gravely concerned about the conflict a team physician has between his duties to his patient, the athlete, and his client, the club. Under such a circumstance, can there be such a thing as the sanctity of the doctor-patient relationship? When does the physician knowingly or unknowingly harm his patient in order to take care of his client?

The 1981 season was tough on Thornton because he was disabled in spring training through the first weeks of the season and again from August 24 to September 8. The season was interrupted by the longest strike in baseball history. Approximately one-third of the season was lost, but free agency was protected as the owners were repelled in their efforts to destroy it.

Andre Thornton hit six home runs, scored 22 runs, and drove in 30 runs in 226 at bats. This equates to 14 home runs, 50 runs scored, and 68 RBI during a normal season. Clearly, 1981 was a year in which Andre was off-stride.

The 1982 season was a dramatic contrast to 1980 and 1981. Andre Thornton was named the American League Comeback Player of the Year and was selected to the All Star team. He hit 32 home runs, scored 90 runs, and drove in 116 runs, his all-time high. The 1983 season was a solid season for Thornton, but not nearly as good as 1982 had been. Andy hit 17 home runs, scored 78 runs, and drove in 77 runs.

With one year to go on his contract, I asked Phil Seghi if the Indians wanted to extend Thornton's contract. Seghi was in agreement that an extension would be appropriate. He had developed an enormous amount of respect and a fondness for Andre. Given the rapid escalation in player salaries, Phil knew that the Thornton contract had become a bargain for the Indians.

During spring training of 1984, Seghi and I met in Tucson. He was prepared to extend Thornton's contract past its 1984 expiration date if Gabe Paul would agree to do so. Seghi said he was having no luck with Gabe Paul, so we both met with him. Paul simply shook his head "no" when I asked if he wanted to negotiate an extension. I then said, "I guess you want Andy to play this year and see what his value is at the end of the season." He nodded his concurrence.

When I reported the results of my meetings to Andre, he was disappointed but not really surprised. He simply stated, "I guess I'll have to show them I can play for more than one more year." The tone of his voice, though, revealed his hurt in being reminded of the harsh reality of dealing with Gabe Paul.

The club officials knew that Andre Thornton did not want to leave Cleveland, and they were using this against him. This was ironical because most players did not want to play in Cleveland. But I also believed that Gabe Paul did not believe that Andy could play as well as he once could.

As usual, Thornton accepted his fate with equanimity and worked to play at his best. His efforts paid off, for he had a great year in 1984. He hit 33 home runs (tying his all time high) scored 91 runs, and drove in 99 runs. He was selected to the All Star team for the second time. *The Sporting News* selected him as a member of their Silver Slugger team.

*   *   *

The baseball winter meeting in 1984 was held in Houston, at the downtown Hyatt Regency. Little did I know that, thanks to collusion, this winter meeting would be the last "honest" meeting until 1989.

As the meeting approached, my brother Alan told me that I had to wear a suit each day of the meeting. His mandate had a familiar

Hendricks bark to it, a bark that means, "I am so serious about this that there will be no debate unless you are prepared to do battle." Alan's view was that since Houston was our town, we should look professional and serious—sort of de facto hosts. So no jeans was his edict.

We command each other with some regularity. It works because we know there are no ulterior motives, no manipulative components. Thus, there is instant credibility to the commands we issue to each other.

I chuckled to myself: "What a pain, a suit every day. But he's right about our host role. Besides, it will convey the message that we intend to get some deals done." Most of all, I wanted to get Andre Thornton signed. He was in line for a sizable contract, so I had him fly to Houston for the winter meetings.

Paul Hoynes of the *Cleveland Plain Dealer* was on the same flight as Thornton. When I met them at the baggage claim, Hoynes was both friendly and dour. He clearly anticipated Thornton leaving Cleveland, even though he wished him the best.

At my house we reviewed the situation carefully. We had received an offer weeks earlier from Tal Smith, a private consultant acting as Cleveland's representative. It was a three-year proposal at $600,000 per year. I rejected it on the spot. At the other extreme stood the Orioles. We had a 9:00 A.M. meeting scheduled with them for the next day. For a variety of reasons, including Cleveland's offer, Baltimore loomed as Thornton's first choice.

We concluded our get-together with a prayer from Thornton asking for divine guidance as he prepared to make his decision in the upcoming days. As I prepared for bed, I thought, "Baltimore."

The next morning, Alan, Andre, and I walked into the Orioles' suite at the Hyatt Regency. We were greeted warmly by owner Edwin Bennett Williams. Williams was one of America's most powerful lawyers. He was near legendary and was the consummate Washington insider. He carried himself with confidence, well aware of his fame and stature. I believed that he considered his fame to be an asset and an advantage to him in the negotiations. Supremely confident, he negotiated as if success for him were preordained. Also present were club counsel, Larry Lucchino, who later became a co-owner of the club, and Hank Peters, the general manager. Both were cordial, but reserved. This was clearly Williams' show.

Several weeks earlier I prepared a four-year guaranteed contract at $1,100,000 per year, plus numerous award incentives. Every aspect of the contract, including the guarantee language, was complete, except for a blank space for the club name. This was the proposal for Thornton that I proffered to all interested clubs. In deference to the weak financial condition of the Cleveland club, this "standard" Thornton contract deferred a substantial amount of each year's salary, but at an interest rate of 9 percent. A deferral can benefit a club with cash flow problems, and it can benefit a player by compensating him over a period considerably longer than his playing career.

After giving a speech about why the Orioles were an appealing club to my client, I presented the detailed contract to the Orioles officials. My guarantee language was both tightly drafted and appropriate to a player of Thornton's stature. Larry Lucchino responded that he believed that guarantee language should be uniform, no matter what the bargaining power of a particular player is. This was an obvious reference to the contract I had recently completed with the Orioles for John Lowenstein. While the position taken by Lucchino had merit, I demurred in this instance, because I believed I could achieve our goals, and I therefore did not foresee the need to modify my most preferred guarantee language.

Williams, sensing that his club was the leading contender, agreed that Baltimore and Thornton were well suited for each other, but explained that a three-year contract was preferable to a four-year contract. He also said that a salary of $900,000 per year was more appropriate than $1.1 million. The requested interest rate of 9 percent was too high, he concluded.

I pointed out that the Orioles could find an annuity that paid a 9 percent return, making the requested rate reasonable. Williams ignored my comment and explained that prevailing interest rates would likely decrease, thus making a rate of 6 percent more appropriate to him.

I sensed that Williams was using our obvious interest in his club as a bargaining chip against us. As I sat in the Orioles' suite, I reflected on Andre Thornton's history with Cleveland, especially how inappreciative Cleveland had been when he was injured. The Indians' low offer, clearly revealed as such by Baltimore's 50 percent higher offer, served to stoke my intensity.

I thought that the way Williams was bargaining was typical of the nature of contract negotiations in sports, where timing, talent, and leverage inevitably dictate the outcome of negotiations. There sat Andy, Alan, and I, with an extremely attractive situation for Baltimore, and the club was going to engage us in the usual offer-counteroffer process.

I also thought, "Williams does not understand that just because the Orioles are our first choice, it is not inevitable that he will sign Andy." I knew that other clubs, especially Minnesota, were interested in signing Andy. So rather than bargain, I suggested to Williams that each side carefully consider the other's position. We arranged to meet at 5:30 P.M. that same day. I knew that Williams must be eager, since he did not even want to wait a day to reconvene.

As we were preparing to leave, Williams told us the story of how he had signed star running back, John Riggins, for the Washington Redskins. He told us that, after the basic salary was agreed upon, Riggins and his representative, who was also his brother, had one more demand. Williams recounted that, as he held his breath, they demanded that the money be deferred, but without requesting the payment of any interest on the deferred amount. After Williams indicated to us that he had quickly agreed to the Rigginses' "demand" (one which decreased the cost of the contract to the Redskins), he laughed heartily.

Alan and I stood in the hall, alone, with Thornton nearby. I said to Alan, "Do you realize how much he insulted our intelligence, especially with that Riggins story?" Alan concurred. We agreed that Williams believed that he was totally in control of the situation. Williams struck me as both roguish and charming, a man used to being in command, but one who, like many I had encountered before, would eventually discover that he was not going to command me.

Shortly after lunch, Tal Smith sent word that he wanted to meet with us. Smith was entrenched in the Indians' suite, playing an active negotiating role under new club president Peter Bavasi. Alan, Andre, and I were debating whether or not to meet, and we happened to be on the floor where the Indians' suite was located. Tal Smith came into the hall and saw the three of us. As he approached, Alan, with whom he had always been on the most cordial of terms, initiated a conversation. Andy and I casually moved away.

As they talked, Andre asked me if we should even bother to meet with the Indians. At that point, it was clear to me that in his mind Cleveland was history. I could surely understand why he felt that way. After all, given everything that had transpired with him and the Indians' front office, why should he hold any expectation or hope that Cleveland would now conduct its business differently?

Alan approached us and said that Tal wanted to meet that day. It was then about 2:00 P.M. I said, "Tell him we'll meet at 3:30." Andre interjected immediately his view that we should not meet and subject ourselves to any more patronizing offers. I told Alan to tell Smith that we would give him our answer within five minutes.

As Alan walked towards Tal, I told Andy that not only did we have nothing to lose, but that clubs often make last minute major moves in their negotiating position. Thornton was very reluctant to meet, but I persuaded him to trust my judgment. His confidence in me was such that he agreed to meet, even though I knew his heart was not in his decision.

I walked over to Alan and Smith and said that we would meet at 3:30. Smith said he wanted the meeting to be kept a secret, so I suggested meeting two blocks away, at Baker & Botts, the law firm at which I had practiced after I graduated from law school. Baker & Botts was counsel to the Hendrickses, and thanks to senior partner Tom Berry, an old friend and confidant, I had a conference room at my disposal during the winter meetings. Smith agreed to the meeting place, whereupon Alan, Andre, and I proceeded immediately to the offices of Baker & Botts.

We received a call from Smith requesting that the meeting be moved back to 4:30. I figured that one hour was adequate to hear Cleveland's proposal and make the 5:30 meeting with Baltimore, so I agreed. I had little expectation that the Cleveland meeting would be productive.

At 4:30, the Cleveland brass — president Peter Bavasi, general manager Phil Seghi and hired gun Tal Smith — arrived. The seating at the conference table was hasty but exactly proper. At the far end, away from the door, sat Andre Thornton. I sat to his right, with Alan next to me. At the other end of the conference table sat Peter Bavasi. To his right sat Tal Smith, and next to him, Phil Seghi. I quipped, "We did this much quicker than was done at the Paris peace talks," a reference to the haggling over the seating and configuration of the table at the talks to end the Vietnam War. Everyone laughed.

I looked at the Cleveland contingent and quickly realized that Bavasi would be the spokesman. Alan and I had known Bavasi from his days as president of the Toronto Blue Jays. He had been very marketing-oriented at Toronto, and he would likely be the same way at Cleveland. Bright and with a quick, often acerbic wit, Bavasi was from an old baseball family.

Bavasi spoke first: "Andy, we're here because we want you on the Indians. You're important to the team and to the city of Cleveland. I've talked to many people in the business community. . . ."

As he continued, I thought, "Great speech, and true, but do you have anything materially new to offer?" At this point, words were not going to get the job done, numbers were.

For about five minutes, Bavasi continued his stirring speech about Andre, the club, and what Peter planned to achieve in Cleveland. As he talked, he pulled out of his briefcase the contract that I had prepared, the one at $1,100,000 per year, for four years, guaranteed. Bavasi went on to say, "and to prove the sincerity of my position, I'm signing the contract Randy prepared, exactly as it is, without changing a word."

Peter Bavasi then signed the contract, with much flair, rose from his chair, and put the contract in the middle of the conference table, within easy reach for Andre Thornton.

Andre did not make a move toward the contract. He looked directly at Peter and commenced a speech the equal of Bavasi's. Thornton began, "Peter, I've enjoyed my years in Cleveland. I've enjoyed the club, the community. Cleveland is my home. Randy, Alan and I have thought matters over carefully. . . ."

I stared at the contract, listened to Thornton intently while reflecting on his calm and collected speech. I then focused on the tension in the faces of Bavasi, Seghi, and Smith.

Andy concluded, ". . . so we decided on certain terms and conditions for Cleveland. I decided that if Cleveland met each and every condition, without exception, that I would sign. And Peter, since you have met those terms and conditions, I will sign with the Cleveland Indians," whereupon he reached for the contract. I quickly supplied the pen for his signature.

The room lit up, as we spontaneously jumped to our feet to celebrate. As Bavasi congratulated Thornton warmly, Tal Smith approached me and said, "You did an outstanding job for your client." Phil Seghi was beaming. He told me, "It's a lot of money, but if any player deserves it, Andy does." And I had no doubt that he was as happy for Thornton as was anyone in the room.

Bavasi came over and said, "Well, I'm a lot easier than I was in Toronto. You won this one, but we needed him." I told him I understood, and said, "Peter, you won, too, and your boldness made the difference."

The moments following Andre Thornton's acceptance speech will always be special to me. The competition was over. Everyone was relaxed and happy. The room was full of old baseball acquaintances, and the deal was done.

I thought of the tradition of hockey players shaking hands after a game and how the players on the softball team I played for always shook hands with the players on the other team after every game. I thought how I loved those traditions and believed they represented how competition, in and out of sports, is supposed to be. You cannot compete without other competitors and that reality bonds you to your opponent. You define each other. I was content as was everyone else in the room. It was a serendipitous moment.

Peter Bavasi asked how soon could we have a press conference. Suddenly remembering Baltimore, I said, "7:00 P.M.," and immediately asked Alan what time it was. He said, "5:30."

I took Alan aside. "We must see Baltimore immediately. This will not be enjoyable, but Baltimore had its chance and wanted to bargain and stall, so they lost." We quickly walked back to the Hyatt Regency and proceeded up to the Orioles' suite. As we entered, Williams was smiling and relaxed. That would soon change.

We sat down and I said, "Gentlemen, when we left earlier today, everyone agreed that you understood that you had no exclusive, that if we reached an agreement with another club between the time we left and this meeting, there would be no hard feelings." Williams, Lucchino, and Peters nodded in unison. Their expressions changed as they realized the consequences of my opening remarks.

I continued, "Well, we've just come from meeting with Cleveland, and Andy has signed with Cleveland." I thanked them for their interest and reiterated that my client had been sincerely interested in Baltimore. Hank Peters asked immediately if Cleveland had agreed to our proposal. I said Cleveland had. He smiled slightly at me. I interpreted that slight smile as disagreement with Baltimore's strategy, and an acknowledgement that I had achieved my goal while his owner had not achieved his goal. Larry Lucchino was ever gracious. Williams strained to be gracious, but to no avail. It was clear that he viewed the news as a loss, and he certainly did not like to lose. After exchanging some parting comments, Alan, Andy, and I exited rather quickly.

Cleveland's press conference, which convened thirty minutes later, marked the first major signing of the 1984 winter meetings. After the announcement was made, Andre Thornton gave a fine talk and answered the usual questions posed from the reporters in the audience. Once the formal segment of the press conference was completed, many reporters came to the podium to ask Andy and me questions. Two of those reporters were Thomas Boswell and Hal

Bodley. They were obviously impressed with Andre Thornton, the man, and asked insightful questions about his life, rather than just focusing on the usual baseball questions.

Ten minutes later, Alan joined us and said that most reporters were guessing the contract to be $600,000 per year for three years. I smiled, knowing that Andre's contract was the highest in baseball history for a designated hitter.

Murray Chass of the *New York Times* came up to introduce himself. He knew Alan, but he and I had not met. He reiterated what Alan had said about the reporters' estimates being $600,000 for three years. Murray said he thought those guesses were too low.

Could I reveal the terms? I thought of how resourceful reporters were at asking questions. They usually try three different ways to ask a question, hoping you will finally answer, sort of like how a kid bugs his parents to go to the movies. I thought, "What the heck, the numbers will be out by tomorrow."

"They're way too low," I said to Murray. "How about the highest paid DH?"

Without missing a beat Chass said, "900 for 3."

"How about 1.1 for 4?" I said. Murray's surprised expression turned into a big grin, and after chatting for a few more minutes, we parted.

Within minutes of the close of the press conference, a report of Andre Thornton's signing with the Indians was announced at a Cleveland Cavaliers basketball game. The crowd rose and gave a standing ovation. That showed how well liked and respected Andre Thornton was in the Cleveland community.

Within a day, Texas signed designated hitter Cliff Johnson, and the Orioles rebounded by signing Fred Lynn. That is how the free agent market often works. After the player who is the highest in demand signs, clubs focus on the next tier of available players. One signing dominoes into another.

As I drove home with Andre, I reflected upon the importance of the timing of a player's performance and his contract rights. He had played for five years at $370,000 per year, while the value of comparable players had escalated rapidly. Because Thornton's old contract was signed at the tail end of the era of the $400,000 star player, he had been distinctly underpaid for six straight years, though he did have the security of the multiyear guarantee in his contract.

Thornton had been a power hitter deluxe, and he had endured

the unseemly injury mess with the Indians. Now, I thought, he may end up being overpaid in the latter part of his career, especially in years three and four of his new contract. He would be 38 and 39 years old during those contract years. Overall, I concluded, my friend and client would probably be paid, in the aggregate, what he had been worth as a player. Most importantly, he would be paid by Cleveland.

I said to Andre, "It is simply justice that Cleveland pays you on this new contract. If you had signed with any other club, they would be paying you money that Cleveland owes you."

Chapter 10

1994 and Beyond

Baseball has served as a metaphor for poets and philosophers, who have romantically chronicled its exacting nature. "Casey at the Bat" paints a common picture for those who have played the game at various levels of skill, for all baseball players have at one time been humbled by a strikeout in the clutch. Its constants give baseball a timeless quality.

Regrettably, a timeless quality of ownership has been the facile use of the hollow cry "wolf" regarding impending financial disaster in the game. As *Business Week* reported in its August 17, 1992, edition:

> To hear the lords of baseball tell it, this is a lousy time to own a team. With player salaries still rising and TV revenues headed for a fall, "baseball is poised for a catastrophe, and it might not be far off," Major League Baseball Commissioner Fay Vincent warned in 1991.

The *Business Week* article noted the ever increasing prices paid for baseball franchises. While the sales of the Houston Astros to Drayton McLane and the Detroit Tigers to Mike Ilitch were the focus of the article, the prices paid for those clubs were dwarfed by the $173 million paid in bankruptcy court in 1993 for the Baltimore Orioles, nobody's definition of a large-market club. Such hefty increases in franchise values are hardly consistent with a game poised for a catastrophe.

The Orioles recently rebounded not only on the field, but

290

because of the field. Camden Yard, the Orioles new stadium, is at once nostalgic and modern. The stadium "understands" the intimacy and tradition of baseball, and since they built it, the fans did come. New stadiums in Cleveland and Arlington should do for the Indians and Rangers what Camden Yards did for Baltimore.

The expansion Colorado Rockies set a major league record for attendance in 1993, as 4,483,350 fans saw an ever improving club. The other expansion club, the Florida Marlins, also played well for an expansion club and recorded attendance of 3,064,847. The fan support for the two expansion clubs should have provided reassuring proof to skeptics that the game's timeless quality is a magnetic attraction.

Despite ever increasing franchise values and successes by nonlarge-market clubs, representatives of ownership continually preach doom and gloom as they seek to impose a salary cap on the players during the 1994 collective bargaining talks. Richard Ravitch, the head of the PRC, stated his case in the "Backtalk" section of the July 4, 1993, *New York Times*. Ravitch wrote:

> San Diego Padres fans have a right to be upset with the trading last week of another of their stars — this time Gary Sheffield. The passionate loyalty of fans is the backbone of major league baseball, and if they weren't angry, baseball would be in big trouble. The problem is that the anger is misdirected. It is the system, not San Diego's management, that has brought about the current situation.
>
> The Padres are not unique in the current environment. Pittsburgh, Milwaukee and Montreal, to name a few others, have similar problems and have been forced to reduce payroll. The Players Association has long claimed that the free marketplace should dictate salaries; if the owners couldn't pay, they wouldn't.
>
> When economic conditions force a club to cut its payroll, however, the fans, the players and the press immediately call for action to prevent a market correction. A sound economic system is urgently needed to bring order to the game and prevent exactly what we are seeing happen with growing frequency.
>
> In "Without a Commissioner, Padres Unload Their Stars" (The *Times*, June 27), much space was devoted to the lack of a commissioner to halt these trades. But only a cynical reference was offered regarding the economic problems of a small-market club and of baseball itself. This, of course, is really the story. San Diego was referred to as being a "so-called" small market club in these "so-called" troubling economic times. The innuendo is clear.

The Padres play in a market surrounded by an ocean, a foreign country, a desert and the Dodgers/Angels market. Is this not a tough market to develop broadcast outlets and increase a fan base? And as for troubling economic times, when an industry is facing a huge decrease in revenues and is unable to negotiate its collective labor costs, is there not a need for a warning flag?

Tom Werner and his associates bought the Padres with a good-faith intention to keep the club in a difficult geographic market and to put any profits back into the development of the club. In fact, the then commissioner, Fay Vincent, solicited the investment by Werner's group to preserve baseball in San Diego. The commissioner also approved the level of capitalization.

Since purchasing the club, the Padres owners have lost more than $10 million. These losses were unforeseeable because baseball's current system provides no rational relationship between revenues and player costs. The Padres' actions have been of sad necessity. No other owner would have acted differently under the circumstances unless the owner had the personal capacity and desire to make the club the object of perpetual charity.

Moreover, how could any commissioner with integrity require the club to perpetuate operating losses, particularly having encouraged the purchase originally?

Baseball urgently needs to usher in an era of economic reform, which will provide for small-market clubs to compete satisfactorily with large-market clubs. With all teams drawing from the same pool of players, no small-market club can expect to have a payroll comparable to a large-market club as things now stand.

The economic reform that the player relations committee of major league baseball is trying to bring about contains two essential elements that would address these problems:

1) It would set player salaries as a negotiated percentage of baseball's gross revenues so that players and owners would share the benefits of good times and the burdens of bad.

2) To equalize competition, club payrolls would be negotiated to a level of comparability and a new formula for revenue distribution among the clubs would be set to provide small-market clubs with an enhanced ability to meet a greater payroll.

San Diego's problem is another wake-up call for baseball to set its industry on a prudent financial course, lest we continue to see the haves and have-nots grow further apart, creating a system where fans are deprived of top competition. These economic reforms are critical, not for the profitability of the owners, but for the benefit of the fans and the stability of the game.

Many independent observers are not convinced that Ravitch has accurately defined the problem or the solution. The April 2, 1993, *Wall Street Journal* ran a front page article by Timothy K. Smith and Erle Norton. The headline was lengthy, but appropriate: "Throwing Curves, One Baseball Statistic Remains a Mystery: The Real Bottom Line. Owners Have Been Warning of Catastrophe for Years; Economists Are Skeptical. The Games Accountants Play." Smith and Norton wrote:

"Professional baseball is on the wane," in the words of Albert Spalding, a former player and league executive. "Salaries must come down, or the interest of the public must be increased in some way. If one or the other does not happen, bankruptcy stares every team in the face." Granted, Mr. Spalding has been dead for 77 years, and he issued this warning in 1881, but he said, in a nutshell, exactly what baseball-team owners are saying today.

... Economists, and players, consider grim diagnoses of baseball perfectly accurate according to generally accepted accounting principles — and, broadly speaking, baloney. A baseball team has three strong incentives to show paper losses: to obtain a tax write-off (usually to offset profits from the owner's other businesses); to present a bleak picture in labor negotiations with players; and to scare municipalities into subsidizing baseball with additional tax dollars (for a new access road, a parking lot or a whole stadium).

... The scant figures that have trickled out over the years indicate that team owners go to considerable lengths to inflate expenses and deflate revenue. Turner Broadcasting System Inc., which owns the Braves, paid the team $9 million in 1991 for a TV contract that observers say is worth several times that. Anheuser-Busch Cos., which owns the St. Louis Cardinals, runs concession revenue at Busch Stadium through an affiliated corporation, and it doesn't show up on the Cardinals' books. Owners commonly form a corporation to buy a team, lend the corporation the purchase price and collect interest from it, pocketing the interest payments while increasing team expenses.

Owners pay themselves multimillion-dollar salaries and consulting fees, and they pile expenses into the "general and administrative expense" column, economists say. "You're always on club business. You get an unlimited expense account," says Gerald Scully, an economist who wrote "The Business of Major League Baseball."

Ravitch's goal of a salary structure where players are paid "a negotiated percentage of baseball's gross revenues" would create a salary cap in baseball. His other goal of "a new formula for revenue distribution among the clubs . . . to provide small-market clubs with an enhanced ability to meet a great payroll" is conditioned upon securing the salary cap from the union.

The owners voted in February 1993 to "link" the second goal to the first. Predictably, union chief Donald Fehr was unimpressed:

> Maybe one day they'll explain to us what the linkage is. I'm glad they did it; I'm sure they got an enhanced feeling of solidarity. I hope they feel better. But the real linkage is the big-market owners won't share with small-market owners unless the players give them back the money. That's the only linkage we've heard about.

Fehr and Ravitch were interviewed by *Skybox* magazine in its spring 1993 issue. Their answers to questions posed to them were particularly revealing.

> Ravitch: My objective is to have a system in which the owners know what their costs are going to be as measured by a percentage of our gross revenues . . . (The current) system cannot work in a period of declining revenue.
>
> . . . In the 1980's owners didn't particularly care whether they had annual operating profits because their franchise values were going up. Now, neither is happening. Their asset values are going down, and they are not making operating profits.
>
> Fehr: I think arbitration is the whipping boy. The kind of fundamental change that Dick Ravitch is talking about is placing some sort of artificial limitation on the market for player salaries. That is what a salary cap is. The clubs come in and say, "Please agree that under no circumstances will the players be paid more than X dollars in the aggregate." But sooner or later in the negotiations, you ask what happens if we don't agree, and the owners say, "We'll pay you more." That makes such negotiations difficult.
>
> What the players want is market value for their salaries. That is a pretty hard thing to argue with. What the clubs want is for the players to subsidize them by taking less than market value for their services. As for arbitration, if the clubs had been willing at any time since 1976 to say, "We'll make all of the players free agents," you probably would not have arbitration now. But they know that arbitration is better for them than the players' being free agents, and that is why they prefer it.

... Everyone knows that baseball's particular revenue-sharing formulas do not share local revenue generated from broadcast to any significant degree, and that such revenue has become an ever-increasing source of baseball income, so that the relative proportion of income generated by large and small market teams has grown farther and farther apart. The revenue-sharing rules should be re-examined and viewed in the context of today's income streams as compared to what they were 25 to 30 years ago.

The owners have great difficulty doing that because the large market owners would rather keep the money than give it to the small market owners. That produces labor problems because when the small market owners say, "Help us," the large market owners say, "We won't give you any money but we'll help you get it back from the players." Large market owners know that if the players' salaries can be lowered to an artificial low level, then maybe they'll hear less bitching and moaning from the small market owners and in the meantime, the big market owners will make a fortune.

Ravitch's proposal is founded on the premise that baseball is entitled to both immunity from normal business cycles and predictable labor costs — as if such goals are normal and generally attainable by traditional businesses. In a typical business, when revenues decrease, or profit margins are squeezed, the owner and his managers evaluate how to decrease costs, among other considerations. Baseball should take such a self-disciplined step, rather than seek to create an artificial limit on player salaries. The players understand that the artificial limitation of a salary cap hinders movement by free agents, as has been the case in the NBA and NFL. They also understand that teams in the NBA and the NFL have worked overtime to create and utilize loopholes in the salary cap system.

Enlightened baseball clubs are already taking steps to reduce costs. As reported in the October 13, 1993, *Houston Chronicle*, the Chicago White Sox's Jerry Reinsdorf publicly announced the club's plan for its payroll to "be down considerably" in 1994, to coincide with lowered television revenues.

The *Chronicle* also reported that the 1993 World Series champion Toronto Blue Jays, who turned over one-half of its 1992 world championship club, would also reduce its player costs:

"We're going to try as much as possible to hold this (1993) club together," said Jays general manager Pat Gillick, "but unfortunately, throughout baseball, because of payroll considerations you have to break up some of these ballclubs."

The changes in personnel from 1992 to 1993 obviously did not harm the quality of the club the Blue Jays fielded.

On June 25, 1993, Fehr and Ravitch jointly appeared before the Associated Press sports editors' annual convention in New Orleans. Ravitch continued his campaign that the owners would agree to do that which is in their collective interest (i.e., revenue sharing) only if the players would agree to do that which is not in their collective interest (i.e., a salary cap). Harry Shattuck of the *Houston Chronicle* filed the following report from this particular round of the Fehr-Ravitch debates:

> The San Diego Padres' trade this week of All-Star third baseman Gary Sheffield to the Florida Marlins illustrates baseball's critical problems, the owners' chief labor negotiator said Friday.
>
> "Sheffield is a sad example of what's happening in baseball," Richard Ravitch, president of the major-leagues' Player Relations Committee, told the Associated Press Sports Editors. "Baseball is in trouble. Revenues are going down. Teams in small markets can't compete on an equal basis. And small-market clubs are beginning to peel off their payrolls. It's going to create a competitive imbalance."
>
> But if that's the case, Major League Baseball Players Association executive director Donald Fehr said, the owners have only themselves to blame.
>
> "Baseball simply isn't organized well," Fehr said. "And they've made it clear they aren't interested in the players having a say in major decisions. They didn't even notify the players about the most recent television agreement."
>
> Fehr and Ravitch will have leadership roles over the next few months when owners and players attempt to negotiate a labor agreement.
>
> During a joint appearance at the APSE annual convention, Ravitch called for a salary cap — or, in Ravitch's words, "a floor-to-ceiling plan" — similar to that utilized in the NBA and soon to be adopted by the NFL.
>
> Under that plan, Ravitch said, "The owners and players would ride up and down with the game."
>
> But Fehr said he finds the idea of a cap "disturbing" and countered: "It's an extremely difficult thing for the players to swallow when they're asked to make concessions because of failures caused by others."
>
> "And then what are we supposed to do? Leave the same people minding the store?"

Ravitch said he does not blame the players or their union for the dilemma he describes.

"The player compensation system we have now was fairly negotiated," Ravitch said. "It has just had unintended results."

Ravitch expressed concern that baseball is losing its market share of the entertainment dollar. And advertisers, Ravitch said, consider those who watch the sport "too white and too old to attract the top advertising dollars."

Ravitch also emphasized his belief that adoption of a revenue-sharing plan to assist small-market teams is essential.

But he conceded that owners have spent months without agreeing even among themselves on how such a plan would work.

Ravitch cited San Diego as a special victim of baseball's current plight. Club management reportedly has been forced to cull the roster of high-salaried athletes in order to trim costs. And Sheffield's departure Thursday angered fans and his Padres teammates.

"The San Diego story is a case where just a few years ago, a group of guys in the entertainment industry made some money," Ravitch said. "Not super money. But they used it to buy a baseball team.

"They bought the Padres franchise for $75 million to $80 million. And they borrowed most of that. They didn't buy the team to make more money. They bought it for fun or for civic pride.

"Then, they got into this system, and all of a sudden they started losing a lot of their money. They've lost $12 million over the past year.

"Now, what are they supposed to do?"

Fehr offered a different interpretation.

"A group of people bought the team, and then they found out they didn't know how much it was going to cost," Fehr said. "Why not? They never asked us. Shouldn't they have known?

"The truth is that the people running baseball would all like to say, 'I didn't know this,' and 'I didn't know that,' but 'I would like to keep all my best players and pay them less.' It doesn't work that way in any other business."

Fehr downplayed Ravitch's projection of gloom for the sport, saying: "The notion of survival is not one that's relevant," and stressing anew his position that more input by players could help the game prosper.

Amid much fanfare, the owners assembled in Kohler, Wisconsin, the week of August 9, 1993, to vote on revenue sharing between the clubs. Ravitch confidently stated before the meetings that he believed he would secure the twenty-one votes necessary to implement his revenue sharing proposal.

The projected decline in revenue from the national television contract fueled the push for revenue sharing. Under the terms of the final year of CBS' four-year contract with baseball, the network paid approximately $401 million in 1993, or $15.4 million per club, to the twenty-six nonexpansion clubs.

Beginning in 1994, the lucrative CBS contract was replaced by a six-year joint venture agreement between the twenty-eight major league baseball clubs and NBC and ABC. The joint venture partners produce the games and sell advertising. Revenues to the joint venture are divided between the partners, although the lion's share goes to the baseball clubs.

According to Philadelphia Phillies President Bill Giles, one of the members of baseball's television contract negotiating committee, 1994 revenues to the clubs are estimated to be $200 million, or $7.1 million per club for all twenty-eight clubs. No observer doubts the projections of a decline in revenues from national television in 1994. Some observers believe the decline will be short-lived, while others see the decline as permanent. Still other observers opine that any decline in national television revenues will be offset by an increase in revenues from local broadcast rights.

As the Kohler meeting proceeded, it became clear that all clubs had become resigned to operating on less national television revenue in the near future. This served as a catalyst for so-called small-market clubs to ask their large market brethren to share the wealth. Despite Ravitch's optimistic prediction, the revenue sharing proposal failed to gain the necessary twenty-one votes. Reports indicated that only eighteen clubs voted for the revenue sharing proposal.

A committee was later appointed to attempt to construct a revenue sharing plan acceptable to at least twenty-one clubs. Members appointed to the committee, according to USA Today's Hal Bodley, were George Steinbrenner of the Yankees, John Harrington of the Red Sox, Rusty Rose of the Rangers, Paul Beeston of the Blue Jays, Jerry Reinsdorf of the White Sox, Dave Montgomery of the Phillies, Jerry Bell of the Twins, and John Ellis of the Mariners.

A by-product of the Kohler meeting was the announcement by Ravitch of a no-lockout pledge. Apparently, the owners voted on this pledge in June but delayed its announcement until the Kohler meeting in order to have something positive to announce in the event the revenue sharing proposal failed to pass.

Ravitch reduced the no-lockout pledge into a written form and delivered it in a letter to Fehr. The letter was released to the Associated Press in New York, which reported its contents on August 18:

> We do not want any artificial deadlines to disrupt the bargaining process . . . .
>
> Therefore, as long as the MLBPA does not strike, the clubs will not unilaterally implement a player-compensation system that would interfere with or alter the 1993-94 free-agent and salary-arbitration contract signing season. Further, the clubs will not lock out the players during the 1994 season. . . .
>
> This commitment should provide the parties with ample time to negotiate a new Basic Agreement without the need for a destructive work stoppage . . . By removing the possibility that economic action might threaten the 1993-94 free-agent/salary-arbitration contract signing season, I hope that the clubs have convinced the MLBPA of our strong desire to reach a negotiated solution to the difficult issues confronting the game.

A cynic would have suggested that the no-lockout vote was conditioned upon a revenue sharing plan not passing in Kohler. Had a revenue sharing plan passed, the owners would have likely pressed the union immediately for a salary cap. Since a revenue sharing plan was not instituted, the owners merely postponed a confrontation with the union under the guise of a desire "to reach a negotiated solution to the difficult issues confronting the game."

Support for such a cynical interpretation can be found in a candid statement made by White Sox owner Jerry Reinsdorf, named the most powerful man in baseball by *Baseball America* in its January 11, 1993, issue. Associated Press reporter Ronald Blum wrote a comprehensive story on August 30, 1992, concerning the possible removal from office of Commissioner Fay Vincent and economic issues then confronting baseball. In his story, Blum quoted Reinsdorf on how to deal with the players' union:

> "You do it by taking a position and telling them we're not going to play unless we make a deal, and being prepared not to play one or two years if you have to," said Chicago White Sox owner Jerry Reinsdorf, widely regarded as the most influential voice on management's Player Relations Committee. "You have to have 75 percent (of the clubs) with you. If they're not, then we shouldn't

attempt (a lockout). I can survive. This ballclub isn't one of the teams that's going to go broke."

Whether the owners put the players "on hold" until the owners adopted revenue sharing and were therefore in a position to initiate a confrontation with the players, or whether the owners are sincere in their written declaration to peacefully negotiate a labor agreement, will be revealed over time. It is clear that the owners find it easier to agree to the goal of a salary cap, the price for which will be paid by the players, than a plan of revenue sharing, independent of a salary cap, the price for which will be paid by the wealthiest of clubs.

The small-market clubs were disappointed that their large-market partners agreed to revenue sharing in principle but would not agree to a specific plan in Kohler. Predictably, the small-market clubs weighed their options. One of those options was reported by Ronald Blum of the Associated Press on September 16:

> More than a dozen of baseball's small-market clubs are threatening to black out all non-network games next season as a way to force a revenue-sharing agreement.
>
> Five sources connected with baseball, including owners, officials and lawyers, told Associated Press that without revenue sharing, at least 15 clubs will scrap decades-old agreements that permit teams to televise games in their local markets.
>
> The sources spoke on the condition they not be identified.
>
> If the teams carry through with their threat, the only games guaranteed on television would be the 12 national network broadcasts on ABC and NBC, and broadcasts on ESPN, which will televise approximately 75 games to each market next season. In addition, teams would be able to cut separate deals with opponents for each individual game.
>
> Without the agreements, which can be terminated when five teams in a league give notice, superstations such as WGN, WTBS, WPIX and WWOR would lose much of their most attractive programming.
>
> Large- and small-market teams are battling over the amount of revenue they split, with several small-market teams saying they need a larger piece of the pie in order to survive. Ten large-market clubs broke away and formed their own caucus at a major league owners meeting last month, forcing extended negotiations on a revenue-sharing deal. Talks are ongoing, and 21 votes are needed to pass any proposal.
>
> The National League Broadcasting Agreement was signed in

February 1956 and the American League Broadcasting Agreement in December 1965. Each deal automatically renews each year unless at least five teams in that league decide to cancel.

Currently, superstations make payments that are split among all teams, and clubs split a portion of their cable revenue, after deductions for expenses. AL teams share 20% of their cable money and NL teams give visiting teams 25% of the cable money attributed to each game.

Sources said the Padres, Astros, Marlins, Pirates and Expos were the five teams that instigated the move in the NL, and they later were joined by the Reds, Cardinals and Giants. At least seven clubs in the AL have given notice to terminate their agreement, including the Brewers and Twins.

On January 6, 1994, the owners reassembled at the Hyatt Regency in Rosemont, Illinois, to consider new plans for revenue sharing. In contrast to his pronouncements prior to the Kohler meeting, Richard Ravitch was silent about the prospects for passage of his new revenue sharing proposal. Ravitch's new proposal was "totally different conceptually from" the revenue sharing proposal defeated in Kohler. "There is no resemblance whatsoever" between the two plans, Ravitch told the press.

Ravitch had spent the intervening months between the Kohler and Rosemont meetings attempting to formulate a plan acceptable to at least twenty-one clubs. His efforts convinced Florida and Texas to join the eighteen clubs who had voted for his plan at Kohler. However, his new, and undoubtedly watered-down, plan fell one vote short, as Baltimore, Boston, Colorado, Toronto, St. Louis, Los Angeles, the New York Yankees, and the New York Mets voted against the revised PRC plan.

The eight dissident clubs introduced their own revenue distribution plan, but it garnered only eleven votes. John Harrington noted that this plan would have tripled "the amount of money transferred among clubs." With no prospects for the passage of either plan, the owners adjourned the Rosemont meeting with the goal of attempting to pass another revised plan at their meeting scheduled for Fort Lauderdale on January 17. "I'm optimistic we can get it done there," de facto Commissioner Bud Selig told the press.

Ronald Blum of the Associated Press attended the meeting and reported Ravitch's reaction to the 20–8 vote on his plan: "I'd be a liar if I said I hadn't hoped we'd come to a conclusion today. We've been at it a long time and it would be nice if we got on to the main event of negotiating with the union."

The proposed revenue sharing plans were conditioned upon the clubs negotiating a salary cap with the union. As reported by *Houston Chronicle* reporter Alan Truex, Selig said, "There will not be revenue sharing without a salary cap."

Yankees owner George Steinbrenner told Hal Bodley of *USA Today*, "The big battle to get this (revenue-sharing) is not going to be among ourselves. We're facing the biggest challenge when we go to the union (asking for a salary cap)."

The owners were at a crossroad as they prepared for the Fort Lauderdale meeting. The clubs in the largest markets or with the highest attendance were opposed to the Ravitch plans proposed in Kohler and Rosemont. The eight holdouts recognized, however, that some type of revenue sharing plan had to be adopted. This realization led them to develop the alternate plan, which was defeated in Rosemont.

Most analysts agreed that it was time to restructure the division of income between the clubs. The economics of the game had changed over the years, and the disparity in income between clubs had grown larger.

Currently, American League clubs pay 20 percent of the gate to the visiting club and 3 percent of the gate to the league. National League clubs pay the visiting club 72 cents out of each ticket over $1, but the visiting club must, in turn, pay the league office 28 cents. The home club thus retains the lion's share of all revenue generated at the ball park, including all concessions and parking. Income from licensing, national television, copyrights, All Star games, and super stations are divided equally. American League clubs divide 20 percent of each club's cable income, after expenses, while each National League club pays the visiting club 25 percent of the home club's average cable income per game.

While the clubs recognized that they were "partners" in a common endeavor, the significant differences between them made arriving at an agreeable formula difficult. Large-market clubs were reluctant to increase the split of revenues, not only because it would have resulted in a loss of income to those clubs, but because it could have caused a decline in franchise values.

In essence, revenue sharing is not only a transfer of income, but can become a transfer of franchise values as well. George Steinbrenner will not readily agree to transfer part of the income and franchise value of the Yankees to prop up the Padres. Steinbrenner told Hal

Bodley of *USA Today*, "We have to decide if these cities that are struggling should really have teams." While Steinbrenner acknowledged the need for some form of revenue sharing, he told Bodley, "This is basically socialism at work."

Many of the best club operators do not respect the business acumen of their "partners" who run inferior operations. Those top notch operators believe that revenue sharing is largely a subsidy to inefficient or incompetent operators. They want no part of a welfare system designed to aid those who are disadvantaged largely due to their own inability to organize and operate a first-rate organization. While most club officials avoided stating this publicly, Dodger owner Peter O'Malley could no longer restrain himself during the weekend prior to the Fort Lauderdale meeting. Ross Newhan reported O'Malley's frustrations in the January 15, 1994, *Los Angeles Times*:

> Amid increasingly strained relations between baseball's large- and smaller-revenue teams, Dodger President Peter O'Malley said Friday that he is outraged by suggestions from some of those smaller teams that the big-market teams aren't seriously trying to negotiate a revenue-sharing formula.
> "The clubs putting money into the pot have made an extraordinary effort to be creative, to reach out and satisfy the *quote* smaller *unquote* teams to the maximum extent that we can," the normally low-key O'Malley said.
> "If the smaller clubs feel we aren't, I'm sorry about that, but we can't be expected to pay for their mismanagement."

It became clear that to be acceptable, a revenue sharing plan had to recognize the inherent differences in franchise values and not undermine those values. Every legitimate variable influencing how clubs win and make money had to be recognized, so that superior organizations would not become unduly penalized.

It became even more clear that a simplistic plan would not pass, since twenty-one votes were necessary for approval. If a plan proposed only a token reallocation of revenue, the small-market clubs would reject it. If a plan proposed a large reallocation of revenue, the large-market clubs would reject it.

The eight holdout clubs stood firm as the Fort Lauderdale meetings opened on January 17, 1994. It was clear that a new, innovative proposal was needed to unplug the logjam. One was forthcoming on January 18. The author was St. Louis Cardinals President Stuart Meyer.

Meyer was assisted by Mark Gorris, the Cardinals Vice President for Business Operations. Meyer and Gorris developed their proposal after the Rosemont meeting failed to produce an agreement.

The St. Louis plan passed 28-0. Murray Chass of the *New York Times* reported on the strategy behind the Cardinals' plan.

> "People got stuck on names of plans," Meyer said, alluding to the "big-market" plan and the "small-market" plans that had been rejected by each side. "We decided to come in with a one-club plan. If we had come in with it six months ago, it probably would have been thrown in the trash."
>
> . . . "We said neither one of the plans was going to pass so let's come up with another one," Meyer related. "One thing that helped sell it was it wasn't from a group of clubs."
>
> The presence of the Cardinals in the high-revenue group was somewhat puzzling and Meyer acknowledged, "We're really a middle-market club." But he explained the club had joined with the high-revenue clubs "because of our philosophies."

The St. Louis plan created three classes of clubs. The effect of the plan was that clubs with high revenues would transfer money to clubs with low revenues. Clubs in the middle would neither pay nor receive. Clubs could change from one class to another, depending upon year-to-year revenues.

Once their aggregate revenues crossed a threshold, believed to be $50 million, the top clubs in revenues would contribute money to their poorer relations. Once the threshold was crossed, a regressive "tax" rate would be applied to the excess revenue. The result of the somewhat complex formula would be the amount of the "tax" paid by the wealthy clubs.

Because American League clubs currently share a greater percentage of revenues than do National League clubs, the clubs likely to incur the greatest cost under the formula were the New York Mets, the Los Angeles Dodgers, and the Colorado Rockies.

There were "safeguards" built into the formula to motivate the recipient clubs to operate in a competent and competitive manner. Those safeguards included conditions under which a recipient club could forfeit its subsidy. Tracy Ringolsby of the *Rocky Mountain News* reported the next day that a

> . . . team would lose eligibility for financial assistance if it exceeds the minimum payroll by more than 14%, according to sources. Franchises that have received money, which are either sold

and/or moved to another city, would have to repay a portion of the aid they were given. Eight teams — Milwaukee, Montreal, Seattle, San Diego, Pittsburgh, Minnesota, Kansas City and California — initially would qualify for help that will be on a sliding scale with an estimated maximum of $9 million for the neediest franchise.

After leveling charges and countercharges of greed against each other, the owners were now in a celebratory mood. The atmosphere at the press conference announcing the agreement was festive.

A triumphant Bud Selig said at the press conference, "For an industry that has been portrayed as rudderless, aimless, it did something tonight that it had never done and never even contemplated." While Selig's giddy perspective on passing a revenue sharing agreement was understandable, his pronouncement failed to acknowledge that the owners were, once again, going into collective bargaining with the goal of dictating the terms of the final agreement to the players.

The revenue sharing agreement was conditioned upon the union agreeing to a salary cap. Said Ravitch, "This plan will take effect when there is a new basic agreement with a salary-cap arrangement." He admitted, though, that "it won't be easy" to sell the concept to the union.

Hal Bodley reacted to the announcement with less enthusiasm than Selig. He wrote in the January 19 *USA Today*:

> This battle major league owners won Tuesday over revenue sharing is as exciting as watching grass grow.
> They've been pounding us with those words for more than a year, insisting revenue sharing had to be part of our baseball vocabulary. Just like collusion was in the '80s.

According to Chris Haft of the *Houston Post*, Selig "termed the revenue-sharing accord 'historic and meaningful.'" Alan Truex of the *Houston Chronicle* reported that Selig said, "Even this morning, if you had told me we would have gotten a 28–0 vote, I wouldn't have believed it. To me, the unanimous vote is very important."

It sure is easy for the owners to vote 28–0 to take the money from the players. There is nothing historic about owners voting to control the game and take back freedom and income from the players.

In a fashion reminiscent of the 1990 labor negotiations, Ravitch said during his extended press conference, "there's a real determination in baseball on part of the ownership to change the economic system in baseball, to try and embark on a new era of relationship with the players." Ravitch continued by saying, "The owners have historically misunderstood the unity and determination of the players. I hope the players do not make the same mistake this time that the owners have made in the past."

Ravitch subsequently spoke with Hal Bodley, who reported the management negotiator's new found confidence in the January 21, *USA Today*:

> "Work stoppages occur only when people misunderstand the leverage the other group has," says Ravitch. "Here, you have 28 owners who have agreed to share revenues because they want a salary cap, a more competitive game. They're determined to bargain a bit differently with the union.
>
> "We agreed to forgo the strongest economic weapon we have — the threat of a lockout. I hope the owners stick together, because if they don't, they will not be successful. That's why I was so pleased with the 28-0 vote (on revenue-sharing)."
>
> Fehr said Thursday, "We have all the objections to salary caps we had before. If there needs to be more revenue-sharing, what's that got to do with the players?"

Alan Truex of the *Houston Chronicle* reported the union leader's amplified response to the owners' proposal for a salary cap:

> "The notion of a salary cap is troublesome. It's a very difficult proposition. If the owners want to share revenues, they should just share revenues. They don't need a salary cap to do that.
>
> "If the players agree to accept a percentage of revenue, then you have to deal with the question of how the revenue will be generated. You have to have players in key management positions — a partnership."
>
> Ravitch argued that professional basketball and football have salary caps, and "in neither of those cases do the players have control over the business of conducting football or basketball."
>
> He added, "I do think it's important that the owners and players work together to market their game. I hope we can work together for this common benefit. We're far behind the other two major sports in working together to enhance the attractiveness of our product."

Perhaps Jackie Autry, Executive Vice President of the California Angels, best understood the clarity of the disagreement over the salary cap. She told Ross Newhan of the *Los Angeles Times*:

"I really have to wonder if we're not just spinning our wheels on (revenue sharing) because everything I've read seems to indicate the union won't accept a salary cap anyway."

The Fort Lauderdale meetings were expected to produce a new baseball commissioner. The two leading candidates were reported to be Northwestern University President Arnold Weber, and U.S. Olympic Committee Executive Director Harvey Schiller.

Chris Haft reported the owners' decision in the January 20, *Houston Post*:

These meetings began with expectations that a new commissioner would be recommended, if not named. Baseball has functioned without a chief executive since September 1992, when Fay Vincent was forced to resign.

Bill Bartholomay, the Atlanta Braves' chairman who directs the commissioner's search committee, said that his group has examined 382 candidates in its 344 days of existence and has interviewed 46 people.

But Bartholomay said that during Tuesday night's prolonged talks to form a revenue-sharing agreement, he received a document endorsed by 11 franchises stating that given the industry's state of turmoil, they would prefer not to bring in a new boss until labor negotiations with the players end. Other clubs, said Bartholomay, joined in that sentiment, bringing the total number to "16 or 17."

This left the owners no choice but to persuade Selig, the chairman of their Executive Council and thus the sport's unofficial czar, to remain in the post indefinitely.

Murray Chass reported in the January 23, *New York Times* the rationale behind the move to keep Selig in place:

Acknowledging that the Montreal Expos were one of 11 clubs to sign the document given to the committee, Claude Brochu said: "We have tremendous support for Bud Selig and we just felt under his leadership we have come such a long way in the last year and a half, it would be unfair to change things midcourse. We like the way it's set up for the time being."

Bartholomay told the reporters covering the meetings, "Many of the clubs advised the search committee that they would not vote for a new commissioner until the labor situation was resolved."

Hal Bodley reported the reaction of Senator Howard Metzenbaum of Ohio in the January 20, *USA Today*. Metzenbaum interpreted the inaction on the selection of a new commissioner as a further indication of the arrogance of the owners, a reiteration of their desire for unlimited power over baseball. Senator Metzenbaum said:

> "The owners are looking to maximize their profits and don't want a commissioner around looking out for the good of the fans," he said. "Baseball owners have broken faith with the fans and cannot be trusted with an antitrust exemption."

Unfortunately, Senator Metzenbaum ignored the fact that the commissioner of baseball has always been an employee of the owners. The election of a new commissioner, beholden only to the owners, would not institute the changes the Senator seeks. Only when a commissioner is elected by the owners and the union, with a mandate to serve both parties, protect the integrity of the game, and serve the interests of the fans, will the Senator's objectives be met.

On January 19, 1994, the owners voted to amend the Major League Agreement, restructure the office of the commissioner, and disband the PRC. Hal Bodley reported the changes in the January 20, *USA Today*:

> Baseball owners approved sweeping changes to the 70-year old Major League Agreement Wednesday that essentially eliminates the Player Relations Committee and gives the commissioner more power, especially in labor negotiations.
>
> "The changes eliminate much of the ambiguity that existed," said Player Relations Committee President Dick Ravitch, who remains baseball's chief labor negotiator.
>
> A crucial battle between the PRC and Fay Vincent about whether the commissioner should have power to get involved in labor negotiations was one of several issues that led to Vincent's forced resignation Sept. 7, 1992.
>
> Under the changes adopted Wednesday, the commissioner will have sole authority over labor with the negotiator hired by him and working under him. The commissioner can also be involved as is the case in the NBA and NFL.
>
> Another important change requires 75% approval by owners to approve future collective bargaining agreements, lessening the chance a coalition of clubs could press for settlement as has been the case in the past. Previously, labor agreements required only majority approval, including five clubs in each league.
>
> Changes, however, do not include whether a commissioner

can be fired by ownership. Vincent insisted, under terms of the Major League Agreement, a commissioner could not be fired.

Milwaukee Brewers President Bud Selig, who agreed to continue as interim commissioner, stressed the need for a strong commissioner. He said, although the PRC will be dissolved, there will be a committee of owners that deals with player matters. Selig also said that he would hire an administrator to help run the Major League office in New York and that the office would not be moved to Chicago as some speculated.

Ravitch explained that the change requiring a 75 percent vote to ratify a labor agreement was an outgrowth of the vote on revenue sharing. Murray Chass wrote that, "if negotiations necessitate changes in the revenue-sharing plan, it could not be approved by a majority of clubs after it took three-quarters to adopt the plan in the first place."

Ravitch would continue to represent the owners in labor negotiations until a new collective bargaining agreement was reached. At that time, a new commissioner would be elected.

The job description of the new commissioner should lay to rest any illusion that a new commissioner, as proposed, will represent anyone but the owners. The owners wanted a counterpart to the head of the union, and they created one by redefining the responsibilities of the future commissioner.

While the owners increased the power of the new commissioner to become involved directly in labor negotiations and preserved his right to act in the best interests of baseball regarding on-the-field matters, the owners stripped the office of the power to invoke the "best interests" clause on economic matters. They insured that there would be no new Fay Vincent dictating solutions on the division of expansion rights fees, league realignments, or super station issues.

The office of the commissioner would resemble the position of chief executive officer of a corporation, with the owners resembling the directors and stockholders. On February 12, the owners released the new rules governing the powers of the office of the commissioner. Associated Press reporter Ronald Blum cogently evaluated the changes:

> The power of the baseball commissioner—a job vacant for nearly 1½ years—was sharply curtailed Friday when owners issued rules changes that prevent interference with their business decisions.
>
> Until now, commissioners had virtually unlimited power to

take actions "in the best interests of baseball." The amendments announced Friday prevent commissioners from using their "best interests" power to affect the World Series and postseason play, scheduling, interleague play, divisional alignment, expansion, the sale of teams, the relocation of teams, revenue sharing or broadcasting agreements.

"Basically, the commissioner seems to have no portfolio, power or job. That's what it looks like from a distance," former commissioner Peter Ueberroth said. "I think the changes dramatically change the position. There will be the appearance of more responsibility, but substantially less authority. That's the recipe for a non job."

The office of the commissioner has been vacant since Fay Vincent's resignation on Sept. 7, 1992, which came two months after he angered owners by unilaterally realigning the National League. Owners decided last month not to hire a new commissioner until after they reach a new collective bargaining agreement with the players, which isn't likely until the second half of this year.

"They are wrong, but time will correct it," Vincent said. "Eventually it changes back."

Because of the absence of a commissioner and the move against the powers of the office, Congress has been considering proposals to strip baseball of its antitrust exemption.

"I think overall the office is clearly strengthened," said Milwaukee Brewers president Bud Selig, chairman of the ruling executive council. "This brings the whole structure and office into this decade and gets ready for the 21st century. I think the key is it clears up the ambiguities."

Although clubs formally put labor relations under the power of the commissioner and eliminated the Player Relations Committee, they decided "the powers of the commissioner to act in the best interests of baseball shall be inapplicable to any matter relating to a subject of collective bargaining between the clubs and the Major League Baseball Players Association." That prevents a commissioner from unilaterally ending a management lockout, as Bowie Kuhn did in 1976.

New York Mets president Fred Wilpon, co-chairman of the restructuring committee, defended the changes, saying they made the commissioner's job more attractive because the role was more defined.

"He's involved in the integrity of the game as well as the chief person running the game," Wilpon said. "He's the chairman of all the major committees. That's a very powerful position."

The changes were contained in a restructuring report adopted by owners on Jan. 19. Lawyers have spent the past three weeks drafting the necessary amendments to the Major League Agreement, which governs baseball.

An accompanying news release said "owners have enhanced the authority and independence of the baseball commissioner" and changes were made "to clarify" the best interests power. However, officials speaking on the condition they not be identified admitted the "best interests" power was essentially gutted.

"The best interests clause is effective where it's most needed, in protecting the integrity of the game," American League president Bobby Brown said. "The only thing they were trying to do was eliminate the possibility of some move that didn't make an awful lot of sense."

The report didn't resolve whether owners have the power to fire commissioners, the central dispute in the battle between them and Vincent.

"There are people who have felt the commissioner could, and there are people who feel strongly he cannot be fired," Wilpon said.

The amendments announced Friday place the league presidents under the power of commissioners, who now will have the power to approve their hiring and re-election. In addition, the amendments specify that league presidents may be fired by a two-third vote of clubs in their league.

In addition, the executive council may now, by majority vote, declare a commissioner incapacitated and take over his power.

Ueberroth said the changes will lead to teams taking in less money, and predicted owners will raise ticket prices to make up the difference.

"When you have a committee make business decisions, it usually doesn't produce very positive results," he said. "Baseball is certainly run by the owners, and that may be proper for a while, but I agree with Fay that eventually their own actions will force a way back to a more traditional commissioner, like basketball or football."

Marvin Miller summarized the "real" power of the commissioner in *A Whole Different Ballgame*:

> He served for a specified term and could be replaced when his term was over, and his contract could be bought out at any time. In other words, whatever power a commissioner thought he had over the owners, the truth was that he was their man and was chosen to represent their interests, and if he ever became forgetful of this, he could be quickly reminded. Landis and Giamatti died in office.

Every single commissioner between them was decisively reminded where the real power was situated.

Criticism of the changes in the powers of the commissioner prompted de facto commissioner Selig to state on February 15 that the "commissioner has more power than any other human being I know of, including the president of the United States. But there's now different lines of accountability to reflect the era that we live in."

Senator Metzenbaum was not impressed. He held hearings on the antitrust exemption in Tampa, Florida, on March 21, 1994. Associated Press reporter Ronald Blum attended the hearings. His reports were carried in the March 22, *Houston Post*:

> Baseball's top executive clashed with U.S. senators who on Monday accused owners of lying and gutting the power of the vacant commissioner's office.
>
> During a contentious 2½-hour session across the street from a spring training ballpark, executive council chairman Bud Selig repeatedly attempted to avoid direct answers to questions from Sen. Howard Metzenbaum and advanced a new theory about the powers of the commissioner.
>
> "You don't have to be a genius, you don't have to be a Philadelphia lawyer, you don't have to be a Supreme Court justice to understand that under this new agreement you have denigrated the position of the commissioner," Metzenbaum told Selig, the Milwaukee Brewers president.
>
> "Senator Metzenbaum, I must say to you with all due respect, I disagree, and I disagree coming from a background in baseball," Selig replied. "That man has as much authority in this industry as any human being in the United States of America."
>
> Owners voted in January to strip the commissioner of his "best interests" power over most business decisions, an authority that had been upheld in federal appellate court.
>
> Selig testified several times that the commissioner—an office vacant for 18 months — still had broad power because of his authority to protect "integrity and public confidence in baseball."
>
> "He has more authority in those areas than he ever had in the past," Selig said.
>
> "I say BS," Metzenbaum shot back."

A new contender for the redefined position of commissioner emerged in the person of Senator George Mitchell of Maine. Murray Chass of the *New York Times* reported on this new development. His story was carried in the April 13, 1994, *Houston Chronicle*:

In removing himself from consideration for the U.S. Supreme Court, Sen. George Mitchell put himself in position Tuesday to be named the next baseball commissioner.

Baseball officials would not say that Mitchell was their man for the job, which has been unfilled the last 19 months. But people familiar with their thinking said they were prepared to move quickly to get him before someone else did.

Mitchell, D-Maine, who announced last month he would not seek re-election, has not said that he would accept the job of commissioner if it were offered. But at a news conference in Washington Tuesday, at which he announced he had withdrawn his name from consideration for the Supreme Court, he said in response to a question, "If the position is offered to me, I will consider it at that time."

Major-league club owners decided last January that they would not fill the vacant commissioner's office until they negotiated a new labor agreement with the players. No one knows how long that process could take, but their stance presents no problem for Mitchell because his term in the Senate, from which he is retiring, runs until next January.

Furthermore, the people who talked on the condition of anonymity about the current thinking of baseball officials said Mitchell could be named well before he would take office. They cited the precedent of the election of Peter Ueberroth in 1984.

The owners elected Ueberroth on March 3, 1984, knowing he would not be able to assume the position until the following October because he was president of the Los Angeles Olympic Organizing Committee.

Alan Truex of the *Chronicle* offered his reason as to why Mitchell had emerged as the leading candidate. His comments appeared in the April 17, *Chronicle*:

What hiring Mitchell, a Democrat, will do is protect major-league baseball from Sens. Howard Metzenbaum of Ohio and Joe Biden from Delaware, Democrats who have been trying to remove baseball's antitrust exemption. That is what the movement toward Mitchell is all about.

*   *   *

The owners should adopt a revenue-sharing plan and not condition it upon a salary cap. The St. Louis plan represents a good place to start. There are also some other ideas the owners should consider.

Every club should "tithe" 10 percent of its revenue to a central fund. The criteria for the distribution of the central fund could be based upon a variety of factors. A couple of examples of how the fund could be distributed follow.

Since major league clubs develop their players through farm systems, a club should be entitled to draw a stipulated sum from the increased central fund in order to be reimbursed in part for the loss of those players who leave the club through six-year free agency. A reimbursement amount for each year of a player's first six years would be set. If the player were traded, the right to receive the reimbursement for each year would either follow the player or the reimbursement could be retained. The reimbursement amount could be either a fixed amount per player or a variable amount based upon sophisticated performance criteria. The purpose of the reimbursement plan would be for a club to use the money drawn from the fund to help replenish its farm system.

Winning should be rewarded. A bonus payment from the central fund of $8 million to the World Series winner, $4 million to the World Series loser, and $1 million to the other playoff clubs would ensure that each club had a motive to win. Fan disenchantment would increase if the public recognized the number of teams in professional sports who treat winning as a subordinate goal to making a profit. I have no quarrel with any owner who strongly desires to make a profit. However, I believe that if a person wants to own a professional sports team, subsidized by public money in the form of a public stadium and training facility, he should be required to make a genuine effort to win.

Ironically, the clubs previously agreed on one form of reverse revenue sharing. The cost of the $280 million collusion settlement was divided evenly between the twenty-six conspiring clubs, even though the benefits of collusion were undoubtedly not distributed evenly. Clubs with higher payrolls during collusion generally benefited more from collusion than did clubs with lower payrolls.

*   *   *

Whether the need of owners to control players is pathological or based upon economic considerations, that need has been constant over the history of professional baseball. Since the Messersmith-McNally decision in late 1975, the owners have been obsessed with reversing its effect. The owners tried a lockout during spring training of 1976 in an effort to take back from the players the benefits gained from the decision. The collective bargaining agreement of August 1976 was an outgrowth of the Messersmith-McNally decision and the failed lockout. That agreement created the six-year free agency system still in effect.

In collective bargaining in 1980, the owners tried to thwart free agent movement by requiring that a club signing a free agent pay onerous compensation to the player's former club. The free agent issue was postponed until 1981, when the players were forced to strike for one-third of the regular season to protect their right to meaningful free agency.

The amount of the pension contribution, rather than free agency, was the major issue during collective bargaining in 1985. The issue was settled after a two-day strike during the regular season. The owners' acceptance of free agency during bargaining in 1985 was undoubtedly a smokescreen to mask an impending plan to control player movement. Collusion in the free agent market dates back to the 1985 season and lasted for four years.

In collective bargaining in 1990, PFP represented a different approach to controlling player movement. Since directly controlling player movement had failed repeatedly, the owners tried to control player movement indirectly. The discredited owners' proposal was summarily rejected by the players.

Rather than exercising restraint and control, the owners find it easier to ask for modifications in the current system. They prefer to shackle the players through a salary cap than deal with free market forces. They show no compunction about asking for a subsidy from the players through a salary cap. They show little sensitivity for the freedom issue, which motivated and sustained the player movement, since salary caps inhibit player movement.

Negotiations for a new collective bargaining agreement commenced on March 7, 1994, in Tampa, Florida. Richard Ravitch made his "pitch" for a salary cap to the players in attendance. They were unimpressed, and expressed their desire to continue the current system of compensation. A repeat performance was held in Phoenix, Arizona, on March 30.

Because of a lack of progress in negotiations, the players considered the possibility of a strike. The Associated Press report on this development was contained in the April 20, 1994, *Houston Chronicle*:

The executive board of the Major League Baseball Players Association will meet on July 11, the day before the All-Star Game, to consider the status of labor talks and a possible strike.

"This is what we normally do in negotiating years," union head Donald Fehr said Tuesday.

In 1985, the year of the last strike, the board met in Chicago on the day prior to the All-Star Game in Minneapolis and set an Aug. 6 strike date. The two-day work stoppage was settled the following day after the intervention of commissioner Peter Ueberroth.

Fehr said the meeting may take place in Pittsburgh, the site of the All-Star Game the following day, or in Cleveland or possibly another city near Pittsburgh. Fehr has said a strike is a "real possibility" because of the lack of progress in negotiations and the fear owners may unilaterally impose a salary cap after this season if there is no agreement.

"I don't have any comment to that," said Milwaukee Brewers president Bud Selig, chairman of the ruling Executive Council.

There have been just four negotiating sessions since owners reopened the labor contract Dec. 7, 1992, and there has been no substantive bargaining. Baseball has been interrupted by four strikes and three lockouts since 1972.

Fehr said the site of the meeting will depend on whether the commissioner's office makes hotel rooms in Pittsburgh available to the union.

Don Fehr spoke to the National Press Club on April 5, 1994. Hal Bodley of *USA Today* reported on his speech, which included the primary reason why the players had to consider a strike:

> Major League Baseball Players Association head Don Fehr says that as long as the game's 72-year-old antitrust exemption exists, it increases the likelihood of labor disputes between players and owners, including work stoppages.
>
> Using a "best-of-times, worst-of-times" theme, Fehr also told the National Press Club Tuesday that if owners and players cannot get together on a new collective bargaining agreement — the latest one expired Dec. 31 — this season could be interrupted, most likely right before the postseason, when owners get most of their TV revenue.
>
> "It's going to take a lot of hard work and more than a little bit of luck," Fehr said. "It would be very difficult for the players to go into the offseason without an agreement."
>
> Fehr said losing the protection of the antitrust exemption

would make owners more interested in reaching fair and timely agreements with players. He also said the union still is waiting for detailed financial information promised by the owners during a March 7 negotiating session in Tampa.

Owners are pressing players to agree to a salary cap, which Fehr says is really a way for large-market owners to funnel the resulting savings to small-market owners, rather than have to divert income they now are receiving.

Richard Ravitch, Player Relations Committee president and owners' chief negotiator, bristled Tuesday over Fehr's remarks.

"The implication we are not meeting our obligation is both inaccurate and unfair," said Ravitch. "Immediately following that meeting (March 7) we sent them a draft of a confidentiality agreement, in a form owners sign when they exchange financial information with one another.

"The lawyers are in the process of settling the terms of the confidentiality agreement. As soon as it's signed, the financial data will be forthcoming. Mr. Fehr knows that very well.

"The public ought to start asking why is he constantly trying to imply bad faith when none exists."

Fehr criticized the newly restructured Major League Agreement, which details duties and powers of the commissioner, and said the players keep asking who's in charge, who's running the show.

"I'm not sure it *is* being run," he said, adding it is ridiculous for owners to say they cannot hire a commissioner until a labor agreement is reached. He says a commissioner could be up to speed in 4-12 weeks. "The entire federal government can be turned over between November and January."

Ever intent on flaunting their antitrust exemption and increasing control over players, the owners in March 1992 initiated a new rule in the amateur draft. Under the new rule, major league clubs were granted five years to sign a player drafted out of high school. To justify their rule, the clubs cited the "noble" reason that they did not want a high school player to "feel the pressure" of having to decide between playing baseball while attending college or signing immediately with a professional baseball club.

The union reacted swiftly to this new rule. It challenged the rule as a tool through which the clubs reduced the bargaining strength of high school players selected in the draft, since the rule eliminated the leverage created by the possibility that a high school player might go to college.

More importantly, the union charged that the rule violated the collective bargaining agreement. Gene Orza argued before permanent arbitrator George Nicolau that the new rule increased the value of draft choices to the clubs. Because draft choices are compensation awarded to clubs losing Type A or Type B free agents, an increase in the value of draft choices would constitute an additional impediment to a club seeking to sign a ranked free agent.

In a July 1992 decision, Nicolau ruled that the new draft rule constituted a change in the system of free agency, and therefore had to be bargained with the union, rather than being unilaterally imposed by the clubs. Needless to say, the union rejected the change, and the old rules on the amateur draft were reinstated by the clubs.

Controlling players has always been "the owners' game." Even PFP was not a new idea. Dan Okrent and Steve Wulf wrote in *Baseball Anecdotes* about John Montgomery Ward, a renaissance man and baseball player who played in the latter part of the nineteenth century. After detailing Ward's remarkable life in their book, the authors wrote:

> But Ward's boldest act occurred during the 1889 season, when the owners adopted a salary classification plan, under which every player would be "graded" and assigned a grade-related salary between $1,500 and $2,500 a year. On July 14, 1889, Ward urged a meeting of players to do the unthinkable — to form their own teams.

*   *   *

The Economic Study Committee on Baseball issued its report on December 3, 1992. In the Introduction to its report, the committee stated its concerns:

> Our primary concerns are whether, and to what extent, the health of baseball is threatened by economic pressures, and the possible implications of these pressures for owner-player relations. We do not believe that health can be determined simply by analyzing whether the returns available to baseball owners are comparable to those in other industries, or even whether the returns justify the prices paid for particular franchises in the past. What does matter is whether there is a continued interest by existing owners in building their franchises and maintaining their competitiveness and whether owners who wish to sell can find responsible and willing buyers.
>
> In other words what is critical for baseball over time is not maintaining particular franchise values, but that there be reasonably

stable ownership able and willing to maintain the continuity of their clubs and franchise location, to pay enough to attract exceptional athletes to baseball and to their team, to justify the large capital expenditures for stadiums (whoever directly bears that cost), and to maintain fan interest and healthy competition.

As the history of baseball suggests, this does not require every club to be profitable every year. As in the past, the overall profitability of baseball may vary over cycles. But to have any reasonable assurance that owners, existing and new, will be willing to operate and acquire baseball clubs, and be able to make the requisite investment, there should be some reasonable prospect of achieving revenues in excess of expenditures most of the time.

For civic or avocational interests owners or ownership groups may sometimes be willing to support a particular club through even extended periods of losses. However, we believe that a healthy outlook for baseball does require the prospect that with effective management the industry as a whole be able to cover operating expenses, with a reasonable margin to cover necessary investments and to maintain continuity during inevitable difficult years. That situation would usually be reflected in significant franchise values. The absence of such franchise value for a significant number of clubs, reflecting an inability to "earn their way" over the long haul, would be disruptive not just for those clubs, but for the stability of baseball as a whole and thus to its appeal to the public.

The committee also offered an observation:

Overall, baseball generates more than enough revenue to thrive; only greed, rashness, or a lack of reasonable cooperation can preclude economic viability for both owners and players.

The committee focused on three major areas—competitive balance, the manner in which player salaries are determined (including salary arbitration), and revenue sharing between the clubs. The committee had no trouble in concluding that competitive balance existed in baseball:

A reasonable degree of competitive balance is essential to the excitement of baseball. One of the great attractions of baseball is that on any given day any team may beat any other team. Tight pennant races, Cinderella teams, underdogs, and David-and-Goliath contests are all part of the lore and attraction of the national pastime, perhaps more so than in other sports. The practical question, therefore, is whether financial imbalances among teams have undermined competitive balance sufficiently to be "a problem."

· · ·

The Committee found no evidence that such a problem has existed in the past two decades. The 1991 World Series involved two clubs that were last in their division's standings in 1990. Six of eleven teams alleged by the clubs to be in chronic financial difficulty finished in the top third of their respective division races in 1992; two won division titles. As the staff report shows, clubs in large markets enjoyed an advantage on the field of 2.5 games during the period from 1984 through 1990. Staff estimates indicate that a club in a market four times as large as that of another club would win from 2.5 to 5.2 more games than the smaller market team. Staff analysis finds no evidence that competitive balance has decreased and some that it has increased since the advent of free agency.

In reviewing why there was competitive balance between small-market and large-market clubs, the committee cited a myriad of on-the-field reasons as to why large-market clubs had not dominated despite having greater resources. Perhaps for political reasons, the committee failed to cite the primary reason — the quality of ownership and front office management.

Because economic studies often infer reasons for behavior from statistical data, the quality of management — a variable difficult to quantify — was referred to only obliquely in the report. The managerial skill of correlating the performance ability of a player to his cost (i.e., assessing the "value" of a player), was not even discussed in the report. The committee noted that player salaries represented the largest expense to clubs:

> The future financial health of baseball as a whole depends on whether player salaries will adjust to any slowing of revenue growth. The players assert that just as salaries responded to the growth in revenues they will respond to decline or slowing in growth. The clubs contend that salaries will not respond because of long-term contracts that promise salaries based on more bullish revenue expectations and because arbitration tends to pass on to "poorer" clubs the salary costs paid by "richer" clubs.

The committee concluded this section by recommending "that the parties move to extend free agency to players in the three-to-six year category. We have not agreed to recommend any changes in the rules governing player compensation other than the reduction in the service requirement for free agency from six to three years."

Unfortunately, the committee's reasoning was influenced by the notion that salary arbitration represents a market aberration. Thus, the committee reasoned, "in the absence of other compelling arguments restrictions on contracting between the parties should be minimized. The burden of proof is on those who would restrict the ability of individual players and owners to contract freely with each other."

Salary arbitration is summarily dismissed based upon the philosophy that players and clubs should be able to "contract freely with each other." After speculating on the side effects of its recommendation, the committee report stated "if the enlargement of free agency produces such significantly larger movement of players as to decrease fan loyalty to teams, it would be in the interest of the parties to negotiate subsequently some small deterrent to movement by players in the three to six year service group."

The committee cannot have it both ways. It should have "stashed" the fancy rhetoric about contracting freely, if it wanted to suggest limited free agency for three-to-six year players. The history of free agency in professional sports is replete with "deterrents," which effectively rendered free agency meaningless.

The committee concluded that attendance and competitive balance have never been better than during the period of free agency. The committee should have reached the conclusion that since the current free agency system has more efficiently allocated player talent, increasing the supply of free agent players should produce even greater competitive balance. Instead, the committee suggested adding "deterrents to movement," a contradiction to its stated philosophy that players and owners should be allowed "to contract *freely* (emphasis added) with each other."

The committee justified its departure from its philosophy based upon the possibility of a decrease in "fan loyalty to teams." This standard is so subjective that it is essentially meaningless. Ownership has for years cited similar subjective reasons to justify its control over players. Concerns about fan loyalty were cited by representatives of ownership in the mid-1970s as a reason to oppose free agency.

When a free agent player leaves one club for another, the former club's loss is the new club's gain. While the fans of the former club may be disappointed, the fans of the new club may be equally excited.

There is no question that free agent signings generate much excitement in the city of the new club.

Citing the subjective concept of fan loyalty to justify an infringement on the freedom of movement by players is regrettable. Fan loyalty in baseball, as in every sport, attaches only to great players and to winning teams. This form of baseball Darwinism is a fact of life. Another, less charitable interpretation of this fact of life is that fans tend to be "front runners." With the exception of fading former superstars, I cannot recall an example of a significant number of fans becoming distraught when a marginal player was released by a club.

It is curious, indeed, that a committee composed of such distinguished members would recommend more free market movement and more free market contracting — the fundamental right historically sought by all sports unions — and then suggest that these rights be "deterred" if "fan loyalty" were to decrease. One would assume that this distinguished group could have stated "a decrease in attendance" if it meant to use an objective standard.

I am inclined to believe that in this instance the committee members followed a time honored tradition of many educated men. Faced with predicting the consequences of their recommendation, they elected to disengage the left sides of their brains and opted instead to use the right sides of their brains. They departed from objective standards because they believed they "intuitively understood" what fan loyalty meant. The same type of "reasoning" led to the opinion written by Oliver Wendell Holmes that baseball "would not be called trade or commerce in the commonly accepted use of those words." Fortunately, the committee could not agree "to recommend any changes in the rules governing player compensation other than the reduction in the service requirement for free agency from six to three years."

During the discussion period following my appearance before the study committee, I stated that I would not object to trading salary arbitration for free agency for the three-to-six year players, since free agency had been the overarching issue pursued by players in all team sports. However, the committee's treatment of salary arbitration as a whipping boy was inappropriate.

The salary of each salary arbitration eligible player does not directly track the salaries of the highly paid free agents. The salaries of players eligible for salary arbitration more frequently correlate to the salaries paid to similar players within the same service group than to the salaries of free agent players who performed similarly during the prior season.

Over 80 percent of all three-to-six year contracts are negotiated by the player and the club. Arbitrators in salary arbitration do not set salaries independent of what players and clubs do on their own. A "bad decision" in salary arbitration does, though, cause an unsettling effect on many of the participants in the system. Ignoring the bad decisions, one is left with the criticism that the salaries paid to players in the salary arbitration system are not free market salaries.

If all three-to-six year players were made free agents, many would receive larger salaries and longer contracts than they would receive as salary arbitration eligible players. If a particular player received a significantly higher salary in salary arbitration than he would have received as a free agent, then it would seem that the club did not focus on "value" when it decided to keep that player on its roster.

Many of the clubs' complaints about salary arbitration are rooted in their long standing reverence for seniority. Because of this view, clubs have failed to properly value senior players with declining skills. Since the salary arbitration system now recognizes that talent is more important than seniority, clubs can effectively use the salary arbitration system to their benefit if they keep this in mind.

Clubs are now cutting the salaries of veteran players and "nontendering" contracts to salary arbitration eligible players. There is ample evidence of this in the market place, so an enlightened club should not be forced to "overpay" a salary arbitration eligible player with declining skills. If a club fears that the possibility exists, it has the option to "nontender" the player and put him "at large" in the market place.

As salaries drop for free agents (including nontendered free agents with less than six years of service) of average skill or with declining performances, the salary arbitration system will incorporate this trend from the free market system into the arbitration decisions rendered. The Staff Analysis for the study committee implicitly recognized such a close correlation when it stated that "arbitration salaries respond to free agent salaries with very little lag— sometimes there is no lag at all, sometimes the lag is about a half-year."

The clubs' obsessions against salary arbitration is inextricably linked with their neurotic need to control players. If clubs would give little credence to seniority and focus on the "value" of a player, the salary arbitration system could continue to be an effective system in which to negotiate contracts and resolve contractual disagreements for the three-to-six year group of players.

The study committee devoted a significant amount of its report to the "Economic Condition of Baseball," especially club finances. The committee calculated that the net operating before tax income of clubs averaged slightly more than 6 percent of their revenue over the period 1985–91. Club revenue ranged from a low of $39 million to a high of $98 million in 1991.

The players association and its expert analysts have long distrusted the data produced by the clubs. One of the reasons for this distrust is the clubs' related party transactions. The committee addressed the issue of related party transactions:

> The players have long alleged that such transactions cause baseball profits to be systematically understated. The clubs acknowledge that some minor distortions may occur, but hold that they do not much color the overall picture of baseball's economic condition.
>
> . . .
>
> The Committee concludes that the profits of a small number of teams, most of which are profitable, are somewhat understated because of related party transactions. The financial condition of some other teams may be affected to a relatively minor extent. In the aggregate, baseball is probably slightly more profitable than the statistics submitted to the Commissioner suggest. But this Committee does not think that its comments about the future or its recommendations would have been changed if teams transacted all business completely at arms length.

Like the union, I have long distrusted the financial data released to the press by the clubs. It is useful propaganda for a club to assert that it loses money, while arguing that players are greedy. Teams in all sports routinely use this tactic to justify increased ticket prices and to shift the wrath of the fans from the owner to the players. Study after study has demonstrated that supply and demand for tickets, not player salaries, determine ticket prices. Regrettably, most beat reporters have not investigated club released financial data or evaluated underlying economic conditions to determine whether the club data and assertions made from it deserve to go unchallenged.

The category of general and administrative expenses for clubs often contain many inappropriate and unnecessary expenses. A club can pay the owner or the owner's relatives very large salaries. A club can convene a meeting far from its home city in a warm, resort surrounding. Such expenditures should be categorized as "paid out of operating profits" to more accurately reflect the profitability of a club.

The Staff Analysis attached to the study committee report expressed bewilderment at the lack of correlation between the profitability of a club and the price at which that club recently sold: "It is puzzling that this variance in sale prices is so small, with so little premium paid for having positive operating income. Why will prospective owners pay $90 million to buy a club that is likely to lose money on average, and only an extra $10 million for a club that is likely to make money on average?"

Among the explanations offered by the staff was the following insightful one:

> Given the difficulties in measuring true baseball profits recounted earlier, one possible explanation for the discrepancy between income and asset values is that operating income is still not measured well, despite our best efforts. In this case one would place credence mainly in the asset value.

In his Supplementary Statement, committee member Henry Aaron wrote:

> The other explanations for high asset values in the face of indifferent operating income seem far more reasonable. Operating income or cash flow may in fact be greater than is apparent.

When it focused on the topic of revenue sharing between the clubs, the committee minced few words in one of its primary recommendations:

> A principal finding of this Committee is that the owners now face a set of conditions and economic prospects which requires a basic restructuring of the rules and processes that determine how and to what extent various sources of revenue are allocated to individual clubs or the joint enterprise.
>
> . . .
>
> The rules that govern the distribution of revenues among the clubs need review. As far as the Committee can tell, revenue sharing arrangements have not been updated to reflect enormous recent changes in revenue sources. The fixed nominal payment to visiting clubs in the National League represents a steadily declining share of steadily rising ticket prices. Such practices may have made sense a century ago. They are now inadequate to bridge current disparities

in revenue among the clubs. In short, baseball's revenue sharing rules produce a much different result in the early 1990's from that of a generation ago.

．．．

While, as reported below, no overall problem of competitive balance in major league baseball has existed or exists now, the committee judges it important to make sure that financial imbalances do not create such a problem. In particular, the financially weakest clubs must not be led by low revenues to slash payrolls dramatically by selling off their star players in an effort to reduce costs and become profitable. Such practices would produce what is essentially minor league baseball in which some teams make no meaningful attempt to produce winning teams, would break faith with the public in the affected cities and harm baseball as a whole. Increased revenue sharing, we believe, would reduce the likelihood of such unfortunate behavior.

．．．

Whatever sources are selected, we recommend that the current level of twenty-five percent shared revenues should be considered as a floor, and that significant increments in this percentage should be achieved promptly.

．．．

Our analysis and the discussion between the players and owners persuade us that both parties, players as well as clubs, have an enormous interest in the additional financial stability that extended revenue sharing would bring to baseball. The fans and the communities served by major league baseball have an even larger stake.

The study committee did not express an opinion on a "floor-ceiling" salary cap or on a designated percentage of income being allocated to player salaries. However, in one of its most foolish conclusions, the committee noted that a prominent advantage of a system where players are paid based upon a percentage of combined revenue was that it "may increase management-labor harmony by focusing contract negotiations on exactly how much of the pie labor will get, and then fixing that for the duration of the contract."

Given the NBA Players Association's intention to terminate the salary-cap system in professional basketball and the anathema to a salary cap held by the baseball union, player agents, and baseball players, the suggestion that a salary cap will increase labor harmony in baseball is sadly misadvised.

The committee was far more realistic when it stated the disadvantages of a salary cap in baseball:

> The Committee recommendations with respect to players with three to six years of service would in fact allow the clubs to negotiate all of their player costs clearly and specifically. Any minimum-maximum proposal would add nothing except to limit the ability of players to negotiate with individual clubs and to artificially restrict clubs from paying what they think players are worth. If, as basketball has found to be necessary, and as the clubs proposed in 1990, an exception to the maximum permits clubs to resign their own players without regard to the maximum, free agency would be essentially eliminated, since bidding clubs would be subject to the maximum while the players' current clubs would not. The result would be to reduce total player compensation and, as in basketball, might be to seriously affect competitive balance. If no such exception were made, clubs with payrolls now in excess of the maximum would be required to reduce the salaries of their present players and would be powerless to bid for any players at all.
>
> If total player salaries are contractually tied to revenues, the players would insist on the right to have an equal voice in the negotiations and decisions which the clubs now make unilaterally that directly affect revenues, such as franchise sales and moves, new franchises, television and cable contracts, ticket prices, revenue sharing, etc. Finally, any direct tie to gross club revenues would require a relationship of trust in the accuracy of club statements as to revenues; it is clear that, at present, the union does not have the requisite level of trust.

The Supplementary Statement of committee member Henry J. Aaron could be described as both a concurring and a dissenting opinion. Aaron concurred with the recommendations that players become eligible for free agency after three years of service and that the amount of revenues that are shared between the clubs be increased.

He noted that the report failed "to clarify the nature of the disputes between players and owners and fails to explain the structures underlying this unfortunate relationship." Calling the failure a betrayal, Aaron stated:

> The report skirts central issues. It substitutes hortatory and saccharine rhetoric appropriate to childrens' novels or sentimental movies for clear analysis. And in an effort to fashion language all members could accept, it becomes obscure and contradictory. Confusing what should have been the educational objectives of its

report—which require clarity—with mediation and negotiation—which require compromise of conflicting interests, the majority blurs disagreements in the pursuit of consensus.

Aaron argued that the report contained a misplaced emphasis on the importance of net operating income. The Brookings Institute economist concluded that not only could net operating income be greater than apparent, but:

> Civic altruism may cause club owners to bear losses for the good of the communities in which they reside. And the sheer fun and community prestige from owning a baseball club may cause owners to accept returns that would be insufficient to induce them to hold more pedestrian investments.

He also reviewed the large-market/small-market issue. In noting that small-market clubs have done quite well at winning, the namesake of one of baseball's greatest players astutely summarized the quandary in which all baseball people are caught:

> No one is good enough at predicting which players will play well *next* year or what combination of players will jell into a winning team to permit those with deep pockets consistently to buy on-field success. Small market clubs have remained competitive.

Henry J. Aaron cogently analyzed why the players would resist a salary cap, and why all of the owners would want one. He dryly observed that a salary cap would increase income for the clubs, with a resulting multiplier effect on the value of all clubs. He was also displeased with the report's innuendos about future economic problems:

> Through roughly 9,000 words of text, however, the majority report leads readers up one blind alley and down another, suggesting that an industry whose companies are valued in the market at prices as high as, or higher than, ever before is on the brink of some vague sort of economic trouble.

The real problem, Aaron said, was that there was no mechanism to enforce greater revenue sharing between the clubs. Until that problem was addressed, "labor management peace will never come to baseball."

The committee report made astute observations about the state of marketing and promotion by Major League Baseball. The committee recognized that better marketing and promotion could increase income to all involved in the game. One area of "opportunity" cited was "cable distributors and other outlets for baseball programming other than national over-the-air broadcasters." A portion of the committee report follows:

> Some of the clubs do a remarkably sophisticated job of selling local media rights to their games. But most TV markets now have 300-400 games per season available to the viewer; these games are available helter-skelter and often are not effectively promoted or scheduled so as to maximize audience and advertising potential. It is ironic that of the major sports, the only one with a judicially sanctioned anti-trust exemption is the one which makes available its entertainment product on the least controlled, least effectively marketed basis. The present price of most regular season games sold to local cable systems can range anywhere from $15,000 per game on the low end to $100,000 and higher per game on the upper end. Local TV may replace national broadcasting as the fastest growing source of revenue for baseball. While this revenue picture will certainly be affected by the general slowdown in TV revenue growth we have described elsewhere, baseball as a whole has a tremendous stake in maximizing the growth of local TV audience and revenue in the future. Many clubs presently do a professional job of selling and marketing their games on a local ADI (Area of Dominant Influence, a television marketing term referring to the population of a geographic area in which a particular set of VHF stations are the principal ones received) basis. But the increasing availability of multi-channel TV in markets all over the country, increasingly refined market segmentation programming strategies, and the profusion of other sports events available to distributors and local systems, are beginning to give an enormous advantage to any sport or entertainment which does an aggressive, nationally coordinated job of packaging, scheduling, selling and promotion. The Committee feels this opportunity should be a major focus of baseball's efforts in the future.
>
> The Committee makes no recommendation on how the players and clubs should organize to improve the marketing and promotion of baseball. We note simply that increases in overall baseball revenues create the potential for both parties to gain, and that "growing the overall pie" is a vital objective that the owners and players share in common. We think that cooperative efforts to increase revenues may be more important in the 1990's than they would have been in the 1980's.

Perhaps due to either labor conflict or ineptitude, baseball has done a poor job, compared to the NBA, of marketing its superstar players to the public. When the committee focused on promotion of the game, including promotion of its star players, it recognized that cooperation between owners and players was crucial. The committee firmly stated that "a broad and durable partnership" was needed to achieve better results:

> Although fan support of baseball is near all-time highs, the Committee judges that aggressive promotion of baseball can produce even better results. To realize this potential will involve looking at a wide range of matters, including how to make playoff and championship competition more attractive; exploring the possibility of more international baseball competition; additional ways to market local television rights; and possible restructuring of league structure and season length. These issues can be addressed only through disciplined and effective cooperation between players and clubs. Indeed, the very challenge of more effective national marketing for baseball underscores the need for a broad and durable partnership between players and owners. Marketing in baseball means marketing the players, particularly the stars; and the only way that can work is for players and owners to share a vital sense of their very real common interest and to develop a pattern of cooperation which allows them to build on that common interest.

On May 20, 1993 Don Fehr appeared on "Up Close" with Roy Firestone. Don and Roy discussed the image of baseball players and how the game could be better marketed. The well known ESPN sports interviewer asked the union head why baseball players are not more highly regarded.

> Fehr: There is much more of a focus on baseball players. There is much more of an expectation of responsibility.
> Firestone: You make a good point. There isn't that same type (in the other sports). Basketball players are making the same kind of money, maybe more, average salary, than the major league baseball players. But you don't hear (fans) say: "Those greedy basketball players." Why?
> Fehr: Cause the basketball owners don't run down the players that the fans come to watch. Baseball owners do. And, after fifteen years of complaining by baseball owners, if you listen to them, they've been in business a hundred years and no one has ever made a penny, and it's always the players' fault. After a while, fans come to focus on that, and begin to pay attention to it.

Firestone made the point that some baseball players have appeared callous in their public statements and "have to be careful how they talk to the fan." Don Mattingly was quoted about a degeneration of respect between players and fans.

> Mattingly: The fans have gotten nasty. . . . Those people are mad at us; they are angry.
> Firestone: Why, if that's true? How has it gotten to that point?
> Fehr: Oh, I think it has, and it comes from a number of different ways. You even see it on the field. . . . Then you have something else. It's what I call the Hollywood phenomenon, for lack of a better term. Players are treated as celebrities. And, when someone gets into an incident or a scandal, or a potential one, they're followed around and intimate portions of their lives are exposed and all their friends are asked about them. . . . (Players) are tired of it. There is a "leave me alone". . . . The result is that people get covered, not games.

Firestone asked Fehr his reaction to a recent public opinion poll of students in grades six through twelve. When asked to name their favorite professional sport, the students responded: professional football — 39.6 percent; professional basketball — 28.4 percent; professional baseball — 18.4 percent.

> Fehr: We really need, on an industry-wide basis, to make an overt effort to go back out to those groups that perhaps we're missing, focus in on them, resell the game and the high points about it. That's been lost most of the last ten years. And, a real concentrated effort needs to be made in that regard. . . . It's going to take some joint effort between the players and the clubs. If they don't set up the promotional programs, it's going to be very difficult for players to have a meaningful impact. But it needs to be done.

The interviewer and his guest discussed how football and basketball have done a better job of promoting the images of their players through national television sports.

> Firestone: When's it going to change (in baseball)?
> Fehr: I don't know. I was hopeful things were going to change going into the last television negotiation. They haven't. We knew absolutely nothing about it. What we did know came almost the night before and was, at best, extremely oblique information. And it's distressing, because it almost indicates an ongoing lack of desire

to try and have the players involved. You can't sell this game without the players. It's not possible.

At the risk of citing "hortatory and saccharine rhetoric appropriate to childrens' novels or sentimental movies," I quote the Preface of the report, for it states my sentiments as well:

> The world of baseball provides our country with some of its most wonderful moments of athletic competition. Baseball is part of our history, part of our character—a never exhausted outlet for hope, and a continuing drama of grace, timing and achievement on the field of our dreams.
>
> It is also filled today with money, conflict, and distrust.
>
> The history of relations between owners of Professional Baseball Clubs and the Major League Baseball Players Association has been characterized by repeated and acrimonious disputes. Six rounds of collective bargaining have been marked by three strikes and three lockouts.
>
> We believe that prolongation of the past pattern of strikes and lockouts in baseball would inevitably damage the short and long term interests of both the clubs and the players. Unseemly contests between club owners and players would only sour public attitudes toward the game as a whole, with a consequent long-term reduction in both profits and salaries.
>
> While public attention will shortly focus on the preliminary skirmishing surrounding collective bargaining between the clubs and the players, we believe that baseball faces a challenge far broader and more critical than simply reaching a labor agreement. That challenge is to arrest the decline and embitterment of baseball in American life, and to forge a framework in which owners and players can go beyond their individual financial interests to pursue constructively, fruitfully and together their shared interests.
>
> Baseball must be reconceived by its participants, the owners and the players, as a genuine partnership which pursues competitive excellence, leads by moral and athletic example, resolves labor disputes through negotiation rather than by insulting the public with lockouts and strikes, and tempers financial greed with a sense of mutual cooperation and accountability to the public.

How should baseball proceed to build a "genuine partnership" between the players and the owners? It should start with institutionalized respect for the rights of players.

Baseball players have had to rely upon the wisdom of baseball's permanent arbitrators, rather than the United States Supreme Court, to secure and maintain their freedom. Like all other citizens of the United States, baseball players should be able to market their unique skills without unnecessary restraints.

Unfortunately, the players' fight for free agency and against ownership control has produced years of distrust and acrimony. That distrust is difficult to overcome.

The change in ownership of many clubs has resulted in more enlightened individuals becoming involved on the management side of baseball. Many individuals in current management positions are former players, who have lived through the fight for free agency. Except for a few who have abandoned their heritage, most of these former players are empathetic to player rights even though they must debate what a particular player should be paid. Of course, none of these players are owners.

If ownership can resist its natural urge "to control and dictate," the present climate in baseball is more ripe for a true partnership than most observers realize. The first place to start is with a change in the public and private attitudes held by the participants. One of my objectives during the 1990 lockout was to depersonalize matters, stop the public attacks and concentrate on the economic variables in order to arrive at a mutually beneficial agreement.

Richard Ravitch spoke of the need for this type of change at the Associated Press sports editors annual meeting in June 1993. Ben Walker of the Associated Press reported the following from the meeting:

> "The game needs a collegial approach," said Richard Ravitch, president of the owners' Player Relations Committee. "I've never seen a situation where there is as much hostility between two sides."
>
> Donald Fehr, head of the Major League Baseball Players Association, agreed that the spirit of cooperation was missing. He blamed owners.
>
> "When we talk about a collegial atmosphere, it's difficult to tell the players you want to work together when you've just signed a six-year television contract, the most important document in our industry, that players had no input on," he said.

Don Fehr is correct. The owners have tossed around the word "partnership" without any intention to negotiate a true partnership. Rather than rhetorically using the word "partnership" as an artifice to impose a salary cap, the owners should recognize the need to share power and share decision making.

The players association should be granted meaningful power in a true partnership with ownership. The union should be involved in television contract negotiations, as well as in defining the office of the commissioner. The players should have a vote in selecting the commissioner. The players should help market and promote the game, help decide which cities are granted expansion franchises, and be involved in many other important areas that affect the economics, marketing, and governance of the game.

Peter Ueberroth used the words "cultural change" to rationalize collusion by the owners. Baseball needs a true cultural change by ownership, one that respects player rights and admits the players into the power structure of the game as true partners.

Jerry Reinsdorf said to me in 1990, "I didn't think you had it in you," after I helped mediate the final labor agreement. Reinsdorf is a good example of an owner who both understands what a true partnership is and yet seeks to control the players. He is smart, insightful, and a big fan of the game. Reinsdorf has it within himself to either travel down the road of a traditional confrontation with the union over control of the players, or down the "road less traveled" toward the creation of a true partnership with the players.

To date, not one legitimate effort has been expended by ownership to create a true partnership. Hal Bodley of *USA Today* editorialized in the December 7, 1993, edition that baseball needed a true partnership. Bodley asked Don Fehr about "the progress" on forming a true partnership:

> "There has been no meaningful suggestion from the owners that they wish our involvement in anything," says Fehr. "We know nothing about their committees, nothing about their reorganizations, nothing about their renewed marketing plan, nothing about revenue-sharing debates, nothing about their collective bargaining position. We know nothing about anything."
>
> Could a partnership happen? Fehr's not optimistic.
>
> "It's become clear to me at the very least the best you can say is that they're not ready to tell us anything." he said. "I conclude all the stuff we heard about changing environments and involving the players either was just public relations stuff or whatever."

The challenge is for leaders of the ownership group, like Jerry Reinsdorf, to rise to the occasion and create an appropriate partnership with the players, rather than scheming to find new ways to control the players. Unfortunately, the public comments of Richard

Ravitch, following the Fort Lauderdale meetings, lend scant hope that the owners are interested in a true partnership.

Former Commissioner Fay Vincent had it backwards when he addressed the National Press Club on April 22, 1992. While he appropriately observed that the parties need "to do away with the constant bickering and the four-year confrontations that are so difficult" and do not "have a common attitude toward solving the problems," he inappropriately placed the blame for the economic woes of baseball on the players association when he stated:

> Until the players association begins to work with the owners and construct a more stable economic environment, baseball will continue to endure and suffer labor confrontations, and perhaps worse, every four years.

New Astros owner Drayton McLane was on target when he said in the October 3, 1993, *Houston Chronicle*, "90 percent of the problems with baseball is the owners. They make the decisions. The pilots crash the airplanes. The passengers don't crash them. The pilots make all the decisions."

Richard Ravitch publicly acknowledged on December 15, 1992, that the reason the players have won every major battle over the recent past was due to the players' side having been represented by smarter and more capable people. He said, "The owners have always underestimated the leverage of the players. The union has always been smarter than the owners."

Ravitch was correct. The players association and the top agents have done a much better job than have the owners and their employees. For nearly two decades, the players association, the top agents, and the players have used their abilities and unity to defeat the owners' efforts to control the players.

The owners might be in for a delightful surprise if they would work with us, instead of against us. They would discover that our abilities could be utilized to achieve mutual objectives — advancement of the economic interests of owners and players, better promotion and marketing of the game, avoidance of labor strife, and a better public image to our customers, the fans — all of which would make the title of this book (*Inside the Strike Zone*) apply only to an umpire's call.

The evolution of a sports agent/attorney — Randal Hendricks in 1976 . . .

. . . and in 1979.

Cleveland Indians spring training in Tucson in 1981. Left to right: Andre Thornton, Randal Hendricks, Len Barker, Rick Waits, and friend, Don Heathcott.

The Hendricks clan in the summer of 1981. Edith Hendricks seems to say, "What's a mother to do?" with daughter Carol and sons David, Randy, Alan, Clint, and Rick.

Hendricks Sports Management was the first sports agency to represent both Cy Young Award winners. Left to right: Randal Hendricks, Mike Scott (National League 1986 winner), Roger Clemens (American League 1986 winner), and Alan Hendricks.

The post-1987 season arbitration case of American League Most Valuable Player George Bell settled nearly thirty minutes after its scheduled start. Left to right: Blue Jays assistant general manager Gord Ash, Randal Hendricks, Blue Jays general manager Pat Gillick, George Bell, David Hendricks, and Alan Hendricks. Blue Jays president Paul Beeston dodged the photograph by claiming that there was not enough room to fit him in the photograph.

Randal Hendricks family at home in 1991. Left to right: Daehne, Randy, Jill, Kristin, and Bret.

1990 Cy Young Award winner Doug Drabek with Randal Hendricks at the Houston Astros spring training complex in Kissimmee, Florida, in March 1994.

Index